ALSO BY WENDY SHALIT:

A Return to Modesty: Discovering the Lost Virtue

the good girl
REVOLUTION

the good girl REVOLUTION

Young Rebels with Self-Esteem and High Standards

Previously published as *Girls Gone Mild*

WENDY SHALIT

BALLANTINE BOOKS
New York

2008 Ballantine Books Trade Paperback Edition

Published in the United States by Ballantine Books,
an imprint of The Random House Publishing Group,
a division of Random House, Inc., New York.

BALLANTINE and colophon are registered trademarks of Random House, Inc.

Originally published in hardcover in the United States by Random House,
an imprint of The Random House Publishing Group, a division of
Random House, Inc., in 2007, under the title *Girls Gone Mild*.

ISBN 978-0-8129-7536-9

Printed in the United States of America

www.ballantinebooks.com

2 4 6 8 9 7 5 3 1

Book design by Simon M. Sullivan

For my husband,
who makes being good seem so easy

See, cursing was cool when nobody was doing it. Or just a couple people. Like, if everybody wears the same clothes, then it's, you know—it ain't cool no more. You're trying to be different. One can't be different by being racy today. It's not interesting anymore. See, sexiness was in the mind. It was in your imagination. When you lose that, then . . . it's just old skin.

—PRINCE on *Tavis Smiley,* February 19, 2004

Every revolution was first a thought in one man's mind.

—RALPH WALDO EMERSON, 1841

The journey we're about to go on is a tale of paradox and unintended consequences. It is about how we can be sexually liberated and at the same time emotionally stifled—connected with a touch of a computer mouse to anyone on the globe, and yet often lacking genuine friendship. Well-meaning experts and parents say that they understand kids' wanting to be "bad" instead of "good." Yet this reversal of adults' expectations is often experienced not as a gift of freedom but as a new kind of oppression.

To find out why, my book draws on over 100 in-depth interviews I conducted with girls and young women, ages twelve to twenty-eight; fifteen interviews with young men; and over 3,000 e-mail exchanges with young people who wrote to me or my website, ModestyZone.net, during the years 1999–2006. These individuals came from diverse racial, economic, and religious backgrounds. Some identified themselves as liberal, others as conservative. Some of the young women called themselves "feminists" while others were uncomfortable with the term. But the one thing I heard over and over was how desperate they were for a new set of role models.

Since those who contact me are obviously a self-selected bunch, I made an effort to seek out others who did not share my views in order to better understand their perspective. I found forty-two individuals through news stories, on planes, and sometimes just hanging out at malls. Ten were parents. I also spoke with counselors, psychiatrists, and sociologists from around the country; attended conventions on abstinence in Los Angeles and Washington, D.C.; and visited a high school on Long Island that had canceled its prom. As I swam deeper into the subject of this book, I grew bolder, even going undercover at a Cuddle Party—although I can't disclose where, since Cuddle Parties are rather secretive (see Chapter Five).

What does liberation mean to you? In her excellent book *Female Chauvinist Pigs,* Ariel Levy introduces us to nineteen-year-old Debbie, who experiences regret after doing a "scene" for a *Girls Gone Wild* video. Her regret was not that the producer, Joe Francis, has made millions by using girls like her, while all she got for disrobing was a T-shirt. Nor did she regret (as others have regretted) that she was encouraged to masturbate on camera. Rather, Debbie was upset about "not doing it right" when, for some reason beyond her grasp, she couldn't get excited during the proceedings. I found this detail particularly sad. Debbie doesn't realize something basic: Women are typically paid to appear in pornography precisely because being a sexual object for strangers is not usually fun. Like many young women today, Debbie is publicly sexual while remaining utterly alienated from her own sexuality.

This book is about my search for an alternative to our *Girls Gone Wild* culture. It's about finding a way to acknowledge sexuality without having to share it with strangers. It's about rediscovering our capacity for innocence, for wonder, and for being touched profoundly by others. My goal is not to attack those who want to be "wild," but rather to expand the range of options for young people, who I believe are suffering because of the limited choices available to them.

Warm regards,
WENDY SHALIT

CONTENTS

My Bratz Problem—and Ours

•

You've gotta look hotter than hot! Show what you've got! . . . Ready or not!
—lead song from *Bratz Babyz: The Movie*, September 2006

On television, cartoon baby girls shimmy in their underpants as our wide-eyed toddler multitasks, sucking on her pink floral pacifier and learning to flirt at the same time. She may not be potty-trained, but soon she will know just how to flutter her eyelashes and sway her hips suggestively. She has studied, over and over, her favorite part of the Bratz DVD, where strobe lights flash and the "Babyz" coo about looking "hotter than hot!" and showing "what you've got."

"Ready or not"? One ventures to guess—not.

These days when you walk into a toy store, it's not clear whether you actually made it to the store or accidentally landed in a red-light district. A friend recently had a baby, so I went to buy a doll for the baby's older sister, since everyone knows that it's crucial to pacify the older sibling. At the precise moment, no doubt, that the girl was feeling appalled by the arrival of her baby brother, I was reeling from shock at the store's section for girls. For one thing, I was greeted by the melodious strains of "When I get that feeling, that *sexual feeling* . . ." piped through the speakers. In the doll section, only dolls in tight-fitting, provocative outfits stared out at me, all wearing heavy makeup and self-satisfied, flirty expressions. The young sprite browsing next to me, who looked about seven years old, wore a purple cropped top and peep-toe wedges with heels two inches high—an outfit that seemed to mock the very idea of finding a suitable doll for a little girl.

Bratz Babyz makes a "Babyz Nite Out" doll garbed in fishnet stockings, a hot-pink micromini, and a black leather belt. To look "funkalish" (whatever that means), the baby also sports a tummy-flaunting black tank paired with a hot-pink cap. Dare one ask what is planned for "Babyz Nite Out" and what, exactly, she is carrying in her metal-studded purse? Is it pacifiers, or condoms? It might be both: "These Babyz demand to be lookin' good on the street, at the beach, or chillin' in the crib!" The dolls are officially for ages "four-plus," but they are very popular among two- and three-year-old girls as well.

I've always found the most disturbing thing about Bratz to be their over-size baby faces. Many of the "Babyz" on MGA's website are posed very seductively, showing off their slick lips and teeny-weeny underpants. The Bratz Babyz doll "Phoebe" is garbed in a fluffy pink fur with matching lingerie, and her twin, "Roxxi," is stuffed into red-hot lingerie and a black leather jacket. In days of yore, you actually had to undress dolls to see their little white bloomers. But these days, right out of the box, the Bratz Babyz "Nita" shows off heavy red lipstick and bright toenail polish to match red panties, while "Cloe" has pink lipstick to go with pink panties. Since these dolls bare the chunky legs of babies who are still crawling, to me they are not "fashion forward"—just plain creepy.

Younger girls are already under the frightening influence of the Bratz doll companion books. "Ages three and up" can use fifteen "stylin' glitter body stickers!" that come inside *BRATZ Yasmin: The Princess Rules!* and do some coloring of Yasmin's makeup and outfits for "daytime and night." Presumably, the littlest preschoolers will not be able to fill in "When I want to look hot for an extra special occasion I'll put on _____" or take the quiz about what to do when "the boy of your dreams has just asked you out. . . . Do your pals . . . help you put together a look he'll just die for?" But perhaps a parent or an older sibling can fill in the blanks for them. (For instance, "When I want to look hot for an extra special occasion I'll put on *my big girl pants—no more diapers!*")

The book *BRATZ Xpress Yourself!* teaches girls to express themselves, for example, by writing "about the boys you know. . . . These are cool *boys* I know: _____ . . . This is the most *surprising* thing (name of boy) once did: _____ . . . The *Hottest* Boy Award goes to _____." You get the idea. The *BRATZ Holiday Shoppin' Spree: A Guide to Totally Hot Shoppin'* is a cool, sparkly paperback shaped like a purse, which enables a little girl to keep track of what she wants to buy her friends and her "crush." If she shops for herself, she might want to keep "Jade" in mind (according to Bratz literature, Jade wears only "the hottest fashions"). And—this is crucial—she should never to forget to take a quarter, to call a parent "when you're all shopped out!" It would indeed be poignant for a little girl to be stranded, with a present for her crush in one hand and her new hot clothes in the other.

The illustrations in these books are much more disturbing than the Bratz dolls themselves (which is saying a lot): the girls have extreme come-hither looks; their hips are thrust out to show off their exposed midriffs; and some even touch their rear ends suggestively. When I called MGA Entertainment, the maker of Bratz, its representative was very coy about what age group these books are targeting. Still, peddling so many "hot" products to young girls seems inherently problematic—even if you dub it "funkalish" instead of sexy. This suggests what we might call the funked-up principle: If a little girl is young enough to be coloring and wearing glitter stickers, then she's probably still too young to be worrying about boys and looking "hot."

Bratz already puts out a magazine that's like *Cosmo* for eight-year-olds, spotlighting a "flirty denim skirt," a "divine golden halter top," and Paris Hilton's "alluring outfit that can't fail to impress!"—all in the August-September 2006 issue. After the editors field a heartrending question about divorce from a nine-year-old, who fears that her father prefers his girlfriend to her, since he spends so much time with the girlfriend—"What should I do?"—they then go on to their main business, asking their readers questions like, "Are you always the first in your group to wear the hottest new looks?" and "Do you love it when people look at you in the street?" Though surely the editors do not mean to imply this, if I were the nine-year-old, I might come away with the impression that I had to dress sexy to win back my father's attention.

In the same issue, two girls from Washington who built a "Bratz town" have mailed in their photographs, which are jarring. One blond pixie named Maggie, who looks about seven or eight, is wearing a cropped pink top and low-rider jeans that show both her tummy and her blue bikini underwear. She has a wide, innocent smile and adorable bangs, and she stands next to a backdrop of Bratz dolls in slinky lingerie. All this is unsettling—especially since it makes you worry that she may be showing her underwear on purpose. "My birthday was da bomb!" Maggie writes. "If you remember, my fave Bratz girl is Jade and my fave color is green—just like Jade!"

Two women I interviewed for this book had friends who photographed their baby daughters in bikinis, spread out on the hood of their cars. They imagined that the adult pose was "cute," and they had brought the photos to work. I hadn't heard of this, but around eight years ago, when a friend's daughter turned one, a fellow partygoer pronounced the birthday girl's fuzzy pink coat "sexy." When everyone giggled, I realized that I must be old-fashioned, but "sexy" and "baby" are two words I don't like to hear in the same sentence. This attitude—"You're never too young to be sexy!"—predated Bratz by several years. Something in our underlying idea of female empowerment became corrupted long before it became commercialized.

Walking into that toy store made me feel ancient at age thirty, for when I was little we played with Cabbage Patch Kids. With their soft fabric bodies and one-of-a-kind visages they were all the craze, and I named mine "Patsy." I fretted for several months until Patsy's official "birth certificate" arrived at our door, thus confirming that she did in fact exist. She smelled of vanilla, had beautiful brown yarn hair, and was very lovable.

In fact, I loved my doll so much that a tiny part of me began to wonder if she was real. At seven, I was old enough to guess that she probably wasn't. But on the other hand, there was that birth certificate, which looked so official. (It even came with a "seal of authenticity," which clearly meant something.) In the end I devised an experiment to resolve once and for all whether Patsy was real. I would toss her, and if I felt a twinge of guilt, then clearly she had to be real—well, at least a little. The moment is still vivid in my mind: I took a deep breath, steadied my nerves, and quickly bashed her against my yellow floral-print wall. Patsy still smiled (she was always such a good sport), but nonetheless, she no longer looked her best. For my part, I felt truly awful seeing her crumpled on the floor: "Oh, Patsy, I'm so sorry! Are you OK?" And then it hit me: *Oh my gosh, this means she is really real.*

These days, the way dolls are dressed, the question is not so much "Is my dolly real?" as "How much does she charge per hour?" In April 2006, Hasbro, the second-largest toymaker, announced plans to launch a line of dolls modeled after the Pussycat Dolls, for girls as young as age six. Since the Pussycat Dolls perform highly sexualized song and dance routines, you can certainly understand Hasbro's thinking: Wouldn't it be terrific if six-year-old girls could model themselves after these pioneers?

Hasbro claimed that the dolls were suitable for young consumers because they "reflect the styles and fashions that are popular in the world today," but under pressure from groups such as Campaign for A

Commercial-Free Childhood and Dads and Daughters, it canceled the deal just a month later. The bad news is that the doll market is already saturated with Pussycat Dolls—if not in name, then in spirit.

"Inside every woman is a Pussycat Doll. . . . It's about female empowerment, about being confident with who you are," explains Robin Antin, the group's forty-four-year-old founder and choreographer. Whether or not dolls explicitly modeled after the Pussycat Dolls are on the shelves, this brand of "confidence," certainly, is sold to girls from the get-go. "Kim Possible" by Disney and Lisa Frank "Fab Friends" dolls also send the message that girls need to show a generous portion of tummy in order to be powerful. "My Scene Bling Bling Barbie" wears more diamonds than she does clothes: a jeans micromini barely covers her underwear; it is paired with tall boots and a filmy silver top that resembles a necklace; her back, shoulders, and stomach are exposed; and her heavy-lidded eyes have a pouty, jaded expression. Competing with the Bratz pack has taken its toll, and not just on our fairy-tale princess.

One older teenager from Virginia wrote to me:

It's revolting how much young girls are encouraged by these toys to act older than they are, including acting and dressing as if their bodies are appealing to men, to be so concerned with their looks and so self-centered. To focus on one's appearance is really not natural for little girls, especially if it means an awareness of sexuality. I can't believe that women actually want their young girls to be playing with dolls that look like prostitutes. It's so sad for the little girls. We actually have two little girls who live on our street who are maybe five and seven who dress in platform shoes, miniskirts, belly shirts, etc., and watch so much TV that they know way too much for their ages. Another neighbor who babysits for them told us that one day they saw some boys playing baseball on the field near our house and got all dressed up with makeup, purses, etc. to walk down there and show off. It's horrible that young kids are allowed or even encouraged to act this way. Most of them grow up soon enough without starting off like this.

People wonder why thongs for tweens are now a million-dollar industry: there's the "Hello Kitty" thong; there's the "Care Bear" thong; and by the time girls turn fourteen, as one daughter wearily explained to her baffled mother while they were shopping, "basically, every girl at school is wearing a thong." Given the popularity of oversexualized dolls and cartoons—as well as music videos, magazines, and games that prominently feature strippers—it makes sense that Target's website would hawk "Xhilaration Juniors Ruffle Edge TBack Thong" in girls' sizes, with orange lace and red string. According to the ad copy, "bows and lace thong panties feel sexy under your favorite clothes"—just don't forget to brush your teeth!

In 2002, Abercrombie and Fitch sparked a scandal by marketing thongs to ten-year-old girls (the undies had "eye candy" and "kiss me" printed on the front). But just five years later, most major retailers carry thongs in the girls' section, and nobody blinks. One mother told me that she felt "in the minority" for not wanting to see "stuff that looks like what you'd see on prostitutes" in a Candies boutique for juniors. "Conversations with friends reveal me to be an old fogey on this topic," she confessed, and I can see why. Limited Too, a store catering to preteens, now offers lace and rhinestone low-rise panties to its young customers. Hot Topic, where twelve-year-olds shop, sells black and red satin bustiers and see-through undies, which make the store's astonishing array of Hello Kitty thongs actually look conservative by comparison. And so the debate has shifted. Parents no longer debate the merits of thongs for tweens but instead whether I'M TOO SEXY FOR MY DIAPER is a "healthy" message for an infant girl's onesie.

Even Kohl's department store—not exactly edgy—features padded push-up bras with flirty patterns in its girls' "first bra" section. Shops catering to preteens already sell double-A, padded push-up bras, a product which is inherently puzzling. Why is there any need to show "breasts" at an age when a girl isn't even beginning to develop? The answer is that being a child is no longer a valid excuse not to be sexualized.

A Philadelphia reporter tried to explain why two eleven-year-old girls—Brittany and Lily—were regularly shopping at Victoria Secret's PINK line: "Marketing experts call Lily and Brittany's yearnings 'aspirational,'" Jane Von Bergen wrote, "and that aspiration may explain why the girls and many of their friends are regular Victoria's Secret customers, despite their tender age." Professor Martin Rogoff, a visiting professor of retailing at Philadelphia University, said that this is "something we call age compression." I suppose that sounds better than "childhood compression," but in my view, the store's appeal to youngsters is far more mundane. Its "extreme low-rise string bikinis" are available in colors called "pink puppy love" and "blue puppy love"; and its company's stuffed "pink mini-dog" is given away "Free! With any PINK Purchase!" on its website. (Since 2004, Victoria's Secret has insisted that its youth line is aimed at college students, but the last time I checked, college women weren't collecting pink stuffed animals.)

Don't get me wrong: I don't have anything against lingerie or even against teenagers shopping at Victoria's Secret. But when my friends and I were in high school in the early 1990s, the place still had the aura of mystique; even though we shopped there, we understood it to be a store for adult women: "Ooooh *là là!*" We would tease one another mercilessly, "What did you get at Vic*tooooooria's?*" The problem I have with sexy underwear for tweens—and the Playboy bunny pencil cases and stationery, and all the rest—is not that these items are "inappropriate." Yes, there is a certain creepiness when adults seem to expect you to be sexual. It is also misleading, because a Hello Kitty thong sends the message that sex is just like cartoons. And it is not in the least like cartoons. But perhaps just as important, young people report that trivializing sex also takes the fun out of it. Studies show that kids as young as ten are increasingly ambushed by unwanted online pornography; seventeen-year-old Emily Duhovny from Marlboro, New Jersey, told CNN that she now finds X-rated images "annoying." There can be no dipping your toe into mature waters when you're already swimming in a triple-X lake to begin with. There is no longer any mystery or power to sex—it is just expected that everything will be sexual, and so nothing is. There is nothing to wait for, or to look forward to. And that seems to me to be the real crime. Liz from Maryland, a mother of two girls, complained to me, "Many girls seem to have no childhood at all. Once you get beyond size twelve to eighteen months, the clothes begin to look trashy." It's as if the concept of innocence were illegal. Even owners of nail salons, while happy to have the business of four-year-old girls who now get pedicures, are disturbed by how much these pretweens know. "A six- or seven-year-old is looking up to someone who is twenty," says Mr. Labrecque of the Paul Labrecque salon in Manhattan.

. . .

But just when you think the experts are about to object to all this, at the last minute they always pull back. Consider *Packaging Girlhood,* a well-conducted survey that appeared in 2006 and decried the hypersexualization of girlhood today. The educators Sharon Lamb and Lyn Mikel Brown visited (for example) Claire's Accessories, a trinkets store for girls, where they found a "Hottie Handbook" announcing: "Attention girls. . . . If you have a boyfriend, don't bring him around me because you won't have a boyfriend anymore. . . . I sizzle. I scorch, hotter than any flame." This handbook, the "dirty girl" cleansing products, the "little hottie" tees, and all the girls who dress up "like hookers" for Halloween understandably concern the authors. Quite rightly, they argue that a young girl is boxed into a "narrow sexy image" before her time. But then they offer parents this curious counsel:

> While many parents may be tempted to point to this name-calling [i.e., the word "slut"] as an example of why girls should be careful about their image and whom they act sexy around, think this one through. The message is not, "Don't dress sexy because other people will call you a slut"; the message is how unfair it is that girls are so closely watched, so easily put down.

This sounds good, until you reread the last sentence. After everything the authors have depicted, it's perfectly legit for prepubescent girls to wear "little hottie" tees? And is the only difficulty with those who notice and "closely watch" the girls? That can't be right. I certainly agree that the word "slut" isn't the best way of starting this conversation, but let's not forget that there is an objective problem here, one that is not merely in the eye of the beholder.

Next, Lamb and Brown lament that twelve-year-old girls are listening to Ludacris singing about "ruff sex": "make it hurt/In the garden all in the dirt." (They did a survey, and that's what the girls were listening to.) Their advice? Parents should tread very carefully:

> You can't just dismiss an individual performer or group out of hand. The same group that sings "Don't wanna squeeze triggers just wanna squeeze tits" . . . is the same group that asks "Where is the love" in a beautiful antiwar, antiracism rap. . . . Dismissing a group or an artist because of one song is only going to make you seem reactionary and out of touch. Let's not forget that in the sixties the Beatles were considered junk by many parents, mindless noise that was corrupting the ears of youth. Today we think of their music as almost classical and savor the love songs as well as the ironic and experimental tunes of their later years.

Are these authors serious? Do they really see no objective difference between "I wanna hold your hand" and "just wanna squeeze tits"? The latter sentiment, if you can call it that—or "make it hurt/in the garden all in the dirt" for that matter—plainly has a very different effect on the imagination of preteens. Sex as divorced from relationships, sex as something that is supposed to hurt, is a much more unhealthy and misogynist message than simply, "I wanna hold your hand." And I don't think these destructive lines are something we should ever try to get used to or "savor" for twelve-year-old girls (or boys).

I counted on finding, at the very least, some advice about restricting television, but the *Packaging Girlhood* authors are suspicious of that too. Although "you may think it's best just to turn off the TV," we would be wrong to entertain such a notion; that "won't work"—"at least not for long." In the authors' view, a parent can't even decide what a preschooler should be watching (apparently that's an infringement of the tot's freedom): "preventing TV is an ostrich-with-its-head-in-the-sand maneuver." Even when you see, for example, "a four-year-old girl on a commercial [who] tells us, 'I'm shaking it!'" all you can do is "sit down beside her to teach her to be a critical consumer. . . . Preschoolers are not too young to hear (and imitate) your questions and observations." If you don't have time to do that, then at least do the next best thing:

> Let's be realistic. Most parents sometimes use TV as a babysitter. . . .
> While you're getting that last bit of work done and your daughter is
> watching cartoons, ask her to come get you when she sees an example
> of a cool mom or two girls helping each other and succeeding! She'll
> keep an eye out for the good stuff as well as what's missing.

Do you know of a child who would willingly interrupt television viewing to tug at Mommy's skirt and exclaim that she just saw an empowered woman? I certainly don't know of any. The kids I know are unwilling to pull away from television at all. If a visitor, even a beloved relative, arrives from out of town, they won't be able to turn their attention away from the TV unless it is switched off and unplugged, and perhaps the remote control is hidden as well. The druglike effect of television has been documented in numerous studies, and now that its content is more explicit and faster-paced than ever, the ability of tots to pull away will probably not skyrocket after a lecture on female empowerment.

That Lamb and Brown care deeply about young women is evident on every page. Unfortunately, however, the impotence of the "realistic" brand of parenting is thrown into stark relief when juxtaposed against our over-sexualized culture. We seem to have lost the ability to say that some toys, clothing, songs, or programs are simply inappropriate for children. Why?

As I was making my way through *Packaging Girlhood*, my friend Michael called to say he had just seen a nine- or ten-year-old girl in the At-lanta airport, wearing a shirt that read THIS T-SHIRT WOULD LOOK BETTER WET. That was tame compared with a shirt my friend Elizabeth saw in New York City, on a ponytailed young woman who was out lunching with her mother: I'D F——K ME, it read (naturally, without the dash). We all wonder in such cases who was really "out to lunch." Did some morally ob-tuse parent pay for the shirt, or did the girl buy it with her hard-earned al-lowance? But *Packaging Girlhood* suggests a third (and in a way, more troubling) possibility: Perhaps intelligent, caring parents bought it, after objecting to its "message" and discussing it with their daughter—which, as far as they were concerned, discharged their obligation.

It's not that parents don't recognize the inappropriateness of such shirts. I believe they do. Lamb and Brown, surely, would not have written their book if they thought everything was just peachy. Nor do I believe that par-ents are allergic to saying the word "no." I think the root of our dilemma runs far deeper and is, ironically, a reflection on what good parents Lamb, Brown, and others actually are. Most good parents don't want to say no un-less they can say yes to something else.

The real reason parents have trouble objecting to the bad-girl ideal, I suspect, is that they don't see an alternative to it. Even some abstinence groups now push "Hot Virgin" tees, and the Candies Foundation sells tank tops with BE SEXY in hot-pink lettering—to prevent teenage pregnancy. Exactly how BE SEXY prevents teenage pregnancy isn't immediately ob-vious; but below this phrase, in almost unreadably small lettering, we are told: IT DOESN'T MEAN YOU HAVE TO HAVE SEX. Though it's certainly funny to imagine a young man approaching a girl in a revealing BE SEXY tank, only to be disappointed by the fine print, what's less amusing is that being publicly sexual has become the only acceptable way for girls to demonstrate maturity.

Across the political spectrum, many have expressed dismay that the leg-endary porn star Ron Jeremy was mobbed by families at Disneyland who wanted to have their picture taken with him, or that thirteen-year-old girls told the porn star Jenna Jameson at a book signing that they look up to her as an "icon." Reportedly, both Jeremy and Jameson were shocked to learn of their young fan base.

But if we don't want this kind of thing to happen, then it seems that we need new role models. And we need them fast. For girls to have meaning-ful choices and genuine hope, the "wild girl" or "bad girl" cannot seem like the only empowered option. So in this book you will hear voices of young women who chose to rebel, in various ways, against cultural messages to be "bad"—as well as my analysis of why this is happening now.

We are living through a unique cultural moment, society moving on two tracks simultaneously. In some obvious respects, the STDs, the violent music, the oversexualized dolls all seem to be getting worse; and yet despite this —or perhaps because of it—a rebellion is already under way. Obvi-ously, part of the reason I've written this book is that I was inspired by talk-ing with these young women, and I certainly hope that you will enjoy reading about them. But I also firmly believe that the direction society takes depends on you, the reader: what we value and what we devalue.

If I can persuade just one person inclined to make fun of the "good girl" to reconsider his or her scorn, then as far as I'm concerned, this whole en-terprise has been worthwhile.

the good girl
REVOLUTION

CHAPTER ONE

"Hi, Slut!"

·

There is a metal go-go cage in which a group of Duke girls clad in tiny denim skirts and halters perform a modified pole dance, but no one seems to be watching. . . . Much to the disappointment of many students, female and male, there's no real dating scene at Duke—true for a lot of colleges. "I've never been asked out on a date in my entire life—not once," says one stunning brunette. Nor has a guy ever bought her a drink. "I think that if anybody ever did that, I would ask him if he were on drugs," she says. Rather, there's the casual one-night stand, usually bolstered by heavy drinking and followed the next morning by—well, nothing, usually. "You'll hook up with a guy, and you know that nothing will come out of it," says Anna. The best thing you can hope for, she says, "is that you'll get to hook up with him again.

—JANET REITMAN, *Rolling Stone*, June 1, 2006

When *Rolling Stone* magazine starts to read like the *National Review*, then clearly something has gone very wrong. Not since the Cuban missile crisis of 1962 has there been such bipartisan agreement that we have a problem. It is certainly puzzling. On the one hand, girls are more educated and women more successful in business than ever before. At the same time, girls report that in their private lives, they are feeling enormous pressure to be sexually active and don't know how to say no. Numerous studies from left, right, and center have shown that when women get to college, they are extremely dissatisfied with the lack of a "dating scene." They long to be taken out but instead are made to feel they are weird if they don't "go with the flow" of the hookup scene instead. "The guy means nothing to you" is the socially correct view to adopt. Even an article in a women's magazine encouraging the sisterhood to be happy as singles—"Down with the Husband Hunt!" was the charming title—the author had to admit that she "succumbs . . . from time to time" to the theory "that we are living in a lopsided dating universe in which the cards are all stacked in favor of the guys." Kerry Ball, twenty-nine, of Miami, told her, "Men are just looking for girls to mess around with rather than have a relationship with or even simply date. There are so many single girls looking for relationships that these guys have no trouble finding someone to sleep with them." The number of unmarried women between ages thirty and thirty-four has more than tripled during the past thirty years, and the percentage of childless women in their early forties has doubled. You might say that the "glass ceiling" has shifted from work to women's personal lives.

At this writing, something called PSD is all over the news, and perhaps it may be helpful. I first read about PSD in *Wired,* and since *Wired* is a technology magazine, I assumed it was referring to Photoshop files (which have PSD file extensions) or that the writer had misspelled Canada's PST, provincial sales tax. Neither assumption was right. But this new breakthrough is revolutionizing people's intimate lives.

PSD stands for "pre-sex discussion." As Regina Lynn glowingly reports, the sex therapist Roger Libby has recently discovered that if you get to know the person you're about to have sex with, even a little bit, the sex itself is improved. "Sex is so much more than intercourse and [in his new book] he encourages readers to have an extensive pre-sex discussion, or PSD, before becoming sexually involved with a partner."

Is sex more than just intercourse? This idea is not old-fashioned, like modesty or courtship, you understand. This is a modern thing. Libby is an adjunct professor at the Institute for Advanced Study of Human Sexuality in San Francisco, and his advanced studies of humans have led him to conclude that young people, especially, should conduct PSDs. (His book is billed as *A Guide to Intelligent Sexual Choices for Teenagers and Twentysomethings.*) Then we come to the actual elucidation: "A PSD is an intimate and entertaining conversation that informs prospective lovers about each other's feelings, desires, expectations, fantasies and her/his sexual knowledge and sophistication. It's an introduction to the possibility of a sexual relationship or encounter." Indeed, "a properly conducted PSD . . . includes the meaning of sex."

Whenever I hear experts marketing older notions as newfangled radical concepts that have just occurred to them, like PSDs, it makes me wonder HDDTTPA?—How dumb do they think people are? It takes a college-educated expert to be infected with the opposite notion in the first place; hence the surprise at the "revelation" of PSD, known to the rest of us as common sense.

But I can certainly appreciate the need for a verbal paint job. After all, look at what happened to me. Around ten years ago I began to notice that many young women were becoming disenchanted with casual sex, but it was equally clear that waiting for "the one" was seen as a bit pathological—only for those with hang-ups. Single at the time, and not yet living in our moment of heightened PSD awareness, I decided to pen a defense of sexual modesty. I knew that my arguments—that preserving the erotic depends on a sense of mystery, for example—might be challenged; but nothing prepared me for the tongue-lashings I would receive from my elders for questioning the ancien régime of the 1960s. The alarm was sounded, and all the professional smirkers were dispatched to the front lines. Katha Pollitt called me a "twit" who should be in charge of designing "new spandex chadors for female olympians." Camille Paglia simply declared, "Oh, she makes me sick!" In a sense, it was touching to see sworn ideological enemies join hands and come together—at long last—for the purpose of descending on me: feminists, antifeminists, libertarians, pornographers. At least I was a uniter, not a divider. *Playboy* featured my book under the heading "A Man's Worst Nightmare," and *The Nation* solemnly foretold that I would "certainly be embarrassed" and regret my stance "in a few years." I should be ashamed of myself. To some baby boomers, it seemed, modesty is much worse than adultery.

I trudged on, under the heavy burden of the Scarlet M, baffled but fascinated by the eruption I had instigated. After the *New York Observer* printed a front-page caricature of me as an SS officer, it dawned on me that my opponents were illustrating their intolerance far more colorfully than I could have done on my own. Although we live in a supposedly liberated age, our hysterical witch-hunting of those who question our ideal of recreational sex suggests something else: that our liberation does not extend quite as far as we imagine.

But I wasn't discouraged, not even when I received death threats, because I was too busy reading fascinating letters from young women. Precisely because being a romantic is nowadays an unpardonable sin, these young women, thousands of them, had been sure that something was very wrong with them. Seven years later, I still receive the same kind of letter, and it never fails to touch me. Here are excerpts from various letters; you'll notice a common thread. First, from Rachel:

> You basically laid out almost exactly how I felt as a woman. I am twenty years old and have been asking myself questions like, "What's wrong with me? Why haven't I had sex yet?" . . . Anyway, reading your book, my faith was restored. I am a romantic. . . . I couldn't figure out why I hadn't just slept with this guy or that one like my friends do. And I'll say I was so close to doing that just because I thought it would help me grow up. Be more my own age. Even my mother wanted me to do it. And that's why I thank God I read your book when I did. I began crying toward the end when I realized that nothing was wrong with me and that I was lucky to still have what I have. My desire to be with one person isn't childish or immature. . . . I'm not scared; I just don't have an interest in [sex] as a sport.

From Carrie:

> Your book honestly helped me make sense of a lot of what I had experienced. I went through a bad stage in college where I remember thinking that my instincts (that what I was doing was bad) were irrational and struggled to adopt an "it's no big deal" attitude. Your book was the first time I really sorted through things enough to recognize that our instincts are there for a reason and that the "it's no big deal" attitude is such a horribly depressing view to accept.

About 70 percent of these e-mails and letters indicated that the writer felt that wanting marriage and children was an aspiration she needed to "hide." (From J: "Have I ruined something wonderful by giving in and hiding what I really wanted—marriage and children?") This did not surprise me, but I was shocked that according to nearly half of the letters, a girl's own parent thought something was wrong with her for not being sufficiently casual about sex. Here is one example, from an e-mail sent in October 2004:

> Somehow with it being perfectly normal for twelve- to fourteen-year-olds to have field/bush parties, getting drunk and having sex and doing whatever the locally available substances were, I managed to be one of

the few that "escaped with my dignity intact," I guess. I did end up getting ditched after eight months by a guy because I wouldn't have sex with him. . . . I just didn't like him that much. But I certainly did feel ashamed and embarrassed about remaining a virgin so long. . . . I am twenty-three now. My mother freaks out if I want to borrow the car to drive a friend back to [a nearby town] and return in the dark, but when I'd just turned twenty, and she and I went to Michigan to visit a guy I wasn't technically seeing at the time, and to see the tall ships in Bay City, and I ended up in his hotel room, which was next door to ours. He was better at conversation and had something more interesting on TV, and Mom was staying up reading and watching QVC, so I wouldn't be able to get much sleep there, either. After she found out that we hadn't had sex, she asked me whether I was frigid or gay. He was nearly forty! Perfectly fine for your twenty-year-old daughter to screw a guy twice her age, just as long as she doesn't return *your* car after dark when she's going somewhere that's all of forty-five minutes away. My mom thinks I'm a freak.

Usually these stories were depressing, but I did hear one that was priceless. A friend of a friend, in her late twenties, returned from a romantic weekend and was sharply interrogated by her mother—but not in the way you might expect. When she found out that her daughter hadn't slept with the new boyfriend after a whole weekend away, the mother warned her ominously, "You're gonna lose him!" (She didn't; they eventually got married.)

Parents want to know how to speak to their children about sex, and kids certainly want to hear from parents. ("Teenagers Want More Advice from Parents on Sex, Study Says" is a typical news headline.) And the experts tell us that parents are the biggest influence on whether a teenager decides to have sex. Yet there is one big stumbling block: Often parents don't realize that their sexual revolution has become the entrenched status quo. Today many young women feel oppressed by the expectation that they will engage in casual sex, just as their mothers once felt oppressed by the expectation that they would be virgins until marriage. Parents in the grip of a notion that they need to be "cool" want to show they understand that the kids are going to "do it anyway." Ironically, this adds to the pressure. For boys too, *You're liberated, so get going!* doesn't always translate into an "I care" message. William Nobel, M.D., of the Pediatric Association of the University of Texas, shares a story about his practice:

Recently Todd, an anxious fifteen-year-old male patient, presented to clinic with vague reproductive tract complaints. He was accompanied by his mother, who returned to the waiting room after the initial interview. His history gradually revealed a series of sexual encounters with a woman several years his senior. The sexual liaisons included other risks as well, including alcohol and substance use. The teen's anxiety resulted from an awareness that his behavior placed him at risk for HIV. He requested HIV testing. While discussing the testing and evaluation for other sexually transmitted infections, the boy began to cry.

"I don't think that my mom loves me," he sobbed.

"Why do you say that?" I responded.

"She doesn't care where I go or who I'm with or if I come home at night. I don't have a curfew and she never asks what I'm doing."

Reluctance to set limits is not simply a U.S. phenomenon. Because of the challenges parents face after divorce—or many times simply because they believe freedom is the better approach—mum's the word. "Parents often don't want to be in their kids' bad books," says Sara Dimerman, a child and family therapist who is based in Toronto. After a twelve-year-old girl was stabbed on a street in Toronto's entertainment district at two-thirty AM one Saturday in May 2006, many people wondered why a twelve-year-old girl had been partying at all hours in the first place. The answer, apparently, was that eighth-grade graduation now resembles a high school prom, and many twelve-year-olds party all night like older teens. Coed sleepovers and all-night clubbing often have the parents' blessing: "Twelve is the new fifteen," said the local papers.

In a survey of 1,000 girls in Britain, seven times as many teens picked "lap dancer" as a "good profession" over being a teacher. And Jessica, a twenty-one-year-old camp counselor in Paris, tells me she cannot believe the way the twelve-year-olds speak to one another: *Les garçons disent aux filles, "Je veux te niquer," et les filles répondent, "moi aussi." C'est comme si ils se disaient, "Comment vas-tu?" et "ça va bien."* (The boys say to the girls, "I want to f——k you," and the girls say, "me too!" It's like saying, "How are you?" and "I'm fine.") *Si la fille ne répond pas "moi aussi," ils se moquent d'elle en disant "es-tu homosexuelle ou quoi?"* (If a girl doesn't say "me too!" then it's like, "Are you gay or what?")

Who is countering these pressures? Well, there's Sharon Stone, who travels around the world and hears from young people while she is signing autographs. Often she is asked, "What to do if I'm being pressured for sex?" In March 2006, asked this by yet another girl, Stone saw fit to make public the advice she's been giving teen girls for a while: "I tell them what I believe—oral sex is a hundred times safer than vaginal or anal sex. If you're in a situation where you cannot get out of sex, offer a blow job." This advice was widely circulated. One Internet-based sex educator who works with teenagers thanked Stone for her "frank discussion"; he also "thought of teens I've talked to while doing sex education who have had sex when they really didn't want to." On the other hand, he "worried she may be unaware of the many STDs that can be transmitted via oral sex."

Sexually transmitted diseases are indeed a problem: over 4 million new cases are diagnosed each year. But the reason Stone's advice is awful goes far beyond STDs, I'm afraid. If a girl doesn't want to have sex, why can't she just say no, without having to offer an oral consolation prize? Nowadays, girls are made to feel that they have to offer *something*, and it had better be more than just the pleasure of their company.

The sad fact is that much of the sex teen girls have is unwanted. In a study of 279 female adolescents published in *Archives of Pediatrics and Adolescent Medicine* in June 2006, about 41 percent of girls ages fourteen to seventeen reported having "unwanted sex." Most of the girls had "unwanted sex because they feared the partner would get angry if denied sex." And even when sex is wanted, it tends to be regretted soon after—especially by girls. According to a study done by the National Campaign to Prevent Teen Pregnancy in 2004, two-thirds of all sexually experienced teens said that they wished they had waited longer before having sex (in studies in both 2000 and 2004, the number of girls who regretted sex was consistently higher than the number of boys).

People are always surprised to learn this—as Diane Sawyer was when her famous special on Norplant in urban high schools turned up this unforseen fact. All of the sexually active girls the reporters talked to wished they had waited until marriage. The adults in the segment were strongly in favor of Norplant for teenage girls, so hearing the girls confess this came as a shock.

The marriage educator Marline Pearson, who teaches at Madison Area Technical College in Wisconsin, described the pressure on girls "to have lots of casual sex." By the time girls are fourteen to sixteen, according to one of her young students, "they don't have any concept of sex as something special. After awhile it makes them feel worthless. There is no pleasure. They aren't enjoying it." Pearson sadly remarks, "I increasingly hear girls talk about sex as something you just do. Get it over with, get desensitized, so you don't think or expect too much of it. Sad commentary."

In a survey done in 2005, the steamy adult series *Desperate Housewives* ranked as the most popular network television show among kids ages nine to twelve. That means they are soaking up story lines such as "Bree" and her teen son competing to bed the same man, or glamorous "Gaby" trashing virginity:

> "Are you sure she's a virgin?"
> "Yeah, I wouldn't just bash her for nothing."
>
> "Rich men don't marry virgins, for the same reasons they don't hire chauffeurs who can't drive. They value *experience*."

Yet in real life, the more experiences teens have, the more likely they are to be depressed and commit suicide—again, this is particularly true of girls.

In May 2006 a study supported by the National Institutes of Health found that among nearly 19,000 teens, girls were about four times more likely to be depressed if they experimented with sex, and that the depressive symptoms generally increased as the risky behavior increased. Girls who abstained from sex (or drugs) didn't have significantly different rates of depression from boys who abstained, but as soon as boys and girls started experimenting, girls were much more likely to become depressed "from engaging in low to moderate risk behaviors." These symptoms of depression included "a loss of appetite, feelings of sadness, . . . a loss of interest in areas in which they were previously interested, and a hopeless feeling for the future."

In an important study from the Pacific Institute for Research done in 2005, the authors concluded that "sex, drugs and alcohol among teens actually precede—and apparently lead to—the onset of adolescent depression, which contradicts the common belief that depressed teens may be 'self-medicating' through substance abuse and sex." For some time now, we've known that sexually active teenagers—particularly girls—are more likely to be depressed and to attempt suicide, but there is some kind of fortress or wall of denial between the facts and the advice that is given to teenagers. Yet their unhappiness can be ignored for only so long.

Every emergency room is seeing girls who have deliberately cut themselves badly, and psychiatrists who work in ERs tell us that self-mutilation is usually caused by feelings of anger and rejection. The authors of *Packaging Girlhood* tell us not to worry too much: "Researchers tell us that cutting is not as severe a symptom as it may seem. It serves two purposes: It brings stress relief when a child feels overwhelmed, and it helps her feel real in a world that doesn't know her, doesn't see her." Leaving aside the fact that the girls themselves report being miserable, and even if you accept the whitewashing—that they merely do not feel "real"—isn't this strange enough? Suddenly girls do not feel "real," in a society which is supposed to have girls' liberation as its goal.

This, I would submit, is because conforming to badness is ultimately more oppressive than conforming to goodness. Badness demands that you lose your virginity ASAP, to whomever, as long as you get rid of it. You don't have to like the person you're hooking up with; as long as you go along, we won't throw tomatoes at you. And if you *really* don't want to have sex, then you must offer secondary sexual favors instead (as recommends Sharon Stone). Could it be that badness requires more suppression of individual preferences than goodness ever did? As the old guides for young people make abundantly clear, the point of delaying gratification was precisely to preserve your individuality, preferences, and goals—and your long-term happiness.

In contrast, a groundbreaking 2003 study of 372 college students appearing in the *Journal of Sex Research* found that both male and female students "hook up" primarily because of peer pressure, not because they themselves are really comfortable with uncommitted sex. This phenomenon is called "pluralistic ignorance," a wonderful term coined by Floyd Allport in 1924. It's what happens when individuals in a group each imagine that their private feelings or judgment diverge from the norm, but they nonetheless conform to that norm because they want to be seen as a desirable member of the group. Each believes that others behave a certain way because they truly want to, when in fact everyone else also has private qualms about the norm. As applied to uncommitted sex on college campuses, where "hooking up has become the norm for heterosexual sexual relationships," researchers in 2003 found that it works like this:

> Since the great majority of students do in fact hook up, it appears that most students believe that others are comfortable—more comfortable than they are themselves—with engaging in a variety of uncommitted sexual behaviors. . . . Consistent with other pluralistic ignorance re-

search, this study showed evidence of an illusion of universality. The students failed to appreciate the extent to which others have different comfort levels with hooking-up behaviors. That is, students wrongly assumed that the attitudes of others about hooking up were more homogeneous than they actually were.

Similar to other researchers, we found that men expressed greater comfort than did women with sexually intimate hooking-up behaviors. In the context of hooking up, this could lead to serious consequence. Our study suggests that men believe women are more comfortable engaging in these behaviors than in fact they are, and also that women believe other women are more comfortable engaging in these behaviors than they are themselves. As a consequence, some men may pressure women to engage in intimate sexual behaviors, and some women may engage in these behaviors or resist only weakly because they believe they are unique in feeling discomfort about engaging in them.

Everyone swims toward the norm and imagines that others are having a great time, when in fact many are drowning. Disturbingly, the authors conclude that "it is possible for a woman to experience sexual assault but not interpret the behavior as such, believing it to be normative behavior with which her peers are comfortable." Of those college students who do regret hooking up, men tend to say a hookup was a "terrible experience" because of too much alcohol, or because the woman wanted a relationship (i.e., had the temerity to hang around afterward). For many women, on the other hand, a "terrible hookup" is one in which they are pressured to go farther than they wanted. People disagree about when unwanted sex becomes sexual assault, but one thing seems obvious: The hookup scene is not quite the endless party it is made out to be.

Why are college students having sex they don't really want to have, and why should teenage girls feel that they "cannot get out of sex"? The reason is that sex has become political. Looking "wild" and acting "wild" are supposed to be empowering, but more often they lead to misery, especially for young women who quickly learn to put their emotions in a deep freeze in order to do what is expected. Irene, fifteen, hooked up with a boy for some time—"we basically became friends with benefits," she confided to a reporter for *The New York Times*. Unfortunately, the boy never got around to asking her out on a real date, as Irene was hoping, so she was "devastated."

But she says, "Since then, I've become really good at keeping my emotions in check. I can hook up with a guy and not fall for him." She doesn't get this backward reasoning out of nowhere. Voicing a common view (and in the same *New York Times* piece), Jeanette May, cofounder of the Coalition for Positive Sexuality, declares that girls "are better served by having sex for their pleasure, without a lot of emotional attachment." This explains why, instead of learning from her mistake and not giving herself so easily to the next guy, Irene turned on herself and her sense of right and wrong and saw her own capacity for feeling as the problem. After all, if she could purge herself of all feeling, there would be nothing standing between her and the casual sex she was supposed to enjoy.

Studies have shown that the fewer sexual partners adults have, the longer their marriages tend to last (and the happier, healthier, and more successful people are in general). Also, marital sex was found to be more physically and emotionally satisfying than sex among singles or those who cohabit. And yet, we still pretend that the more promiscuous and public sexuality is, the more exciting it is, even when the participants themselves do not experience it that way. Experience and social science lead to one conclusion; conventional wisdom and peer pressure recommend an entirely divergent path.

When you examine why young women are told to sleep around for the sake of feminism and "positive sexuality," even when it makes them unhappy, the reason often comes down to a corruption of the idea of "girl power": Girls must do everything boys do, even if it's not working. Margaret Atwood, among others, believes that real equality "means equally bad as well as equally good." Similarly, many people, noticing that men seem capable of sex without emotional consequences, conclude that jadedness and disconnection are now the goal for all humanity. As various media have reported, "slut" has become a casual greeting among girls ("Hi, slut!"), and many girls now compete at how "skanky" they can be. Our experts on teenage girls talk about how we needed to "reclaim" the word "slut" in order to fight against the "double standard." If only we can glorify young women sleeping around the way that we embrace it for young men, then—supposedly—no one need feel bad. Apparently, now that girls greet one another with "Hi, slut!" we have achieved our goal. Yet when experts invoke a single standard, they always seem to mean a single low standard. So what's the great achievement here?

The ideologues have long claimed that the only reason the promiscuous girl is unhappy is the "stigma" imposed on her. If we didn't ostracize her, if we accepted—nay, promoted—her, then she'd be flying high with notches on her belt just like Don Juan. I think it's safe to say that we can test, and now discard, this theory. We live in an age when sex tapes are star-making vehicles, when strippers are teen girls' role models, and when Slut lip balm and Dirty Girl body products are all "super stylin'." And still, Doña Juanita is typically not the happy camper we have been led to expect. Witness Jessica Cutler, twenty-seven, a former aide on Capitol Hill who detailed her multiple Beltway conquests online, including flings with married men. *The Washington Post* praised her for being "free of romantic illusions" and an "American über-individualist," yet her own perspective on herself was somewhat less stellar: "It probably is just a huge defense mechanism, dating several men," she admitted. "Because you are, like, if it doesn't go well with this guy, there's always the others. . . . All your relationships are kind of half-assed." A year later, Jessica told *New York* magazine that she was secretly hoping one of her "psycho" lovers would kill her, because "what a relief that would be." A joke? Perhaps. But it takes a certain degree of self-loathing to joke about such things.

Being "equally bad" in an attempt to quash the double standard doesn't seem to work very well. In 2005, Andrea Lavinthal and Jessica Rozler made a splash by proposing that the "walk of shame" be renamed something with "a more positive ring," such as the "I Got Booty Boogie" or the "Post-Seduction Strut." The authors say that "conflicting social messages" are why it's no fun to step out on a Sunday morning in Saturday night gear and smudged mascara. I'm not convinced. More likely, if you don't know the man well enough to have had a change of clothes at his apartment, the walk home is a stark reminder that you may have just exchanged bodily fluids with a virtual stranger. Instead of trying to reprogram women to feel good about this when clearly they do not, wouldn't it make more sense to try to revive a single high standard?

Yet those who prop up the ideal of the bad girl always seem to take their cues (from the "strut" to the "booty") from the most adolescent boys. In other words, it's a rather immature and sexist sort of equality. You rarely hear someone say, "Gee! Scrapbooking is becoming so popular now among young women. Let's get the boys to scrapbook too, and then we can all be equal!" It's never the boys who must learn to scrapbook in order to lead us to utopia; rather, the girls must learn to sleep around and suppress their emotions.

Men report that the number one reason they are choosing to marry later, if at all, is that sex without commitment is so widely available. Yet curiously, the majority of advice books for women instruct them to be casual about sex—and specifically to deny even wanting to get married—in order to be "liberated" and attractive to a man. *The Hookup Handbook: A Single Girl's Guide to Living It Up,* for example, doesn't quite live up to its promise, fielding such depressing questions as, "We've hooked up three times; shouldn't he ask me out?" and tackling "*the booty disparity (noun):* The difference between what you think a hookup meant and what he thinks it meant." As one might expect, there is no real cure for this booty disparity, according to the authors: "Dating is a thing of the past, gone the way of dinosaurs and stirrup pants. It's extinct. Kaput. Over." But if dating is kaput, and nonetheless there is a "booty disparity" to contend with, what is a young woman to do about those nagging hopes for something more? As twenty-six-year-old Frances asks me: "It's like I'm supposed to pretend I'm not me—don't want marriage—in order to be attractive, but then how do I know that my boyfriend really loves the real me, if he doesn't know what I really want?"

A conundrum indeed, yet this is only one of many contemporary love problems. Increasing numbers of men are finding it impossible to perform with their girlfriends and wives because sex has become so "demystified." Shockingly, when given a choice between a real woman and Internet porn, many men choose the porn. There is now talk of a nasal spray, PT-141, a "libido-enhancer" that takes effect in just fifteen minutes. Apparently, we need it.

In 2005, Professor Chyng Sun of New York University was shocked when she worked on a documentary about young people and pornography, so she wrote an essay in *Counterpunch* urging her fellow liberals to take pornographic images more seriously. As she found, it wasn't just that in many porn flicks abuse and mistreatment of women are the whole point; it was also that viewing these images was damaging young people's relationships.

In my interviews, it was painful to hear how both teenage boys and girls feel pressured to have lots of sex, often emotionally detached, at a younger and younger age; and how so many young women feel obligated to please men sexually because they believed that it was their role as a woman. A twenty-year-old female college student thought back to her teen years and said that often she felt that her body was not hers but was for others to look at and gain pleasure from. It is also alarming that many young men and boys have watched a lot of pornography before they have opportunities for sexual intimacy. Some developed a fear of women when they found that real women's bodies were not as smooth and shaven and that real sex was nothing like the sex depicted in pornography. It is clear that pornography not only hurts women but also hurts men on many different levels.

Meanwhile, members of Single Mothers by Choice search online for the right sperm instead of the right man, who often takes too long to appear. One member, Lori Gottlieb, wonders: "Was believing in love today akin to believing in Santa Claus, the Easter Bunny, and age-defying cosmetics?" Indeed, researchers from the University of Chicago and UCLA who have been tracking and quantifying loneliness for thirty years have found that it has reached epidemic proportions.

Then there are the difficulties caused by the general collapse of boundaries. A young mother of two—call her Andy—attends a black-tie holiday office party, where she is serenaded "at least four times" by an annoying rendition of the Pussycat Dolls' "Don't Cha." "Don't cha wish your girlfriend was hot like me?" the singer croons, as the women in the audience shift uncomfortably in their seats, hoping that this entertainer in the slinky cocktail dress will just go away. Instead she sings over and over, "Don't cha wish your girlfriend was raw like me?" Having spent hours prettifying themselves, and with husbands or boyfriends in tow, many had been hoping for something more along the lines of Peggy Lee's "When a Woman Loves a Man." Later in the same month, Andy will attend a show to benefit her daughter's school for developmentally delayed children. This time she and the other tired mothers are looking forward to a night out for a good cause, but instead they are confronted by anorexic-looking women modeling provocative clothing, and by a master of ceremonies joking about "hookers." There are children in the audience. Andy is the epitome of the modern woman—she even "swears like a sailor," as she jokes to me. But she is fed up. She wonders, "Isn't there such a thing as the right time and place anymore?"

To me it raises another question: If doing away with "repression" was supposed to be liberating, why are things now so bad? It is sad enough that we cannot seem to protect children, but the attractive, intelligent women surfing for tadpoles and grown men trading intimacy for inflated megapixels do not exactly seem to be thriving, either. Amy Sohn, one of the more articulate sex columnists, became famous detailing her trysts for the *New York Press* in the late 1990s. Today she asks, "What is the point of casual sex if the sex part isn't any good?" An excellent question. It is now sex therapists who are encouraging women to "raise your standards" and "avoid the booty-call blues"—not for any moralistic reason but simply because casual sex doesn't deliver the goods: not sexual fulfillment, and not long-term commitments either.

Ian Kerner, the most popular sex therapist of the moment (he's even been a guest on Howard Stern's show), delivers the news gently, telling women, "Not to say you can't have casual sex, fall in love, and live happily ever after, but it's less likely." For those who wish to leave marriage aside, Dr. Kerner still issues a caution: *"It's your call,"* he writes in his latest book. "You can have sex like a man but just know that the more casual the situation," the "less likely" you'll achieve satisfaction or indeed "any emotional state of happiness." So why is no one burning him in effigy? As an author who has written about how to satisfy your partner, Dr. Kerner is perceived as having authority in this arena. Lending him extra credibility, to be sure, is the fact that he is a man, and he can admit that casual sex is "hollow" for men too: "You can teach yourself to have sex like a man," he counsels, "but that doesn't mean that men, deep down, wouldn't rather learn to have sex like a woman." In other words, just as George Gilder noted back in 1973, it turns out that men are also better off being married and integrating their emotions.

Does the success of Dr. Kerner mean that the tide is turning? Yes and no. It's certainly refreshing that someone in his field can finally be honest about the emotional and physical dead end these casual flings have led to, instead of the mush we are usually bombarded with: "All choices are equal until you kill someone." (And even that may be OK if you had a bad childhood.) Still, we have known about the side effects of promiscuity for years, and many counselors and opinion leaders have proved themselves remarkably capable of ignoring the misery all around them.

Listen to the executive director of California's National Organization for Women (NOW), Helen Grieco, who recently rushed to the defense of the *Girls Gone Wild* videos: "I think it's about being a rebel, and I don't think it's a bad notion," she told Elizabeth Strickland of the *San Francisco Weekly*. That's because "flashing your breasts on Daytona Beach says, 'I'm not a good girl. I think it's sexy to be a bad girl.'" Being good is seen as the worst possible thing a girl could be.

And so the bad-girl wave continues to crash through our lives. In its undertow, neither facts nor tears seem to matter at all.

From where does it draw its power? Perhaps the bad girl is simply the common erotic object of most men and women today; the men still seek her, and the women still try to be her. If this requires emotional disconnection, then so be it.

She has become our new norm.

EXERCISE:
FINDING YOUR OWN AUTHENTIC SCRIPT

A few years ago, I was invited to be part of a televised dinner program on PBS, "If Women Ruled the World." The other eighteen women included Sandra Day O'Connor, the first woman justice of the U.S. Supreme Court; Lin Chai, the leader of the Chinese democracy movement; and Kim Campbell, the first woman prime minister of Canada. Naturally, I felt honored to be included among such distinguished ladies, and I kept a low profile. The producer called me afterward to set up a private interview—as he had with the other guests—and my comments would be interspersed with the dinner footage.

We were about to set a time when, to my surprise, the producer began to explain what he wanted me to say: that a certain second-wave feminist (another guest) had saved womankind and that I, as a young woman, was grateful to her. Well, I told him, I couldn't exactly say that, as I didn't agree with this woman's idea that housewives were "parasites" or with a number of other things she had written, although I did have respect for her. I myself did want to get married and didn't see my inability to cook as an advantage. It was then that the producer began to get impatient: "What you're saying," he sputtered into the phone, "isn't in the script!" "Oh, excuse me," I replied. "I didn't realize there was a script—I thought we had all been invited to express our different opinions in our capacity as 'powerful women.'" The producer valiantly tried to run through my "script" once more, and to state the conditions under which I would be filmed; and I recapped that there was no way I was going to say something that I didn't believe. I'm afraid the conversation did not end well, and needless to say, he never did come to film me.

For a moment after I was cut out of an opportunity the other guests had been given, I felt anxious and wondered whether I had made a mistake. But then I realized the comedy of the situation. Here was this man, making a movie supposedly to celebrate "women and power," and yet the power was all his, and the script was all his. To me it was an allegory for the experience of being a young woman in today's society. In many small ways, usually a bit more subtle than this producer's behavior, we are notified that we must "liberate" ourselves by disrobing, "empower" our sexuality by being indiscriminate in our choice of partners, and strive to see other women primarily as sexual competitors. But for many of us, we soon learn that this path requires repressing our ideals. To many of us, the script is for the entertainment of adolescent men—it is not our own.

Think about the "script" you grew up with, and the one you've adopted now. What are the ways in which it is working and not working for you? How much of it comes from the media, and how much from your own heart? I would never want my script to be yours, because obviously you deserve your own. But whatever it is, may it be authentic.

CHAPTER TWO

The New Bad-Girl Script
and Its Limitations

Sibyl, just promise before I leave you that you will be a good girl, that
you will make goodness the first thing in life. If, for instance, we were
never to meet again—of course we shall, thousands of times, but just
suppose, for the sake of saying it, that we did not, I should like to know
that my little girl put goodness first. There is nothing else worth the
while in life. Cling on to it, Sibyl, cling tight hold to it. Never forget—

—From *Daddy's Girl* by L. T. Meade (1891), part of a little speech a father
gives to his daughter before going away on a long journey.

Mollie, a sophomore in high school, was upset when she came home
from school one day in 2001. Her English teacher had told her,
"Why don't you lose the glasses? Get a crop top. Go tell that hunk over
there that you want to have a good time for an hour." The comment "did
touch on her insecurities," explained her mother, in Nina Shandler's book
Ophelia's Mom. The teacher defended her tactics: "I thought I was being a
caring adult." She was only trying to keep Mollie abreast of the new expectations.

In all likelihood, poor Mollie was all too aware of these expectations. In
October 2006, a girl named Regina said to me in an e-mail, "I know many
teens are having sex at fourteen, but I, at fourteen, still haven't even kissed
anyone. I know a kiss may seem like nothing, but I just haven't found anyone to kiss, anyone I truly like." She tells me about the T-shirts that read
SPANK ME, IT'S MY BIRTHDAY!—these are popular among her peers—and
why she refuses to wear one: "For me a line was truly crossed when my
eighth-grade teacher made '69' jokes. . . . My past two male teachers have
made sex sound like an animal act." One teacher had actually advised her

that "sex is something you should be doing after the third date or get ready to be dumped." This is what coeds were told when I was in college. Regina continued: "When I told him I thought he was wrong he told me that I'm not facing reality and I need to open up my eyes, but in my heart I truly think sex is an act of passion and love between two people with mutual respect for each other. I don't care if romance may seem hopeless, I'm going to wait until I find someone who truly respects me, appreciates me, and loves me." She later sends pictures of herself by e-mail (she is attractive and rather angelic-looking) because she wants me to know that "PS: The reason I haven't kissed anyone isn't because I'm unsure of my looks, or myself. . . . It's just when I tell people I've never kissed anyone their assumption is I'm ugly or I just stay at home."

Whatever your views on the sexual revolution, surely we can all agree that it's sad when male teachers instruct fourteen-year-old girls that romance is "hopeless," or when it's conventional wisdom that sexually inactive girls are "ugly." Where are these messages coming from? Where *aren't* they coming from would be easier to answer.

When I log on to one of the best websites of political commentary, *Salon*, I read that Miss Alabama "has a lovely voice . . . but she moves her body like a girl who hasn't yet had sex." Later I get behind the wheel to run some errands, and find a local suburban dentist advertising his skills with this enormous placard: WE'RE BRINGING SEXY BACK, BY REPLACING ALL THE TEETH YOU LACK.

A visit to the bookstore is no escape; occupying a prominent spot in the main display area is a *Striptease Kit: A Guide to the Art of Striptease*. For $24.95 I can learn "Everything you need to take it ALL OFF." Really, how hard can that be? Apparently, it's complicated, requiring moves, props, and practice. The kit is said to be "full of great advice and instructions from strippers themselves" and comes with "red sequined pasties with adhesive, sheer black scarf, body glitter, 10 fold-out cards with step-by-step routines." There's something contrived about these cards—two of which are "Boudoir Betty" and "Girl Next Door"—evoking not so much Eros as desperation.

Indeed, women now are installing poles in their living rooms and kitchens, and according to *The Philadelphia Inquirer*, those whose husbands have left them "for the other woman" hope that stripping will banish "self-doubt." There is a college grad who can't wait to "learn to dance like the women she'd seen at strip clubs." The demand is so great that entire fitness organizations are remaking themselves as "tantric" or "flirty girl" fitness, offering classes that run the gamut from pole dancing to stripping, even lap dancing. Manhattan alone has New York Pole Dancing, Exotic Dance Central Inc., My Pole, Passion Play Inc., and S Factor—to name just a few studios for "everyday women." Why waste time merely exercising, when you could be learning to give a good lap dance at the same time? This reminds me of the people who used to say that "housekeeping is great exercise," an idea widely lampooned during the women's movement. (Cleaning is usually enough to exhaust you, yet somehow not enough to get your heart rate up.) Who could have predicted that this notion would be replaced by "Stripping is great exercise!" Aradia Fitness, with locations all over Canada "for every woman, any age, any fitness level," offers not only an Intro to Lapdancing and Stripping Techniques for Women class ($69), but also $490 brass poles for home use. This is important: "When Aradia Fitness first opened their studio doors, it was not possible to purchase brass removable poles, making it difficult for the average woman to practice or demonstrate her pole dancing skills at home." A company in Chicago, caught up by the zeitgeist, names itself "Empowerment through Exotic Dance, Ltd." The way they present history, it's as if women were held back because they couldn't dangle upside down in their living rooms.

I'm not so sure. Having a large brass pole permanently affixed to the ceiling in the center of your living room certainly gives new meaning to the idea of "entertaining." But what happens when your guests notice the pole, and you're not feeling up to doing your shimmy? If you play the piano, you know how annoying it is when people spot a piano and expect you to play: "Oh, come on, you're wonderful!" "Sorry, I haven't practiced in ten years." "But the piano's right here!" Well, picture eight guests munching on chocolate cake, all expecting to see your new sexy moves.

In London, there is a doctor who prescribes pole dancing lessons for patients suffering from depression, and a gym teacher in Northumberland claims that she has the support of parents in teaching kids as young as age twelve how to pole-dance. In the United States, many people remain troubled that teenage girls are taking strip aerobics classes, but if stripping and pole dancing are truly routes to self-confidence, then it makes sense to start young.

In a doctor's office, I pick up *Marie Claire*, and five "confident" women smile out at me—a nurse, a musician, a dancer, a sales agent, and a proctor at a testing lab—all of whom have posed in the buff. We are told,

"These women are actually more confident naked than clothed." Then the editors pointedly ask, "Are you?" In case you missed the lesson, if you don't want to show your naked tush to millions of strangers, then, baby, you've got a confidence problem—at least according to the mainstream media.

There are people who blame "commercialism" and "sex sells" for our exhibitionist extremism, but can these really be the cause? After all, we've had capitalism for a while now, and women were crazy about, say, toasters, not about labiaplasty—surgery to make your privy parts resemble the childlike labia of porn stars. According to plastic surgeons, "feedback from male partners is the number one reason women request the surgery. . . . 'The most common reason we hear is that they have had a negative comment made by a male sexual partner.'"

Formerly, labiaplasty was the province of porn stars; now these "adult entertainers," with their waxed and altered genitalia, are perceived as our aesthetic ideal. One doctor tells the reporter Sandy Kobrin, "I can't tell you how many pages and pages of pornographic material women have brought into me saying 'I want to look like this.'"

Even realms thought to be on a higher level, such as poetry, also showcase the porn star as an ideal to aspire to. The hip, acclaimed poetry magazine *Fence* featured a naked "Suicide Girl" on its cover in 2005 because, according to its editor, Rebecca Wolff, "alternative porn" models like their cover girl are "answering strictly to themselves." (A damper was put on that claim when some models for the Suicide Girls later alleged that the site owners, one of whom is male, were mistreating them.)

Seventeen-year-old Audrey from Fort Wayne, Indiana, tells me, "Being 'bad' is like normal now." She notices that "There's so many people that are, like, 'bad,' but for them it's just normal because they don't know the difference."

Indeed, in 2004 a survey found that most adults and teenagers agree that teen girls "often receive the message" that "looking sexy is one of the most important things teenage girls can do." So the problem is much larger than merely the fact that commercialism or pornography is mainstream. The problem is our underlying attitudes, and they run very deep. When Naomi Wolf wrote in 1998, "There are no good girls, we are all bad girls," it was as if an X ray had captured our new set of expectations. Wolf meant "bad" in "the very best sense of the word," but as it starts to become a virtual requirement to be publicly sexual—and, increasingly, for younger girls—we're starting to see that "bad" can, well, have its bad side.

*   *   *

The May 2006 issue of *Teen Vogue* opens with a two-page spread from Nike: an exuberant young woman wearing a sports bra and pants, doing a very wide plié. Centered in the ad are these words, set like a poem:

> There's a HOT CHICK IN THE MIRROR. . . .
> Her pelvic thrusts are THE STUFF OF LEGEND . . . even
> her earrings have attitude.
> I can't believe THAT HOT CHICK IS ME. But I give her
> a thumbs-up.
> She gives me a SEXY SMILE. And I'm flattered. But
> hey, I HAVE A BOYFRIEND. . . .
> JUST DO IT.

This appeared in a magazine for teenagers that has 1.5 million readers, and that twelve-year-olds (and younger children) are reading. There is something about all the CAPS in the AD that is a little too MENACING. The subtext seems to be: "This hot chick HAD BETTER BE YOU." I canvass a number of young women about it, and they all say that the ad is "dumb." One has an interesting slant: "It's a little too in-your-face about 'empowering women'—I get the feeling that a man wrote it. It just screams to me, 'This is what *strong women* are supposed to think and feel.' It's sexual but in a really weird, unappealing way."

I share her suspicion, so I contact Nike to see who wrote the ad. Nate Beckenson tells me, "We generally don't call out the person or persons involved in an ad, because it's a team effort."

The team effort needs work. The same issue of *Teen Vogue* features an interview with Mandy Moore, a gorgeous twenty-two-year-old actress who plays Sally Kendoo in *American Dreamz:* "Mandy Moore Learns That Being Bad Suits Her Just Fine." This message is underscored in the text: "Being bad [in her movie role] is something at which Mandy is actually quite good." Also, "this isn't the actress's first walk on the wild side." Now we know the "dark side of America's sweetheart," and so on. Another profile, of a twenty-year-old "vixen," Vanessa Lengies (from *Stick It*), also talks about how being "bad" in her movies is "awesome. . . . Everyone should try playing the bad girl once in her life."

So much badness, so little time. But in the back of the magazine, the reader learns about eighteen-year-old Claire, who contracted HPV and has precancerous cervical cells, although she always used a condom with her boyfriend. HPV can be spread in skin-to-skin genital contact, a little-known fact. Claire's boyfriend then broke up with her, not wanting to believe he had HPV (men don't always have symptoms). Now Claire wants to warn other teens: "Even kids who don't have sex, who just fool around or whatever, can still get it." Claire has to go to her doctor every three months for loop electrosurgical excision to scrape cells from her cervix, and "as my surgeries add up, so does the probability that if I have children in the future, I'll give birth prematurely." Each operation shortens the cervix and makes it more likely that she won't be able to carry a child to term, so Claire decided to speak out: "When you have sex, you don't think about things like how it's going to affect you in five or ten years. I assumed that using a condom and being on the Pill was enough."

It is so typical: *Be bad, bad, bad;* and then the blip—PS, this often doesn't work out.

Christina Aguilera, according to her producer, Linda Perry, released the single "Dirrty" (2002) in order "to show everybody that she's not some goody-two-shoes." Even after getting happily hitched, Aguilera felt the need in 2006 to let the public know that she was keeping her bad-girl bona fides. She reassured *The New York Times:* "Just because I have this new-found love in my life, that doesn't mean I'm going to play it any softer, or that I'm going to change my point of view on sexuality. . . . I still got the nasty in me." One can only hope that, in time, she will recover from the damage done to her by marrying such a nice man.

I think there is a misunderstanding here. We continually malign the good girl as "repressed," while the bad girl is (wrongly) perceived as intrinsically expressing her individuality and somehow proving her sexuality. Taking off your shirt is a way to "be part of history," according to a professor who has studied the *Girls Gone Wild* phenomenon. Leave your clothing on, and who will notice you or know that you are proud of your body? Modesty is always taken to be shame, although they are two distinct words and two very different concepts. The prevailing view is that if you think sexuality should be private or special, then you must be ashamed of it. You're a prude. Conversely, if you are "comfortable with your sexuality," then you should be "cool" with lifting your shirt for strangers or cheering on your man as he enjoys a lap dance with another woman.

If you're like me, you may wonder how this harem mentality is liberating for women. Now that some *Playboy* bunnies are defecting, admitting publicly that the sex at the *Playboy* mansion is actually quite awful, the time is perhaps ripe to discard some of our assumptions. Even non-bunnies, such as Jennifer Saginor—whose father was Hugh Hefner's "doctor," in charge of providing diet pills and breast enhancements for Hefner's "girls"—felt she was damaged by seeing nineteen-year-old girls dying of drug overdoses, and girls whose last act on earth was performing sexual favors for men in public. Today she admits that seeing sex so violently dissociated from emotion has made it "difficult to be intimate. Very difficult."

History has taught us a surprising lesson: Intimacy flourishes where there is also restraint. Having sex for its own sake, without waiting to integrate our deepest emotions and hopes, at best becomes boring, fast. At worst, men and women end up competing over how cruelly they can use one another. And in between, there is much confusion.

Over and over, girls who fool around with "friends with benefits" wonder why they are left without friends, and without benefits. Or the older ones will go along with the hookup scene but suspect that there is something wrong with them for wanting more than just a string of physical encounters. After being cheated on four years ago, Jen Singh, thirty-two, decided, "Screw relationships—I'm a single woman, it's strictly booty calls." And yet she admits to a reporter in *Toronto Life:*

> There are times when I wish I could have someone who could just
> come over and snuggle up and be there for me. The idea of growing
> old alone is absolutely petrifying. Especially when I know I have so
> much to offer a man. I stay awake at night thinking about it. It just eats
> away at me. Technically, I've been single since 2002. That's a long time.
> I wish my booty call would just wake up and say, "You know, I want to
> be with you. You're so good to me."

Unfortunately, that kind of thing doesn't usually happen with booty calls or hookups. Ever on the ball, *The Hookup Handbook* encourages women to sign a "hookup contract," not with their prospective or past partners—who are either long gone or will be soon—but with themselves. This contract features such self-brainwashing mantras as "I will resist the urge to mentally combine my first name with a hookup's last name 'just to see how it sounds,'" "I will not drunkenly dial him," and "I will not wait in obsessive agony for him to call me." Instead:

> I will give myself permission to call him. However, I must not do so in
> a passive-aggressive manner that will put the ball back in his court (i.e.
> leaving a message on his cell phone while he is at work . . .). I will come
> to terms with the fact that this is a vicious cycle that always concludes
> in the same manner, with me waiting for the f——king phone to
> f——king ring.

Although *The Hookup Handbook* is quite bouncy and pro-hookup on the whole, it's impossible not to detect a tiny kernel of disappointment here. The f——king men are not picking up their f——king phones. Even a girl who has signed a contract stipulating otherwise can still be undone, apparently, if she doesn't get her post-hookup checkup—even when she knows that technically no checkup is owed to her. To appreciate how absurd this situation is, it's useful to recall that in a different age, a young woman could assume that a man wanted to marry her if he simply spent a good chunk of time with her. This passage comes from an etiquette manual of 1887:

> *A Gentleman's Conduct Toward Ladies.* Gentlemen are at liberty to invite
> their lady friends to concerts, operas, balls, etc., to call upon them at
> their homes, to ride and drive with them, and make themselves agree-
> able to all young ladies to whom their company is acceptable. In fact
> they are at liberty to accept invitations and give them ad libitum. As
> soon, however, as a young gentleman neglects all others, to devote him-
> self to a single lady, he gives that lady reason to suppose that he is par-
> ticularly attracted to her, and may give her cause to believe that she is
> to become engaged to him, without telling her so. A gentleman who
> does not contemplate matrimony should not pay too exclusive attention
> to any one lady.

I'm hardly saying we should go back to 1887. But it strikes me that it's per-fectly reasonable to be attached to someone you've just been extremely in-timate with. For most of world history, society acknowledged that men and women could become attached after having intimate *conversations.* So it is really quite normal after exchanging kisses, and being as close as two humans can physically be, that you may be experiencing emotion of some kind, and might wish to know what happened to that darling person who was the proximate cause of those emotions. I think that this is a good thing, not something to cure. Scientists have triumphantly uncovered oxytocin as the culprit; apparently it is the source of the "problem" of women's becoming emotionally attached to their sexual partners, even when they do not mean to. (Perhaps someone will come up with an antidote.) But I think the cause is just being human, and having an awareness of how precious we really are.

Yet all the voices around young people tend to promote a cavalier attitude toward sex from the get-go, often under the guise of "health."

Consider a fifteen-year-old girl in Boston who is on the fence. Her boyfriend is pressuring her for sex and she's not quite sure what to do. Everyone—the pediatrician, the school nurse, the girl's therapist—is encouraging her to use birth control. Her mother (whose sister contacted me) is looking for a doctor who will recommend abstaining from sexual activity, but she can't find one. She keeps hearing, "The kids are all doing it anyway; you'll be saving her life." Today it is nearly impossible to find a medical professional who cares enough to ask a girl, "Why do you want to go on birth control?" Or to take the time to point out, "If he's pressuring you for sex, he probably doesn't love you." But at least this mother was really listening to her daughter—and listening can no longer be taken for granted nowadays.

Richard Blaquiere, a teacher from New Brunswick, came on the popular radio show *Sounds Like Canada* in 2004 to defend his school's sex-ed program. The program, for grades six, seven, and eight in Woodstock, New Brunswick, includes explicit pictures, information on how flavored condoms taste, and an exercise in which each student must write a "positive slogan" for a hypothetical condom vending machine. Traci Taylor's eleven-year-old daughter, when told about the exercises, simply said to her mother, "I'm not taking *that*." Another student, Tim, said "There's stuff that we don't want to know half the time!" Mr. Blaquiere, who works at the school, insisted that the program was important. But at the end of this defense, offhand, he let slip that "by the way," his own daughter did not want to take the course. "Well, I don't really want to take it," she had said. His ideological response was to force her. "Take it," Blaquiere ordered, "and let's talk afterward." He then laughingly said that his daughter didn't want to talk afterward, either.

Somehow I don't find this as funny as he does.

* * *

Hearing this story helped me to appreciate my mother, who pulled me out of sex ed from fourth grade on, after I didn't develop a fondness for the curriculum. ("It's just like talking about an elbow!") I attended public school in the Midwest (Wisconsin) before the Internet explosion and before eight-year-olds started to wear thongs, so on the whole I would say I had a fairly innocent childhood. For fun I arranged my Snoopies into pyramids and took Polaroid pictures of them, played "Kaboom!" on Atari, and built secret forts in the backyard with my friends.

I mention this not to evoke nostalgia for the 1980s but merely to point out something that rarely gets mentioned. Even though I had a quite sheltered childhood, at a time when the media and clothing styles were far less sexualized than they are today—and when the most popular dance for preteens was not yet pelvic thrusting—I never felt that there was any expectation for me, as a girl, to be "good." What was expected was the same for girls as for boys: academic achievement.

Certainly no one ever said, "Be a virgin until marriage," or anything remotely close to that. I grew up in an academic, Reform Jewish home; but when I compared notes with my religious Christian friends, most of them had never heard it either. Any normative advice that did trickle down was of the opposite nature.

The concept of sex as "nothing to be embarrassed about," was of course impressed on us in Human Growth and Development class from the very first day. Sex was "no big deal." As we grew older, my friends and I would joke about how our parents were concerned if we didn't go out to party— were we normal? No parent wanted his kid to be truly bad, but a certain nice random sampling of badness was proof of one's psychological health. In 2006 in Germantown, Maryland, the police busted an underage sex-and-drinking party. Unfortunately, the ritual of calling the parents to pick up the drunk kids was complicated by the parents' enthusiastic support for what their kids had been up to. As Marc Fisher hilariously reports in *The Washington Post*, one father "arrives [to collect his son] and immediately asks to speak to the sergeant: 'Don't you guys have any real crime to take care of?'" Then a mother arrives to pick up her daughter: "'It's okay,' she tells her child, 'these police are just harassing kids.' She raises her voice so the officers can hear. 'They're just trying to spoil your fun.'" Another parent from Montgomery County is precise and thorough: "I want my child to be experienced, as long as he doesn't get killed on River Road."

When I was eleven, my friend Amy celebrated her twelfth birthday, and for a treat we all got to watch *Harold and Maude* on the big screen (her father was the owner of a local theater). I enjoyed the party because Amy was always a cool person to be around, but I just couldn't get into the movie. Amy would later laugh about how "all the girls there thought it was the dumbest movie ever." It wasn't the May-December romance between Harold (twenty) and Maude (seventy-nine) that bothered me. Most of us had already read V. C. Andrews and we were well versed in allegedly exciting nontraditional love affairs, including incestuous ones. What I found grating was the facile anticonventionalism of the film. Maude would say "carefree" things like, "Vice, Virtue. It's best not to be too moral. You cheat yourself out of too much *life*! Aim above morality." She was trying to be anticonventional, but I saw her as a bit of a phony, a poseur, since to me she embodied the new conventions. Even the fact that I was watching this bizarre parent-approved film at age eleven was proof enough to me that these ideas were nothing big. A truly rebellious film, then and now, would have been a young couple defending virtue.

Some people were taken aback when, in 2005, a "career day" speaker told thirteen-year-old students at a middle school in Palo Alto that stripping was a lucrative profession. As part of his presentation—somewhat comically entitled "The Secret of a Happy Life"—this speaker, a sixty-four-year-old salesman named William Fried, explained that strippers can earn as much as $250,000 a year. According to one student, Fried also said that large breasts are essential. When approached by members of the media, administrators pointed out that only two parents had complained.

I wasn't fazed by the fact that a man in his sixties was extolling the virtues of stripping to middle-schoolers. In 1993, when I was still in high school, an attorney in Milwaukee advised a group of thirty seventh-grade girls not to get married, because marriage interferes with careers: "Frankly, sleep around all you want, but whatever you do, don't get married." I wish I could do a longitudinal study of how many twelve- and thirteen-year-old girls took her advice to heart. It could be that when they grew up they were among those who ostracized a twenty-one-year-old woman, in 2006, for wanting to marry her boyfriend. This young woman wrote to *Salon* for advice about the "abject horror or resigned sorrow" that greeted her "bourgeois" plans for marriage to a man she called "the best human being I've ever met." Even her older friends, "mostly thirty- to forty-year-old teachers, poets and activists, are too enamored of my youthful freedom to bear talk about settling down." Her mother's response was to sneer: "She couldn't believe I was her daughter."

· · ·

Twenty-nine-year-old blond, willowy Sarah from New York was so annoyed with family members pressuring her to lose her virginity that in August 2006, she turned to *Jane* magazine, which proposed a sort of public deflowering. *Jane* agreed to field offers from strange men (whom the readers voted on) who wanted to do Sarah the favor of ridding her of her burden. Sarah agreed to sleep with one of them by her thirtieth birthday, which was November 7. What happened if she didn't come to love (or even like) any of those men? Would she sleep with one of them anyway? Apparently she would, just to get her family off her back: "Seriously," she wrote on her dating blog, The Virgin Chronicles, "there is nothing stranger than having your relatives at a family dinner rattle off who they know might be a 'good first.'" The editors of *Jane* agreed, adding that they are surprised to hear Sarah is a virgin, since she is "a veritable hot chick" who has "a nice rack." You see, only ugly, small-breasted women stay virgins.

I followed in horror as Sarah's father voted on candidates for her deflowering—certain select males had the honor of being "Sarah's Dad's Pick!" And I found myself wondering how more experienced young women viewed things. Were they grateful for all this encouragement from adults? Significantly, even those who had positive premarital experiences all reported that they felt it was "wrong" or "weird" of adults to add to all the sexual pressure surrounding them.

For example, Cece, an attractive brunette from Manhattan, compares a friend's story and her own: "One of my good friends lost her virginity in college when she was twenty-one. I guess that was considered really old and there was a lot of talk about it." Cece, now in her mid-twenties, lost her own virginity when she was sixteen, "and I remember really wanting to do it because others were, and I had the chance to get it over with." She considers herself "one of the lucky few," because she actually cared for the boy she lost her virginity with. "Other people felt it wasn't the right time, or the guy wasn't the right person, or he was mean afterward. So, my friend who lost her virginity late, her parents loved her, but they were like—get out there and do it already!" *Get out there and do it already.*

Under these influences, no wonder twenty-five-year-old virgins are afraid that they are "freaks," and are told in women's magazines like *Cosmo* to "downplay" their virginity to a prospective mate, who may worry that "afterward, you'll cling to him like a tee shirt on Pamela Anderson." *Cosmo*'s resident male expert gives this advice to a young woman who is "scared" to confess her virginity: "Say something breezy like, 'Listen, I should have mentioned it before, but I've never had intercourse. It's not a huge deal.'" One might be forgiven for thinking the subject under discussion is herpes: "Because the guy cares about you and has been willing to take things slowly, my guess is that he'll take it in stride." So if you apologize for your innocence and offer your virginity to him in just the right, pseudo-casual "breezy" manner, it's possible that you may be forgiven. There is an unmistakable misogyny in our attitude toward the virgin, which becomes all the more obvious when this philosophy is carried to its logical conclusion.

Amy Alkon, the likable and syndicated "Advice Goddess," has a problem with virginity and calls girls "chattel" if they wear rings indicating their commitment to abstinence. Although chastity rings are sold for both men and women, her view is that they should be called "Women As Chattel Jewelry" because that's "more to the point." She adds, "I hate the term 'losing your virginity.' . . . Quite frankly, it really isn't the big deal it's cracked up to be." Like Amy, I am conflicted about whether it's best for all teens to make private choices public by wearing "purity rings," but describing virgins as "chattel" seems extreme. The words "love" and "caring" are mentioned nowhere, not even in Alkon's online comments section.

Is it really radical to view virginity as a boil to lance, something to get rid of? Or has that become the predominant view, especially among the intelligentsia and our team of advisers? Take a closer look at another popular advice site for teens, Scarleteen.com, which is "committed to delivering the best contemporary teen sex-ed on the net since 1998." Indeed, it comes highly recommended by the American Library Association (ALA) as an "honest, fresh, and fun" resource for teens. Certainly Scarleteen's philosophy is nothing if not down-to-earth: "Sexual intercourse doesn't have to be the biggest deal in the world or a major drama. When you subtract the factors that might make it so," such as "being irresponsible about your sexual health" or "having unrealistic expectations," then "it can actually be amazingly normal, healthy, safe, loving and fun." So if you expect teen sex to be special, it probably won't be; but if you don't have "unrealistic expectations," then it might just be "amazingly normal" (that's code for disappointing). Perfect—because you've already prepped yourself to be disappointed by securing those low expectations in advance. This is fascinating, and yet rather an indictment of the whole enterprise.

If a teenager somehow stumbles upon Scarleteen's sexual abstinence page (it's not on the main menu), she is quickly navigated away to a very long essay putting her on the spot, "Why Choose Celibacy?" The bait and switch is revealing. The teen chose to read an essay entitled "Does Abstinence Make the Heart Grow Fonder?" and now she has "celibate" slapped on her, a word that evokes nuns or priests, and not getting married—ever. We are taught that a teen may choose "celibacy" for a variety of reasons: to prevent STDs or, even more legitimately, "Perhaps you were raped, sexually traumatized, or your last sexual experience left you feeling bad or confused," "or [you] are feeling 'sick of sex.'" This last business is something we all go through; "we all will go through these stages at least once or twice" in our lives, and we just need to "work through them." Guess how.

You can end your bad feelings right here and now by keeping this time of "celibacy" in your life as short and sweet as possible. The implication is that trauma is the real motivation for a teenager to postpone sex. It couldn't possibly be idealism or waiting for someone wonderful to share a life with. The good news, though, is that—much as with head trauma—if you are treated properly and immediately, you will be OK. "All of those reasons— and others—are excellent and valid reasons to be celibate for a while."

Note how nonchalantly "for a while" is slipped in at the end. You hardly even notice it, but this sneaky addition becomes pivotal. For when the teen advances to the next screen—which virtually demands to be read, given its engaging title, "So, You Want to Be Celibate"—she is told, "Choose a timeframe. How long are you going to be celibate for? A month, a year, five years? Rather than choosing an event which will determine when you stop (which takes your own power away from you), like yes, marriage, pick a manageable time period that you can work with."

Your own choices and ideals, you see, "take your power away from you," whereas sex advisers who want to take your choices away from you seek only your betterment. Then, incredibly, the advice gets more condescending: "Your sexual choices and sexual identity [are] your own, and it's about you—not some magical, mystical gift someone else gives you with a ring and a minivan." If hope stubbornly persists, a teen might deal with it thus: "Write it down somewhere." With a few key changes, naturally: "For instance, instead of saying, 'I'll wait until I'm married,' if that's what you want to do, which puts a little undue pressure on yourself and your psyche (and has made people jump into marriage unduly a time or two), start in month-long blocks."

To sum up, if you're a teen who wants to wait until you're married, this choice simply vanishes from the Scarleteen screen. You are told that this is not a realistic or "manageable" choice; not a healthy choice; and not an autonomous choice, since power will be taken from you. Finally, you are tarred with the deeply cynical implication that someone waiting for marriage really seeks the external trappings—"a ring and a minivan"—rather than a spiritual bond or the special intimacy that flows from commitment. So, poof! Sorry, waiting until marriage is simply not a choice that is open to you. However, if you make the "correct" choices instead, a whole world opens to you—and, incidentally, so does the online Scarleteen shop. There are T-shirts reading, I [HEART] GIRLS WHO LIKE LATEX and I [HEART] BOYS WHO WEAR CONDOMS; there are a variety of condoms; and you can even visit the "wonderful babes" who run an online sex toy shop.

Another site the ALA recommends for teens' sexual health is Go Ask Alice, Columbia University's sex and health information website, staffed by writers in consultation with doctors from the university hospital. The site has come under fire for, among other things, giving teens detailed instructions on how to clean their cat-o'-nine-tails when it draws blood. (Answer: It depends if it's rubber or leather, and also if "there has been a heavy flogging.") But what is mainly striking is how "Alice" answers a sixteen-year-old girl who is nervous about her first kiss. Afraid that others will find out how inexperienced she is, the girl is told, "No need to get your knickers in a twist over your very first kiss," and that she should get "relaxed." She does not "need to tell any potential partner about your kissing, or non-kissing, history." So the girl's sense that her first kiss is significant is not validated, while her sinking feeling that there is something wrong with her inexperience is confirmed. Yes, she is essentially told, if people were to know of her deep dark naïveté, it would, in fact, be awful, but no one needs to know. Contrast this hush-hush treatment with how understanding "Alice" is about bestiality: "Sexual contacts with animals might be stimulating for some people because they are secretive, forbidden, and dangerous. An animal doesn't 'kiss and tell,' nor do his or her expectations 'get in the way.'"

The problem with this attitude is not just that the website is visited by readers in over fifty countries, or that it is recommended by the ALA for minors. I think the problem is much larger. It's the way that anything "transgressive"—even drawing blood or sex with Fido—is automatically taken to be cool and "stimulating," whereas innocence is seen as inherently problematic. This is downright nihilistic in my view, to the extent that we were all innocent once.

As several women who went to college in the mid-1970s made clear to me, "the idea of sleeping around as a power thing" was already well in place by the time they arrived. Margaret, a mother of two teens who lives in the Midwest, recalls:

> If you were a virgin it was like, "What's wrong with you?" Everyone was piling up at the health center for whatever kind of contraception was available. And there was a reading dynamics poster—you know, for Evelyn Wood? It used to be, "Read fast, and go to law school!" Well, the posters started to change and this one poster had a very slim good-looking woman with a pencil and her glasses down saying, "*All* my men read 1,000 words a minute." God, we loved that poster. That was the first time I saw women who would use their sexuality as a power thing. At the time I thought it was a fad thing with women on the East Coast, since I was from the Midwest.

As it happened, this was not a fad. The experiment lasted for about thirty years, and started creeping to younger and younger kids. Eventually, it led to today's situation, where doctors are expected to put teenagers on the Pill (in London, girls as young as age ten); and in the United States, a girl as young as thirteen can be a victim of statutory rape by her thirty-seven-year-old gym teacher, and a taxpayer-funded clinic will provide ongoing contraception so that no one need ever know about it. On occasion, mothers actively procure their daughters' sexual partners to make sure it is all handled with dispatch. In September 2005 a woman in White Plains, New York, pleaded guilty to second-degree rape for providing a hotel room and beer so that her thirteen-year-old daughter and a fourteen-year-old friend could have sex with two men (ages eighteen and nineteen) they ran into at a local mall. This telling detail is from the Associated Press report: "The woman, whose name was withheld to protect her daughter's identity, allegedly told investigators it was time for her daughter to 'have sex and get it over with.'"

You may insist that this is a crazy example indicative of nothing, but less than a year later we were presented with this story from Michigan:

> A woman afraid of "losing" her boyfriend while she was recuperating from surgery arranged to have her fifteen-year-old daughter be his sex partner for two months. . . . Evidence against them includes testimony of a written contract signed by all three that specifies the sexual services and the "pay" the girl would get, including clothing and body piercings. . . . [Detective] Mahan said Fitzgibbon [the mother's boyfriend] and the fifteen-year-old girl had sex "close to 20 times" during June and July. The girl testified in court that she chose to put on a mask when she had to have sex with Fitzgibbon. The mask was described as a sleeping mask.

This is shocking, but in a culture so hostile to the idea of innocence, not entirely surprising. If the best thing for our daughters is really just to "get going," then why not with those nearest and dearest? That way, everyone can be happy. And yet, the daughter told the court that "she never wanted to have sex" with her mother's thirty-seven-year-old boyfriend, so perhaps this philosophy is not good for our girls, after all. A woman named Amy commented, in reference to this case,

> I know a couple of girls (women now) who were abused by their mother's boyfriends (one in particular was abused by MOST of her mother's numerous boyfriends from age ten on). The mothers in question were aware of the abuse and essentially told the daughters to put out so they (the mothers) could keep their boyfriends. This has resulted in permanent damage to the way these two women see most men (and of course what you perceive is what you draw to you, so it perpetuates endlessly).

The right wing is generally in favor of parental notification laws for abortion and contraception, so that we can know if children are victims of statutory rape, and the left generally opposes such legislation. Both sides assume that parents who know about such activity will try to stop it. But the debate over parental notification obfuscates a more disturbing reality: If parents knew, many would not mind and might even be relieved that the child was "getting [his or her] groove on." Our expectation that young people will be sexually active, and cavalierly so, is clearly making it difficult to call child abuse by its proper name.

Glorifying casual sex and making a swear word of "innocence" have had devastating consequences. In her harrowing memoir, *Smashed: Story of a Drunken Girlhood* (2005), twenty-four-year-old Koren Zailckas looks back on her tumultuous adolescence: "My hang-ups [were] even worse than my hangover." Later, as a student at Syracuse, Koren hatches a plan to resolve her resistance to casual sex. She gets so drunk that she passes out completely, thus getting rid of her virginity in a state where no "hang-ups" are possible. Chillingly, she loses her virginity to a boy she actively hates:

> I barely know Skip, but I know I don't like him. He is smug in a distinctly male way. . . . The one time we spoke, he made it clear that the feeling is mutual. . . . I decide he even looks like he's swaggering when he's sleeping. He is facing me, with his eyes pinched closed and his lips pulled into a pout. I'm not happy that I've passed out here, but I'm not alarmed by it—not until I move my hands under the quilt to quietly roll myself away from him, and realize that I am as naked as the day I was born.

During another night out on campus, Koren relates calmly, "a man I barely know bites my armpit, leaving a vampire-like ring of teeth marks and bruises that lasts weeks." (She noticed it only after she sobered up.) Her friend Elle reassures her, "Whatever. If you can't remember it, it never really happened, anyway."

Although we are supposed to live in an age of heightened awareness of sexual assault, our expectation that "liberated" girls have to be sexually active—and also blasé—in practice undermines girls in ways that would have been unthinkable to previous generations.

Incredibly, even after Koren has several hospitalizations for alcohol poisoning, her mother prods her to order white wine for her twenty-first birthday and her father presents her with a bottle of Malibu rum. She polishes the rum off a few days later, and not surprisingly is then date-raped once more.

It's easy to wonder what Koren's parents were thinking, but the reality is that parents also face a lot of peer pressure, to enforce our new low expectations. Paige (not her real name) is a mother of teenagers in a Chicago suburb. She is the odd parent out, since about two-thirds of the parents in her community are in favor of coed sleepovers:

> My daughter was invited to a coed sleepover and the parents are going to be home, she said, and they think it's okay. So what am I going to do? First of all you talk to the parents, then they say oh, come on now. Wouldn't you rather have your kids just finding out what you found out in college, in your own house? I mean we live there. I said, wait a minute, whatever we did or didn't do in college, we did with a huge dollop of guilt because we knew that parents had certain rules, or if you want to put it religiously, then if you choose to distance yourself from God you have made the choice to put a barrier there and that is a bad feeling. To take that away from them, to not give them that relationship with their morals is denying and hurting the kids. You are denying them, and they are not getting what they need from you. So suddenly the room got very quiet.

Debbie, in Montgomery, who does not let her sixteen-year-old daughter Cait attend coed sleepovers, tells the reporter Emily Wax that "the fact that so many other teenagers are allowed to go makes it harder to say no." What are the other parents thinking? Some of them are in la-la land, assuring me that kids at these parties "are just like brother and sister!" Perhaps, if you're talking about the brother and sister from *Flowers in the Attic*. Others have an illusion of safety: "I've talked to them about birth control." Still, if not all the teens want to fool around but a parent's sponsorship of the party gives them the idea that sexual activity is expected, birth control won't really help.

When a group of thirteen-year-old girls in Brockton dressed up in fishnet stockings, tube tops, miniskirts, and high heels for Halloween, telling a *Boston Globe* reporter, "We're ho's," the clinical psychologist Catherine Steiner-Adair explained, "It's almost like kids go from elementary school to teenagers. There's no pause." But granting that tweens want to look grown-up, why must they look like prostitutes? Surely there are other ways of growing up.

One mother, Alma, unwittingly got to the core of the problem when she explained to the CBC why her twelve-year-old daughter, Amanda, wears "very sexy" clothes: "I would probably prefer if she wore a baggy T-shirt and baggy jeans, but she would not like it though. She wouldn't be herself." I heard this catchphrase from countless parents across North America, but no one could explain to me how, exactly, a girl's truest "self" was embodied by sexy clothes. Amanda was much more practical than her mother, admitting that "being sexy is, like, I guess you have to follow trends. . . . You're more popular if you're sexy. . . . Nobody wants to be, like, a loner."

Elizabeth Wurtzel was onto something when she wrote: "Obviously, in the pageantry of public life, in the places where women invent persons, the one statement a girl can make to declare her strength, her surefootedness, her autonomy—her self as a self—is to somehow be bad." This is very well put; but to the extent it is true, it presupposes a society where most girls are socially pressured to be good. And the obvious difficulty is that now bad-ness has become normative. Self-actualization through badness may have been theoretically possible when the norm did not celebrate badness— although ultimately this posture has its limitations, too. But today it's hard to argue that internalizing all this prepackaged badness is the Path to the True Self.

The plain fact is that girls today have to be "bad" to fit in, just as the baby boomers needed to be good. And we are finding that this new script may be more oppressive than the old one ever was. The psychologist Nina Shandler offers a shrewd insight: "The conformist mentality has been resurrected from the fifties—only today the badges of belonging have a higher price tag." Consider how girls today need to be thin, available, and always sexy. At the same time they are supposed to have no hopes, no messy feelings, no vulnerability. They must be aggressive, yet somehow inviting. It's complicated, and to rebel against the new bad-girl script takes enormous confidence. But, as I learned, it can be done.

* * *

Sixteen-year-old Lauren is a lovely blond girl who lives in Indianapolis. She teaches dance, is very fashionable, and does well in school, but she doesn't like coed sleepovers: "At a personal level, I'm sorry, I don't know why you would even *want* to be, like, with a bunch of boys all night." She confides to me, "I like having girl time with my friends." For example, her best friend just came over to watch movies and stage an (unplanned) noodle fight. "We had so much fun!" She laughs. Even though she seems very innocent, Lauren knows all about what's going on. In fact, she actually knows more than I do—the colors, for example:

> Basically, I don't know, I think they came up with it in fifth grade. You've heard of the expressions like if you're yellow, that means you haven't kissed a boy? If you're green you haven't made out with a boy, and then if you're like pink you've gone further and like red you've had sex—no, black you've had sex; and I think red you've given oral. I think people just now, like, they just use the term green as naïve, so I'm green. Or green is sometimes just "the G card." And that's all the colors they use.

Lauren is wary of coed sleepovers because she knows they can be "uncomfortable" for the girls: "Just because like you never know if they could push you into anything." She's had a number of friends who have been in "those situations" and "they've done things that they regretted."

Lauren attends a "huge school" of about 4,000 students, so "we have a lot of bad girls, and a lot of like prude girls." It is more socially acceptable to be a bad girl than a "prude girl," she explains to me. At her school and other schools, "we have a lot of what we call 'sluts and hos,' and that's like a cool thing, and I think that they do this in a way to persist. Sometimes they think that if they don't please the guy, the guy will stop talking to them and then they'll be a square. They'll lose their status or something."

Lauren knows all about losing your status by being perceived as "square," for she herself is starting to acquire a "bad name": "I feel like a lot of girls my age, you know, the whole hookup thing that they do . . . I don't know. . . ." She trails off. "I've never had a serious boyfriend and I'm not into doing physical things with boys or anything but I think that for me to do anything, I'd actually have to go out with someone, and like for a long time. But because of the label guys have on girls now, the girls think it gives them a bad name if they haven't, like, done anything, and I know that."

There are obviously a number of high school kids who haven't had sex (estimates are typically around half), but they often don't tell their friends what they haven't done. Lauren's problem was that she spoke up: "Yeah, I told my friends that I will not have oral sex—or any sex—until the day I get married." It all started because one girl in their circle had sex "with like eight different people and she's done drugs, pot, and drinks a lot, and now she has to live up to her reputation and it's hard for her." So Lauren told her friends "No, I have respect for myself."

The reputation the "prude girls" have is that "they're not comfortable in themselves," but "I'm comfortable in myself and I'm very talkative," Lauren says. Indeed, she does have a straightforward manner that's very engaging, and she seems quite self-aware for someone so young. There are girls who are "prudes," she acknowledges, who don't seem to have self-confidence, but Lauren, it is clear, is not one of them. This makes it all the more puzzling to her that she is ostracized sometimes.

> I was with my friends last night and they were like, you're the good girl in the group, and I said, "Well, I guess I am." But I don't know why people have to point it out to other people. Like sometimes if I'm—if one of my friends—like basically I met some new boys and like I wouldn't say anything but my friend just goes up and tells them, she's like "Now don't try to be with Lauren, because she's not a booty call!" Then they kind of got scared of me, and so I talked to them. They're like "Yeah, we're kind of scared to talk to you because we don't know if you're going to hate us or something." I was like "No, I'm not going to hate you," I was like, "but I'm *not* a booty call, but just because I'm not, doesn't mean that you guys can't *talk* to me." And they were like, "Oh, OK." She had made it sound like I'm some good girl and I'm going to hate them!

Notice how "good girl" is the lowest of the low (even as far as Lauren is concerned). Some of her friends—a lot of people at the school, actually— smoke pot, she explains, and people are starting to not tell Lauren when they do things, because they're afraid that she "will say that they're bad." After finding out about this, she tried to clarify her position, partly because she didn't want to be cut out of the loop but also because she genuinely is not the judgmental type: "I said, I don't think you're bad or anything, and you make your own decisions; I don't make your decisions for you."

In general, though, Lauren has given up trying to justify her existence to her peers, and is fine with people not accepting her. By now, surely, all the parents reading this book are wondering how to raise a girl like Lauren. So, folks, here's the scoop: "My Mom isn't controlling. She never told me I 'had to' do anything. She never said, 'Stay a virgin!' She just raised me really well. Almost, I have this thing if I do anything and I get caught with it I feel I'm going to disappoint her." Lauren has even told her mom why she isn't drinking: "There's two reasons why I don't want to drink. Number one, I hate throwing up; and number two, I don't want to disappoint you."

Instead of getting drunk, Lauren and her friend will have shaving cream fights for fun, or in the summer they'll just make a big bonfire. There is a local mall where recently many kids have been "skittling"—taking little red pills that are basically speed. In lieu of this, Lauren is teaching gymnastics to seventh-graders, but this is not entirely an escape, she explains to me, because many of these seventh-graders have big problems. In fact, Lauren worries that they may be much worse than her peers. It never fails to amuse me the way everyone (even a sixteen-year-old) thinks that younger people are much worse off; but Lauren stands firm: "When I was in seventh grade, it used to be, 'Oh, he gave me a hug!' And like you could get excited about that, and now I do know that some seventh-grade girls just have sex with different guys. It's just so wrong."

Kids might tease girls like Lauren for not being a "booty call," but the reality is that she is admired by her peers and by adults who are friendly with her mother. With the self-confidence that comes from having ideals and sticking by them in the face of pressure, girls like Lauren are ready for anything.

That is good, because let's face it—high school is only the beginning.

· · ·

When I arrived at college, I was excited to think that I had a secret admirer. Little red folded cards with hearts began arriving in my box at the student union. Alas, I had no "Valentine"; the red cards were only impersonal notices from "Peer Health." One read, "What the well-dressed Eph wears on Valentine's Day," an "Eph" being a student at Williams (named after Ephraim Williams), and then when I opened this missive, a packaged condom would slip out and land on my shoe. I adjusted to this kind of thing soon enough, but I never could shake the feeling that Peer Health needed some help with marketing. One poster in particular always annoyed me:

COME ON DOWN! AND SEE OUR NEW ORAL SEX HOW-TO GUIDES! To me, it evoked Bob Barker on *The Price Is Right*—not a very sexy connotation ("*C'mon down!* You're the next contestant to . . . have the honor of servicing me!"). On the other hand, Peer Health did operate from the basement of our main student center, so it may have been referring merely to its physical location. During Women's Pride Week, Women of Williams distributed SHAMELESS HUSSY stickers that we were all expected to wear, to prove that we were proud to be sexually active. They also distributed stickers reading F———K THE PATRIARCHY that seemed to be in conflict with the first set of stickers (unless they meant F———K THE PATRIARCHY literally).

Perhaps the best illustration of the tenor of campus discourse was provided years later, when it came to light that one undergraduate was a porn star, and a lively campus discussion erupted over who was worse, she or I (my historic crime was having objected to the coed bathrooms). It was decided that I was much worse, because, as one man put it in an online alumni forum, "Say what you will about the porn star, at least she's contributing something unique to the discourse of Williams rather than merely rehashing conservative arguments so old you can stick a fork in them." Although some women were developing urinary infections because they weren't using the toilet enough (they were too embarrassed), it was "old" to call for separate bathrooms and a bit of privacy, whereas having sex on camera was *au courant*.

I would have transferred, except that some of my professors were excellent. More to the point, I actually knew a few people who had transferred both to and from Williams, and the consensus among them was that campus life was pretty much the same elsewhere, if not worse. At least we never went as far as Bucknell, where in 2006 many campus groups cosponsored a $1,920 sex show, called "a celebration of whore culture," and featuring phone sex operators, prostitutes, porn stars, and a man lubricating himself. Maybe they were trying to top Wesleyan, which invited Annie Sprinkle to lecture on the wonders of prostitution, and where Professor Hope Weissman used to require her students to produce a work of porn as their final project. Tripping over themselves to appear cutting-edge, educators at Occidental College offer a course called The Phallus, which not only includes "the meaning of the phallus, and phallologocentrism," but also examines "the lesbian phallus, the Jewish phallus, the Latino phallus, and the relation of the phallus and fetishism." And an employee of Miko Exoticwear,

Megan Andelloux, recently descended on Brown to give a "workshop" for the men on campus, telling them that "sex toys are your friends," because "they cut your work in half." Student-produced sex magazines can now boast of having university financing and even faculty advisers.

Clearly, what would be unique on campus today would be a show not of porn but of modesty. In nearly all colleges and universities in America students of the opposite sex can sleep together in each other's rooms, leaving when they please—a policy administrators coyly call "twenty-four-hour intervisitation" or, more suggestively, "intervisitation unlimited." Many people, until they arrive on campus, do not realize that this applies even to supposedly single-sex floors, often making the bathrooms de facto coed. As Dean Joe Tolliver of Haverford put it, "the students tell us that what we don't know is that after 5:00 P.M. all the bathrooms become coed." Also, the students become "evictable" from their rooms; hence the "sexile" phenomenon: getting kicked out of your room when your roommate is hooking up.

The days of *in loco parentis* are long gone—even at many conservative schools. (At Villanova University, which is Catholic, students are merely encouraged to write a "roommate contract.") If you think single-sex schools are any different, you're dreaming. At Bryn Mawr, men not infrequently roam the halls and stay overnight. "The only problem we have," an official in the residential life office explained, "is if a guy is there for weeks and weeks and starts giving out one of our students' addresses as his own." In this case, the school's concern is economic: "We don't offer free rooms here."

When the universities abandoned parietal rules, in theory they expanded students' options; in practice, it wasn't so simple. In fact students could always sneak in and did. Maybe they had more fun, too, for they could never think intimacy wasn't significant when they had to work for those stolen moments. As Lynn Peril notes in her wonderful history *College Girls*, in the 1930s "there never was a rule that a cunning college girl couldn't break or at least seriously bend as needed." (Brothers or cousins were generally allowed to visit until a later hour, so during the course of a year a girl might discover she had ten brothers and twelve cousins.) Universities created a logistical nightmare when they failed to build hotel complexes specifically for their newly condoned sexual activities, instead plopping young men and women on the same floors and relying on peer pressure and the most aggressive to battle over turf for themselves. The epidemic of date rape is only one aspect of the problem. It's time to face the fact that college administrators' wholehearted endorsement of premarital sex has been an unmitigated disaster. Those who choose not to participate are now stigmatized, kicked out of their rooms at odd hours, and made to feel prudish if they don't favor coed bathrooms. Yale's website says it all: "Students who for some extraordinary and compelling reason need to be assured housing with a single-sex bathroom must petition the dean in writing." If you put it like that, what "extraordinary and compelling reason" could one possibly have? Oozing red sores from head to toe? (Incidentally, I'll bet you that the 1960s-era administrator who crafted this gem of a rule still ensures that his office washrooms are quaintly marked "Women" and "Men.")

One notable exception to the overall chaos in dormitories is the historically black colleges and universities (HBCUs). At Spelman, which is a women's college, men have to be off campus by 11:30 P.M., and after midnight they can be charged with trespassing. Is that rule really enforced? I ask when I ring up the residence hall office. "Oh yeah, that's a rule here," says Sandra. "They don't play here—oh, no. They'll run 'em off campus." There are "people who try to slip through the gates, climb fences, and get all dressed up, thinking that they're gonna go somewhere, and they actually wind up having to go back and change their clothes and go back to their room. They *thought* they was going somewhere, but they wasn't."

One residence hall director, Jackie Clifton, twenty-six, lets her students know that they should tell their guests to be outside the building by 11:30 P.M. If a man is in the building after then, he will no longer be allowed to visit (the information is logged using IDs). "For the most part the students really appreciated the rules," Jackie tells me. She herself lived in a coed dorm at South Carolina University, where she was also an RA for three years. Sometimes Jackie thinks that the women at Spelman are "sheltered a little," but she adds, "I don't think it's a bad thing." There are real advantages to the way Spelman does things: "There is that structure, there's a time limit. You know that from six to eleven-thirty, I may not be able to get in my room; but after that, at least—at eleven-thirty I'll be able to get in my room. Whereas at a liberal arts school, it will be, like, it's two-thirty in the morning, *what do you mean I gotta leave?!*"

In retrospect, college institutions that touted modesty may have been, paradoxically, more pro-choice. The need for privacy and a little peace and quiet was taken for granted, yet if one was resourceful, one could still find a way around the rules. Lest I be misunderstood, I should add that I am not advocating sneaking in. I am merely observing that when there are rules, one always has the choice of observing them or bending them. By contrast, when college administrators expect—more often, explicitly endorse—casual sex, young people often end up with fewer choices. It's much more difficult to opt out of a drama swirling all around you.

A student poll from the Harvard yearbook of 1957 quizzed the students about the parietal restrictions, and half of them expressed a desire to end visitation hours at midnight instead of at eight. Yet "complete abandonment of all prohibitions was propounded by a surprisingly small 20 percent of the romantic youths." It's interesting that 80 percent of Harvard men wanted some sort of curfew. Did they intuit that something ineffable would be lost by seeing the girl next door shaving her legs in the sink, or that some mystery between the sexes hinged on not brushing teeth side by side before going out on a proper date? Maybe it was neither of these reasons, and they just wanted to study.

In any case, the situation is clearly different now. The night before finals, students run around Harvard Yard completely naked. In January 2006, one junior at Harvard told her friend Meghan (who then wrote to me) that she planned to streak although she didn't want to, because she *could not come up with a valid reason not to.* I wrote back, suggesting several reasons. *Objectification:* drunk nerdy guys ogling your naked body. *Squeezification:* otherwise known as harassment, or people you don't like squeezing your derriere. *Rejectification:* to some, the worst humiliation of all—people assessing your naked body and *not* seeing you as a sex object. And *Facebookification:* fear that your genitalia will end up prominently featured in the Harvard Facebook.

I wonder if the young woman ended up streaking or not. Perhaps I will hear from her someday. Peer pressure can be very strong. Studies have indicated that especially as regards the opposite sex, young people are profoundly influenced by peer pressure even when they do not perceive themselves to be. I've heard of women dumping perfectly wonderful boyfriends because they were so thoroughly persuaded that they had to sleep around. Amanda, a twenty-two-year-old recent graduate, writes that last year her best friend "broke up with her boyfriend of four years because she was convinced she was 'supposed' to date lots of guys. Then, when the first guy she got together with treated her really badly, she realized what a mistake she was making and got back together with her boyfriend. They are still trying to heal the damage done to their relationship. . . . She always says she wishes she had realized sooner that she did not have to give in to societal pressure." After this, Amanda learned the importance of speaking out about her views, since "so many people are afraid to admit they feel the way we do that it is very easy to feel alone." There have been times when Amanda "had to pay dearly" for her views, for instance:

> Last spring I took a fiction writing class in college in which I wrote stories that portrayed romance and faithfulness as a positive thing. This evoked brutal hostility from the other students, who said my work was sentimental and unrealistic and that my characters' feelings qualified them as insane. While such criticism was hurtful, I could deal with it from my peers but thought it was completely inappropriate when the instructor decided to join them. At one point he told me to "find something to write about besides policing men's sexual desires," and he was constantly insisting that I "revise" my stories in ways that would alter their message. When I refused to alter that aspect of my work, since I felt no teacher has a right to dictate a student's moral beliefs, he docked my grade in response. It continues to baffle me as to why our beliefs evoke such extreme hatred like this.

Over the years I've received countless e-mails from students who find their professors' treatment of sexuality very crude. One senior at a university asks me, in reference to professors who use the f-word and then criticize her for being unable to "handle" the class discussion, "Of course much of literature deals with love and sexuality, but why must they always deal with it in such a demystified way?" In an important sense, the tension between the students of the sixties era and the administration has been virtually reversed. Today students are more likely to be trying to rein in their own professors than vice versa.

Professor Susan Shaw, director of the women's studies department at Oregon State, shares an intriguing story. For several years she has been showing her undergraduate students a film involving S&M practices (not because she is in favor of sadomasochism *per se* but rather to expose the students to different lifestyles). Over the years, she tells me, instead of becoming more and more accepting of the film, her students have become less and less so. Last year, to her great surprise, one of her students piped up:

"Professor Shaw, you know, maybe we really need to *rethink* our support of this, as feminists." The other students nodded in agreement and looked at her quite pointedly.

There is something undeniably encouraging about this story. Kids are funny this way. You want them to go down a certain path, but then they question it. They want their own path. When they're oversaturated in sex, sadomasochism isn't so exciting. The web acronyms "WDUGU?" (Why don't you grow up?) and "YOOC!" (You're out of control!) are not boomer locutions. I think many boomers have yet to appreciate how oppressive the "bad girl" script can be for young women.

But it doesn't really matter anymore, because the girls are growing up, and they are writing their own scripts.

EXERCISE:
CONFRONTING YOUR BABY BOOMER PARENTS

●

After being asked time and time again what to say to one's parents if they think "you're weird for being a virgin" or for not wanting to be casual about sex, I've come up with a sample script you might want to use. Feel free to tailor it to your individual needs, but here is the gist:

Mom, Dad, I know you love me and that you're concerned about me, and I appreciate it. I realize that you think I'm a bit weird for not sleeping around and not taking advantage of the sexual freedoms you fought for, but I've been noticing that a lot of my friends are just not happy after losing their virginity, or hooking up, and I really want to wait until marriage or until I meet someone I can trust and truly respect. I know it might be hard for you to believe, but this is really not because I have hang-ups. I've actually been exposed to more sex than you ever were in your day. I think of myself as being idealistic, and I hope that you can too. I also want to preserve my sensitivity for my future spouse, and not become jaded and cynical. There is so much pressure from the media and my peers to have casual sex, and your adding to that pressure really doesn't help me, even though I know you mean well. I hope that even if you don't understand my choices, you can respect my high standards—it would mean a lot to me to have your support until I find that special person I'm looking for. Thanks for taking the time to listen to me, and, here, you can take back the condoms that you gave me—I won't be needing them.

CHAPTER THREE

It's Midnight: Do You Know
Where Your Role Models Are?

The adolescent must learn . . . , as a mature adult member of a
community, . . . to find satisfaction and happiness through long-range
planning, and not require immediate satisfaction of all his impulses. . . .
Real life prince charmings and beautiful princesses aren't just made to
order. They grow and develop same as you. Neither can you make
another individual fit into your individual dream pattern. It requires a
very special person, like Cinderella, to fit your slipper. He or she will
come along quite naturally to fill the bill, if you'll only WAIT. Don't
dash out and demand any old misfit. In your haste, you feel like doing
just that. And then instead of the smoothness you wanted, you get
squabbling, or one or the other of you becomes possessive, or jealous, a
nag or a doormat. You just can't rush real love. It happens when
everything else is in order. You can push the physical attraction into a
seeming romance, but you'll only wind up empty handed or holding the
bag—and have to start all over again.

—LOIS PEMBERTON, from her 1948 guide for teens

The old advice is sounding new again. Fifteen-year-old Taylor Moore
bounds into the room, wearing jeans, a jeans jacket, and a tan baseball
cap, flicked to the side in the style of the hip-hop stars. She is small and
cherubic, but walks with confidence, which I'm glad she's got because she
has the toughest, most unforgiving audience of all: her peers. About 180
teenagers from all over the country—most of whom are older than she—
have gathered in Los Angeles to hear her speak. There is no small talk, and
Taylor starts up with a bang: "I wanted to tell you, don't let being a statis-
tic interrupt you from your dreams." The media and society all expect her

to fail, she explains, just because she's from a single-parent household, "so just for that, I make sure I give it my all, because people expect failure." She mimics the postmodern adult: "'Your hormones are just *raging*! You're going to have a baby before age nineteen.' Well, just for that, I'm gonna wait till I get married." A few teens start clapping.

Taylor is often asked about peer pressure. Her advice is to go on the offensive. Instead of apologizing, she advises teens to "peer-pressure your peers. Say, 'Hey! It's OK to be abstinent.'" Then, suddenly, she looks vulnerable, admitting, "I've been talked about for not going with a guy, for proudly saying I'm a virgin. But we have the power to change what other people think, so peer-pressure your peers! We're not here to make out and have an HBO show right in the middle of the hallway. We're here to be educated, to be all you can be."

I glance behind me, and everyone—boy or girl, black or white—is transfixed, hanging on Taylor's every word. The boys who were slouching are now at the edge of their chairs, and several girls are taking notes in the furious way that girls do, as if their very lives depended on it. In this case, they well may.

Taylor recounts how people test her: "Is this for real?" The other day she heard from a boy who said, "You know, Taylor, you've got your head on straight; I like you." She laughs and says that the boys always open with a line about her head being on straight: "Is there like a handbook you guys are all getting this from?" People snicker, but the fun has just begun. One guy came up to her and, "He was like 'Dang, girl, why you always have to be the president of something? Re-*laaaaaax*, be like me and do nothing!' I'm like, that's why I can't be with you, because you're doing nothing, man." As the kids nod in agreement, paying rapt attention, she then walks her audience through all the typical lines "players" say, and coaches them.

"'*If you don't get with me, someone else will.*' Whoa! That's the *wrong* thing to say. That means you're asking for more than my friendship." So here, finally, is the correct response to Sharon Stone, who advised teenage girls to perform oral sex if they were feeling pressured. Indeed, why should anyone feel entitled to ask for more than your friendship? From the back rows someone shouts, "You go, girl!" And Taylor is on a roll, debunking the games people play.

"'Oh, you look *good*!' Well, I'm not at all flattered by that," she declares, and a few girls look up from their notes, surprised. "That's because my mom tells me I look good," she explains. If you get it from home, then you don't have to look for that kind of appreciation from others. And if you can't get it from home, if your family is unstable, then, "Find someone who's not looking at you sexually but someone who can mentor you. Don't be on a lookout for someone to tell you that you look good." Otherwise, Taylor warns we could end up being played by "suspicious kinds of characters, and you know you're worth much more than that." There is something very endearing about a fifteen-year-old warning her peers and elders to stay away from "suspicious characters."

Taylor's talk is called "Girl, Interrupted," but I quickly see that it's about how not to get interrupted. "People go through so much mishmash on the phone for twelve hours: *'No, you hang up,' 'No, you!'* Hello? You could have been doing your algebra by then," she points out. That's why Taylor encourages students to be passionate about music or their education, since "it keeps you from being interrupted." But what about teens who have made mistakes? "Some of us have gotten knocked down, but the important thing," she stresses, "is don't stay there. Don't make friends with the rocks. Just start over."

Taylor then shares a few of her musical compositions with the crowd. First a peppy little rap, "A-B-S-T-I-N-E-N-C-E, Abstinence is the choice/ I choose for me/A-B-S-T-I-N-E-N-C-E. . . ." It has a catchy beat, and when everyone is clapping along, she has something even more tuneful in store:

> Don't want to toss away my pride.
> I'm worth waiting for. . . .
> Friends with benefits
> Just can't get with it.
> What's wrong with being a good girl?
> I can make a difference in this world!

Taylor has a powerful voice for someone so small, and I find myself thinking, *Wow, this girl could really give Christina Aguilera a run for her money.* Then I observe her mother, Trudy, manning a video camera and making mysterious hand signals like an umpire. Taylor quickly wraps up. The teenagers are supposed to go to their next session, but they all want to stay and talk with Taylor. She is graceful and hugs everyone who approaches her, but the organizer is firm and herds the throng away. I'm glad about this, since I've arranged to talk with Taylor privately. Was she always such a force of nature? In a word, yes.

When Taylor was three, it emerges, she could sing like anything and speak very well. "My mom could see that there was this natural God-given talent that was within me; and with her supporting me"—she smiles modestly and pats her mother's shoulder—"I was able to mature in my ability to stand in front of audiences and speak." At age nine, Taylor was asked to speak at her first school rally.

At the time, Trudy was working for *Jet* magazine where she had been a feature editor for fifteen years. She worked hard to arrange her schedule so that she'd be there when her daughter came home. Taylor was always her priority. Hearing the story of Taylor's birth is amazing, and it reminds me of the Jewish tradition of the Nazirite, a child dedicated to God:

> I'm a single mother and when I was carrying Taylor I just prayed and asked God to, first of all, just forgive me. And I promised Him that if He would give me a normal, happy, healthy child, I would dedicate her to Him, just getting his Word and doing His will. And it has been such an awesome responsibility and by the grace of God we have persevered, and He has made a way for us. I took a drastic pay cut to spend more time with Taylor, but I always instilled in her that God had ordained sex for marriage, and I told her, "If you just stick to that." She was little when I said, *"When God will send you a husband . . ."* People say, "Oh, how can I talk to a child about sex?" But there's a way to do it in an age-appropriate manner.

When Taylor talks about abstinence, her peers realize that she is facing the same pressures as they are. Taylor tells me that the pressure all flows from people who misunderstand the good girl:

> The media portrays bad girls as the outgoing, spontaneous-type thing, getting the men, and I think the whole way that a bad girl is perceived is essentially as being out there, being provocative, being available. It's always, "Right, yeah, I'm the baddie; don't you have a good time being the bad girl?" It's like if you're a good girl, you'll have a *baaaaad* time, you're going to be boring or something like that. But there's nothing wrong with being a good girl! Because, you know, you put yourself in a

position of being a girl who's classy and having dignity, and eventually people will treat you as such. I think it all comes down to vibes, the vibe that you give up. If you give a vibe "OK, just take me!"—you know what I'm saying—then that's the vibe that people will pick up, and they will approach you as such.

Taylor explains that she often sees girls who "kick out those vibes" get taken advantage of. But instead "if you are like, 'Hey this is me, I have dignity, and I'm fine with being classy but at the same time hip-hoppish and cool,' then people will generally accept you."

At the same time, she adds, "The whole thing is not about other people accepting you, because you're always going to have half and half—people who don't accept you. So all you can do is make sure you stay true to who you are, and then everything will work out in the divine order. But if you're trying to please the lovey crowd and the hatey crowd, forget about it."

Taylor has spoken to teen audiences—her "lovey crowd"—around the country; and in March 2006, as the keynote speaker for a teen program in Philadelphia, she drew nearly 4,000 eighth-graders over three days. Teens will often scream "We love you, Taylor!" or "You're my hero!" and mob her for autographs when she's finished. But all this doesn't seem to faze Taylor. She's simply too busy. As a gifted percussionist, she has already performed in such diverse venues as *Showtime at the Apollo* and the Ravinia Music Festival in Highland Park, Illinois (where she was the first female percussionist ever selected for the Jazz Scholars program). In her spare time, Taylor became a certified cable television producer and host who now has three shows on the Chicago Cable Access Network. (She also speaks about excellence and nonviolence, in addition to abstinence.) Somehow, through all this, she manages to study and be at the top of her class academically.

In fact, Taylor is so articulate that when I'm talking to her, I temporarily forget that she is only fifteen. In one of the more comical moments of our interview, I ask her where she grew up and she replies, "On the South Side of Chicago"; then, forgetting that she is still growing up, I ask her where she lives now: "Um, I'm still on the South Side of Chicago, yeah." We both laugh.

Where Taylor and Trudy live, there are of course gangs to be reckoned with, but that, Taylor insists, is not why she doesn't play outside. Some of the kids on the block ask her, " 'How come I never see you outside, like you live around here?' I'm like 'Yeah, I sometimes come outside,' but it's not because I don't feel safe, it's just that when I get home from a speaking engagement I want to go to sleep, you know?"

Recently, Taylor met a friend at one of her speaking engagements, and they've been in contact since. He invited Taylor to his church picnic, which she says was fun, and they've also played catch football and gone to the All-Star Basketball game together.

Trudy always came along, since she chaperones all of Taylor's mixed events. "Yeah, she went with us," Taylor notes breezily, "so, right, we went out for pizza and stuff like that, rode on our scooters." Then they all went and saw some fireworks—Trudy too.

I find this nearly incredible. I've never even heard of a chaperone in this day and age. But Taylor doesn't seem to mind at all: "She's there. She's with me for good." In fact, if a "player" is "playin'" with Taylor, she notes with an impish smile, "all I've got to do is say, 'OK, great, do you mind if my mom comes?'" And that takes care of him. "I could tell his intentions were not good from the start," she deadpans, giving me a knowing eye. This is a very effective weeding-out mechanism.

The reality is that it's also hard for Taylor to make female friends, since so many girls are "hung up over guys," and that's all they want to talk about. "So there's that separation," she notes. Enter Trudy: mother, chaperone, business manager—and friend.

A lot of girls her age just make her sad. On their way to Los Angeles, for example, in the airport they saw a group of girls, who "couldn't have been older than sixteen," and these girls were wearing "stiletto heeled boots and their hair all spiked." Taylor wondered, "Why are you trying to grow up so fast? Last year I was getting ready to turn fifteen and I was like, Wow, I can't even fathom being behind the wheel of a car because I felt it was so far away, like it was going to be so long before I will be driving—but then, Wow, now I'm driving. I look up and it's right here. So why are you trying to push it?"

Taylor points out that her mom always dresses nicely—she is indeed a very classy lady—and so Trudy was always a role model for her: "I can't go into her closet and pull out a pair of stilettos. Like when I was little, growing up, I would play office or church or something like that." Taylor would go into her mother's closet, and there would be a briefcase and a business jacket, "so I would dress up like a businesswoman, and not one of those women on the corner you see. You don't always have to look like you're in an MTV video, you know." I listen and nod. "I know," I respond; "I agree with you."

Thinking about Taylor dressing up as a little girl inspires my protectiveness and starts me thinking. Taylor is almost sixteen, and she is juggling so much that I feel conflicted. Before you know it, she'll be seventeen, and much as I support her message and think she is doing great things, I also worry that she is working too hard. I consider bringing this up with Trudy. But then, as if reading my mind, Taylor tells me about a party where she arrived late, when she was ten. All her elementary-school friends had been complaining, "Hey, you never go to any parties or anything."

"I'm thinking OK, this is an elementary school, I'm at a school party, it can't be that bad—you know what I'm saying. So we went to the party. I had some other errands to run, and I think a speaking engagement too, so by the time I got there the party was over." After Taylor arrived late, her friends filled her in about what she had missed: "I went downstairs in the basement where the actual party was, and they were covering up this big hole in the wall from a guy and a girl juking—they had put a hole in the wall. I'm like 'Oh, my' and I was just ten years old." I don't get this, because I don't yet know that "juking" refers to "dry sex." Taylor patiently explains to me how their activities led to a hole in the wall: ". . . Yeah, so they went through the wall, right; and I'm like, we're ten years old. And I'm like, if you're doing this when you're ten . . . So it's a good thing I wasn't at that party."

It makes sense to me. Trudy looks a little sad at the memory of this incident. It happened during a time when she was more lax. Naturally, she was right outside in the car the whole time, but still. As usual, though, she has a good attitude: "It was something that she had to go through that day. I said OK, I'll take you by, we'll just go by there for a little while. And I parked right outside and she didn't stay in there that long. She's like, 'Oh, Mom!'"

"Oh, Mom" is right. "Juking," Taylor later explains, was supposed to be a type of dance. It began as a word to say, "Get a party pumped or started or get it on—like the party was juking, you know, like the party was hot, it was live, it was banging. But then it turned into . . . what it turned into, and now that's what happens at parties." So it's hard to say that Taylor is really missing much in the way of wholesome childhood activities by not spending much time with her peers. Her music and her inspirational speaking help many others, to be sure, but they are also saving Taylor Moore. Governor Rod Blagojevich of Illinois gave Taylor the Outstanding Community Leader Award in February 2005, saying: "This young lady could one day be president of the United States." So far, at fifteen, she's certainly accomplished more than several presidents combined when they were her age. But then of course, as a young woman, Taylor has to keep busy or she could get "interrupted."

The following summer of 2006, I check in with Taylor to see how she's doing, and naturally, she's just won a scholarship to a two-week theater program; and after that, she will be interning at a local bank because she wants to "get a feel for what it really means to work a nine-to-five." Now sixteen, Taylor reflects on the freedom that being abstinent has given her:

> I've been living my life to the max. I'm not sitting around waiting for a boy to call. I'm not crying because I think my boyfriend is cheating on me with another girl. I'm not worrying about whether I'm pregnant. I'm not thinking about whether I've been exposed to some sexually transmitted disease. I'm simply living my life to the fullest.

• • •

Taylor was one of many speakers at the Abstinence Clearinghouse's annual conference in August 2005—that's how we met. The conference began with a salute to the American flag and a rousing rendition of "The Star-Spangled Banner" by the vocalist Deanna Grimm. I actually started to tear up a bit, but I couldn't tell if the reason was Deanna's beautiful voice, a sudden surge of patriotic sentiment, or simply that this was the first day I'd been away from my infant son, who was nestled in a bungalow in Hollywood Hills under the expert care of my husband. Before I could consider the matter properly, the gears quickly shifted and 100 colored beach balls were released into the audience to the tune of the Beach Boys' "Get around round round I get around/Get around round round oooo/Wah wa ooo!" An odd choice, I would have thought, for an abstinence conference; but then as everyone tossed the balls around, I got it: Abstinence programs are spreading—getting around. Over 1,000 people involved in different abstinence programs throughout the world have come together to share ideas, sell material at their booths, and form alliances.

The Abstinence Clearinghouse in Sioux Falls, South Dakota, began ten years ago with an all-volunteer staff and now has almost 3,500 affiliates worldwide. Although most people don't know much about it, it is the organization everyone loves to hate; many suspected a prank when Google Maps in 2005 directed people who searched for "brothels" to its doorstep. ("We've been seeing some strange men stopping by the office," Leslee Unruh, the founder of the Clearinghouse, commented at the time. "They're clearly looking for something." But she managed to keep her sense of humor: "We do have a red lamp near the window. I told my staff, 'We have to get that out of there.'") Abstinence education, of course, is a hot-button political issue of our time. Now that federal dollars have been funding abstinence programs in addition to many comprehensive sex education programs around the nation, abstinence has become even more controversial and any discussion of it is highly charged. You might deduce from the media hype that abstinence education has supplanted sex education, but nothing remotely like this has happened; dollars allocated to abstinence education programs are still significantly less than the overall allocation to sex education and contraceptive programs.

On the other hand, many involved in the abstinence movement would like to take credit for the decline in the teenage pregnancy rate over the past ten years, but it's difficult to isolate all the variables and know this with any certainty. Since there are many different trends all taking place at the same time, anyone who claims to be 100 percent sure of what's happening is probably giving you a political answer. It could be that abstinence education has caused the turnaround—certainly its timing does correspond to when the teenage pregnancy rate started to go down. But it is inconsistent to say that abstinence programs are only a drop in the bucket compared with the many entrenched sex-ed programs, and at the same time maintain that this drop in the bucket is solely responsible for a cultural turnaround. Certainly abstinence education has been an extremely valuable influence, and one that cannot be measured by allocated dollars alone (since many involved are volunteers). However, many young people also seem to have gotten sick of our oversexualized culture on their own. Perhaps the millennial generation is turning out to be more conservative in general, in ways unrelated to abstinence education. A Hamilton College/Zogby poll in January 2006 found that two-thirds of high school seniors favored more stringent parental notification laws for abortion. William Strauss, a noted playwright and director who cofounded a nationwide high school theater program called The Cappies, told me that in his experience, young people are "the first to suggest that a sexual innuendo should be removed from a play. There is definitely a re-norming going on. I heard a teenage girl saying, 'We're the establishment, because nobody else wants to establish things.'"

Complicating matters is the fact that, as with much else in the world, some abstinence programs are clearly superior to others. For example, the Best Friends program in Washington, D.C., which stresses self-control and self-respect, has been astonishingly successful.

In general, I think the debate over abstinence would benefit by being de-politicized. Let's separate the merit of different abstinence programs from whether it's acceptable for teens to choose abstinence for themselves. Teenagers are looking for more than just "the facts"; they also need a positive goal to aspire to. The best abstinence programs do cover this, but even if they don't, that doesn't mean it's wrong for individual students to choose to postpone sex. Too often, those who oppose abstinence education and call it "ignorance-only education" end up sounding as if they oppose the actual choice to postpone—that choice is "unrealistic," they will often say. I think this is a destructive message, because when teens sit down to make their choices, the table is already set for them with the expectation that they are going to have sex right this minute. In spite of all the talk to the contrary, teens who pledge abstinence are less likely to engage in risky sexual behavior than non-pledgers (and pledgers are also less likely to have children out of wedlock, to have sex before age eighteen, and to have extramarital affairs as adults). So individual abstinence commitments are something I think everyone can support, even if he or she is opposed to particular curriculums.

No doubt those pledges are a lot easier to keep when young people have role models. The three-day abstinence conference, at least, is teeming with shining examples.

* * *

Lakita Garth, taking the stage in a golden-yellow skirt suit with pearls, is to adults what Taylor is to teens. Everyone wants to have a picture taken with Lakita. An alumna of the University of Southern California and a talented singer who was once a runner-up for Miss Black America, Lakita is the rock star of this abstinence convention. She may, however, be the only rock star who is a thirty-six-year-old virgin. But just when you're starting to get worried, this turns out to be a victory speech of sorts, since in just a few days (August 12) she is going to walk down the aisle and kiss her boyfriend of two years for the very first time. In lieu of wedding presents, the couple are asking guests and supporters to help them build an orphanage for African children who have lost parents to AIDS. (In addition to speaking to 500,000 children each year, Lakita is also a sought after consultant on AIDS/HIV, and on preventing STDs.)

She is also a bit of a ham: "Once upon a time, long, long ago," she begins in a dramatic hush. Then she reconsiders—"Oh not *too* long, but long ago . . . I was born a poor black child. Actually I *was* born a poor black child!" She was born and raised in a tough part of San Bernardino, California, and it was hard for her to find role models.

> All the women in my community were either on government assistance, or they were pregnant by the time they were fifteen. Many of them now, many of my peers, actually have four kids each by a different man, and so that was kind of the scenario that I had growing up in my community. Yet I was a lady in waiting, I was looking for someone to be that example and I was always told that if you can't see something you can't be something, and therefore the only role models in my community were the drug users, the pimps, and the pushers, those who were involved with gangs—and those were the only role models that our community had. Being an African American woman not much has changed, because if you are African American and you're on TV you're either a comedian, an athlete, a hoochy, or a criminal—or you might find a weatherman once in a while.

Then she started to notice that her grandfather would get up every morning "at the butt side of dawn" to walk two miles to the cemetery. Lakita wondered why he was doing that, and finally she got up the nerve to ask him. "He told me, 'I walk two miles every day to sit next to your grandmother's headstone,' and he would sit there. And he told me he would talk about children, grandchildren that have come in, that she hasn't seen, and he would talk about times that they'd had." Lakita thought it was sweet, but still she wondered why. "Because your grandmother was my best mate," he said. They were married for almost seventy years and had twelve kids.

Lakita's father died of cancer when she was young, and her mother was left a widow to raise Lakita and her four older brothers.

> One day my mother said, "Your father wants to speak to you," and I went into the hospital room and my father said something I will never forget, and he said, "You know, the reality is this: I am not going to be here to walk you down the aisle but I know you will grow up to be an incredible woman and I don't want you to ever forget this: If you live your life trying to please a man by how you look and being concerned over what he thinks about you, you'll never please God."

And conversely, he explained, if she pleased God, then she could have the man she respected the most. Just when her speech is getting heavy, Lakita jokes about her mentioning God and how that's going to get her into trouble. "Now, some of you don't get bent out of shape and say 'People were preaching!' and all that—I'm just telling you the last words my father said!"

Lakita compares her late father's words to a movie in which a dying father told his son to go out there and sleep with as many women as possible: "Oh, not the ugly ones, he said, only the superficial good-looking ones." She started to think more about her father's words compared with what she saw and heard around her, and that's when she realized "that high self-esteem didn't come from what I looked like. Self-esteem comes from doing what is right. There is no greater feeling, even if people are dogging you out and talking about you, than that you know you have done the right thing."

Other kids would make fun of Lakita and her family because they didn't have "nice clean white Air Jordans" and they had to be in the house when the streetlights came on. Her mom limited their television viewing and actually made them crack the books. Lakita would regularly get eggs and tomatoes pelted at her in school—well into high school—because she wouldn't sleep with the boys. Yet oddly, she insists that her decision wasn't "hard."

Today when she appears on television shows (such as *Politically Incorrect* or *The View*), people always want her to talk about her hard life: "'Well, tell us how you really wanted to fit in.' I didn't want to fit in—I'm not trying to get your vote. 'Well, you know, tell us about how you felt really bad,' and—I didn't feel bad! I didn't feel bad at all. I mean the reality was, I had the best contraception ever: four older brothers who were very big boys, all of them over 200 pounds. That's some serious contraception and my momma made sure it was with me all the time."

Seriously, she adds, "Keeping my virginity was not hard—you know why? Because I had conviction." Although Lakita has been challenged in the past, "there's not one brother who approached me and I looked back and thought, 'Man, I should have given up the panties for him.' I never look and say, 'Man, I should have, I would have, I could have,' and I look forward to next week and I am really excited that I can look my husband in the face and say, You know what, I loved you before I even knew you. I've saved myself just for you."

When Lakita was fifteen, she sat down and wrote a letter to her future spouse. She encourages young people to write down their visions because "when you make it plain in front of you, when young people write down their dreams and their visions, they have more probability of accomplishing those things." Mulling this over reminds me of Scarleteen, the website that specifically instructs teens *not* to write down the goal of waiting until marriage—because, you'll recall, this dream is not "manageable." The implication is that the writer is protecting teenagers from dashed expectations and disappointment. Or perhaps the guardians of the status quo are afraid that teens may actually achieve their dreams. Then society might change, too.

There are people who do seem to feel that postponing sex will "set women's rights back," or that it is "oppressive." Just as I am thinking this, Lakita addresses this very point, and her response is interesting:

> You know, I'm president and CEO of my own company. All of my employees are men, and you know what? Pretty soon, hopefully, I'm going to have my own little office, maybe a little office building strip mall off somewhere, and I have to hire a janitor, you know, to service my building, and you know what I'm going to do? I'm going to have to have some applications before you can even see my face. And then there's the interview process, when you sit across from my table in my office and my building. I want you to fill in an application with your full name, not "Mooky" or whatever alias you're going by this week; and I want all your telephone numbers, not just a cell or a pager. I want to see some previous work experience, I want to see if you have a criminal record, and as a matter of fact, I want some character references. I want you to write that all down, and that's just to clean my toilet, and most women don't have that much sense, to get a last name from guys who will take off all their clothes and have sex with them.

She turns the question of women's rights around: "In many ways, women got the opportunity to go out into the workplace and do a lot of different things, but in a lot of other ways we lost. Because free love meant free from obligation, free from the commitment, free from intimacy, and free from any of the responsibilities. Really the freeing thing is for the men not the women, because the men got off the hook."

Lakita's perspective on responsibility is interesting, because her concept of personal dignity is very much tied to the civil rights movement. Every summer while she was growing up, in fact, the Garth family would all pile into a car and drive to Montgomery, Alabama. They would sit at her aunt's and uncle's feet, and they would talk about growing up in the segregated South. Eventually, they would entertain Dr. Martin Luther King in their home and strategize the Montgomery civil rights march together, but in the beginning King was just "this really cute pastor" people came to hear.

Lakita's grandfather was a pastor of the Sixteenth Street Baptist Church in Birmingham that was bombed and where four little girls were killed. He was preparing for Sunday school on the morning that the bomb went off, and that changed things:

> There was an adultness that our parents put into us. . . . And as I grew up I began to understand that people can stand up at a microphone and scream about their rights and I have a right to this and a right to that, but every right demands a responsibility and you know, there's no need for another civil rights movement. We need a personal responsibility movement so we can responsibly execute the rights that we have. Why is that important? I began to realize that what was going on in the roller coaster as a teenager, was that I was different than a lot of my peers, than most of my peers. Things that I valued were different.

Christina and Jason Evert are also "different" in a good way. After Lakita's talk, I duck into the "Youth Track," where this young married couple is taking questions from teens. Jason, tawny-haired and handsome, talks about why he had saved sex for marriage and why you should be wary of a partner who pressures you: "No one would take a date he liked to the Grand Canyon and say, 'Hmm, how far could I go without dropping her?'" He notes that individuals who remain virgins until marriage have a 50 percent lower divorce rate than other individuals, and that couples who saved sex for their wedding night have a divorce rate three times lower than that of other couples. His wife, Christina, a shyly smiling, beautiful brunette, talks frankly about how she lost her virginity at age fifteen: "I know what it's like to wake up the next day when the party's over and the friends are gone, and I'm alone. The next day the fun and games were over and I knew it wasn't worth it. I never had any peace until I started respecting myself."

With Christina being the experienced one and Jason the one who waited, this is an interesting reversal of the sexual double standard. But these teens don't even seem to notice; most are just excited to find out it's OK to wait. Mike from Alabama, a broad-shouldered, sporty-looking sixteen-year-old, tells me later, "Yeah, it's all about respect. You want to see what your relationship is based on when you take sex out. My parents are divorced and I want my marriage to last." Melissa, a twenty-two-year-old from Salina, Kansas, muses, "It's always been interesting to me how this generation, this millennial generation, wants to be the opposite from what we see." Even her long-sleeved blue top is cinched with a bow—very retro.

In the hotel lobby, some African American girls with large hoop earrings are giggling together. I plop down on a couch next to them to see what they make of it all. They are quite stunning, and poised for teenage girls (all six extend their hands and say, "Nice meeting you!"). I ask them how they got interested in abstinence, and they fill me in on their high schools in Michigan.

Rachel, who is sixteen, explains that it was largely a function of her school: "They came into my school and did an abstinence program for a couple of months, and I joined the program. That's how I first heard that you could be abstinent." Darcia, fourteen, simply says firmly: "I *will* remain abstinent until marriage." Leoeneye, also fourteen, entered a program through her church. How do they resist the pressure to have sex? Each girl has a different answer:

> I resist the pressures because a lot of my friends had something that happened to them in the midst of what they're doing. And I feel it's a sign to tell me to wait.

> My cousin just had a baby and she's very young, so I feel I have to stay focused. I know I'm not going to follow in her footsteps. I'm going to follow in my own footsteps, to keep my goals in life.

> I'm abstinent because I have a goal in life. I want to be a doctor or a registered nurse. If I have a baby or something that blocks my goal, I'm

not going to be able to achieve that. So being focused and staying in school is my main goal right now.

My mom had me at a young age, and I see her struggle, so I don't want to go through that with my child. I don't want to have to tell my child, "No, you can't have this because I don't have the money," and I don't want to have an abortion, because I think that's the worst thing you can ever do to somebody—not even give it a chance in life.

The upshot is that not wanting a baby is their main reason for delaying sex, which raises the question: Haven't they heard of contraception? True, condoms can break, but in talking with these young women I came to see that having a baby symbolizes being "stuck," being set back—whether it's because of an STD, emotional heartbreak, or the responsibility of raising a child without a father. For them, postponing sex is a way to stay an "individual" and to attain their goals.

After I talk with the girls from Michigan, something strikes me. I start to recall all the college-educated white women who have written to me saying that they agree with me but are "afraid to speak out." They don't like coed bathrooms, or they don't want to hook up, but they imagine that they are the "only ones," so they don't want to object to the status quo. But never has an African American girl come up to me to lament, "Wendy, I'm afraid to speak out." The cultural pressures African Americans face can be even worse, but they're more likely to laugh about men's insults instead of taking them so seriously and being intimidated. "Yup, you know, I'm a *playa hata*," declares Beth, a young married mother from North Carolina. She had written to my website, and we became friendly, exchanging e-mails and talking on the phone one evening when both our babies were sleeping. Beth was funny and, with a lilting Southern accent, she reminded me of Scarlett O'Hara in *Gone with the Wind*. But then her phrase "playa hata" shattered my preconceptions. "Wait, what's a playa hata?" I ask. She laughs at me: "You know, *player hater*, someone who doesn't like players. That's what they'll call us. Girls who don't want to have casual sex."

It suddenly dawns on me that all the writers who have attacked me, calling modesty illegitimate and an "elite white" concept, are in fact elite white people themselves.

. . .

And so it is perhaps no accident that my last stop on the tour to interview abstinence leaders should find me in Washington, D.C., to meet twenty-six-year-old powerhouse Rashida Jolley.

Rashida was born and bred in Washington, D.C. I visit her on Martin Luther King Day at a brunch celebration in her family's cozy home. I feel a bit guilty about intruding, since the house is already filled to the brim with her four brothers, their wives, two younger sisters, and what smells like some good pancakes, but everyone is so warm and friendly that I'm quickly made to feel as if I've known them all for at least twenty years (and possibly that we may even be related). As adorable toddlers with ribbons pop out of nowhere, Rashida shares that she loved growing up in a big family because "there was always some type of excitement; you were never bored." I can definitely see that.

It may be her beautiful smile that won her the title of Miss District of Columbia in 2000, but Rashida's talent as a harpist and vocalist has already influenced thousands through her debut album, *Love Is Not a Game*. Her whole family is musical (one brother is studying at Peabody, another is a jazz pianist, another a drummer—they were all playing professionally by age thirteen). Her late father, Noble Jolley Sr., "my best friend, mentor, and the greatest father in the world," was a professional jazz guitarist and Howard University's first jazz graduate. He wrote Black Entertainment Television's first theme song and was then offered a record deal. Rashida's father could have made a lot of money, but he would have had to travel a lot, which he didn't want to do, so he turned the deal down in order to be able to work from home and raise his kids. His main goal in life was to be a good influence on them—and it seems that he certainly was.

In addition to personally lugging Rashida's harp to all her musical events, Rashida's father let her know that, as she says, "if she got pregnant or had sex, period, and he found out about it, that I would have to move to another *planet*, so it was pretty much written in stone that I would be abstinent." Although this was the message given to all the children, obedience goes only so far. When Rashida was fifteen years old, she was having a discussion with her cousin when they both realized that they wanted to postpone sex of their own free will: "It wasn't about our parents anymore, but realizing that we wanted to be respected in all aspects of our lives, and that's when I made really a vow to God that I would wait until marriage before having sex."

Later, over coffee at Kramer Books, Rashida reveals something fascinating: that whether people are impressed or annoyed by her decision tends to depend on their age. Although her choice does go against the norm, among young people, she says, abstinence is becoming more and more popular:

> The best example I can give is that when I go to speak in urban areas and talk about the decision I made, 90 percent of the kids start applauding. That's something special to them. I talk about believing in yourself and not allowing someone else's opinion to become the reality for you. I tell them if you're different, that's not a bad thing! That's a great thing. You know we're honoring Dr. King today, and that's what he did; he went against the norm. Because of his courage to be a leader, all of us have been positively impacted. I talk about going against the negative majority and leaving a positive legacy, and making decisions that are healthy for you.

Rashida's inspirational speeches are nationally known and immensely popular among young students, but the people who have given her the most trouble have been the teachers. "I went to speak a few years ago [at] a school in New York, and before I got up to speak I was told, 'Now, you'll probably only be able to speak five minutes, and people have had things thrown at them, and at that point, when that happens, it's probably best to end it right there,' and you know, 'we will not be held liable,' and all that. Well, I was twenty-three at the time, and I said, you know, I'm just going to go in there and talk to them like I'd talk to anybody else."

So Rashida talked about dreams, as she usually does, and she said that abstinence begins with a dream of one day being married. As with anything else, you've got to take steps to accomplish your dream, but "first you have to have a vision for your life." Right away a teacher raised her hand, in the middle of the speech, "waving her hand all over the place, so what could I do?" Rashida said, "Can I help you?" The teacher couldn't wait until the end of the speech; "she had to interrupt it. I was like, 'Thank you very much,' but I called on her, I was like, 'OK!' And I'm thinking to myself, *I don't know if I'll be able to remember what I was saying before you interrupted my presentation,* but OK!" To herself, Rashida wondered, "What do you have to say that is so important you couldn't wait 'til the end of my speech? Do you gotta go to the bathroom or something?" What the teacher had to say was this: "Well, *I* think the problem with talking about dreams to young people is that we tell them to dream too much." That's what she said, and Rashida was "just boiling mad."

Now, Rashida is an extremely gentle person, so for her to get "boiling mad" seems highly unusual. But the teacher blathered on: "Yeah, and we have these high expectations for them, and then they can't really accomplish it, and then they feel frustrated and they feel defeated, because they haven't been able to reach their goals that we encouraged them to reach."

Rashida was very upset by this, and also dumbfounded, but before she could so much as open her mouth to respond, a fifteen-year-old boy raised his hand and said:

> "Yo, Miss Jolley, can I respond to that?" I said, "You go ahead." And he stood up and looked the teacher dead in the eye and he said, "No. Far too often, it's the adults who are saying we can't accomplish our dreams, and they expect us to fail instead of encouraging us to aim high. We may be upset if we don't accomplish our goals, but if you would stand up and set the bar high, and encourage us and have high expectations for us, then you would start to see the change."

Rashida was amazed by this, particularly because many of the kids at this school have had legal trouble, drug trouble, and family problems, yet this young man was able to stand up to his teacher. The things that adults say often mystify her.

Like the view that any reticence about sex is a "privileged, elite Victorian notion." She explains: "People like to stereotype African Americans as animalistic or whatever, and I find that to be very offensive and very racist to say that we don't have control over ourselves." To her "it's about being educated about the options that you have, and many young people do not even realize that they have an option. Those same individuals want to target urban schools and set up clinics and they make an assumption that we are just going to have sex anyway, and we aren't capable of anything else, and to me that is *extremely* demeaning."

It is hard, she concedes, for young people who don't have a father around to encourage them, as Rashida did; but even so, "I have seen transformations in their lives, for people who have people who believe in them." A big point for her is "parity," that teens need to see options other than what they see in the media and all around them.

Even if Planned Parenthood doesn't come into their school with the condoms, they're going to get it just by turning on the TV. They're going to get it just by walking down the street. There's not going to be a day that goes by where they're not inundated with a sexual message. We are just a small minority with the abstinence message; we are not dominating the media and society. And they want to take away the abstinence message and fight over any money the programs are getting? It's ridiculous, because they've already got the other side.

Rashida stresses to heartbroken young people that dating is always a challenge, but "if you don't give your whole self to the other person, then at least you have the ability to walk away." But it's so easy to be seduced by an imitation of love:

For example, my niece, when she was three, she said, "Oh, Rashida, I love you, I love you, can I have a cookie?" And I said, "You can't have a cookie; it's eight AM!" So she said, "OK, then I don't love you no more! I want my mama and I want to go home!" I was like, "Wow, and she's only three." That's the kind of love people refer to, mostly, when they talk about love today.

Real love, she explains, was the love between her mother and father. When her mother would sigh and observe that there was no Ben & Jerry's ice cream in the freezer, "I would have just told her to dream about it, frankly, but my father, he would go out in the middle of the night to the 7-Eleven, and get her that Ben and Jerry's." Her father showed her that real love is about service to others, not manipulating another person to get what you want.

For the most part, Rashida tries to give young people practical examples. She'll tell them to imagine someone "really fine," and they get all excited, the boys usually thinking of Jessica Simpson and the girls thinking of their favorite "hot guy." There is pandemonium in the audience, and it's almost impossible to calm the students down. "Now imagine that this person is coming toward you and is going to have a conversation with you!" Now everyone gets even more excited: "Whoooooo! *Whoooo!*" the kids say.

And imagine you just got paid so you've got some money in your account and you're feeling good about yourself, and the person comes up to you and says, "Hey, could I have your ATM card and get your password?" What would you do? They go from "Whoooo, whooo!" to "Aw, NO! No way!" "You must be craaaaazy!" The kids are all, "I would never give my money to them; I would *never* give them my ATM card!" So then I say, "Well, if you wouldn't give them your money, why would you give them your body? Your body is far more valuable than any of the money in this world. Oprah, Donald Trump, P. Diddy, all their money combined isn't even 1 percent of your value." And then I'll leave them with that and I'll get a bunch of them who are like, "Wow."

I'm in awe too. As we leave the bookstore and Rashida and I walk down the street together that mild January afternoon, I am briefly thrown by how much taller she is than I. But her genuineness has a way of making other people feel a bit taller too. We then discover a chance coincidence; Rashida's mother, like mine, pulled her out of sex ed from fourth grade on. (Her mom, who is a lawyer, gave her a substitute sex-ed class in her office, complete with charts, diagrams, and Rashida's favorite food, chicken teriyaki.) But instead of being sent to the library as I was, Rashida was sent to a special-ed classroom. It's the kind of thing that could cause a lesser person to take offense, or at least scoff. But Rashida just says, sincerely and sweetly, "I still have very nice memories about that class, actually."

Postponing sex until marriage, of course, puts Rashida in the minority, but that, she advises me, is something she's quite used to and comfortable with. "You know, my grandmother actually did the same thing that Rosa Parks did, refusing to give up her seat on the bus for a white woman, and to me, going against the norm of society like I'm doing now, and encouraging positive change, is part of the same thing—taking a stand for something that is not accepted by society, to try to make that society better."

* * *

There is no doubt that on the ground and in the trenches, young African American women are leaders in what you might call a personal dignity movement. The question is why. All the experts I speak to seem to be afraid to theorize, race being a taboo subject. Undeniably, there is the painful legacy of slavery, which often tore husbands from wives and children from mothers. Today black leaders such as Dr. John Diggs, A. C. Green, and Rodrick Glover, who want to give disadvantaged young people a head start in life, often talk about repairing the family; and for obvious reasons, self-control and sexual morality are a big part of that effort.

Yet it is undeniable that African American women seem to have a special gift in arguing for fidelity and premarital chastity. Finally, I track down a respected sociologist who tells me, off the record: "The fact is, black women have paid the heaviest price from the sexual revolution in the United States. There are many socioeconomic reasons for this, but both as individuals and in their communities as a whole, they now see the value of abstinence as a way to renew family life."

Perhaps. But a few months later I will have the rest of the answer, when a woman I don't know emails me in September of 2006. She apologizes for "venting," but I am thrilled to hear from her because she puts all the pieces of the puzzle together:

> I am twenty-nine and I still resent that stupid teen "narrative" that claims it's natural (and typical) to have sex and mess with drugs and alcohol, among other things, when you're a teen. WHATEVER! Why is it so bad to be good? When did doing the right thing became wrong? And when did getting drunk and doing drugs become a benchmark of the supposed awesomeness of our teen years? I just do not think that one has to do a little dirt in order to have a meaningful and authentic teenage experience. I'm not saying I never messed up, but, according to friends, I was still a Goody Two-shoes.

She then tells me that she wants to work with "young women of color (I'm African American) because I want to talk to them about the representations that are out there of us. I feel like it's a battle right now and young women of color are under siege. If white girls have *Girls Gone Wild*, girls of color have a whole aspect of hip-hop with those horrible videos and the rise of the hip-hop honey or video girl."

At the turn of the last century, she explains,

> Black women formed clubs in a major movement to fight against the racist negative images of us as lascivious, and modesty on all fronts was a major tactic. I'm beginning to feel like I need to do something like

that again: a return to respect, a call for common sense because our image is so tarnished and disrespected, especially in popular culture. A young girl of color will have the darndest time looking for a role model who looks like her who is not oversexed (otherwise there's a long list of half-naked, shiny, R&B black girls like Beyoncé, LOL). There's Raven-Symoné, maybe Alicia Keys, at least, but it is slim pickings, unlike if you're a young white woman. I'm not always sure where I stand on the various permutations of modesty, but I know it can't hurt to tout modesty with the same vigor that half-nakedness is touted in our culture.

Cantice Greene, a young teacher at Spelman, gives me the scoop when I contact her a few months later. The voices that inspired her were those of crisis pregnancy workers, "mostly middle-aged white women who'd been 'doing' abstinence for years, but they were new to me as the movement became relevant to my life." Today, she says, "the anomaly of an attractive black woman standing for abstinence" is coming "in a world where African American women are the largest racial group of single mothers in America. Add the STD and HIV/AIDS epidemics and it just makes sense. Marriage in the African American community is at an all-time low." Still, for Cantice, "the heroes are those who've quietly worked in the trenches, in schools and women's health services all along, who've consistently maintained their abstinence stances. They are old and mostly white crisis pregnancy workers and old black teachers and church mothers who've been saying the same thing for years."

*   *   *

Whether members of the millennial generation are listening to these elders in a way their own parents did not, or are challenging our assumptions about sexuality on their own, young people are shifting societal attitudes significantly.

In 2004, Capitol Records invited 6,000 girls to a series of parties promoting a teenage artist named Skye Sweetnam, and the company was surprised when the girls critiqued her clothing. Since eight- to twelve-year-old girls are considered trendsetters, Capitol responded by making her image more conservative.

In the United Kingdom, *Mizz* magazine, which is aimed at preteens, promoted *Playboy* stationery on its cover and as a giveaway. *Playboy* stationery is also available in WHSmith, next to Disney and Winnie-the-Pooh stationery, so in July 2005 seven fed-up schoolgirls ages eleven to fifteen picketed outside the WHSmith in southwest London to try to get it to pull the *Playboy* stationery.

More broadly, in 2002 and again in 2003, the National Campaign to Prevent Teen Pregnancy consistently found that adults were twice as likely as teenagers to believe it was "embarrassing" for teens to admit being virgins. In other words, the teens didn't think that virginity was such an embarrassment, but many of their parents did. And in a 2004 study, 71 percent of girls ages twelve to nineteen and 61 percent of boys "agreed strongly" with the statement "I believe that sex should only occur in a long-term, committed relationship." These generational differences were confirmed by a Harris poll in 2006; this poll also found that younger adults (ages eighteen to twenty-nine) were much more likely than older adults to view abstinence education as effective.

Things may get worse before they get better, but it's clear that the tide is turning. In a society where college bureaucrats pass out condoms and parents cross-examine kids on whether they've gotten rid of their virginity yet, young people seem to want to change course.

At Notre Dame in 2004 a group of students launched the Edith Stein Project to explore a "new feminism" that would stress the dignity of women and "the unique role of women in society." (Madeleine Ryland, a sophomore philosophy major who is an advocate for victims of rape and a mentor to girls, says she became involved in the project to "raise awareness and combat the pressures in society that can negatively impact women as they search for acceptance and fulfillment.") In 2005, a bunch of students at Princeton founded the Anscombe Society to bring speakers who would support the "inherent dignity of every human person," and "to provide the often missing support and encouragement for those students either already practicing or striving for a life of chastity." At Arizona State in 2006, a group of students formed a club called the New Sexual Revolution to "revolt against cultural messages that separate emotional value from sexual relations." Started by Rosa Camou, a senior majoring in computer information sciences, the New Sexual Revolution seeks to "open up a dialogue . . . about leading a healthy and happy sexual lifestyle." Also with an eye to promoting premarital sexual abstinence, a new student group at Harvard called True Love Revolution distributed chocolates and personalized valentines to all freshmen girls in 2007. How thoughtful of the older students, who had received only condoms, to send chocolates instead.

People wonder why the rate of virginity among teenagers has risen for the tenth straight year when this is not at all what we see and hear about in the media. Perhaps not in spite of the popular culture but because of it, some young people are seeing the limits of the "let it all hang out" philosophy. Perhaps Janet Jackson's exposed nipple at the Super Bowl in 2004 caused a stir not because it was shocking but because it was boring. Janet showed everyone that it just wasn't fun anymore. When the culture is already a veritable museum of pornography, more exposure doesn't have much cachet.

Total exposure may be omnipresent on the screen, but the moment you get a coed alone, she'll confess that she wishes for more romance and less explicitness, or at the very least for a "dating scene."

One young woman, Helen Vera, wrote in the *Yale Daily News:*

> At the risk of sounding old-fashioned, I think that I speak for a lot of us when I say that the dating scene at Yale is in a little bit of a rut, and I don't think that online dating, Sex Week, or even the *Herald*'s illustrious front page feature with step-by-step instructions on how to get a hook-up will make things any better. . . . I propose that we give an old system a new whirl: boys should develop a thicker skin and ask girls out on dates. A girl, in turn, should accept the offer unless she has a very good reason not to.

Miss Vera hastens to add, "Of course, the modern woman has the luxury of taking control and initiative when it comes to her love life, and I commend that as well." On the other hand, "ask almost any girl at Yale—really, any single woman you know—and she'll tell you that she'd be very happy to be asked out for a drink or a milkshake."

While members of the new generation are pining for courtship and milkshakes, all they get fed is more explicitness, which only increases their longing. Sex may sell, but at our current degree of saturation, mystery and honor will sell even more—something movies as diverse as *Titanic, Pride and Prejudice,* and *Lord of the Rings* have all tapped into. We are hungry for examples of uniquely human striving, to be reminded that we can still experience genuine feeling and not just bodily contortions. *Harvard Business*

Review warned its readers in February 2007 to "think twice" about touting sexually explicit video games: "Businesses that have relied on sex to sell products . . . could provoke boycotts or outright bans." Soon, today's sexy marketing campaigns "could come to be seen as relics of a decadent past."

What young people need now is a vocabulary to express their disenchantment. As Lakita Garth tells me, her mentor—who was a professor at Berkeley in the 1960s—used to say, "He who controls the language controls the culture." That's why she is suspicious of words like "chastity" that have a lot of "baggage." Instead she talks about setting boundaries or "modeling the message." Her biggest opposition doesn't come from the kids, who she says are "pragmatic" and don't want to get diseases or become pregnant. Instead, like Rashida Jolley's, her critics are almost without exception older adults: "Baby boomers . . . view any retreat in premarital sexual activity as the imposition of morality on themselves."

But their objections may be too late. Thanks to role models like Lakita Garth, a popular uprising seems just around the corner. Our vision of a rebel is a member of a motorcycle gang. You know the type: He walks into a bar, and the place clears. But when piercing, swearing, and "friends with benefits" are the new norm, perhaps the real rebels today are those who stubbornly insist on the right to define themselves.

EXERCISE:
MILD GIRL ACTIVISM—TAKE BACK YOUR ROOM

Don't wait to be "sexiled." Two college students told me that they weren't even given the consideration of being kicked out beforehand; the drunken encounters happened at night (often after one roommate had turned in), so they would get woken up.

If you are a college student, don't let this happen to you. Use your leadership skills to start a campus-wide initiative to be called "Take Back Your Room." Put pressure on the administration to reinstitute "visiting hours," let's say between 7:00 and 11:30 P.M., when persons of the opposite sex would officially be allowed to visit private rooms. Don't let your administrators off the hook if they insist that they are only "letting the students decide." Point out that without the support of the administration, you are powerless to enforce your right to live in your own room (yes, even in single-sex dorms), and you, after all, are paying tens of thousands of dollars a year for this privilege. Obviously, signing in visitors and enforcing these hours won't be feasible now that the administration houses men and women on the same floors. However, having times that in theory are devoted to "visiting," and times earmarked for studying and sleeping, will empower students who are being taken advantage of. Now you will be able to say, "I'm sorry, but I just can't be flexible about visiting hours tonight; I have tons of work to do," or "I need to go to bed early." At least in this scenario, those who want to breach visiting hours will be on the defensive. By contrast, now you are "the poor sport" if you want to stay in your own room. This will give all students more leverage in the sexile wars.

And if you don't win this battle, then at least you can tell your grandchildren that you tried.

CHAPTER FOUR

Against Repression (Emotional Repression, That Is)

•

So right away on the trip, a bunch of the girls—most were eighteen or nineteen—end up sleeping with some of the older guys in their twenties, you know, "no strings attached." Then they all later individually come up to me because they're concerned that something is wrong with them. They wanted to play by the boys' rules, "no strings attached," you know, spend the night together but not spend any time together during the day. Only they didn't see it as the boys' rules; they saw it as their rules too, that they had agreed to. Well, soon they started to feel bad about the arrangement, and the longer they were together at night and didn't spend any time together in the day, the worse they would feel. But they couldn't figure out what it was. I mean, they were able to articulate to me *that* they felt bad, but since they had all agreed to "no strings attached," they didn't know *why* they were feeling bad. It was kind of funny how each one came up to me, separately—but also sad, I guess.

—C, a thirty-two-year-old kayaking instructor in British Columbia

I am not a sheltered person, but I was surprised to read in *New York* magazine that a swinging couple could "certainly teach most couples a thing or two about communication." Professionals in their mid-thirties, the man and woman—I'll call them M and W—are nonmonogamous and in general could not be more liberated. They refer "to their additional partners as living, breathing sex toys." M takes nude photos of the other girls he's with, then sells the photos in various venues. W, meanwhile, is allowed to "veto" women who are too attractive. Disappointed by the infidelity of a previous boyfriend, W has now made up her mind not to care anymore: "It's like, you have this best friend, and you want the best for him. So if he's hot for that chick over there, you want to be like, 'Yeah, go for it!'"

You may want "to be like, 'Yeah, go for it!'" but if you really were, then why use the word "want"? Our desire to appear cavalier often, apparently, exceeds our capacity. Clearly, if M were to come home one day and tell W he loves her so much that he can't even dream of being with another woman ever again, it's likely that W would be thrilled to pieces. But if W insisted on monogamy, her demand would pretty much end M's entire lifestyle and career. After reading the article, I was left with the impression that their relationship was a bit off-kilter, fulfilling one man's wildest fantasies at the expense of a woman's day-to-day emotional needs.

Then I happened to visit M's blog seven months later, and it emerged that he and W were then struggling over whether to have a baby. ("To Breed or Not to Breed" was the day's entry.) W, who is not getting any younger, has apparently raised the presumptuous question, and though M reports that he is "torn and she feels the same," it turns out that one side is a bit more "torn" than the other: "I resent a biological clock imposing its will on my girl," M writes. "I resent that it's one-sided. That in just a few years I will still be able to have a child, but she won't." Even worse, if they did have a child, M would need to curtail his "sexy bohemian open relationship" and, he protests, "I love our life so much right now." So he signs off: "I have more questions than answers, and not enough time to answer them all. Story of life, I suppose." Meanwhile, W waits and waits.

All the commentators on the Internet are very supportive of this couple's lifestyle; M in particular is an "inspiration" and "so impressive a person." In one online forum I ask if the pair ever got married, since that seems relevant in considering how a child might fare, and the snappish reply is: "They are probably MORE married than most of us could ever hope to be."

M is certainly not without endearing qualities, but it is hard to see a baby fitting into this lifestyle. It's also remarkable how W's desire for a family is so quickly whisked away and coldly intellectualized as a "biological clock imposing its will." W is depicted as a kind and attractive woman with so much going for her that one can only hope she will soon run, not walk, to the nearest exit, and trying not to trip over all the naked women on her way out.

But will she make it out the door? That depends on how she perceives her own ideals and emotional needs. Lately I've been noticing that our war against sexual repression always seems to require another sort of repression, of feeling and caring. This repression, more often than not, is required of the woman.

. . .

One day in mid-February 2006, I was packing my clothes in a hotel in Chicago, when the television suddenly jolted me to attention with a male voice crying "Nutbag!" I thought I had tuned in to WGN news, but could a male anchor be calling a woman a "nutbag"? That seemed unprofessional. It turned out that they were discussing the previous night's episode of *The Bachelor*. A clip was then shown, in which the "nutbag," Moana, a twenty-six-year-old distribution manager from Los Angeles, is told very earnestly by a thirty-three-year-old medical resident, Travis, how much he cares about her. She has already met his parents after two months of dating, and so has her competitor Sarah. Moana is dressed in her finest gown; her face is made up; and she stares expectantly into Travis's loving eyes. It seems that a marriage proposal is imminent, but instead she is summarily dumped. Moana is then filmed sobbing in the car, crying about how vulnerable and hurt she felt—especially to have thought her feelings were reciprocated when they really weren't. Throughout this replay, the anchors at WGN are hooting and laughing at Moana, with her puffy eyes. I feel that I'm missing something, since I don't find this funny at all. Later I consult friends who have followed these reality shows from the beginning; one explains to me that "people just want to see the bachelorettes squabble among themselves and fight for the bachelor's attention." It's like the staged fights in the ancient Colosseum, where lions ate condemned people and the spectators clapped. Will future generations, I wonder, consider us barbaric?

In our defense, we don't get very good advice. When young women in our society cry out that they want to be married, invariably our experts reply, *No you don't!* For instance, *Elle*'s expert on relationships tells a woman who wants to get married that she should marry her dog instead—because he's "the only creature who will love you more than you love yourself." *Cosmo* tells women who are "dying to get married" that they need to try to "enjoy dating" more. "Part of your yearning to marry may come from having a blah single life," the editors counsel. I suppose this could be true, but no one seems to entertain a more obvious answer, that a "yearning to marry may come from"—well, a yearning to marry. If women are supposed to be so liberated nowadays, then why do we require such deprogramming? Why can't we be permitted to want what we want? If women could only be cured of our embarrassing desire for an exclusive love, then, according to postmodern logic, we would experience no pain when we couldn't fulfill our desire. If emotions cannot be compressed, they must be redirected. Where to? The dog, clearly.

But making marriage taboo is the least of our problems. A typical issue of *Cosmo* prints a letter from a woman who is afraid to ask a man "if he's been tested for STDs" because she might "scare him off." *Cosmo* advises women that the number one way to "keep him interested" is to *"Keep your heart under wraps."* This advice is in bold type, because no matter how much you like a guy, letting him know that you do could prove disastrous, and "make him freak out that you'll be one of those superclingy girlfriends." A woman who "made the mistake of dropping the L bomb"—that is, telling the man she was sleeping with that she loved him—is counseled, as if she had dropped the H bomb, not to do it ever again. Over and again, the reader of *Cosmo* is told to "go easy on the love stuff," and certainly never to make the same mistake as a girl who wrote an old-fashioned love letter to her boyfriend, on special stationery, only to be summarily dumped by a response "on a greasy, folded up fast-food wrapper [reading] *'We're done.'"* Let that be a lesson for all of us.

The overall impression you come away with is that women are terrified to broach their real concerns with their lovers, whether the woman wants to get married or wants to avoid catching a deadly disease. It's striking how deeply uncomfortable these women are with the men who share their beds. Young women ask, "How do I turn down a kinky sexual request that skeeves me out without embarrassing him?" (Embarrassing *him?*) And my personal favorite: "Is it OK to run to the bathroom after sex to pee?" If we continue down this path, in a year or so the question might be, "Is it OK to breathe next to the guy I'm sleeping with?" (In case you are wondering, it is not OK to pee. I would have thought that it was, but nope. *Cosmo* clarifies: "You may . . . have heard that it's best to pee after sex to avoid getting a UTI [urinary tract infection] but a lot of guys find it disturbing when you jump off of them like they're the sinking *Titanic*. So lie back and relax for a few minutes. . . .")

The men who share these women's beds are treated like kings or princes whose authority comes from God Himself, whereas the women's own feelings and even their health concerns are restricted in the extreme. The men have the mandate of heaven, but the women don't even have the mandate of the loo. They must hew to a "protocol," literally. "The Booty Call Protocol. . . . Booty-Call Rule 2: Avoid the redial button. If he doesn't answer or call back after you make the first attempt, don't keep hitting redial. He could be sleeping or spending time with someone else, and you're not allowed to mind." You are not even allowed to *mind*, mind you. Must keep those emotions under tight wraps and blast them away before they can come to the surface, escape, and—what, exactly? What are we so afraid of? What is this war on female emotion really about?

Cosmo's August 2005 issue specifically instructs that one way to "Wow Him after Sex" is to "ask for a ride home" just when he expects you to want to stay. It's a dash of reverse psychology meant to pique his interest: "Regardless of how mind-blowing the booty was, guys get antsy in the A.M. and it's up to you to cut the festivities short after you eat." Sprint to the door, and he won't know what hit him. One man, "Miles," twenty-eight, waxes nostalgic about a "chick" who was hip enough to say bye-bye right after the French toast: "I was relieved, because I wasn't ready to spend the whole day with her." I'll grant him his relief, but what of Miles's "chick"? *Cosmo* has a strategy for her, too, a column not surprisingly drafted by a man: "Always Keep Your Expectations Low."

> He slept with you because you let him. You slept with him because he has potential. We know you have standards, which is why we [men] always suspect you may have other ideas of what having sex means for the relationship. "Even if it's all fun and games *before* sex, I'm always afraid that afterward, she's going to assume our commitment level has leapfrogged," says Dan, 28. "But it's not necessarily a milestone for me." So the relationship expectations that you had before you hit the sack should stay the same post sex. Trust me, *his* are.

Should a woman jump into bed immediately and lower her expectations, or should she wait and keep them high? And does it even matter what the women's magazines say? "Serious writers" often tell me that "we all know" women's magazines are not to be taken seriously.

I beg to differ. The intelligentsia's dismissal of *Cosmo* and other such magazines masquerades as sophistication but could hardly be more clueless. While it might be nice for writers to imagine that their political columns have a great influence on wide swaths of girlhood worldwide, that tens of millions of young women in pink bedrooms pore over every sentence of their diatribes and strive to incorporate the columnists' every jot and smirk into their private lives, I regret that such is not the case. *Cosmo* and *Seventeen*, on the other hand, do have precisely such an influence. Perhaps it is necessary to state the obvious: The reason these magazines are available in every supermarket everywhere is that tens of millions of women are buying and reading them.

If there is poison in the tap water and nearly everyone is drinking it, we don't say, "Well, it's just tap water. Who cares? I drink bottled water." Mashadi Matabane, who used to be the editorial research director at *Seventeen*, tells me, "Honestly, I didn't think much of teen mags before working with one (even though I did read *Sassy* and *Seventeen* when I was growing up), but I know that girls take *Seventeen* very seriously. Sometimes it scared me to learn just how much girls really looked to the magazine for advice. You wouldn't believe the kind of questions they would ask—things they should have been asking their parents but couldn't or wouldn't. I'd be thinking, why don't they ask their parents that or a big sister . . . somebody close to them?"

When I mentioned in passing to a modern Orthodox girl that there are people who don't think *Cosmo* should be taken seriously, she was shocked and drew in her breath sharply: "Are you kidding me? *Cosmo*? It's, like, the Bible!" I had to bite my lip to keep a straight face: "The Bible? Don't you think that's going a bit far?"

Now, do not imagine for a moment that this young woman reads *Cosmo* uncritically. In fact she reads it very critically, underlining passages that strike her as ridiculous and triumphantly presenting them to me. But the important thing to note is that she is not so dismissive that she would, God forbid, ever fail to read an issue. Even girls who are critical of *Cosmo* nonetheless learn from it: what to do and how to do it. Because these magazines are explicit and slickly presented, they do have the ring of truth when they advise girls on relationships. But much of this advice, unfortunately, is quite bad.

So our journey into emotional repression does not end with the women's magazines, but it's useful to begin there. For the bizarre advice is not confined to those magazines; it seeps in rivulets all across our culture.

Consider the manual *Swell: A Girl's Guide to the Good Life*, whose authors—Cynthia Rowley and Ilene Rosenzweig—urge girls to try "naked

Saturday" with their boyfriends: "Put on your pair of fuzzy slippers and you're both dressed for the day. Makes chores more stimulating." For even more excitement, you might pretend that someone is chasing you, or "Go on the lam," like so:

> For the price of a night at the multiplex, buy your own Hollywood get-away scene. Instruct him to meet you at the train station. Pretend you've been spotted and have to get out of town on the double. Ask the clerk for two tix on the next train and hurry on board looking suspicious. After a few stops, when the coast seems clear, get off.

If I had done something like this while dating my husband, he would have thought me paranoid or delusional. Still, I can appreciate that people have fun doing different things. But when the authors go on to advise going out with married men "platonically," which makes you a "great broad," they lose me entirely.

These hip authors have impeccable credentials: Rowley is a well-regarded fashion designer, and Rosenzweig is the deputy style editor for *The New York Times*. And their book, which is chock-full of clever illustrations and bright, colorful boxes, is fun to read. But when you take a closer look at this "swell" new girl who is naked on Saturdays, pretends to be chased, and dates married men "platonically," the secret to her "good life" turns out to be the same as always: Bottle up those emotions. Our new swell girl may be adventurous, but she is never so adventurous that she could actually do something like, say, express her true feelings:

> You're pillow-talking: he's in a coma. Hitting the hay is no time to get deep. It's been a long day—and night! The last thing you want is him nodding off in the middle of your account of your parent's second divorce. You're nose-to-nose, just having done the dirty deed, the urge is to share. So talk about your scars. . . . Intimate moments don't have to be heavy. You'll both sleep better if you conk out on a laugh rather than on an issue-stained pillowcase.

If a swell girl still feels close the morning after—"If you open your eyes and after one glimpse think you're still dreaming"—never ask, "What are you doing today?" That "puts him on the spot." Instead, "be cling-free like fabric softener."

But wait—before you take any of this advice you'd be wise to flip to the next page. Yes, it turns out that after you try really hard to pretend you don't care, it's unlikely you'll get to keep the guy, anyway:

The no-pajama party was Saturday. No word on Sunday. What are you gonna do, call your lawyer? Before you slept over, did he sign anything promising to respond within twenty-four hours? You have no case. *Should I call him?* Flip a coin. Better yet, avoid the waiting altogether with the underutilized next day "Thanks for everything" phone call. And his feelings, whatever they may be, won't be changed either way.

Now, if all this emotional repression doesn't even "work," what is the point of it?

The war on emotion seems to have taken on a life of its own in recent years. Not content merely to detail how adult women should black out their hopes, those giving advice to teens now tell them to purge all emotion before undertaking sex. Consider, for instance, Scarleteen's widely circulated "Sex Readiness Checklist," referenced and cross-linked by countless teen advice and sex education sites. This checklist is in a sense the gold standard of what a prepared teen ought to do and think before having sex. Along with "I have a 'sex budget' of about $50 per month to take care of birth control, safer sex items and annual testing and sexual health care," and "I have had regular doctor checkups," the checklist includes some "emotional items." Astonishingly, one of these items is: "I can separate sex from love." That was once seen as pathological but is now taken to be a hallmark of maturity. Being able to separate sex from love is on the list with "I can relax during sexual practices without fear, anxiety, or shame." If you think love has anything to do with the enterprise, then you are not "relaxed" enough to continue. Those who can separate sex from love are sophisticated, like jaded adults. They are ready to embark on a lifetime of meaningless encounters. Conversely, those who still dream of love are immature, and should return to playing with dolls and trucks until they can be callous enough to seek sexual non-intimacy. It's not enough, then, for teens to wear the T-shirts sold in the Scarleteen shop: I [HEART] GIRLS WHO LIKE LATEX and REVERE RUBBER CO. For a totally rubber experience, their emotions can be rubber too. Sex, after all, is no big deal:

It seems that a lot of what we hear in terms of safeguarding our emotions [is that] only sex within marriage is safe emotionally, but that simply isn't so. Sex is not something that need be hurtful, or that we have to avoid so as not to get hurt or hurt anyone else. When entered into with a solid basis of self-awareness, empathy, care, good judgment and an arsenal of accurate information, sex has no more capacity to hurt than anything else in life.

The beauty of this formulation is its circularity. It cannot be disproved. Thus, if you experience negative emotional consequences after having sex—as studies suggest most teens do—it's not the activity itself that is to blame, but rather your failure to separate sex from love. It's your fault for not being mature enough, for not attaining that elusive combo of "a solid basis of self-awareness, empathy, care, [and] good judgment."

Scarleteen may be just parroting conventional wisdom, since campaigning for emotional repression has become widespread. We all tend to seek intimacy and lasting bonds in our own lives, yet we continue to make disconnection a goal for younger and younger girls. You'll recall that Jeanette May, cofounder of the Coalition for Positive Sexuality, believes that girls "are better served by having sex for their pleasure, without a lot of emotional attachment."

To find out more about this, I browsed the coalition's website. The site features posters for $5. These include "Latex: The fashion accessory that goes with everything!" (young women showing off latex gloves and where to position a dental dam); and girls whispering to each other and smiling, next to the words, in bright blue: "The secret to great sex . . . water-based lube!"

The Coalition for Positive Sexuality's main campaign is its "Just Say Yes" initiative. It began as a bright purple "Just Say Yes" flip book, which the coalition distributes and which features a disembodied male member standing at attention on every page (as you flip the book, this image is magically cloaked with a condom). But the first thing that struck me was its main illustration of two androgynous-looking young women. The short-haired one on the left wears boxy overalls, and the tough-looking one on the right a puffy ski jacket. The latter, with arms akimbo, lets loose to her friend this all-caps sentiment: "IF I DON'T GET LAID SOON I'M

GONNA EXPLODE!" Apparently, being on the prowl for a release is considered being "positive about sexuality." There are pages of instruction on where to get an abortion, how to circumvent parental notification laws, and so on. Hard as this is to imagine, many parents who didn't know how to talk to their kids about sex were contacting the organization for these flip books, so eventually the coalition decided that a website would be the most effective way of spreading their "Just Say Yes" message. Today this site features instructions such as: "There are lots of safe and fun ways to get off, which you probably won't learn in school." (Oh, trust me, you will.) Teens are told, "You can do many of these things all by yourself as well as with others. . . . Don't feel like you have to do everything on this page, but don't feel like anything is automatically off limits either." Suggested activities that shouldn't be "automatically off limits" include insertion of vegetables into various bodily orifices of "someone" and attaching clothespins to this someone; and let's not forget to "cross-dress" or "look at sexy pictures and videos"—this time with or without "someone."

Since the Coalition for Positive Sexuality is such a well-regarded resource for teenagers (its website is another one highly recommended by the ALA), I flew in to Washington, D.C., to get a better sense of where it was coming from. I wanted to know if there was a relationship between being "sex-positive" and "emotion-negative," because I was starting to suspect that there was.

The coalition's cofounder, Jeanette May, turns out to be a serious-looking woman in her early forties with short hair. As befits an artist and activist, she wears a black leather jacket and walks unusually fast. After meeting each other at the appointed hour, we make plans to go to a nearby restaurant, but then Jeanette sprints off so quickly that I fear that she is trying to run away. I make a mad dash after her—chasing positive sexuality, as it were, which is ever-elusive—and when I finally huff and puff my way to her side, she admits that she walks fast and that her friends complain about it, too. She is quirky and very likeable.

After we settle in a booth at a busy Mexican restaurant, Jeanette munches on a salad and explains that she was one of about twenty people who founded the Coalition for Positive Sexuality (CPS) in Chicago in 1992. They were primarily activists involved with three organizations: Queer Nation Chicago, Act Up Chicago, and The Emergency Clinic Defense Coalition. But Jeanette is now the main person keeping CPS afloat. They

decided to branch out to teenagers because "we wanted to have sex education materials that were presented in a positive way, that sexuality was good
and natural and wonderful. . . . We felt that a lot of sex education was very
negative, that it was about what you shouldn't do, and about the horrible
diseases you would get if you did do it, and we wanted to turn that around."
I agree with Jeanette that you need to have a positive vision of what intimacy is; but what I don't understand, I tell her, is the way that "positive
sexuality" is always taken to mean "casual sexuality." Why do you have to
be blasé about sex to prove that you have a positive attitude? Can't you
be positive and at the same time seek only one lifetime partner? Jeanette
pauses, and chooses her words slowly and carefully:

> I don't think casual sex is inherently problematic, even for teenage girls,
> if the girls are making choices based on their own needs, if they are not
> being pressured into doing anything they're not comfortable with, and if
> there is a level of pleasure for them in the encounter. Too often what I
> am hearing about casual sex amongst teens is it seems that it's not in the
> best interests of the girls because they're not getting anything out of it.
> But girls *could* be getting something out of it, and maybe they would
> make better choices about the kind of sex they have and who they're
> having it with if they believed that there was something in it for them.

So, just as adult women are coming to terms with the fact that casual sex is
usually bad sex—asking, like Amy Sohn, "What is the point of casual sex if
the sex part isn't any good?"—there are those who still hope that teenage
boys are going to be better lovers than their adult counterparts. Is this wish-
ful thinking, or something else entirely? Jeanette truly believes that if girls
were encouraged to have casual sex and told that they could enjoy it more,
then they would enjoy it more:

> Part of the problem in our society is that we tell girls that there is noth-
> ing in it for them, that sex is for boys, the boys want it and they're try-
> ing, that girls need to protect themselves and deny boys sex. Well,
> maybe girls can want sex too, and then they can make better choices
> about who they're having sex with, what kind of sex it is, when they
> have it, when they don't have it—if they got the message that it was for
> them, that sex was for them, that there is pleasure in sex for women,

and that they should choose it when they thought it was going to be beneficial to them.

Jeanette's good intentions are obvious. But I really don't think societal expectations are causing girls' ambivalence about sex with "no strings attached." The cause is more the nature of the enterprise: If you're with a guy who doesn't care about you much, he's not going to care about your sexual needs either. Of course the "friends with benefits" arrangement ends up benefiting boys more than girls. Why should the boys waste much attention on someone who is merely a "friend"? Wanting a serious relationship does seem to put girls at a competitive disadvantage when casual sex is valued. But instead of turning against their desire to connect (which is, after all, the foundation of civilization), why not give girls more tools to navigate in a culture that's so hostile to their desires? Of a dozen possible topics in sex education, 84 percent of girls asked to hear more about this number one topic: how to say no to a boyfriend's requests for sex without losing the boyfriend.

The sexual messages I grew up with, whether they involved attorneys telling seventh-graders to sleep around or the ironic SHAMELESS HUSSY stickers we were to wear proudly in college, all amounted to a big banner that casual sex was just as enjoyable for girls as for guys. There was complete parity with our expectations. But then, oddly, the morning after, the sexes would divide. It wasn't the guys who led protests against date rape on campus. It wasn't the guys who strung T-shirts together in a "Clothesline Project" with messages like SOMETIMES I DON'T WANT YOU TO MIND YOUR OWN BUSINESS. The pain that young women were experiencing was real, but it was not the pain of a social stigma or a double standard. It was, if anything, the opposite: the pain of feeling that society had abandoned them by failing to inform them of the emotional consequences of sex. Catharine MacKinnon says, "Politically, I call it rape whenever a woman has sex and feels violated," whereas her critics point out that some of this is just plain bad sex. Even so, shouldn't that only begin the discussion? Instead, our public debate always ends in semantics. Katie Roiphe dismisses coeds who say they feel "defiled" and "I long to be innocent again." (She says these women are using "an outdated, sexist vocabulary.") But even if we don't like their vocabulary and even if it is merely bad sex and not rape, shouldn't their feelings still count?

I ask Jeanette May what she thinks the problem is with a girl who is heartbroken after a sexual encounter. She says, "Well, I think the issue is she thought that there was going to be love involved with casual sex and that's because girls are taught that sex is about love. . . . I would rather that they be smarter about what sex is and what it isn't." To her, empowerment means "having realistic expectations for that encounter."

Are low expectations therefore "smart," and high expectations "dumb"? If high expectations for love were truly societal—imposed from above— then perhaps casting them off would indeed be liberating. But after talking to hundreds of young women about their relationship problems, I've learned that girls' natural hope for real intimacy actually protects them from remaining in unhealthy relationships. Consider a nineteen-year-old college student whose boyfriend slammed the door on her foot: Did I think he was abusive? Was she right not to sleep with him even though he was "so mad at her"? Well, obviously she was right.

I think I understand why Jeanette says girls would be better off having sex "without a lot of emotional attachment," but part of what makes sex pleasurable is the emotional attachment; we can relax and know that we are with someone who cares about us and our needs. Lacking that, girls in particular back away, sensing that they are just being used—because, let's face it, they are.

Amazingly, near the end of our interview, after telling me why girls need to adjust their expectations and not look for love, Jeanette suddenly got animated while reflecting on boys' emotions. She brought up the topic: "I think boys are taught in our society that sex is about physical pleasure for them and that there's not necessarily a connection to love, but I have seen teenage boys in *tears,* sitting in a corner of the hallway, because their girlfriends broke up with them. That is not the media representation we get for teenagers." This was the only point in our interview when Jeanette seemed to be really passionate, devoting the next several minutes to detailing how important boys' emotions were. I was speechless.

I would encounter this contradiction over and over again: Emotional, dreamy girls are a thorn in our side, but when boys are romantic, their every tear is precious. It was a mystery to me. On Teenwire, Planned Parenthood's website, you will find the same paradox. On the one hand, girls are discouraged from expressing emotions, which are supposedly culturally based; on the other hand, boys who are emotional are praised:

Dear Experts,

Do guys have the same emotional results from losing your virginity to someone as girls do? Cuz I know that girls become attached to the person they first had sex with and stuff. . . . Does this happen with guys?

mamacita15

Dear Mamacita15,

When it comes to having sex, everyone is different. There is no universal experience or reaction that all guys have, and there is no universal experience or reaction that all girls have. . . . In fact, some studies show that guys, in some ways, may even be more romantic than girls. That's why it's important for partners to talk about their feelings and expectations about sex. Sometimes society places different expectations on guys and girls when they first have sex, but many of these expectations are based on gender stereotypes that do not hold true for everyone.

Unpack this: If a girl is upset after losing her virginity, that is due to cultural programming, since "there is no universal experience or reaction." This is misleading, since well more than two-thirds of girls consistently report that they do in fact regret their experiences. Planned Parenthood deliberately conceals this majority, clouding reality with the specious statement that there is no "universal" feeling. In this case, told that there is no "universal" experience, our teenage girl is made to feel she is on her own if she experiences any bad feelings. Yet once again the companion message is that boys "may be more romantic than girls," and the subtle implication is that this is charming. Why is it bad when girls get attached, but adorable when boys do? The experts at Teenwire are helpful here, actually telling us why: because they are against "gender stereotypes." Get it? I certainly don't. It's not based on any coherent understanding of what emotions are, and the important role that they play in integrated human sexuality. It's just sexism in reverse: Whatever the historical expectations have been for boys and girls, let's just flip that around, arbitrarily.

The Sexuality Information and Education Council of the United States (SIECUS), which is, in a way, the command center for various gloomy teen-sex-ed troops, outlines its challenge with military precision. "It is important to note," I learn from its website, "that although patterns of sexual involvement are increasingly similar for boys and girls, persistent gender stereotypes mean that young women still experience their sexual behaviors quite differently." Later, SIECUS runs through previous studies, in which young women have consistently reported that they were "more likely to regret their sexual experiences, more likely to label the relationship 'love,' less likely to report their sexual experiences as pleasurable, and more likely to bear the brunt of negative outcomes than their male counterparts."

It is difficult to believe that all this is due to "persistent gender stereotyping." Remember, we're not just talking about girls who were raised after the sexual revolution and the women's movement; these are girls for whom the concept of self-determination and "girls can do anything!" was incorporated into their very upbringing. The more obvious explanation is that our experts' pattern of consistently trivializing female self-reporting is caused by persistent *ideological* stereotyping. The girls are always found to be under the mysterious influence of "persistent gender stereotyping," which no girl in fact reported. Even the girls' own sense that they are in love is pooh-poohed by these experts—notice how SIECUS sets off the word "love" in scare quotes—they suspect both their love and their sexual regrets because the boys reported neither reaction. But why would boys be the benchmark for what constitutes legitimate female experience? Apparently, their ideological stereotyping leads SIECUS to believe that the girls' and boys' experiences should always be identical, and so it finds the disparity between girls' and boys' reporting too disagreeable to process in a logical manner.

* * *

How are girls responding to all these signals to stifle their emotions? Not every girl finds it easy to put on a harsh persona and develop sufficient worldly disdain. True, there are dutiful girls like fifteen-year-old Irene, no longer "devastated" by not being asked out on dates. Today, proudly, she "can hook up with a guy and not fall for him," but there are many others who still stubbornly hope for more.

When twenty-year-old Amanda contacted me and invited me to read her Live Journal blog, I quickly saw that she was smarter than all the sex educators put together:

In the July 2005 issue of *Seventeen* magazine, there is an article on page 84 about how to tell if you are ready for sex. This article contains a list of things which you are supposed to ask yourself before you have sex, "not just the first time but every time," and if the answer to even one of them is no, then you shouldn't do it. . . . The list also includes ways to tell if you are emotionally ready for sex, which include the condition of being able to handle it if your boyfriend breaks up with you soon afterward. I never was and never will be all right with a person I have opened up to and tried to bond with leaving me. However, since a certain level of emotional intimacy is necessary before I will even want to have sex, to say nothing of being OK with actually doing it, by the time I have sex I will already be at a point where I would not be able to handle being broken up with.

In my opinion, it is not the girls who say no to this question, but those who say yes, who should not be having sex, since their hearts are not in it and their emotions are not fully engaged. If a girl can let a guy go so easily, then he is not the one for her, unless she is the kind of girl who sees sex as solely a tool of physical pleasure and never wants to bond emotionally with a lover. I don't know how many girls of this type there really are out there, but I am quite sure that it does not include the entire population. By making this one of the conditions for being ready to have sex, *Seventeen* has, essentially, denied girls the right to view sex as an act of love. In order to be ready, you have to view your partner as replaceable. If you care about him too much and can allow yourself to get fully lost in him, then you are not emotionally mature enough.

This young woman, who happened at the time to be in a serious relationship, is convinced that the type of man who would abandon her would be recognizable from the start, and that her current boyfriend is not that type. Amanda could be right or wrong about this, but one thing she argues powerfully is that our equation of jadedness with maturity is misplaced. Later, she makes an equally profound point: If we tell teens they have to be disconnected before they have sex, then, "How can they trust their partners? I think this consideration is crucial. If you don't trust them, how can you believe them when they say they don't have an STD?" Or trust them if they say they handled the contraception: "Did he really put the condom on right? When dealing with STDs and pregnancy, you are, literally, putting your life in this person's hands." (Indeed, about half of college students use condoms incorrectly, although they are assumed to be more responsible than teenagers.) More significantly:

> If you can't trust a person to respect you and refrain from hurting you, either physically or emotionally, why would you want to reward them by giving them something as special as the chance to have sex with you? So, this is my challenge to girls. Don't ask yourselves if you are mature enough to handle it if your partner treats you badly. Instead ask yourselves whether your partner is really worthy of receiving such a great gift from you. If there is a risk he would treat you badly, clearly he is NOT worthy.

But what about the girls who are successful in separating sex from emotion? Sadly, the ones most adept at emotionally disconnecting have typically been abused. These young women rarely experience disconnected sex as empowering, though others may look up to them for their promiscuity. Being admired for their ability to disconnect, which actually comes out of pain, can make their lives surreal. Consider this letter I received in September 2005, from a woman I will call "Katherine":

> First let me say that I am what most people would call a liberal, although I hardly find myself in step with most of the liberals in this country when it comes to sex and the roles of men and women in our society. . . . At eight years old, I was the victim of sexual abuse by my peers. The school system told my parents, who had only an inkling of what was going on, that "boys would be boys." I entered my teen years terrified of sex.
>
> In college, I ended my long period of abstinence by having sex with everyone. Other girls were actually jealous of me and my ability to have sex without getting attached. What they didn't know was that love and sex had been violently separated for me before I ever hit puberty. I hated sex . . . but I didn't know how to say no. I somehow got through that period without any permanent STDs or pregnancy. I did not escape with my sanity; I developed an alcohol problem that drove me out of college and straight into a twelve-step program.
>
> The twelve-step program turned it all around for me. Not just be-

cause of the help I received there, but because of what I saw. I saw men who should know better preying on young girls who suffered from the same delusions that you describe in your book: that virginity is a burden, that having sex with no strings attached is normal, that saying no is wrong. I watched young girls deteriorate and leave the program to do more dangerous drugs and end up worse off than they were before they came in. I fought with these men; I begged these girls not to do it. Yet I was the freak; I was the prude. I was told that I was not the "arbiter of other people's sex lives."

Three years ago, Katherine tells me, she met the most wonderful man in the world, and they have been together since then. She was "shocked that he didn't want to sleep with me right off the bat, but I learned to appreciate it." Now, at twenty-five, she looks back on her past and realizes, "I wish that I could take back every single person I was intimate with prior to him." Her friends think she is "crazy, that I should not regret my past; some still look up to me for it. I try to explain to them that who I used to be should not be anyone's standard. I was miserable!"

Today, Katherine still worries about girls like herself, "raised in the era of sexual liberation and left to fend for ourselves. . . . What makes a group of eight- to thirteen-year-old boys molest and attempt to rape another child?"

Molestation certainly didn't begin with the sexual revolution, but now it is more likely than ever to be thought of as "no big deal." Our legal dockets overflowing with "harassment" cases supposedly indicate how "aware" we are, but maybe they show only how out of control things are. Plainly, making emotional disconnection our ideal is making the "boys will be boys" mentality more dangerous than ever. This isn't "blaming the victim" as some people claim in order to avoid having this discussion—it's defending the victim. The more adults jeer at any sexual reticence or emotion, the more the boys will too. A society that is hostile to innocence is by definition hostile to children. Young people need to be taught that sex is significant and that it has emotional consequences; instead we explain to them that virginity is bad and that private parts are no different from elbows, or that "sex has no more the capacity to hurt than anything else in life." Then when they get hurt or hurt others' "elbows," we act surprised. We may need to rethink the message that sex is "no big deal."

Nearly all of the teens I spoke with said something similar to fifteen-year-old Robin Gunderson in Seattle, though she put it especially well: "I think the best relationships with your friends and stuff are the ones that are emotional and attached. Like when they're really sad and feeling something, you help them through, and that's the point, that you're emotionally attached and that you'll do anything for them." I ask Robin why she thinks adults are telling girls that emotions aren't good, and she has a wonderful insight: "I don't know; it's so strange. . . . It's almost like the adults feel guilty that they were attached maybe, and that they got hurt once." Robin imitates an imperious adult voice: "'Drop those emotions, and be your own person! And be happy!' Like, happiness isn't also an emotion?" Indeed.

In the meantime, women well into their twenties and thirties are struggling with their emotions privately, shamefully. The saddest story I heard was from twenty-seven-year-old Lynn, an attractive raven-haired entertainer who continued to sleep with her ex-boyfriend after he had broken up with her and she had moved out. "We're all just supposed to eat ice cream for two weeks and 'Get back out there!'" she said sarcastically to me, over raisin toast one evening in Manhattan. "You know, be brave new urban creatures." Since Lynn couldn't handle the breakup, for a period she continued their physical relationship even though none of her emotional needs were being met. At least, she figured, it was something. Finally Lynn woke up when her ex remarked to her one evening, "You know, it's hard to have sex with you when you're crying."

Our deepest hopes are always part of who we are, and we ignore them at our peril. Rashida Jolley summed it up best: "People want to remove consequences, but we cannot remove consequences. For every action there is an equal and opposite reaction. You can't change the consequences, you have to change the behavior. Because the only real way to remove emotions is if you are buried, six feet under. Then I guess you can remove emotions." Rashida believes that we have to "take that energy and channel it into getting young people to make better choices," instead of telling them not to have negative emotions. She is right, of course, but it's an uphill road.

The odd thing is that we are currently a society awash in the public venting of emotion. Whether it's President Clinton mouthing "I love you" to his wife Hillary in front of cameras, or witnessing a hail of tears and recriminations on reality television, it would seem that we are a society "in touch" with our emotions. Yet strangely, the private and sincere expression of emotion is more taboo than ever. Several women who have lived through tragedies told me that friends would often direct them specifically "not to cry" and "to be strong."

Ten years after her son suffered brain damage during a terrible accident, a teacher named Orna looked back at those who told her to "be strong and don't cry," and she shared this insight: "You know, crying is not the opposite of being strong. When you suppress emotions, they come up later and it's much worse then. You have to deal with things and permit yourself to experience the pain at the time."

I asked Orna, what are people afraid of when they tell others not to cry? "They are afraid that they will have to take care of you," came her matter-of-fact reply. "But you know what? They didn't have to take care of me. They just had to let me cry."

* * *

Unfortunately, it's not just adult women and teenage girls who are encouraged to be repressors nowadays. Children of divorce are also taught to quash their feelings. In a remarkable book, *Between Two Worlds: The Inner Lives of Children of Divorce,* Elizabeth Marquardt poignantly describes the pain that children of divorce carry inwardly, although outwardly they may seem "fine." Marquardt, who is herself the child of a so-called good divorce (her parents stayed civil), nonetheless shows how often she felt torn in two as she tried to bridge the two worlds and the two homes of her parents. Yet look at the children's books aimed at kids of divorce. In one, *To and Fro, Fast and Slow,* a young child learns about opposites by traveling between her divorced parents' homes; as one reviewer noted, this upbeat book "invites young readers to notice the specific differences between two lifestyles while noting also that this child is really enjoying herself. It is possible, this book quietly asserts, that there may actually be riches gained and experiences broadened by something as theoretically troubling as a divorce." As Marquardt compellingly argues, this may be something a parent wishes to believe, but it does not match the experience of a child.

You're never too young to start smothering your feelings. There are adventures to be had when *Dinosaurs Divorce,* and above all, remember *Don't Fall Apart on Saturdays! The Children's Divorce Survival Book.*

My own interviews with children of divorce suggest that "Don't fall apart!" is not a sufficient directive. Take Izzy—not her real name—whose artist parents split when she was a teenager. Now she is twenty-four. I spot her in a Manhattan steakhouse, wearing jeans and a blue lace shirt, and wave at her to join me. When she smiles back, I notice that her tongue is pierced. This nod to youthful rebellion sharply contrasts with her self-possession, since she has a maturity most forty-year-olds would envy.

I never really intended to go into the subject of divorce with Izzy, but very quickly our conversation takes on a life of its own and becomes personal: "When my dad had an affair with a woman," she begins, in measured tones, "his new wife felt like she'd 'won' my dad—there was no idea of or empathy for the other woman, my mom. It was just like, 'I won' this man." Izzy actually likes her stepmother a lot, she adds, and this is conflicting for her. "But the sense I get is that she feels justified for some reason. I'll hear her talking to my dad about someone who doesn't agree with their relationship, and she'll say it in a way that shows that she has no idea why someone wouldn't support it or understand it. That's what hurt my mom more; she's married to my dad, but it could have been a woman who didn't really even want him—it was just the conquest of it."

Her own attitude toward it all is sympathetic, up to a point: "I wish I could be blasé about all that and say that's normal, and that's human nature . . . that he would want to stray . . . but I can't." Izzy found herself "personally dealing with feelings of jealousy and real grief" because of a boyfriend's infidelity, and "as much as it's normal to feel that way sometimes I just wish I could eliminate that completely from my repertoire of feelings, especially jealousy or envy, which is such a useless emotion. It's horrible. It feels like your heart is being ripped out."

I found Izzy's language arresting and revealing. She wishes she could be "blasé." She wishes she could "eliminate" wayward emotions from her "repertoire of feelings," and her emotions are "useless." When Izzy's parents divorced, she was sixteen,

which is a really hard age to go through it. It affects me every single day because my sister just got very sick and I think she dealt with it better because she was so young . . . but for me, I was just at that age that I was seeking my independence, and because that happened, it caused me to actually go back into my shell. I remember my mom was crying all the time, so it was really hard for me to want to be an adult, sort of. I remember being really afraid of the world. I love my dad. He was my best friend when I was young—I'm lucky because I'm close to both my parents, and I speak to them every day—but . . . I can always feel this underlying sadness . . . the things that aren't being said. At the time I took out all my anger at my mom, and it took me a long time to tell my dad that he had done something wrong, that he had hurt me. You can't talk to my dad; the guilt is so deep he turns it around. He's never just taken it and said, "You're right—that was hard." My mom always tells me to write down my feelings anyway—just to get them out—it's weird. . . . I don't know if I ever fully dealt with it. . . . I don't know if anyone ever does.

Izzy comes across as a brainy person with a very gentle spirit. She identifies "politically as liberal." Still, like many twenty-something children of divorce, she doesn't shy away from using words like "wrong." Having experienced firsthand the pain of disconnecting sex from morality, she has dealt with that by, among other things, resurrecting a moral vocabulary for her own life.

At the thought of leaving her boyfriend during hard times, she asks, "What's the point of going to find someone more fun at that moment, because in the end you're always going to hit reality with him too?"

* * *

The official reason for advocating promiscuity is that modesty was based on "a fear and loathing of sex," in the words of one online commentator. According to one contemporary marriage guide, back in the days when today's grandmothers were brides, "unsatisfying sex was the norm." This is like the movie *Pleasantville*, in which the kiddies had to teach their 1950s-era parents about sex. (Until the 1960s, everyone was apparently conceived by artificial insemination.) Visually, *Pleasantville* is a gorgeous film; when the children enlighten the adults, life, which has previously taken place in black-and-white, explodes into Technicolor. But to take this view of history, you have to ignore certain facts. You have to ignore that for thousands of years, Jewish law stipulated the woman's sexual rights, and that the men were taught to please their wives before themselves. You have to ignore a winsome guide for teenagers that I found on my grandmother's bookshelf, called *The Stork Didn't Bring You!* I learned from this book that "it's all out in the open at last. Today we all know that you are the cooperative product of both a father and a mother; that your mother housed you as a seed, kept you warm and snug inside herself until you were ready and able to make an appearance in this world."

The Stork Didn't Bring You! was published in 1948, hardly a time when "all [was] out in the open." Even so, it has a glossary right up front, with the correct name and a detailed explanation for everything. To be sure, our grandparents did not flash their private parts and discuss every smooch with the entire world on reality television. And this, our experts say, makes them repressed and us enlightened. Carol Queen, a leading feminist advocate for prostitution and stripping, addresses her late mom thus in her chipper "Letter about Whoring": "Dear Mom, I know you and Dad read Shakespeare to each other and wrote each other love letters during your courtship." But to her, her mother's eroticism was "such a closed-off place, like a rosebud half-blossomed that's died for lack of water." Queen says that she "embraced whoring" in part "to have experiences you could never have had . . . to show myself that I would never take after you."

Say what you will about all that Shakespeare and those effusive love letters. Repressed as her parents' relationship may have been, it nonetheless managed to produce Carol Queen. In her ongoing effort to become her mother's opposite, Queen views prostitution as servicing the downtrodden, for "every time I see a client, I know I am intervening in a marriage possibly as sexless and unhappy as yours [her mother's]." To Queen, "sex work" is about "pride in stepping outside the restrictions imposed on 'good girls.'" At the same time, despite her ongoing effort to purge her inner good girl, Carol complains of men who assume that because they're paying for a peep show, they can speak crudely to her. She also laments some of the "not very impressive" sex that she's had. Queen blames "clumsy, selfish male sexuality" for this, but maybe there is more to it. Perhaps our mothers and grandmothers were not as befuddled and half-blossomed as we tend to assume. Perhaps they knew a simple but important truth: that unless our emotions are integrated, sex becomes rather dreary. The old rules preserved its power.

"Theresa," a mother in her late thirties, reflects: "You know, it causes a lot of problems later on when you're trying to have a real relationship and you're still acting like a . . . a porn star. Don't forget, if you're so busy turning yourself off, then you can't just turn yourself *on* when you're with someone you love."

As early as the turn of the twentieth century, radicals were toying with the notion of purging emotion from sexuality. In 1911, Theodore Schroeder had bragged that his "sex-sensibilities" had become "considerably blunted . . . partly as a result of my study of sexual psychology," and wondered if "blunted sensibilities are not a good kind to be encouraged in the matter of sex." "Who would be harmed," asked Schroeder, "if all men ceased to believe in the 'obscene,' and acquired such 'blunted sensibilities' that they could discuss matters of sex—as we now discuss matters of liver or digestion—with an absolute freedom from lascivious feelings?" A hundred years later we have the answer to his question, and it turns out that those harmed are ourselves.

There is a need to push on toward stranger and crueler activities, just to prove that one is alive. *Maxim* magazine runs a feature called "Share Your Girlfriend," offering readers cash prizes for sending in photos of their nude or seminude girlfriends. The "literate smut" site Nerve.com, when I last checked in, was showcasing a defense of bestiality. ("Unlike humans who sleep with other humans," the author pointed out, "the guy who sleeps with his dog doesn't have to worry about being abandoned by his lover, unless he forgets to close the gate.")

For years we have been hearing, "The answer to bad porn is not no porn, but to try to make *better* porn." But better porn does not seem to be forthcoming. By every account, in fact, porn seems to be getting worse. Horrific acts involving the extreme sexual humiliation of women are now completely mainstream. Why? There seems to be a process of desensitization, once sex is disengaged from morality and emotion; when we pursue the physical for its own sake, we require a steady diet of the formerly forbidden to keep us excited.

Yet proving that we are not repressed has, in a sense, become the goal. Consider the new edition of *Our Bodies, Ourselves* (2005), for decades considered the authoritative quasi-medical guidebook on women's bodies. In promotional comments, doctors call it "truly the Bible on women's health" and declare, "If only every little girl were born with a copy of *Our Bodies, Ourselves* in her hands, we would raise a society filled with healthy, confident young women."

Or maybe the young women would just be very confused. The chapter on "Sexuality," for instance, introduces far-out sexual practices as if they were nothing more than a walk in the park: "In penetrating a female partner . . . you can put one or more fingers inside her and, if you both like, gradually put your whole hand inside (called *fisting*). . . . It can feel warm, wet and wonderful."

It's nice that they add, "if you both like." In striking contrast to this beautiful tribute to fisting, the section on heterosexual intercourse is much less warm and much less wonderful: "*If* you make love with a man, you *may* want to have intercourse [emphasis mine]." But "if you are sexually inexperienced, frightened, not ready, not in the mood, or angry with your partner," then penetration "can be boring, unpleasant, even painful." This is no doubt true. Still, one is unfortunately compelled to wonder whether these side effects wouldn't apply all the more to the insertion of an entire fist.

I feel a responsibility to mention that fisting can cause damage in and around the vaginal opening, and severe tearing of the vaginal muscles leading to incontinence. I was able to discover this after a two-second Internet search, yet in *Our Bodies, Ourselves*—all about women's health, supposedly—you have to flip sixty pages over to their chapter on safer sex to learn that fisting "carries some risk." What is this loony advocacy of fisting doing in a mainstream book about women's well-being, especially if the book is meant to be a guide for girls? I suspect for the same reason we are instructed elsewhere that "the institution of marriage has a long history of oppressing women."

The message is about as subtle as a jackhammer. Whatever is "traditionally done" is bad, and whatever isn't—however harmful—must be good. Even Freud feared that "allowing complete freedom of sexual life" would be damaging, since it would mean "abolishing the family, the germ-cell of civilization," but today we are more Freudian than Freud himself. Every bizarre sex practice must be celebrated, while even a whiff of hope for an emotional connection must be stamped out, the very thought of it forever banished.

Sometimes medicine is required. Dr. Paul McHugh of Johns Hopkins tells me, "Women will come in and say, 'Gee, you know, somehow or another I have these experiences again and again and the guy says "I'm not ready"—to get married—so there must be something the matter with me. Dr. McHugh, give me a pill.'" The women have grown accustomed to being prescribed Prozac for their romantic disappointment.

"But there's nothing the matter with you," I tell them; "what's the matter with the world? Let me help you find a way of not immediately hopping into bed with all these guys right off the bat." . . . And by the way, these other men should be shamed and in some way rebuked. Occasionally I get the men in. Some of the "not ready" guys. I say, you know, "What are your intentions?" Like the old dads used to say. They're very surprised: "Oh, you know, I'm just having fun." Having fun at the

price of somebody else? What kind of stuff is that? See, some of them don't get that.

In her wise book *Jane Austen's Guide to Dating*, Lauren Henderson notes that women in Austen's time were much more open and direct about their feelings than women today. They weren't as calculating and didn't play games: "Austen repeatedly emphasizes the opinion that a woman who likes a man should make her preference for him clear—without, naturally, going overboard. She would have no truck with modern dating books that make a science of playing hard to get." Catherine in *Northanger Abbey*, for instance, shows Henry how much she enjoys being with him, and Henry comments happily on Catherine's "fresh feelings."

Here is Henderson's incisive reading:

Catherine doesn't pretend to be jaded or cynical, she's open and direct. When she misses going out for a walk with Henry and his sister because she's tricked into going with John Thorpe instead, she doesn't try to make Henry jealous or play John Thorpe off against him. Instead, she tells Henry immediately, the first chance she gets, how much she likes him, and apologizes for her inadvertent rudeness. "I had ten thousand times rather have been with you . . . ," she says; "if Mr. Thorpe would only have stopped [his carriage], I would have jumped out and run after you." Henry loves it. He likes her better than ever for telling him how much she likes him. "Is there a Henry in the world," Jane Austen asks, "who could be insensible to such a declaration?" Note that Jane Austen says "Henry," rather than "man." Jane Austen is not saying that all men respond well to this. But a man with a good sense of self, a man who doesn't have the kind of low self-esteem that makes him think that if someone likes him there must be something wrong with her, will love it.

This point hit home for me, since if I hadn't been open about my admiration for my husband, we probably would never have met. (I actually asked his rabbi to set me up with him after hearing him speak at a Passover seder.) Today, looking back, it's troubling to think of what might have happened had I given in to all the voices telling women to stifle their feelings and emotional "intensity." If I had made a habit of burying my heart, I never would have known who was wrong for me, or who was right.

But perhaps the main reason I felt comfortable expressing my feelings while dating my future husband was that (having dated according to observant Jewish custom) we didn't even touch each other until we were married. I realize that this will seem preposterous to many people, but the extreme case may prove the general rule. Henderson allows for "a few weeks of anticipation" in postponing sex, but she never really asks why contemporary women are so insecure in the first place. Women were more expressive in Jane Austen's time because they were not as sexually vulnerable. They didn't have as much to lose. They kept a part of themselves in reserve until they could determine that a man was truly worthy of their company.

The postmodern woman is quick to observe that reticence is "artificial," but perhaps casual sex may cause, on balance, a greater degree of artificiality: women giving their hearts and bodies too soon, regretting it, and then having to be false and pretend that they don't care. All the dating books floating around nowadays impose arbitrary rules, without ever challenging the behavior that causes women to feel vulnerable to begin with. Critics of these books rightly ask why the women can't just be themselves. Apparently, women are too worried to be themselves.

Modern dating guides come up with so many artificial rules—never accept a Saturday night date after Wednesday; always wait a ridiculous amount of time before returning his phone calls—because they are trying to help a woman retain some measure of dignity at the same time that they advise her to be completely available, sexually. It's a recipe for attracting exactly the wrong sort of guys. If you care about someone, I think you should show that you do. But instead of giving your body and soul, and then being dishonest about your feelings, I think it makes more sense to be honest but hold yourself physically in check until you have established the other person's character and intentions. This is not "manipulating" anyone, as some would argue; it's taking the time to establish whether you even want to be with a person to begin with. Once you are physically involved, you can forget about being objective. Then, yes, it is all about manipulation.

One of my most admired teachers, Tziporah Heller, once observed, "Everything in life is repressive. Have you noticed that? Do you get up with an alarm because you love your job? No. But it's better than being unemployed. Do you brush your hair or your teeth because you love the motion? No, you just want to look normal enough to go out among other

people. All trade-offs involve repressing A to get B. A good trade-off gets you more than you lose." If we have to choose between emotional repression and sexual repression—as I believe we do—then a better trade-off seems to be fewer partners and more intimacy.

Single or married, we all have a unique purpose in this world. But if we are looking for a lifelong bond, then we need to seek out partners who treat us as whole human beings—including mind, emotions, and hopes for the future—not just as bodies. In seeking a soul mate, in other words, it's helpful not to forget your own soul.

*   *   *

Often the attitude one takes toward emotional repression will depend on one's generation. Consider Erica Jong, famous for her novel *Fear of Flying* (1973), which glamorized the concept of a random, guilt-free sexual encounter between strangers.

Molly Jong-Fast is a child of Erica's second marriage, to the novelist Jonathan Fast. Now twenty-six, happily married, and living in Manhattan, Molly is also a talented writer in her own right—though to some she is still perhaps best known as Erica Jong's daughter.

Instead of running from this legacy, Molly has embraced it, writing a priceless account of her celebrity childhood, *The Sex Doctors in the Basement*. You may think that twenty-five is too young to publish your memoirs, but if when you were a child you fell off a horse, and your arm gushed blood, and it prompted the pediatrician to quiz your mother thus—"Erica, are you working on something new? I loved you on *Donahue* the other day"—then you too might feel impelled to write about your childhood. In this incident, Erica replied, "Well, actually, I'm working on a novel about Venice," and Molly interrupted, "Ohh, I'm sorry, am I bothering anyone here? Don't mind me, I'm bleeding to death." Molly gently yet surgically lampoons her mother's romances—"Evidence that Dart would be a good daddy was everywhere, from his Harley-Davidson motorcycle to his many tattoos"—and her own many childhood analysts, who repeatedly interrogate her: "Do you feel repressed because your mother writes dirty books?" and "Don't you think that admitting your mother's erotic novels have repressed you will set you free?" At the time, Molly was eleven. Then there was her mother's fourth wedding: "When you're twelve, there is nothing funny about your mother's fourth wedding." Molly was the flower girl, and she cringed when Mom read "a truly distressing poem about a horny Boy

Scout and a private plane." But she was not without her coping mechanisms: "I covered my ears and tried to calm myself by thinking about the chocolate-covered strawberries I'd gorge myself on later. To this day I am wildly embarrassed by Mom's dirty poems, and more interestingly, I still love chocolate strawberries."

Although Molly is a comic writer, there is a deeper truth in her writing, which her critics don't seem to get. They tend to smirk at her for being the daughter of famous people, but that is hardly her fault, and such objections miss the point entirely. As I see it, the point is this: What is liberation to one generation can be oppression to the next. That doesn't mean the earlier generation is bad and the next generation is good. I did a television show once with Erica Jong and found her perfectly lovely. Nonetheless, individuals may experience the same thing in genuinely different ways. Writing erotic poetry may be empowering and yet, when your own mom reads it to you, that same poetry can make you cringe. This truth is no one's fault. Perhaps this is just how God designed us, so that society could never go too far toward any extreme, and each generation could correct for the excesses of the previous one—or try, anyway.

Naturally, after reading *The Sex Doctors in the Basement,* I set off at once to meet Molly, knowing that we would have lots to talk about. When I heard from her the first thing I noticed is that she signs her e-mails "mother of Max," signaling—like many twenty-something mothers I've met—that her most important identity is as a mother.

When I meet Molly in a dessert café in Manhattan, she is dressed in a sweat suit and comes across as very genuine. With sparkling blue eyes and a cute, exuberant smile, she wins you over immediately as a friend, and then surprises you with her rapid-fire insights about life.

Despite her obvious love for and devotion to her mother, Molly Jong-Fast has nonetheless dealt with her mother's being the "queen of Eros" in the healthiest way possible: by not reading her books. "It's just so embarrassing," she says to me—or, as she tells her mother more directly, when interviewing her for *Glamour:* "I think I'm going to barf."

These comments may seem unremarkable—silly even, to one who doesn't understand—but insisting on your right to be embarrassed is actually a radical statement nowadays. It is much more radical than being transgendered, in fact, because no student group will fly to your defense if you want to be embarrassed. It is not long before we get down to the shocker:

"So my parents had an open marriage and they were married for eighteen months. . . . I don't know if my mother's parents had an open marriage but my father's parents had an open marriage for a long time. But all it meant was that he cheated on her all the time."

Molly, as it happens, comes from a long line of bad girls. And yet, her mother's philosophy has evolved over the years, it emerges: "It's funny," she tells me; "my mother's really a good example of the kind of woman who has really changed her views a lot, and she doesn't say this but she really has. I was totally surprised because I interviewed her for *Glamour* and she said, 'Yeah, sex with someone who doesn't love you is totally meaningless and it's not pleasurable.' And I was like, Whoa! She's totally changed her tune."

What, then, is the problem with casual sex? Molly explains: "I think the problem is that the kind of really promiscuous sex—like the *Sex and the City* sex—doesn't have to do with the real lives of women." In real life most women get "totally damaged" this way, although Molly admits that "some women experience some degree of temporary power with sex, and that is definitely addictive; there's a high to that." It's just not getting them anywhere in their relationships:

> I've always been amazed with my generation. There's pro-sex literature, sex blogging, just sex sex sex. It's just everywhere. Personally I've always been amazed with how "everywhere" it is. And so it's not shocking anymore. And in all these sex, sex, sex books, let's face it: all these women are really looking for is love. You're always reading it thinking, *Wow, this person is having a lot of sex.* And then by the end it's always: *But why won't he marry me?* So it's always so disappointing to me. If there were people, if there were women out there who were really sexually liberated, then, fine; but even Samantha seems to want a husband by the end! So by the end the women are always wanting a husband or wanting this sort of Edith Wharton rise in society. Sex is just a vehicle for something else.

We then talk about the ideal of the "bad girl" and whether it's workable. Molly says it is not: "I was not un-promiscuous in my day, and you know, it's unfortunate, I think, that I was, because ultimately I was able to come back from that, but I think I was sold a bad bill of goods." Not that she didn't give it her best: "I sort of tried for that ideal of being completely removed from your sexuality and that's not what happened. I did not succeed in that."

"Removed from sexuality" strikes me as an interesting choice of words, so I ask Molly what she means. "I mean separate from my emotionality," she explains. "I had experience in trying for that, and I don't think that it works. And my mother really had that experience, and she also seemed to come to the conclusion that it doesn't work, which is really interesting." I then ask Molly why it's such a radical thing to say that casual sex doesn't work:

> Well, because I think that in the 1950s you weren't allowed to admit
> that you had been that way [promiscuous]. But then in the 1960s you
> weren't allowed to admit that it didn't work. In the 1970s you weren't
> allowed to admit that it doesn't work. And now, it's sort of that same
> kind of thing, you know, where you're not allowed to admit that it just
> doesn't work.

For her part, Molly has no trouble admitting this because she is used to hostility. "I get a lot of hostility because my mother is famous," she says wryly, "and the general feeling is that if they were Erica Jong's daughter, what *they* could do, and I don't know—maybe they could do something really great, you know?" The joke, it seems, is ultimately on Molly's critics, because all the while they have been observing and criticizing her, she has also been observing them.

In a touching essay, "My Mother, My Daughter, and Me," Erica Jong writes that mothers and grown-up daughters are like "glass unicorns who might break each other's horns by kissing too passionately." A wonderful metaphor, suggesting love, fragility, and the potential to do real damage. Sometimes I wonder: If the baby boomers could see that our decisions and way of thinking, so different from theirs, are not indictments as much as attempts to protect our own vulnerability, then who knows? Maybe there could be a truce. Ultimately, we're not trying to break their horns; we just would like to keep what is left of ours.

POP QUIZ:
ARE YOU EMOTIONALLY REPRESSED?

·

1. Do you ask yourself, "How many times do we sleep together before we're dating?" rather than, "How many times do we date before we sleep together?"
2. Are you ever even a little bit ashamed that you want to get married?
3. Do you feel bad that you ever felt bad about a breakup?
4. If you care about the person you're sleeping with, do you ever feel that you have to hide this fact or "tone it down"?
5. Are you worried that you may be too "clingy"?
6. Do you like watching *Sex and the City* for the characters' sporting attitude toward sex, and do you conveniently block out the episodes where their unhappiness is made abundantly clear?

If you answered yes to any of these questions, you could be emotionally repressed. Not to worry, though; if you are still aware of your emotions, that's a very good sign. In the advanced stages of emotional repression, people are completely unaware of having any emotions or hopes for the future whatsoever. If you are merely emotionally repressed, as opposed to emotionally neutered, all you need is a simple paradigm shift. Remember, your emotions make you human, so get out there and find someone you don't have to stifle yourself around, someone who appreciates you for who you are.

CHAPTER FIVE

Excuse Me, Ma'am, Have You Seen My Friends?

•

I have come to have a deep-seated hatred of The Sims. I have had several roommates who were addicted to the game; I'd say, "Hey, let's go get coffee together this evening"—"Sure, sounds like fun!" Come that evening, they'd all be too busy playing with little computerized people to go out and talk to real people.

—JOI, a college student from Los Angeles

I've set out to discover what's become of friendship in contemporary culture, and what better place to begin than with Cuddle Parties.

I first heard about Cuddle Parties from my twenty-six-year-old friend Erin, whose colleague had ambushed her with an invitation. Single at the time, Erin was considerably underwhelmed:

One day at work, a coworker tells me he has a couple of events he'd like to invite me to. Mind you, I think maybe he's in a band, since he has some musical talent. It even would be better, however "inappropriate" nowadays, to get asked out on a date. Nope. He invites me to a "Cuddle Party." I almost laugh in his face. I naïvely ask what it is, hoping against hope it isn't what I think it is. Not only does he tell me exactly what it is but apparently I need to bring my pajamas and fifteen dollars with me. No, I'm sorry, that's the student rate.

Started by Reid Mihalko and Marcia Baczynski in 2004, Cuddle Parties have become a worldwide phenomenon. With Cuddle Party "facilitators" all over the globe, from Alabama to Australia, and glowing coverage on Montel Williams's and Tyra Banks's shows, Reid and Marcia now sit atop a veritable cuddling empire. In their literature, they make a big deal about not offering a sexual environment—"A Cuddle Party ISN'T: A free-for-all, a pseudo-orgy or a grope-fest." This is meant to be soothing, but I found it confusing. If all these thousands of people are really only cuddling strangers, then you have to ask why. Cuddleparty.com says the parties usher in "a safe space for adults to be affectionate with one another without becoming sexual," which makes people "feel safe and feel good." It sounded noble enough, but I had one nagging question: What about those who, free of charge, are "affectionate without becoming sexual"?

That is, where were all these people's friends? Sex, I realize, sells, but emotional intimacy seems more challenging to package.

The official rule at Cuddle Parties is that "you don't have to cuddle anyone"—but as everyone knows, rules are made to be broken. And if everything is nonsexual, why is there any need for "Rule 7: No Dry Humping"? Moreover, if all participants have internalized the concept of not forcing a cuddle, why would they require a "Cuddle Lifeguard on Duty"? The thought of a pajama-clad man veering toward me in his official capacity as Cuddle Lifeguard was not reassuring.

Cuddle Parties also have strict rules about protecting the privacy of the participants—known as Cuddle Monsters—rules that I want to respect. So let's just say that I attend a Cuddle Party in one of the many places where one may: Los Angeles, Chicago, New York, Michigan, even London or Zurich. (OK, not Zurich.) True, there have been "media-friendly" Cuddle Parties, which others have reported on, but I don't want to see people angling for the camera. I want to know what really happens at an average Cuddle Party. Naturally, I have to go undercover.

I pack the night before. The list of "what to bring" from Crafty Snuggles (not her real name) reminds me, pleasantly, of camp:

WHAT TO BRING

- Yourself :)
- Pajamas or comfy clothes (yoga pants and a T-shirt) to change into (think flannel rather than lace and no shorts).
- Your favorite pillow, blanket, or stuffed animal (just make sure they are clean and not covered in animal fur).

- Hairbrush—if you would like to invite someone to brush your hair.
- Light snacks will be supplied but if you would like something in particular bring it along.
- Please try to avoid wearing strong scents, perfumes, or colognes in case we have participants who are allergic. Thanks!!

I pack my bag under the watchful eye of my husband, who is pleased to see that I am not bringing a hairbrush. I am, however, bringing fifty dollars to pay for myself and a friend, Myriam. (I figured it would be safer to bring my own Cuddle Buddy.) My husband, an easygoing and nonjudgmental person, cannot believe it: "They charge twenty-five bucks to cuddle strangers? What a scam." He shakes his head in disapproval. "Well actually, sweetie," I clarify, "it's on a sliding scale of twenty-five to thirty-five dollars, but I figure that twenty-five is fair, since I'm not going to be getting much cuddling out of this." My husband seems uncharacteristically tense, so I say in my best serious-reporter voice: "I just want to understand why so many people would pay to cuddle perfect strangers for almost four hours."

"Because they're nuts, that's why," he says. I'm not sure what to expect.

When I arrive at my Cuddle Party, the atmosphere is benign and cordial. There are pillows and blankets everywhere, and three smiling young women are already sitting cross-legged on the floor, waiting for the other Cuddle Monsters to arrive. Fruit, tea, and cookies are provided in abundance. I am just starting to let my guard down and feel rather cozy when I am rudely yanked back to reality by one of the Cuddle Party administrators, a brunette I will call Spensive Hugs. "Would you like to make your donation to the space!" Ms. Hugs asks me briskly, in a way that is not a question (she is seated near a tin money box). Hugs is in her early forties and has a very authoritative air. I reply, slightly miffed, "Well, is it OK if I get changed into my pajamas first?" She nods and motions to the bathroom.

Dear reader, do not be alarmed. I do not really slip into my pajamas. I suit up in a silk peach robe, which covers me from head to toe (and clavicle and wrist for extra measure). It is almost like a long dress, but the faded ivory floral pattern is serene enough, I hope, to give off a casual vibe. With my robe I am trying to say: *"I morally support you, but I don't necessarily want to cuddle you."*

I feared my robe would arouse suspicion that I was not a true Cuddle Monster, but to my relief, it is a conversation piece. "Do you really sleep in that?" a young fair-skinned man immediately wants to know. I give him a fixed Cheshire cat grin in lieu of an answer. Luckily, he has on a FRIENDSHIP SLUT T-shirt, which I compliment, and soon everyone is briefing him on what it means to be a "friendship slut." There is a lull, at which point I introduce my giant stuffed pet worm, Jerry (whose name has also been changed to protect his privacy).

Perhaps I should explain. Participants and their stuffed animals were labeled upon arrival. Thus, my blue-and-red-striped bug now wears a sticker saying, HI, MY NAME IS JERRY. As I regard Jerry's blank button eyes and motionless antennae, I experience a pang of guilt, for he actually belongs to my infant son. I feel somewhat uneasy dragging an innocent pet worm into this shady business, but there is no turning back now.

By this point there are about twenty people (fourteen women and six men) gathered and sitting together on the blankets. My friend Maud's words of warning echo in my ears. After I reassured her that I planned to cuddle no one, she quipped, "The question is not whom will you cuddle, but who will cuddle *you*." I look around apprehensively. The people are squished so closely together that I congratulate myself on not having bugged Jerry with a digital recorder. (When tapped on a certain button, my recorder rewinds and starts playing, and if my stuffed worm were to suddenly turn and demand, *"Do you really sleep in that?"* I would surely be ousted from Cuddledom.)

What happens first is a long lecture given by Crafty Snuggles.

It turns out that Crafty, your average Birkenstocked dirty-blonde in her mid-thirties wearing flannel pajamas in public, has studied with the best of them. This kind of advanced training in cuddling will set you back $1,000, in case you are wondering, and entails participation in a three-day "Cuddle Party facilitator training program." Unfortunately, at the end of this study period there is no guarantee that you'll be accepted into the certification program. Indeed, only twenty-two people so far have been certified to throw official Cuddle Parties. So I guess you could say that Crafty really knew her stuff.

Crafty leads us in the introductions that make up the Welcome Circle, and the most bizarre aspect of the day immediately comes into focus: how completely normal everyone is. As we take turns giving little speeches on why we are here, my assumption that the participants lack social skills crumbles fast. The people are ages nineteen to fifty-five, and though there is one short, rather creepy married guy in attendance, the rest seem altogether normal. In fact, odd as it sounds, you might even say these people are nicer and *more normal* than average. An attractive coed shyly explains that her friends say she "is too sensitive." It was one of them who told her about Cuddle Parties. Another young woman had also received a referral: "Me too!" she exclaims, "Someone also thought I should come to a Cuddle Party, and so here I am!"

A pleasant middle-aged woman with teenage daughters mentions that her husband has just left her for a younger woman. This revelation is followed by a few moments of awkward silence, as no one knows quite what to say, but her story moves the others to get a bit more personal. People start to make admissions such as, "I'm feeling a lack of touch in my life." Crafty chimes in with a cheerful tale about a man who didn't want to cuddle, so he brought his girlfriend here, to this very room, to get her fill from others. The indelicate thought intrudes—how long is that relationship going to last?

When it's my friend Myriam's turn, she is perhaps a bit too honest, saying that she heard about Cuddle Parties from me and they "sounded hysterical." I give her a little pinch and she quickly adds, "Plus, we thought it would be nice to spend more time together." Everyone smiles receptively.

During the Welcome Circle, I make it very clear that I am married and I will not be cuddling any men. I state this at every conceivable opportunity. For example, when the Cuddle Lifeguard explains that it is unwise to "renegotiate boundaries that are important to you." My anticipated limited participation is taken in stride, although everyone wants to know why my husband didn't come too.

Next, we are told that Cuddle Parties are not sexual, but that if arousal does happen, we shouldn't be perturbed: "We're taught that we always have to act on arousal, but we don't," Crafty explains, looking slightly fatigued. I wonder how many times she has given this speech before.

If something too sexual is observed, a whistle will blow and we will be instructed to grab our Cuddle Buddy's hand and hold it high in the air. (Myriam automatically becomes my Cuddle Buddy; others quickly choose theirs.) All hands in the air will notify the Cuddle Lifeguard on Duty that no one is illegally burrowing under a blanket. A few women look concerned, but Crafty reassures us that this kind of intervention has been necessary only once, in Alabama (of all places). The men seem vaguely disappointed. One jokes, "Well, at least my banana's getting around," in reference to the two women who had shared bites of his banana earlier.

We are then led in a "saying no" exercise, because "it's OK to say no, and it's OK to hear no." In fact, we are told, some people come to Cuddle Parties just to practice saying no. Now our assignment is to ask the person next to us to cuddle, hear him or her say "No!" and then switch roles. Once we have all heard and said no, we are closer to being ready for advanced cuddling on the floor. We must learn to speak out and to be clear about our wants and needs: "If you're a yes, say YES! If you're a no, say NO! If you're a maybe, say NO!"

Suddenly and without warning, our "saying no" exercise is interrupted by a loud rattling of the door. The plaintive cry of a man with an Indian accent echoes through the studio:

"Hello, can I come in? I got lost! *Hello?* Is anyone in there?" Rattle, rattle, rattle.

Crafty is dispatched to neutralize the latecomer: "I'm so *sorry*," she coos in her soft, angelic voice, "but it's too late to come in now. It just doesn't make people feel *safe* when everyone doesn't experience the Welcome Circle." Awkwardly, it appears that the man is not going to go away. He had fully intended to cuddle today: "But I got lost! I had trouble parking!"

Eventually, it takes two Cuddle Lifeguards to subdue him and prevent him from entering: "You can come back another week, but we can't let you come in now." To put his plight in context, he is made aware that "some people come from out of town and even they have to be turned away if they're late."

After a few tense minutes, just when you think a sedative might be necessary, the latecomer reluctantly gives up and the door is secure once more. There is a moment of quiet, and an inexplicable desire to comfort and cuddle the unknown stranger wells up within me, but I quickly suppress it. He is the "other" who must remain outside. He was not part of the Welcome Circle, and he cannot be cuddled. The Cuddle Lifeguards are just.

After this incident, things start to get curiouser and curiouser, as in Wonderland. Some Cuddle Monsters get restless, attempt to get up for a snack, and are repeatedly and firmly told to sit back down. I have vowed to keep a low profile, but my natural assertiveness gets the better of me, and I raise my hand:

"I'm sorry, but I'm confused. I thought you said that the food was for us, but I couldn't help noticing that whenever people get up to get a snack, you tell them to sit down."

A few participants giggle, and I am assured that we will "be able to eat soon, really soon." Unfortunately, though, my clowning exacts a cost: My cover is almost blown. A cool college-age couple who have been canoodling suddenly start studying me intently, then pointing and whispering. This time, I fear that it's more than my peach robe that's caught their eye. The man asks suspiciously: "Don't I know you from somewhere?" "Yeah," his girlfriend chimes in, "you look familiar . . . are you . . . ?" Her eyes narrow and she looks slightly menacing. I remember, in a panic, that someone told me recently that BookTV has been running an old talk of mine. Foiled by C-SPAN! I instinctively clutch my stuffed snake and say the first thing that pops into my mind:

"Oh, are you from Milwaukee, too?"

It's a classic diversionary tactic ("I'm from the Midwest"), which you should not try at home unless you have the accent to pull it off (I do). The pair are thrown off. They say that they're not from Milwaukee but that I "look like someone." They return to canoodling, but I can't shake the feeling that I'm on thin ice. One false move and I could be thrown to the bunnies, cuddled alive.

This is of particular concern because the Lifeguards have just announced it is now time for one and a half hours of "freestyle cuddling." Having mastered the art of saying no, we are now set free to importune others to cuddle us.

To my great surprise, three of the six men invite me to cuddle them, despite my having been quite firm about my boundaries. (My friend, who is both more attractive and more available than I, doesn't get asked at all, so it must be reverse psychology.) Two of the men are young and seem pleasant enough, and they graciously accept my declining their offers.

But the older married man is downright scary. He reminds me of a short mad dog, yipping at everyone's ankles, demanding that nearly everyone cuddle him. He looks frantic and slightly frothy and commands me to cuddle him. It's not just that I've made it very clear I'm not here to cuddle men (although to be sociable I do offer back rubs to the women). I happened to be in the middle of receiving a nice foot massage, and as all civilized beings know, if someone is lucky enough to be getting a foot massage, you do not interrupt. I turn and raise an eyebrow at Mrs. Creepy Married Guy, but she merely shrugs, as if to say, "Why do you think I come to these things? I have to deal with this all the time." But before I can say "Send in the

Cuddle Lifeguard," I turn back, and lo! Creepy Married Guy is on the floor with Crafty Snuggles. He quickly arranges her to face him and lie down with his pelvis thrust up against hers, his legs and arms completely encircling her. If poor Crafty had wanted to move, it's not clear how she might have. Myriam reminds me that it's not polite to stare, but it's hard not to. For a moment I am frozen by the bizarre spectacle, thinking, *There but for the grace of God go I.*

Does Crafty have to cuddle with everyone just because it's her job? Does *she* have the right to say no to Creepy Married Guy? Does she, perhaps, need to work on her own "It's OK to Say No" exercises? True, there was no "dry humping." But then, in what you might call the full frontal koala pose, that would have been superfluous.

No wonder she looks so tired.

Seventy minutes, four back rubs, and three abbreviated life stories later, a clanging call reaches my ears: "Time for the puppy pile!"

It is time for soft music, for deep breaths, and for all of us, alas, to pile onto one another. I find a perfect spot at the outer rim of the pile, resting my head on my friend's stomach and looking up peacefully at the ceiling. Others are not as fortunate. Although, to be sure, there are a few tranquil moments of unity, sharp voices tend to shatter the warm fuzzy feeling and remind us that we're all—well—just strangers piled on top of one another. "Uh, can you not *do* that? Thanks!" and "When you sit on my head, I *cannot breathe.*"

I don't know who the last objection came from, but I can certainly guess who the perpetrator was. After about twenty minutes in the puppy pile, Crafty prods us to form a human wreath, arm over arm. This is called the Closing Circle. I make sure I have women on either side of me, but that does not prevent a young redheaded man from stretching out his hand to stroke my back in annoying little circles. Every time he surreptitiously tries to touch me, I lean away from his direction. But how he accomplishes this feat is truly beyond me. He must have had very long arms, like Batya, whose arm stretched out to rescue the baby Moses, except that in this case his arm stretched out to rescue me from the plight of not touching him—a somewhat less noble endeavor. I guess I could have confronted him, but since Crafty was about to give a speech, it didn't seem the right time to be setting boundaries in a nonjudgmental way.

A hush falls over the Closing Circle. Crafty says dramatically, as if reading from a script: "Look around you during this Closing Circle . . . [long, weighty pause]. A little over three hours ago . . . [another weighty pause] all these people were strangers to you!"

It took everything in me not to blurt out: "And they still are."

The Lifeguards talk about how we might feel a lot of "mixed emotions" after the Cuddle Party, and how we would be wise to face these emotions right away. "The Cuddle Party may trigger intense emotions. Do not, under any circumstances, go to a bar and have eight tequilas. Be careful with these emotions."

What emotions could they possibly mean? Feelings of intense loneliness when people go home and realize that no significant connections to others were actually forged?

(Later I confer with Myriam, who gives me an interesting take: "The part at the end, where they said we all used to be strangers? I saw it as a ploy to try to make people feel loved, so they're happy about spending money to cuddle, but it's not honest. Well, maybe I should say it's insincere, because of course we don't really feel loved when we leave.")

But we haven't left just yet. Crafty is continuing: "People don't have permission to experience their emotions, and here they do." Half of her statement seems accurate enough. Clearly, a lot of people are lacking intimacy and closeness in their lives. But is this really the right environment for them? I have nothing against the founders of the Cuddle Parties, and I don't doubt that they are sincere in wanting to "make the world a better place." But since most of those in attendance were people you might actually want to be your friends, I was left feeling unsettled, wondering why intimacy was so elusive for them.

Naturally, I am one of the first to leave. Crafty intercepts me: "Can I hug you good-bye?" What could I say but yes? It is both the best and the worst hug I have ever received. She is a good hugger—a professional, you might say—but despite or perhaps because of this, it feels fake. She's hugging me as if we're lifelong friends who have just reunited, except that we're not. I will never see Crafty again and I don't really want to.

The only person I wished to stay in touch with was the recent divorcée, but in my rush to escape the Closing Circle, I did not stop to get her particulars.

* * *

The Cuddle Party had its amusing moments, but in general I found it rather depressing. According to a study by sociologists at Duke University published in June 2006, Americans have one-third fewer close friends and confidants today than two decades ago, and the number of people who say they have "no friends" has more than doubled. Researchers speculate that Internet communication and long work hours are creating greater social isolation, cutting back on the contacts that were once formed through clubs, neighbors, and organizations.

Certainly Alice, forty-two, would agree. She used to get together with a knitting group at a yarn store in Chicago. Until, she tells me, one day there was practically no one there.

> I said, "Where is everybody?" And the organizer said, "Oh, it's an important episode of *Will and Grace*" or something like that. Oh, I didn't know; I've never seen the show. And she said, "Yeah, I couldn't make it home tonight but I'm going to record it. I don't normally record it because I like to watch it as it's happening." As it's happening? I'm like, It's not happening! It's been rehearsed to death, and it's already prerecorded! I thought, People would actually prefer to stay home and watch a lame prerecorded comedy than get together with some real people? How sad.

Over time, she tells me, the inability to depend on the group ground her down. Her mother's generation, Alice continues, "just got together and they'd do church things and potluck and things, but I can't imagine having potluck with any of my friends. Getting us together to do something? I've given up on that." Alice tried different knitting groups but always had bad experiences:

> I thought the knitting movement was positive coming back, but there was just too much bitching. There was a woman who considered herself the founder of the group and she was knitting these walls around the group. When I said, "Well, why don't we all get together with the other group at the Yarn Store downtown?" she was short with me: "No! I want to have a separate identity." *Identity?* OK. And then there was another group in the same neighborhood that had been getting together and knitting for like ten to twenty years and they were older women, and I said, "Well, why don't we get together with them as well?" "I don't want to be associated with them." She felt that they knitted like kitty-cat sweaters and she was prejudiced against their age, and I

thought, Well, there is no pleasing you. And then she got somebody to design a logo for the group and the character had on army boots and was muscular: DON'T MESS WITH ME, I'M A KNITTER. And I thought, Wow, this is not the women's group I remember my mom being in. This seems like it's set up to be like an army or something. It should have been a nice way to build friendships, but now it's in-your-face knitting and I'M A KNITTING HO, or FUTURE KNITTING HO baby tees— I was just not into that. It's too political.

I ask Alice if they are possibly trying to overcompensate: "We are not your mother's knitters." She considers it: "Yeah, maybe. I started to knit when I was seven, and if I knit in public or some friends found out I was knitting, they would shake their heads at me, Suzy Homemaker." Suzy Homemaker, Alice explains, was a line of toys. The most popular item was a little oven that girls played with. It was heated by very large lightbulbs and came with little pans and little cake mixes. "You'd add water and you baked your little cake. Knitting was like the Suzy Homemaker oven, which was bad." Understandably, she became a closet knitter.

So Alice took up knitting before it became cool (her grandmother taught her in 1969). The first time I heard about anyone who was involved in feminine crafts was in college. It was 1996, and a friend called me to report on his best friend's new girlfriend, whom he had just met. There are some conversations you never forget, and this was one of them. "She's totally unworthy of him," he pronounced darkly, as soon as I picked up the phone. "What do you mean?" I asked, aghast, wondering what crime she had committed. He elaborated: "All I have to say is, She makes her own pillowcases."

"So what? I don't get it."

"Oh, you know the type!"

Privately, I did not understand what was so terrible about making pillowcases, but I was just nineteen, so my heart went out to this unknown woman. I wanted to call her, to warn her that she was jeopardizing her relationship by pursuing this strange hobby. *Hide the pillowcases! It's not worth it,* I would tell her. Alas, I did not have her number.

A few years later, I began to notice that feminine crafts were being taken up with a vengeance by the women of my generation. Hip young women could be seen knitting everywhere—for example, on buses and subway trains—much to the amusement of older commuters. They were starting "Stitch 'N Bitch" groups all over the country, forming alliances and exchanging patterns and tips about life. Did Miss Pillows start it all? Why would young women be reclaiming the feminine hobbies of their grandmothers? Debbie Stoller, author of *Stitch 'N Bitch,* explains:

> It seemed to me that the main difference between knitting and, say, fishing or woodworking or basketball, was that knitting had traditionally been done by women. As far as I could tell, that was the only reason it had gotten such a bad rap. All those people who looked down on knitting—and housework, and housewives—were not being feminist at all. In fact, they were being antifeminist, since they seemed to think that only those things that men did, or had done, were worthwhile.

Debbie was onto something deep. But her book, which set the tone for the new movement, abounds with messages such as "You Ain't S——t If You Don't Knit." And her sequel is called *The Happy Hooker.* By always bending over backward to prove that they're not like our grandmothers, the stitch 'n' bitchers may also miss out on the fun that our grandmothers had. My eighty-seven-year-old grandmother, for example, has played bridge every other Tuesday with mostly the same people for fifty years. Even after her stroke she has pulled herself together to be with these women. "I don't win, but I always play," she says gamely. Her friends don't go around criticizing the other women or saying, "You Ain't S——t If You Don't Play Bridge!" They have an ease with friendship that some younger women seem to lack.

One point made by the researchers at Duke is that people are vastly overscheduled and overworked, with little time left for friends. Children today certainly do seem to face a bewildering array of scheduling challenges.

When I was growing up, if my mother wasn't home when I got home after school, I would get the house key out of our lockbox, let myself in, and prepare an exciting snack. It was always the same thing: Wheaties with sugar sprinkled on top. My parents were against sweetening cereals, but at a young age I had discovered the bakery cabinet and the great things in life that could be accomplished merely by standing on a chair. I don't know if my mother ever figured out why our sugar supply was so low when it came time to bake a cake for company; in any case, she knows now. Carrying a bowl of my favorite snack, I would leap upstairs, plunk myself down on our guest room bed, and usually watch television for about three hours. Or, just as often, I would ride my bike to the park with my friends. We would sit on the swings and chat about deep matters that concerned us, such as what color ribbons to attach to our bicycles for the Fourth of July, or who had the best sticker collection. Sometimes we would go to Walgreens and contemplate the lip glosses. For the most part, we just hung out. Throughout childhood, in fact, I just "hung out" with my friends, building forts in our backyards or shopping for jelly bracelets. We never had structured play or other activities, but I always had friends. Friends with whom, years later, I remain in touch.

So it is ironic to me that nowadays, activities are so structured and yet real friends seem so elusive. Looking back, I think I may have been part of the last generation of children (the tail end of generation X) that escaped regimented "fun and enriching" activities supervised by parents. With the millennials there was to be no more wandering around. This has had its benefits, but it also has had some drawbacks.

Many grandparents I speak to are confused about not seeing kids playing outside, or their children are confused on their behalf: "My dad is perplexed. He doesn't understand why the kids next door don't play outside." "I just don't see a lot of kids playing outside and I'm wondering, I grew up before there was birth control or abortion and my neighborhood was crawling with kids. You went outside and there was always somebody to play with. Nobody was indoors watching television. You'd feel bad if you couldn't be outside. If you were grounded and you could watch your friends playing outside, it was torture. There was no way otherwise we could get in touch with each other."

Today's teens approach their friends much the way previous generations asked for dates with the opposite sex. They don't want to appear needy, as if they have "nothing to do," so they end up not hanging out much.

Twenty-four-year-old Cece, from New York, sums up the situation nicely: "Literally, every time I go home my fourteen-year-old sister is at the computer. She lives at the computer. She'll be home totally bored and she says she wants to hang out with her friends." Cece will suggest, "Well, why don't you call them?" And her sister looks at her with a horrified expression: "She can never call anybody. She feels like she's intruding or imposing herself on people when she calls, so nobody calls. They all just communicate through IM all the time."

In a curious way, modesty and timidity have reasserted themselves in same-sex friendships, while casualness is reserved for the province of sexuality. This is the phenomenon of servicing the boy next door because you are his "friend with benefits," or FWB. "Friends" who use you are everywhere, but friends without benefits are harder to find—and certainly harder to get ahold of.

Lindsay, a bright fifteen-year-old girl from Indiana, explains to me:

> It's mostly instant messaging to make plans and talk, because a lot of my friends are like, "This boy dumped me online." I think that's just kind of, like, I don't know, pathetic. Because he can't tell you in person or something. And also like a lot of my friends, like they're online all the time and I'm never online and so they're always like making plans and stuff and they'll go somewhere and then I'm like, "Oh, what did you do?" And they're like, "Oh, we couldn't get ahold of you because you weren't online," because they won't call me or anything. On rare occasions they'll call me, but it sends a message. Like I'm the only one that calls.

Her friend Audrey, seventeen, concurs: "You can't just go up and talk to somebody, because they're texting on their cell or talking on their cell, and you can't approach people as easily. It's like there's no way to get ahold of them unless you have their cell phone number or can instant-message them."

* * *

When I studied diaries kept in the 1850s, I was surprised to find out that American women had been so publicly involved in civic life. Such involvement was more than just the custom of "friendly visiting," though it is noteworthy how many close friends a woman could typically call her own. Whether in town halls or other people's homes, whether it was the antislavery movement or political organizing, women were remarkably busy with social activities. By contrast, when no longer shuttled to and fro by her parents, a young woman is likely to be shut in her dorm room. She instant-messages, often furiously, but doesn't necessarily have anyone to get together with.

Karen Hansen, a professor of sociology at Brandeis, writes about the "multidimensionality" of women's lives in nineteenth-century American society, and says that it "challenges us to rethink our picture" of women in times past. For example, one seamstress, Martha, listed nineteen people she met in just one day in 1853—close friends, neighbors, and coworkers—and described plans to attend a meeting of the Anti-Slavery Society: "Am anticipating much pleasure, not only from listening to the speaking, but also in meeting some esteemed friends." This was not at all unusual, Hansen explains: Mary Mudge, a busy schoolteacher living in Lynn, Massachusetts, recounted in-depth visits with eleven people, in a partial diary entry for one day in 1854. (Some of these visits were to repay obligations; others incurred obligations. For instance: "Abba West made me a present of a pretty book.") Hansen notes, "Mary was not a middle-class woman of leisure. She was a working woman, pressed to help her mother and save for her own future." Nonetheless, "her diary is bursting with names, people, and relationships."

I thought of Mary when I fact-checked an episode of *Grey's Anatomy*, and this sad post popped up in the last page of my online search. A young woman calling herself "JustJel Newbie" had written:

> Lately I've taken up the habit of chewing and spitting [out] my food . . . I can't stop. I just started college and I'm extremely depressed and stressed out. My roommate and I don't jive very well . . . and I'm having trouble finding friends elsewhere. I'm not like everyone else that likes *Grey's Anatomy* and whatnot. . . . Watching TV is not my bag. As such . . . I'm having a hard time finding people with similar interests. I've become withdrawn, and the gym is my only escape. Burn off calories . . . no talking to anyone. It's just easier that way. I write this after a chewing and spitting bout. . . . I'm tense and extremely disappointed in myself. . . . I'm scared out of my mind. Can someone please just write *something?* I know this is useless . . . to post, I mean. But, God . . . if someone cared . . . wouldn't that be something?

JustJel had posted this on a "Healthy Place" forum, supposedly "a community of people providing mental health information, support, and the opportunity to share experiences helpful to others." Yet no one responded to her query, although it was evident that thirteen individuals had seen it. So she then posted a follow-up: "Ah yes . . . thirteen views . . . thirteen more people that don't care . . . the story of my life." Her disappointment finally registered with someone who posted a comment, but only to rebuke her:

"Comments like that aren't going to do anything for you, JustJel. They certainly won't gain you friends." The writer blames the poor girl for sounding "defensive," for "pushing people away," and for taking "the wrong tone." If you go to the trouble of posting a reply to someone so obviously miserable, is it too much to ask to offer a few words of encouragement? Apparently, it is.

I've heard a lot of people blame the Internet for the decline of friendship. I don't think that's entirely fair, but with regard to my friends who have weblogs, I do see the point. One by one they have dropped out of sight. We used to talk on the phone and meet, but now they are nowhere to be found. I started to notice this phenomenon in 2003, when I would say to someone, "Hey, I haven't heard from so-and-so for a while; how's he doing?" And the response would be, "Don't you read his blog?" or, "It's all on his blog." If the person himself showed up in public, and I cornered him to ask how he was doing, the knowing, slightly irritated response would be, "I guess you don't read my blog." Frankly, I was just expecting a "Fine, thank you."

If everyone is obsessed with his or her own blog (even if his or her blog is truly wonderful), then the problem is obvious. It's a new twist on the old joke: "Enough about my blog. Let's talk about you. What do you think of my blog?" If all my friends blogged, I would have no one to talk to outside my family, though they would surely all link to me.

CuteCircuit has just invented a "Hug Shirt" (sold as a pair) which is Bluetooth-enabled and beams your pressure and temperature data to your cell phone. When you wear it and hug yourself, your pal or lover will receive the same exact hug in "real time" via his cell phone and actuators in a similar shirt. It's a great concept, and it could enable bloggers to experience something like human contact again, but for me it raises the thorny question of what happens after the breakup, and whether someone could continue to be hugged against his or her will. (I picture a businesswoman delivering a polished presentation, when suddenly she whirls around and screams: "Stop hugging me, you jerk!" Everyone thinks she has gone mad, but then she explains bashfully, "Sorry, I forgot to deactivate my Hug Shirt.")

Eventually, I decided to splash around in the blogosphere myself, to see what all the fuss was about. It was very beguiling: Within a day people from Turkey, Israel, and Ohio were e-mailing me and posting their thoughts on Modestly Yours. It is certainly exhilarating to connect with people you would never have met, exchange ideas, and get attacked by people all over the globe. There really are opportunities to form unique communities on the Internet. But an online community cannot substitute for friends in real life.

In 2003, raven-haired Suzanne Gonzales was depressed and found support from an online suicide group for ending her life. She swapped about 100 notes with people in the newsgroup who told her that if antidepressants weren't for her, then "You can always leave." "Leave" was their code word for "kill yourself." The newsgroup also detailed a variety of effective ways to kill yourself. Nineteen years old and a student at Florida State, Suzanne only delineated her plans to the newsgroup. More than a few users were supportive: "Suzy, I want you to leave us if it will bring you peace," one posted. "I hope your method works for you," wrote another. Unfortunately, none of the people encouraging her to kill herself knew about her beautiful smile, or about all the people back in Red Bluff, California, who loved her. Suzanne beamed one final missive on March 23, 2003: "'Bye, everyone; see you on the other side." She then sent good-bye e-mails to her parents and to the local police, telling them where to find her body. Officers rushed to her hotel, but, tragically, the poison she had swallowed had already killed her. Soon after, her parents had their daughter's hard drive examined, and that was when her visits to the suicide site turned up. When her parents logged on, the site's members were boasting that they were the "only people" who had understood Suzanne. Her father countered, "How dare they say that! They didn't know *anything* about her."

The operators of the suicide site defended themselves: "We believe that every person has the right to choose to take his/her own life, if and when (s)he chooses." I checked back with the newsgroup at the end of 2006, and someone named Lany posted an e-mail similar to Suzy's last one: "My curtain call will be this Friday. I definitely made up my mind." Another visitor, J. T. Laurie, replied, with perhaps a hint of malice, "I hope your bus can leave on time and you arrive according to schedule. Have a nice trip."

"Two are better than one," we learn in *Ethics of the Fathers*, "For should they fall, one can lift the other; but woe to him who is alone when he falls and there is no one to lift him!" How much worse off is one who thinks he is among friends when really he couldn't be more alone.

.   .   .

"Dembe," a twenty-six-year-old designer who has lived in the United States, Africa, and Japan, wonders if the increase in teen depression and suicide could be connected to a false notion of individuality. According to Dembe, women in particular seem to think "individuality means they must do everything on their own." But the idea that you are "enough on your own" she finds "very misleading":

I am all for moments of quiet reflection with yourself because goodness knows sometimes you just need to recoup. But it really can't be a way of life, especially if you are finding yourself lonely and yearning for human interaction. We are social beings and whether we want to admit it or not, our actions do have repercussions and effects on those around us. So if our individuality leads us to isolate everyone around us and we are miserable, then some changes need to take place.

When Dembe moved to America for college, she tells me, she felt a "sharp change" in her interactions with women. Since she is Ugandan and attended a mostly white, elite liberal arts college, she first "put it down to a cultural difference." However, after traveling more and comparing notes with friends back home, Dembe now feels that "the demise in female friendships is true across all cultures":

In my youth I had very strong bonds with women. I have noticed that in their twenties, especially the early twenties, many college-educated women take a less than positive view of female friendship. I have friends still living in Botswana and they have mentioned the same point. It seems that the friendships of our teens, which we felt nurtured us, have turned into very negative interactions. Then if you are trying to be positive you are seen as naïve. I think cynicism has become the norm and that makes me very sad.

Like many women today, Dembe finds herself more comfortable around men:

When I was younger I didn't stop for a moment to notice how precious friendship really is. It was easy to make friends and meet people I could relate to. As I grow older I have found that it gets harder and harder to

meet people I can relate to and want to be friends with. I have more male friends than I do female friends and I find myself—like I said before—yearning for female friends. [But] I don't went to settle for the fake interactions.

Many mothers echo this sentiment. Debbie from Los Angeles says it starts young: "My daughter has friends who are boys, in a brotherly way, and frankly they are far more pleasant to be around than many teenage girls. Teen girls are often brutally manipulative and mean. The boys she knows are far more even-tempered and kind."

The writer Ariel Levy told me that when she visited college campuses in 2006, college girls would often declare, "I'm a guys' girl" or "All my best friends are guys." The girls were "always proud of how many males they associated with; they would say, 'I don't trust women.'"

To Dembe, the main culprit is jealousy: "It plays out that when one woman achieves her ultimate goal, be it starting her own business or getting married—the other woman can't really find it in her heart to be happy for her friend. Instead she wonders, 'Why her and not me?' It is especially volatile when a single woman is friends with either a married woman or one part of a happy couple."

Of all the reasons for the demise of female friendship, I heard this one most often. Even when a woman was truly happy for her friends, her married friends would often treat her differently, causing a rift.

I thought about Alice from Chicago, who had shared this dismal fact: She doesn't get invited to many parties since her friends got married. "It's like, if I show up alone, am I going to be like a problem? I'm just wondering, What do they think of me? Am I going to take hold of somebody's husband?" Although Alice is pretty and does not look her age (forty-two), she is definitely not the "other woman" type: "I have a clear sense of right and wrong." So this attitude is very upsetting to her: "I feel like saying to some of these wives, 'Don't flatter yourselves! Like OK, I dated your husband in college but there's a reason why I don't date him anymore. I know what he's like.' So that bugs me, too. You can't really count on your friends anymore."

I would hear this again and again: There's no longer any sexual solidarity. There's no sense of "OK, this is another woman's husband, so I'm not going to try to be flirtatious and sexy, because why do I need to muck up

their marriage?" Instead it's all about *me* and "*I* need to be appreciated" whether the person doing the appreciating happens to be married or not.

Many factors are blamed for the dwindling of friendship—television, the Internet, the culture of individuality. Still, one factor I haven't heard experts mention is the link between normalizing adultery and the decline of female solidarity.

Consider Cathy Gallagher, a resident of Bethesda, Maryland, who is a former ad executive. Her new line of greeting cards for people in adulterous relationships, the Secret Lover collection, offers cards for any occasion. One holiday card reads, "As we each celebrate with our families, I will be thinking of you." Another, "I used to look forward to the weekends, but since we met, they now seem like an eternity." For a high romantic quotient, there is: "As I lie in bed and think of you . . . I know that we are meant to be with each other. . . . Even though I want you all to myself, I understand that you are not mine completely and I have to share you. Let's trust in our love and know we will be together soon. I love you."

In an article in the *Gazette* (a local newspaper), Gallagher explained that she and her husband personally know many people involved in affairs, so she figured that there was an "untapped market." (Presumably Gallagher would not want her own husband taking advantage of her new product.)

Secret Lover contends that according to its research, 60 percent of American men and 40 percent of women "are involved in or have been involved in an affair." Other studies have uncovered lower numbers, but Gallagher claims that people downplay their affairs to pollsters. Whatever the total, online business has been brisk, and Gallagher is proud to help those who have trouble expressing their tangled feelings: "They're in this conflicting situation. They love this other person but they may not want to break up their family. It's very taboo, but I'm not judgmental about it. I feel like I'm helping them." In fact she goes further, seeming to congratulate customers for their affairs. On her website, visitors are celebrated for their "inherent passion," "deep emotion," and a "deep understanding of that special someone." Joanna Bare, who counsels couples dealing with infidelity, disagrees: "We don't see Hallmark cards about abuse or alcoholism or addiction."

Secret Lover clearly thinks that adultery is different. The website expresses the hope that their cards will aid in "Providing comfort to that special someone during separation and difficult times," "Strengthening personal connections and enhancing the passion with your lover," and "Adding a personal touch to special occasions and holidays."

I'll say.

Secret Lover does promise that "all SLC products are shipped discreetly" and that it will "execute its transactions with the greatest discretion"; the company also pledges that it "will not communicate with customers unless they have authorized us to do so." That's shrewd, for if the company were to call and say, "Hey, Mrs. Johnson, your husband's adulterous greeting cards are ready. Where should we ship 'em?" surely it would not keep Mr. Johnson's business for long.

· · ·

How did we get to this point?

We don't hold male cheaters to a higher standard; rather, for many people, equal-opportunity adultery is tangible evidence of women's liberation. In 2005, writers at *New York* magazine hailed the trend of "marriage with benefits": "Perhaps this time around, seventies-style swinging and slutting will actually be feasible—and fair."

In the same year, *Undressing Infidelity: Why More Wives Are Unfaithful* received glowing coverage in the press for finally redressing the inequality implicit in a man cheating on his wife. At last women, too, could cheat in increasing numbers, the author, Diane Shader Smith, reported, and isn't that wonderful? "Their stories seduced me," she writes, "leaving me envious of their ability to throw caution to the wind and curious as to how they did it. . . . A woman who engages in extramarital sex puts her own needs and desires before her husband's, a concept many women, myself included, find both baffling and compelling." She depicts these "amazing women" as if they were heroines. A few women admit that tearing their families apart was maybe "too high a price to pay" for the affair, but such reports are few and far between. More typical is "Raphael," who enthuses, "It was the best time of my life" and "my affair with Mike was the best decision I've ever made." One woman, "Reilly" is a more practical lady: "At least with two relationships, I have a bigger safety net." Their husbands' feelings are brushed off like stray crumbs. In a particularly cruel description, "Anna" scoffs that when her husband "almost lost me to another man, he had nothing to say. He put his head in the sand. That was the problem with him—he had no spine." The author even burdens us with her temptation to stray from her own husband, Mark, and tells us how deeply wounded he was by her behavior. Is she bragging? In a way, yes: "This book is a love story, about finding my way back to Mark." It's easy to see how this "love story" could be humiliating to her husband, but the men's feelings are not the point. Rather, disregarding the men's feelings is the point.

Nothing can stand in the way of giving women access to equal-opportunity adultery. Whether they are the "other" women having affairs with married men, or wives looking for a little fun on the side, choosing adultery is choosing to be empowered. The book *Homewrecker: An Adultery Reader* (2006) was praised by feminist critics for its "complexity" and for exploring "far more than the psychology of adultery's victims."

To dwell on victims of adultery is today considered *passé*. It's so last century. We have evolved newer and better understandings. In *Against Love,* for example, Laura Kipnis informs us that adultery is "the nearest thing to a popular uprising against the regimes of contemporary couple-dom." The author is a well-regarded professor of media studies at Northwestern, but her support for adultery is indistinguishable from that of Mandi Norwood, who was editor in chief of *Mademoiselle* and the British *Cosmo* from 1995 to 2000.

Norwood is somewhat less sophisticated than Kipnis—one section title in her *Hitched Chick's Guide to Modern Marriage* is called "Monogamy? Schmonogamy!"—but the rationale is e'er the same. These days, "Nothing should be presumed. Not even female virtue. . . . Society cannot expect a woman to conduct herself according to an outdated stereotype."

To her credit, Norwood does briefly note studies showing that affairs cause "a range of negative effects on children," from aggression to eating disorders. And "some women whose parents had affairs remain haunted by them."

But why should these problems get in the way, if equality is at stake? We all know that our husbands would leap at the chance for a fling. Consider thirty-two-year-old "Phillippa," for instance, who had an affair with a famous soccer player.

> [It] was an opportunity she couldn't turn down. "How could I? I would have kicked myself." . . . Good, harmless, bed-notching fun or a serious threat to your marriage? As far as Phillippa is concerned, sleeping with a celebrity is no threat to her marriage. "I mean, if Scott had the chance to sleep with Gwyneth Paltrow, I'm sure he would. How could he not?"

The enlightened postmodern chick is always post-morality. "All Work and Some Playing Around Makes Jill a Typical Hitched Chick" announces the final section title in Norwood's chapter on female infidelity. The implication is that if you don't play around, you may be a bit atypical, and perhaps even a bit oppressed. Before you know it, you could end up like Carmen's mom. Carmen's mom lived in the country and thought that she was happy with her husband, but really, deep down—so deep even she was not aware of it—she was just yearning for some new male flesh to jump on. If you don't want to meet Carmen's mom's fate (which was, by her daughter's own admission, happiness, but never mind), then you too will get out there and do some cheating.

Norwood believes that "Sometimes an affair can have a stabilizing effect on marriage." This is popular to say, but I have yet to see a single study supporting this. Norwood's proof? "Only 25 percent of divorces are filed on the grounds of infidelity," so marriages that have weathered affairs must be much stronger now. Anyone who thinks this is proof of anything other than our desire to rationalize failure is living in a dream world far more isolated than the country home of Carmen's mom.

* * *

Why does any of this matter? I think we need to look at how our post–sexual-morality culture makes it harder to form friendships. Simply put, if you can't trust women, it's much harder to be friends with them. This is our elephant in the living room: obvious, and yet for some reason passed over. But once you notice it, you realize how large it really is. Remember the "Hottie Handbook" for teen girls? "Attention girls. . . . If you have a boyfriend, don't bring him around me because you won't have a boyfriend anymore. . . . I sizzle. I scorch, hotter than any flame." Not exactly the kind of girl you'd rush to befriend.

Then there is RevengeLady.com, where women proudly trade stories of revenge on other women. Their rampages, without exception, are prompted by sexual double-crossing. One boyfriend asks a woman's best friend how he can get his girlfriend back, since they have been fighting; the best friend responds by throwing herself at him, thus earning her the title of "ex-best-friend" and a carful of skunk oil, applied discreetly in the cushions with a syringe. Another woman's husband has a coworker who is constantly flirting with him and calling him at all hours; the wife retaliates by sending subscriptions for fifteen different magazines to the coworker's doorstep with instructions to "bill me later." Naturally, the wife includes porn and baby magazines, "since I know the baby thing is a sore topic for the Witch." One woman decides to sleep with an old college friend's fiancé, so, in retaliation, "I sent her a letter stating that she had recently had unprotected sex with someone who just tested HIV postive. My (fake) organization strongly urged her to get tested immediately. I sent the letter to her job. Her reaction was great! She got very upset, she began breathing hard, and she fainted. They had to call an ambulance to transport her to the ER from work! [And] she stopped sleeping with my fiancé."

One may legitimately question whether men so easily sidelined are worth keeping in the first place. However, some of these cases are fuzzy (as with the married man who was flattered by his coworker's attention but wasn't about to have an affair), and women can very easily make a bad situation worse—or turn it around and make it better. It's now conventional wisdom to pile scorn on cheating men even as we encourage women to imitate them, but in training our eyes exclusively on bad male behavior and never on bad female behavior, we clearly make things miserable for ourselves. What if all this retaliation weren't necessary, and women could simply trust other women?

At the end of our interview, Alice mentioned a friend who is the "other woman": "My friend was like, 'Oh, I'm so happy my boyfriend got divorced!' Yeah, she'd been dating a guy who'd been married for a long time and I felt like saying to the girl, 'Well, thanks so much for lowering the bar on everyone's behavior. I really appreciate it!' She doesn't even want to get married to him; she just wants his undivided attention." Suddenly, Alice didn't feel like getting together with her friend as much.

After three girls violently attacked a thirteen-year-old girl in January 2007 and the video was uploaded all over the Internet, the superindendent of the girls' school in North Babylon, New York, suspended the assailants and declared to the press: "This Internet business is out of control." Well, not exactly; the girls' kicking and punching was over a boy, it turned out. It's really the sexual competitiveness that is out of control.

What if girls wouldn't steal other girls' boyfriends when given the chance? What if, instead of glamorizing infidelity, women would agree not to poach one another's husbands?

Personally, I think this would do more for friendship than all the knitting conventions and cuddle parties in the world. And the reason I venture such a peculiar proposal is that I have actually seen this happen, and it works.

. . .

I don't want to idealize the Orthodox world, but as someone who has lived in both mainstream and religious environments, certain differences have become apparent to me. Married Orthodox women take a particular interest in helping single girls: inviting them over for Sabbath meals, trying to fix them up, and listening to their problems. Their investment in single women really has no equivalent elsewhere—except perhaps the psychotherapists who are paid to listen. Looking at this from a purely sociological perspective is tricky because the women believe that helping others is what God wants them to do. But observant Jewish women also just don't seem to see other women as competing sex objects. Both their marriages and their friendships seem more secure. I've been among secular Jewish women and haven't experienced this feeling. It's a feeling that comes from agreeing on common rules. In this case, adult men and women who aren't relatives don't even hug one another casually, and Jewish men are discouraged from even looking at scantily clad women who are not their wives—to say nothing of adultery. There is no sexual free-for-all (for the women or for the men), yet instead of seeming restricted, the women actually seem more relaxed.

In 2000, when I first visited a seminary for Jewish women in Israel, I was dumbfounded by the way the women would take a break to dance for anyone who happened to be engaged at the time. At ten-thirty in the morning, about once a week, all the girls would put down their commentaries on the Torah, looking mischievous, and the rabbis would take their leave. The doors would close, and suddenly all these serious, educated professional women in their twenties would link arms and dance and sing as if they were schoolchildren. The first time I saw it happen, it struck me as bizarre, and I was even a bit embarrassed for them. The second time I noticed tears in some of the girls' eyes, tears of genuine happiness, not of jealousy—and I thought to myself, "You know, it is nice. But I'm twenty-four already; I'm too old for this kind of thing." The third time, to my horror, someone pulled me into the circle, and before I knew it, I was the one who had tears in her eyes. The idea of women truly being happy for one another, without any reservations, was new to me and also very moving. As Yehudit, a therapist in her early thirties, would later explain to me, "God doesn't do anything that's not perfect. So if your friend gets married, that's

making the world a little better for you too; it's not taking away from you."
An admirable view, when you consider that Yehudit is herself not yet married and obviously wishes to be.

We will never return to the days of the scarlet A, nor would we want to. But perhaps it's not really necessary to direct cheaters to the adultery cards section. Maybe instead of asking if we "play around" enough to be "typical hitched chicks," we can instead begin to ask, "How would you feel if the tables were turned, and someone did that to you?" And perhaps we won't, but the next generation will.

Izzy, the young woman whose family was shattered by adultery, pointed out that "the people who are fine with bringing another person into the relationship, those are the people—if you go back far enough in their lives—those are the people who have serious things to work out. I think that is abnormal, that way of being; it doesn't make sense to me. One person and one person—that makes sense to me."

One person and one person. And if we can find that one person without destroying other women's lives, so much the better.

TEN STEPS TO GREATER FEMALE SOLIDARITY

As suggested to me by Sarah Pevey, a twenty-three-year-old law student at the University of Tennessee:

1. Don't go after guys who are "staked out." But you knew that already.

2. Give thought to your dress in terms of its "threat level." A very sexily dressed girl puts every girlfriend on edge, instinctively. And an intimidated girlfriend is like a pit bull backed into a corner—one wrong move and she'll come at you with everything she's got.

3. Compliment other girls: There are well-coordinated outfits, clever jokes, impressive talents, and considerate actions all waiting to be complimented. Compliments make people feel better, and there's no downside to giving a sincere compliment. It's a sign of self-confidence.

4. Accept that other women will be prettier, smarter, and more popular than you are, and that's fine. It's a big world with lots of opportunities. The goal is not to stand on the top of the pile. The goal is to hold yourself to a personal standard and become someone you would respect if you were someone else. Try to figure out what you enjoy doing and do that rather than looking to others first.

5. Pick your battles carefully. You can't control what others do—you can control only what you do. Sometimes, you need to fight with people who are threatening things that you care about. But chick-fighting is draining and time-consuming. Sometimes the threat is just in your head, and you'll make your life worse by fighting a pointless battle. Realize that not everyone will like you. But you don't have to confront every petty person who crosses your path.

6. When you gossip, assume that what you say will be reported back to the subject. So say only things that you could defend or would say to someone's face. Even if gossip is true, don't say anything that would make you cry, if the tables were turned. Never betray confidences.

7. If you are chick-fighting with someone, don't gossip about her at all. The fuel of chick-fighting is, "Did you hear what she said, or did?" If you don't say or do anything controversial, people will quit focusing on you and will see just her unwarranted attacks. It's best to give diplomatic-style "press statements"—"I'm sorry she feels that way." "I don't know why she is saying that; it's false."

8. When you do something wrong, apologize, even if others also did things wrong and they don't apologize. Remember, you're holding yourself to your own standards and controlling your own actions. It doesn't matter if others retaliate; do the right thing, and you'll feel better.

9. When you confront people about their actions, do not make personal attacks. Personal observations are fine, but a sarcastic attack is counterproductive, as it changes the subject and diminishes the authority of your complaint. It changes other people's focus from what they did to what you said.

10. If another girl has a problem with you and you need to resolve the conflict, say, "I really like you, but I get the impression that you don't like me. What am I doing wrong?" This does a few things. It defuses the situation. It does not back her into a corner, because you haven't accused her of anything in particular, and you don't have to give evidence to back up an impression (as you would with an accusation). It gives her a chance to vent about her problems, but she will probably be more reasonable about them.

CHAPTER SIX

Pure Fashion Divas

[As I] walk[ed] around a crowded city shopping area on a hot day last week, it often felt as though glancing anywhere below head-level in any direction was fraught—yet not doing so could clearly result in a twisted ankle. However, amid the plunging necklines and beltlines, piercings and tattoos, one woman stood out. She was wearing a long white summer dress with a red pattern on it, and she stood out because it made her look . . . pretty! Remember pretty? Ah, yes—I'd almost forgotten it, lost among all the hot, hip, raunchy grrrl-wear that has become the unofficial uniform *de nos jours.*

—Thirty-three-year-old PAUL, from Britain

In the autumn of 2006, a coed at an Ivy League college is approached by one of her professors. Does he want to talk about her last paper? No, he does not. He is curious about why she doesn't dress more provocatively, and sees fit to ask her: "Why do you always dress like an eight-year-old?" Not long after this incident, in Philadelphia, twenty-nine-year-old Carin opens a Christmas package from her loving mother and groans. To judge by her reaction you might think she had received a tacky red sweater with appliqué snowmen, but in fact it is "yet another pair of jeans." For several years now, she explains to me, she and her mother have been engaged in a battle of wills over Carin's discovery that she feels "more feminine" wearing a skirt: "I get jeans from my mom for Christmas each year and into eternity in her hopes that I will dress 'like a normal person' again. Poor Mom. I pray someday she will understand. It was one of the most liberating choices I ever made."

In an age when even an ad for Evian water features a naked woman lying in the snow, and when college officials are proud of their "varsity streaking teams," you have to wonder how it's possible for a young person to rebel.

A twenty-three-year-old woman from Alexandria, Virginia, tells me how. I promise not to use her name and so, giggling, she continues. Am I ready? Yes, I tell her, I think I am. I brace myself for a truly wicked revelation. Instead, "at university," she confesses, "sometimes I would dress up." She looks like any normal college student, in a sensible lavender sweater and jeans. And yet:

> Sometimes I would dress up, and I wouldn't do it a lot because it just wasn't done. I went to Marshall University in the middle of West Virginia—when people dress up, they stick out. And then when I did, people were like, "Oh, why have you dressed up?" I'd be like, "Oh, I have a speech today," or "Oh, I have . . ." Sometimes I would just lie and say whatever—I have a speech or I have a meeting or—and just make something up so they wouldn't bother me about it. Half of them would go to a class in their pajamas, wouldn't wash their hair for like two days, three days.

Hearing this young woman's confession was a surprise but not a shock. I'd come up against this type of thing before in my days at Williams College, when I would receive nasty e-mails addressed to "You Overdressed Little You." I didn't consider a shirt and slacks or a skirt as really "dressing up," but neither did I walk around day after day in the same gray sweatpants—and that apparently constituted an offense. Ten years later, I'm noticing that the dissidents have grown bolder. At the University of Pennsylvania in the fall of 2006, a sophomore, Chloé Hurley, wrote an op-ed bemoaning going "to class in pajamas" and calling for a revival of actually getting dressed in the morning:

> Last spring, I sat next to two senior associate students (the senior citizens who sometimes sit in on classes) during my history class. They told me that in their day, every man in class wore a collared shirt and a tie, and every woman wore a skirt. While perhaps this would be an extreme dress code for Penn, wouldn't it be nice if students' outfits showed they were serious about class. . . . Dressing up for class, in my mind, is a form of respect for your teachers, your peers and, perhaps most importantly, for yourself. . . . Dressing up communicates that you view the occasion as a valuable way to spend your time and have made a commitment to put your best self forward—intellectually as well as physically.

Chloé, a history major who resembles a young Michelle Pfeiffer, has gumption. Her research carries her all the way back to *The College Freshman's Don't Book,* published in 1910. "Don't think that crazy or odd clothes are necessarily 'College' clothes," this guide cautions—advice that Chloé passes along approvingly, albeit with a wink. "Lots of College men do wear crazy clothes; but it isn't so much because they're College men, as because they're crazy." When I contact her, Chloé has already anticipated the objections to her piece, assuring me that she is not a "'girls in pearls, guys in ties' junior member of the DAR"—Daughters of the American Revolution. "Though I am, yes, perhaps, fairly 'mild' in my everyday behaviors, I tend to think of myself as pretty radical in my personal politics."

Strange as it sounds, upholding social standards has become the "radical" position today, especially now that "crazy casual clothes" are fashionable even in grade school. One midwestern mom told me that an event called Pajama Days has become disturbingly popular in her public school district since 2002:

> Now, when I was a kid, if you went to school in your pajamas you would be mortified. I used to have nightmares—Didn't you have nightmares of being there in your pajamas? Well, my son, who's in junior high now, came and told me about it. He doesn't even participate; he just blocks it all out. He just says, "Pretty weird, Mom." And he told me that in one of the classes the kids would get extra credit if they wore slippers, and I was just shocked. I said, "That is so darn goofy." And again, being a boy, he's like totally disengaged from his environment. And the teacher even wore pajamas. It was like, "What?" So I complained about it and I said, "This is all kooky; what's the point?" I was told, "It's school spirit."

It does make you wonder how many kids are nagging their mothers with a new battle cry, "Mom, I have nothing to wear for Pajama Days!" The trouble is that sloppy dressing can lead to sloppy thinking. An older woman I greatly admire likes to quip, "When you stay in your pajamas, you feel like a pajama."

Pajamas in the classroom may seem harmless, but they signal a collapse between public and private realms that is no longer cute. One example of this collapse is the popular MySpace website, where teens often share personal information and expose themselves to predators who want to hand-pick their victims. And so the old jokes are no longer so funny. When P. Diddy inaugurated his new YouTube deal with a video of himself in the bathroom, sharing the wonders of emptying his bladder to the tune of his own tinkling, the reaction in the YouTube community was universally nega-tive. The clip was meant to be entertaining and even included a reminder to viewers to wash their hands, but user "Jay6385" said, "Wash my hands? I need to wash my EYES!" "That's something I never wanted to see," agreed "mcny1971." "Man, this is a new low," pronounced "Veronica Dreadful."

The urge to reveal private matters still presses, but so, apparently, does the urge to cultivate a little modesty. Denise Richards, an energetic thirty-one-year-old mother from Utah, has discovered that many girls around the country are already weary of total exposure. She lets me have an early peek at her documentary film *A Modest Revolution* (2006), which features inter-views with girls from around the country and is by turns compelling and hilarious. "*Modesty?* Is that, like, an SAT word?" one teenager says quizzi-cally, peering suspiciously at the camera. The other girls tend to be more suspicious of today's fashions than of the earnest reporter in front of them. Discussing a popular kind of "too low" jeans, reportedly "designed to show the butt crack," Lindsay from Los Angeles—who looks about thirteen and wears funky green triangle earrings—makes an icky face for the camera at the thought of wearing such jeans: "I don't wanna." Her pony-tail shakes, emphasizing her disapproval: "I see enough of it already!" This is no nun, mind you, just a young woman in a black tank top. Another Pure Fashion diva is born.

*   *   *

It's a beautiful February day in Seattle, Washington, the kind of day that could pass for spring. Finches *chirp-chirp-chirp* in the tree above my head. For the day I've absconded from my home to meet the famous Ella Gunderson—who at age eleven took it upon herself to write to Nordstrom and ask the retailer to carry more modest clothing. Her letter set off a flurry of national media coverage and a worldwide discussion about contempo-rary fashion trends.

As I'm waiting for the Gundersons to collect me at a local Starbucks, looking for the redheaded pixie I've seen in media profiles, I notice a van outside and two blurry figures waving at me. I duck in and it is indeed

Ella, now thirteen, in the backseat—wearing a pale blue tracksuit, wire-rimmed spectacles, and a shy smile. (She is in fact not blurry in person; I just have something in my contact lens.) Her mom, Pam, drives home as she discusses her favorite subject: her daughter and the new meaning she's brought to the concept of youthful rebellion. "You know, Ella used to have spiked hair and piercings all over her," Pam jokes, "but we brought her back from the edge." We grin at each other like old friends.

In ten minutes we pull up to the Gundersons' home in the suburb of Redmond, where I am greeted by Dusty, a wonderful golden retriever who enthusiastically sheds all over my skirt. I take it as a compliment, but I can't spend all day patting him since I have come on an important mission. I want to find out what motivated Ella's crusade, which began a year and a half ago in 2004.

"Oh, I haven't talked about it for so long," Ella sighs in her mature, tranquil way. By now I've slipped onto a couch in the spacious living room next to her harp; and, frankly, it's easier to picture Ella as a little angel serenely plucking the harp than as a young activist urging corporations and her elders to take modesty more seriously. And yet that was what she did. It began innocently enough:

> Well, I was shopping with my older sister [Robin, then thirteen]
> and my mom and my sister's friend and one of my girlfriends and
> we were all shopping and, um, my sister was trying on a pair of
> jeans and they were too tight, so my mom told her to go try the
> bigger size. And when she came out, the salesclerk said to her,
> "No, you don't want *that* size, you want the smaller size, the
> tighter size, because it's The Look."

Robin ended up buying the larger size, even though it wasn't The Look. But the experience left Ella with a bad taste in her mouth: "That was what kind of convinced me to write about it." Pam knew what the clerk had said to her daughters, but she soon forgot about it. Ella, on the other hand, came home and decided to write a letter. "I didn't know she was doing it," her mother recalls; "but then she came out and asked for help addressing it." What Ella sat down and wrote was this:

> Dear Nordstrom, I am an eleven-year-old girl who has tried shopping
> at your store for clothes (in particular jeans), but all of them ride way

under my hips, and the next size up is too big and falls down. I see all of these girls who walk around with pants that show their belly button and underwear. . . . Your clearks sugjest that there is only one look. If that is true, then girls are suppost to walk around half naked. I think that you should change that.

Pam has a copy machine, so "I thought this is really cute; I'm going to make a copy to keep for our memory book." Then Ella "kind of forgot about it," since she didn't really expect anyone to write back. But a few months later, two representatives from Nordstrom wrote separately to Ella, apologizing for her inconvenience and assuring her that they would make an effort to educate their sales force. They even said they would search for a solution to her problem. Ella was taken aback. "I didn't really expect them to notice, but they said they'd try, they'd try to change their fashions."

As it happened, during that week the Gundersons were helping to put on a local "Pure Fashion" show featuring modest clothing, and at the last minute the person in charge of the publicity packet said, "Do you have the letter that Ella wrote? And the replies when Nordstrom wrote back?" Both the letter and the replies were stuffed into the packet—quite as an afterthought—and that's how the media hubbub began. The story of Ella and her sensible letter soon hit the front page of *The Seattle Times*. (The reporter Nick Perry grasped the significance of this story from the beginning.) That day, Ella's fifth-grade teacher read the article aloud in class. Was Ella embarrassed? "Yeah. Yeah." She giggles. How did her peers react? "They were all supportive and they helped me. None of them were, like, I don't know, mad at me or anything, you know, or rolled their eyes. They were all, well, proud of me."

The first day (May 21, 2004) after the article appeared in *The Seattle Times* was a roller coaster for the Gundersons. Ella was kept busy with eight interviews—four on the radio before school that morning, and the other four on television after school. Pam quickly became her press agent:

It was hilarious because we were awakened at about five-thirty or so, and a station out of state was calling to ask if Ella was there. I was like, "Well, she's sleeping! It's five-thirty AM." They said, "We'd like to ask her about the story in *The Seattle Times*." Of course, we hadn't even looked at the paper at that point.

Ella had a solo in a school concert that day, so her parents were in the school building helping to set up. They repeatedly tried to leave, but "the PA kept saying 'Can Mr. or Mrs. Gunderson come to the office?' So we kept having to go back to get phone calls about Ella, and then finally there were really urgent ones—'Please come to the office right now!' It was the *Today* show."

Ella attracted a stream of admirers—parents, teenagers—and for once, the smirkers were silent. Not since 1897, when Virginia O'Hanlon received her answer from the New York *Sun*—"Yes, Virginia, there is a Santa Claus"—had there been such a universally positive reaction to a young girl's letter. Ella was also surprised when Katie Couric ended up agreeing with her on *Today*, since she had prepared herself to be attacked. "She also interviewed Pete Nordstrom," Ella told me, "and it was kind of funny because I had been, like, prepared for her to be, you know, not supportive of me, but she was really supportive of me and not really of him." If the people at Nordstrom had hoped to neutralize Ella by writing back to her, they had miscalculated. The company ended up sounding defensive, in a way that even children noticed. On CNN, Mr. Nordstrom explained that he wasn't surprised by Ella's letter, because he had been fielding similar complaints from teenage girls for years. "Actually, three years ago we had some young women from Orange County, California, write us about a pretty similar subject," he admitted.

Ella observed of Mr. Nordstrom, "He'd try to avoid [reporters'] questions and be like, 'Yeah we're fine; we're doing that; we're chasing the trends.' That's what he kept repeating, 'We're chasing the trends.' But if you're providing the clothes," Ella explains to me in her patient, soft-spoken way, "you set the trends." Pam agrees, adding, "People wear what they can find."

After all those years of mothers' putting their daughters on the spot—"You're going to go out looking like *that?*"—it's funny to see young women putting their elders on the spot: "You're going to sell clothes looking like *that?*" I suppose that it was just a matter of time.

How did Ella process the whole incident? "Well, it all happened so quick. It didn't just stop after that weekend; it actually kept going on for quite a while, for six months. There were still little things going on a year later. But, I don't know, I felt, I don't know . . ." Did she want more? "No!" Ella shouts. Then she laughs. "I wanted it to stop!"

She is, however, proud to have made a difference. The Gundersons keep a large basket of clippings and letters of support, particularly from teenage girls fed up with today's fashions. Pam adds, "Within a month of the whole thing, there was a story in the paper about Nordstrom's annual stockholders' meeting, and one of our friends—I think it was Tammy—said, 'Open up your paper!' It was their annual meeting and some stockholder stood up and asked: 'What do you plan to do about the Ella Gunderson issue?'"

The Ella Gunderson issue did not go away quickly, for one thing because Ella was not a lone voice. Ella did receive the most attention in the media, but Nordstrom, Dillard's, and JCPenney department stores have all reported groups of teenagers submitting petitions for more modest clothing. In Tucson, Arizona, teens collected over 4,000 signatures on a petition asking stores to carry more clothes for girls who didn't want short skirts, low-rise jeans, low-cut tops, or bare midriff tees. Jim Benson, director of advertising and marketing for the Phoenix division of Dillard's, tried to placate the teens with a letter: "We hear what you are saying, and we are working on reacting to your needs." (When that didn't satisfy them, Dillard's eventually put on a modest fashion show at its Park Place location.) What were teenagers responding to? Pam offers an interesting insight:

> When we were in the midst of it, it seemed like what girls are looking for is a way to be pretty, a way to be feminine, and what the stores and the designers are giving them is a way to be sexy. And it's not the same thing. It's kind of like when you're a mom of little people, you have to help your kids because they misidentify their needs. They'll be really, really tired, bone-dead tired, and they'll say, "I'm hungry!" and you have to help them. You have to be perceptive enough to know, "No, honey, you're really tired. I'll put you to bed and then you'll wake up hungry, but you're not hungry now." You get all of those emotions so connected in your brain. Well, it's the same thing with femininity. Sexiness and femininity are not the same thing—they're close in the brain but they're not the same.

The Gundersons were simply hoping that the controversy would sell some tickets to their fashion show, which was to take place a few days later. It did.

In the end they sold 150 in a single day, and 400 total that year (compared with the previous year's 150).

The concept of a Pure Fashion show began about eight years ago, in 1999. It was started simultaneously by moms around the country whose daughters belonged to a Catholic girls' youth group called Challenge Clubs ("Challenge yourself, challenge others, challenge the world" is its motto). Although the origins are Catholic, the goal of the Pure Fashion program is general: for girls ages ten to eighteen to become leaders. (The older girls lead the preparation sessions, which stretch over four to eight months, depending on the city.) In 2006, seventeen North American cities from Calgary to Miami featured Pure Fashion shows; and for the spring of 2007, twenty-two shows were in the works. Within each program, the number of girls involved has kept increasing. In 2004, thirty-seven girls launched the program in Seattle; in 2006, the number of participants nearly doubled. Audiences for these fashion shows have also snowballed. In Atlanta, which puts on one of the more professional shows, the audience numbered 1,300 in 2005 and 2,200 in 2006. In 2006, the show had to be held in the Georgia World Congress Center to accommodate all the ticket holders. It featured the Grammy-winning songwriter David Foster, whom the girls were naturally thrilled to see.

If the Pure Fashion shows are starting to seem mainstream, that's because they are. A fair percentage of the participants attend public schools and are not religious. They join because their friends tell them about it (the biggest advertisement for the fashion shows is word of mouth, girl to girl). And a sizable number buy tickets because they are interested in fashion: They want to see beautiful dresses, often paired with brightly colored long-sleeved sweaters, on happy, healthy-looking girls. "My mom is agnostic," the national director, Brenda Sharman, a former model, told me, "but she still loved the show and the commentary!" Many of the girls, who have had their hair curled and makeup professionally applied, really do look like models as they sashay down the runway, except that, instead of looking jaded and heroin-thin, they all seem to be shining. Pam Gunderson believes that the glow on their faces is more than just makeup: "A lot of people who are not Catholic or Christian or not even God-believing people have a real interest in it. It's just written in their heart. They know truth when they hear it."

Hearing the word "truth" associated with fashion is odd, to say the least. But as I would learn, the Pure Fashion program is about more than just fashion. It culminates in a fashion show, true; but before the girls ever think of clothing, they meet on an ongoing basis to learn about etiquette and community service (a man who works with disabled children gives a popular class). So a Pure Fashion model is not someone who hankers after corsets or crinolines, it turns out. She just doesn't want fashion to be the beginning and end of her self-definition. (Ella Gunderson, for one, hopes to have a career as a veterinarian someday.)

Ironically, in 2001, at about the time the Pure Fashion movement was getting off the ground, the political theorist Katha Pollitt was predicting that nothing like it could ever happen: "As I have outlined earlier, the realities of modern life ensure that there will be no massive 'going back' to premarital chastity and buttoned-up cardigans as envisioned by professional virgin Wendy Shalit." A revolution of buttoned-up cardigans wasn't quite what I had in mind in 1999, but if you want to know the truth, they do seem to be making a comeback. This is not because I issued any orders from my throne of professional virginity (a seat that I believe is already occupied by Madonna) but precisely because boomers like Pollitt seem to expect young women to dress revealingly, and this expectation gets annoying after a while. A lot of young women don't get misty-eyed over today's fashions; nor do they thrill to their elders' expectation that they need to be publicly sexualized in order to prove that they are "modern." Rather, because they have real goals to achieve, they don't want to be sidetracked by pressure to present themselves as porn stars. Even the Pure Fashion etiquette class— which one might associate with merely smiling demurely and not making waves—is experienced by a surprising number of the girls as "liberating" them to be taken seriously.

For example, in May 2006, when I spoke with a group of young women from Fort Wayne, Indiana, the day after their Pure Fashion show (which drew a crowd of 500), several girls, ages thirteen to seventeen, mentioned their etiquette "formation class" as a highlight. To me this was baffling because they seemed so naturally polite, but the girls insisted that they really needed to know more about manners. Dark-haired Elizabeth Harlan, seventeen, who has participated in the program for several years, explained:

> A lady came in and she first taught us, like, how to be a gracious guest
> and how to greet your hostess and things like that you should thank
> them, and bring them a gift-type thing. And then they also said this is

how a table at a fancy dinner would be set. This is how you eat each
thing, and this is how it's arranged around a plate and things like that.
That's so that when we go places, they're not distracted by our really
bad manners and they can actually look into what we have to say.

Many people might assume that girls attending Catholic schools have
teachers supportive of modesty, but today this is not necessarily the case.
Audrey and Stacey Litchfield, sisters who were also involved in the Pure
Fashion program in Indiana, explain that when Stacey, now thirteen, was in
the third grade, their mother started to notice that the girls were wearing
extremely short skirts. Audrey, seventeen, tells me: "Like we had mass two
days a week, and you bow in front of the altar. They had to hold their skirts
down because otherwise their underwear would show." Her mom decided
"it was time to take action and have the school regulate the length of the
skirts because they were becoming so scandalously high," but one of their
teachers fought the regulations for a long time. "I don't know what she really wanted out of it," Audrey reflects. "She was saying that short skirts are
like feminine or whatever. I don't know what she thought it revealed, because it doesn't reveal anything but skin. But she fought for [the mini-
skirts]." The sisters told me that only one or two girls actually supported
their teacher, and the rest just "felt pressure to wear short skirts because you
were looked down upon if you didn't wear very short skirts."

These generational dynamics affect communities across the nation. For
the school year 2006–2007, a school in Arlington, Texas, decided to institute a "cleavage crackdown," meeting with resistance not from students but
from a parent. One student, Tyler Edwards, nodding with enthusiasm, said,
"I think it's good that they're doing it"—the pressure to wear plunging
necklines was getting out of hand. But a parent, Tom Pederson, found it
necessary to vent his concern about the new dress code to a local reporter:
"It puts a little bit of a policeman approach to the educators, and they really
need to focus more on teaching."

I had already heard about this parental approach from a former member
of the school board in a suburb of Chicago, whom I'll call "Sandy":

The first time I became concerned was when a teacher stopped one of
our young ladies—I think it was an eighth-grader—and told her she
needed to go home and change her clothes and get into the dress code.

I think that one wasn't wearing any underwear, she had a see-through shirt or whatever, or she had on what appeared to be like underwear and nothing else. Those were the two big things girls would wear to school: see-through without underwear, or just underwear. So she told her to go home and change and her parents called up and there was a big powwow with the principal about his attitude and how—you know—Did he have bad thoughts? Was he lewd? And stuff like that. It was the principal's and the teacher's problem, according to the parent. That was the first time that we took seriously that there were parents that really didn't share our values or weren't on the same page, and that became more and more obvious over the years. This was about six years ago [in the year 2000]. Generally the community seems to want to hold some standards, but nobody wants—it's hard to be the one who speaks up and draws the line.

At a time when mothers defend see-through shirts, fathers rally for cleavage during the school day, and Catholic schoolteachers advocate for miniskirts for their charges, the entire burden of proof is now on anyone who believes in modesty. As I watch from the sidelines, I'm interested to see that young women are rising to this challenge. At some level they seem to recognize that they are the only ones who can change things. Nene Kalu, a junior at Princeton, says with impressive force and vitality, "It doesn't matter what type of underwear you choose to wear *as long as it is not showing* (neither the lines nor the actual undergarment). This is why it is called underwear; it should be hidden!" There is a note of frustration in this judicious advice, as if to say: enough!

So, naturally, the high school girls lead the Pure Fashion meetings, organizing and presenting the material from the head office. At least half of the meetings feature a "good work" campaign of some kind, and the Fourth Rule in the Pure Fashion creed is "that virtue is the most important 'must-have' for every season." When I met with Ella Gunderson, for example, her group just the night before had "all come up with a different virtue and we like wrote a little thing on it, you know, and talked about why it's important to us and gave examples. And then we went to our local radio station and read them, and he recorded them, and they're going to put them on the air as a little filler in between shows." Humility was Ella's favorite virtue; Heather's was patience; Anne's was authenticity.

To Ella's older sister Robin, brimming with cheerfulness and wisdom, the older virtues are all about authenticity: "It's best just to not care what other people think of you and to be your own person. If you're doing everything because someone else tells you to do it, then you're not your own person; it's not you. If you dress like everybody else dresses, or talk the way everyone else talks, then it's not you talking—it's your friends." Robin is blond, wears a bandanna, and comes across as a very confident and attractive fifteen-year-old. To her, pushing sexualized clothing on younger and younger girls is part of a society that does not value women: "I think our culture values men more . . . [and] external stuff, like 'Make more money; be more independent.'" So for Robin, refusing to wear sexy clothing means refusing to be defined in external terms.

Consider a ninth-grader in Los Angeles—I'll call her Alex—who will soon be switching high schools. She loves swimming, but not the coed swimming "scene," and since sports rotations are not optional, she will change schools to avoid coed swimming. You may already have a few choice words for this girl, but before you tell her to get over her hang-ups, consider that her sensitivity has benefited her fellow students in a different context. A few years ago, Alex's PE teacher quietly asked her if she would mind walking instead of running around the field to accompany a student with a heart condition who could not run well. The teacher had anticipated that the slower girl would get picked on, and she clearly thought highly enough of Alex to ask her to be the escort. And indeed, soon enough a girl—a little meany—did shout, "You guys are pathetic!" But Alex shouted right back, "You'll just have to deal with it!" This made the girl next to her laugh. Swimming is optional at the school Alex will be attending next year, so she has already announced to her mother that she intends to join the golf team instead. (Her mother has "no idea" where that came from, for no one in the family plays golf.)

People are often surprised when the modest girls are also the most outspoken ones, but it's not at all unusual. My twenty-three-year-old anonymous informant from Marshall University—the one who dressed formally, to her peers' consternation—was also one of the few girls in her peer group who refused to participate in sorority games:

I saw a lot of crazy stuff going on at sorority, and a lot of girls would just do things to be cool, like play these crazy games. Like you get a correctly points out that parents need to approve of the costumes, which can be purchased only with a valid credit card. Still, this is hardly comforting.

The problem is that even when it's not Halloween, parents are buying their toddlers tiny tees that say "Shopping Ho." Even when it's not Halloween, girls of eight or nine can be seen in fishnet stockings and wearing full makeup, in the company of their mothers. The new term being bandied about is "prostitots"—very young girls in crop tops, hip-huggers, and long-lasting lipstick. The commentator "Shaggles" on Huffington Post, "raised in the era of miniskirts and hot pants so I'm not exactly prudish," nonetheless called girls' clothing today "sad": "You should see the blank looks on my granddaughters' faces when I start in on how maybe an eight-year-old doesn't need to have her belly hanging out or wear sexy phrases across her chest. Because they think I am wrong: they DO have to wear that to fit in."

Stacey, the youngest of the girls in Fort Wayne, attests that the Pure Fashion movement is all about "having respect for yourself. Instead of trying and making yourself feel better by doing stuff with guys because you think that it's going to help you . . . dressing modestly helps girls feel their own importance." This, she's discovered, leads to better decisions. Just when I forget that I'm listening to a thirteen-year-old, Stacey adds that from her vantage point, another surefire way to be popular is to "smell fruity" because "popular girls usually have to smell like . . . something fruity. Like their hairspray or their perfume? It's always fruity."

Fruit aside, Elizabeth, another member of Pure Fashion, says that a more conservative fashion style helps to put her on her own path; it is a visual reminder that she won't succumb to peer pressure on a number of issues:

> People are like, "Everyone is wearing the same things so I'm going to wear this too." They do this with a lot of things. I say instead, "I know that these kinds of clothes fit me, so I'm going to wear these." It's important for girls to have confidence in themselves in knowing that they don't need to always be like wearing the same thing as their friends. Like they're always, *"I want to be an individual,"* but at the same time, they dress exactly like all their friends do and stuff. But come up with your own style. Say, "I like these kinds of clothes." I mean that's how trends are started, right? Like one person thinks, "Oh, this is cute," and they wear it, and then everyone else is wearing it.

twelve-pack of beer and you get in a room and you pick a guy's name out of the hat, and then you get in a room with him and you're supposed to drink that twelve-pack, whatever, as fast as you can and also get to know the guy? Yeah, right. I did go to some of [the parties]; I couldn't say I didn't go to all of them. But when I heard the themes, the way the other girls just accepted it, I was like, *"What?"* One theme was: The girls would wear white T-shirts, and then, well, the guys would get markers and write crude stuff—like awful stuff—on their chests. While the shirts were on them, they'd just write all over them and then they had to get out in the water and get wet too—it's so dumb.

Because she stayed sober, she started to notice a few things that annoyed her: "There were a lot of guys in our library, looking at porn, and I'm sitting there studying and I look over—it's totally open, like the desks are against the wall, so it's not like it's covered." It's not the pornography that bothers her so much as the expectations men get from pornography. "Even when I went to work [after college] my boss told me that I should dress more revealing, that I was too covered up, and I could do so much for myself if I didn't hide behind my clothes." She rolls her eyes as if to say, "Adults today!"

With all the little comments this young woman has endured, because of her dress and her nonparticipation in certain rites of passage, you might expect her to be racked with insecurity. Instead she seems quite laid back. In a lavender cardigan, she has no desire to make a spectacle of herself. But if she makes a spectacle of herself by not wanting to make a spectacle of herself, then so be it. "It's their problem," she says, shrugging off her boss, the boys in the library, and the sorority girls. Then her eyes flash impertinently.

Pure Fashion programs come and go. In Fort Wayne, earnest fifteen-year-old Lindsay would explain that she "liked the program a lot, but then it was gone like in five minutes." But what has lasted is her "being able to show other people that you can dress modestly, and still look good."

Now that French maid costumes (complete with garter belts) are sold to tween girls, it would seem that this message is needed now more than ever. Brands On Sale, which is based in Los Angeles, does a brisk online business selling "Child Pimp and Ho Costumes" for Halloween. Its creator, Jonathon Weeks, defends his company: "The 'Ho' costume is just there for excitement." Weeks does not indicate whose excitement he has in mind, but he

Every conversation I have with Pure Fashion divas is characterized by this tension. On the one hand, modesty appeals to them because it showcases their individuality. Today, a tastefully, attractively dressed girl is different, "someone special," as one put it. On the other hand, they would be only too happy if modesty were to become a worldwide movement. What, then, of individuality? Audrey clarifies Elizabeth's assessment with a spirited story about Junior Day:

> It's just like what Elizabeth said. Like [most girls] want their own identity but then they all wear the same clothes. At our school a week or two ago we had this big deal with Junior Day where all the juniors dress up. And there were three girls wearing the exact same dress. Like it was just ridiculous because they were complaining, "There's nowhere in town to buy a dress or a skirt!" And like one girl skipped school one day to go shopping to find a dress for Junior Day. It's all because they shop at the same stores. They want their own identity, but they're too afraid to go out to a different store and get it.

So, I tease her, girls can buy their identity at stores? No, Audrey patiently explains; the trendy stuff gets in the way of their identity: "With the trashy stuff, you're wanting to show everybody how good your body is, instead of how you are on the inside. I think it's much better to dress modest so you don't distract other people." When the girls talk about "distracting" others, I would learn, they don't mean what many people might assume—"leading men into sin" or any such thing. Rather, they don't want people to be distracted from their personalities. So the Pure Fashion divas aren't modest for the sake of being rebellious or being different, although they certainly do stick out nowadays. They believe that dressing modestly inherently showcases more individuality. And indeed, if there is one thing that comes across loud and clear, it is these girls' personalities.

Their message seems to be sinking in. Shortly after Ella Gunderson's campaign against Nordstorm, *Seventeen* magazine featured a profile of twenty-year-old "Maggie," who wrote an essay, "The Art of Modesty." "It's not easy getting guys to pay attention to your beliefs and values," she began. "But if you don't let them see too much of what's outside, then they have to pay attention to what's inside." Maggie wears:

knee-length skirts and buttoned-up shirts because I want to send the message that I'm more than my body—and I attract guys who actually respect girls! Once I got to high school, it did get harder to stick to my style and values; I saw my friends in stunning "little nothings" get tons of attention. I was athletic, smart, a singer and actress, and the editor of my school paper, but that didn't measure up to my friends' low-cut shirts. I wasn't even asked to the senior prom! But as I've watched my friends fall for guys who are only into their bodies—and then get dumped and hurt—I'm increasingly happy I've kept my standards high.

Maggie then ticked off the "tons of cool things" she's done "without compromising my values." For example, she's in a band with one of her brothers, Judd. They both sing, and Judd plays the piano while Maggie plays the bass guitar. The energy she lavishes on resisting "sexy, attention-getting clothes" is impressive—"As a young 'rocker chick,' I'm sometimes tempted." But then Maggie realizes that:

> when the show's over and I'm back at home, I'd rather have had one good conversation with a guy who's interested in who I really am . . . than have twenty guys hitting on me because of my short skirt. I think most girls feel like I do and want to be loved for the "right" reasons too. It just seems as if only girls in skimpy outfits get attention, so we tend to settle for less—both in what we wear and who we date. But what I've learned is that you don't have to settle. Since high school I've made tons of great guy friends who respect me and appreciate my personality. . . . The impression I want to leave with a guy is not "She'd make a great one-night stand . . ." but "She'd make a great wife."

This, in the same magazine that features sexy clothing, sexy hair, sex surveys, sexy phone-chat ads, and beauty tips on how to wax your pubic hair in patterns or take it completely off. Just when teen mags seemingly could not get worse, we are starting to see a different worldview.

The Pure Fashion divas do seem to be making a difference. "I actually haven't seen too much of the stomachs anymore," reports Robin Gunderson. Then she beams at her younger sister: "It has a lot to do with Ella." At first I'm not sure whether she is playfully ribbing Ella, but she seems genuinely proud of her kid sister. Not that Robin doesn't have a sense of humor about it. "I should really get discounts while shopping because I am Ella Gunderson's sister," she muses, her blue eyes dancing. "Actually, I think Ella should wear a big sign with arrows when we go shopping, and she could be, like, *'Don't make me write another letter!'*" It's not a bad idea.

But Ella hasn't let her newfound power go to her head. She is benevolent, and quick to praise stores that have featured even minor improvements: "Old Navy used to be one of the worst offenders, and now they turned around. When I last shopped there, they had some pants that fell just below the waist and some a little lower, but I don't think they had the ultralow." Then, of course, there are some stores that are simply unrepentant: "At American Eagle, you know how they have the little signs, and all the jeans on all the shelves—there were two choices, either low or ultra-low . . . nothing for me." They had better watch out now that Ella is on the case.

Two years after Ella wrote her letter, the average clothing store such as H&M now carries shirts with higher necklines and more stomach coverage, and there's no question that the Pure Fashion divas have something to do with this. Their shows might have begun in church basements and hotel meeting rooms, but today local department stores often send reps to Pure Fashion events to see what the girls consider hip and modest. And in response to Ella in particular, and the media flurry she generated, Nordstrom actually created a new category on its website for junior customers called "Modern and Modest."

So the fashion landscape is beginning to look different, but our underlying attitudes have not shifted much. I happened to interview the Gundersons just when the all-nude Hollywood issue of *Vanity Fair* hit the stands in March 2006, with all the attending controversy. Reportedly Rachel McAdams had walked out of a cover shoot when she learned that she was expected to be nude. Tom Ford, the artistic director—whose idea it was to have the all-nude issue—commented publicly that Rachel seemed "uncomfortable" during the shoot. The magazine described her as "a certain young actress" who "bowed out when the clothes started coming off," thus ruining "Ford's plan of having a gorgeous female threesome." The implication was that McAdams was a bit of a prude. Hence Ford needed to step into his own cover shoot to take her place (albeit fully clothed). Ford saw Hollywood starlets as carefree if they took off their clothes for the whole world, but for reasons that eluded many readers, he kept his own clothing on. (So did almost all the other men featured in the issue.) Yet because she refused to strip, one of our best contemporary actresses was deemed unworthy of a write-up anywhere in *Vanity Fair*'s Hollywood issue.

The Gunderson girls viewed the whole setup as unfair, and McAdams's walkout as completely justified. Robin said, "I don't think she's uncomfortable with her body! She's so comfortable she doesn't have to show it off to make herself feel comfortable." "Yeah," Ella added. "She doesn't have to prove anything." The fact that she was strong enough not to be afraid of the consequences of walking away made McAdams a true role model for the girls.

Nowhere is the politicization of dress more evident than in our deep-rooted belief that a girl or woman who undresses for the general public is "comfortable with her body," whereas one who keeps her body hidden is "ashamed of it." Thus, Halle Berry, who had said she would never do a nude scene, was roundly called "brave" when she finally bared her breasts for the movie *Swordfish* in 2001. Never mind that she got paid more to disrobe than to remain clothed; stripping is always taken to be an inherently "brave" act, at least for women. Jennifer Aniston's being named *GQ*'s first "woman of the year" was also supposedly a triumph for womankind, although predictably, unlike the "men of the year," Aniston had to be "brave" and grace the cover topless. Even top-ranking women in the chess world have posed nude for the Russian *Playboy* or *Maxim* in the United States in order to advance their careers.

To repeat: Only women are called on to prove that they are "comfortable" in this way. There is no equivalent for men. Nor does anyone ask men to prove that they are "comfortable with their romantic hopes," for example, by proposing to women they've just met off the street. Why is disrobing in public equated with "bravery" or "comfort" for women in the first place? Robin Gunderson mulls it over: "Most of the time with fashion or with bikinis on the beach, people talk about confidence, but it's not the same thing. Being comfortable is not being confident. Like, you can see people in bikinis who are not confident. They often say, 'I do not think I look good in this,' or something like that." In other words, they seem to need people to reassure them that they have a nice body: "It's like you're downgrading yourself to have other people say, 'No, you're really beautiful!'" At this, Robin flutters her eyelashes in mock pleasure, "Oh, *really?* You think I'm beau-tee-ful?" She really hams it up until all of us are laughing.

. . .

I left Seattle feeling hopeful. Then, after arriving home, I learned of a T-shirt for six-year-old girls featuring the word "Lust" at its center. Bethany, a commentator on ModestlyYours.net, reported:

> I saw a little girl's T-shirt at a store recently with various sins such as PRIDE, VANITY, etc. written on it with curly letters and then the word LUST written very boldly right in the middle. I almost cried. What kind of person would design such a T-shirt for a six-year-old and then what kind of parent would buy it? Probably the same people that wear such a T-shirt themselves. I think parents either consciously or subconsciously usually want their children to be like them. As our culture becomes coarser and coarser so do the "values" that we teach to our children.

The reality, unfortunately, is that because of encouragement by adults, if not outright pressure, the "prostitots" seem to outnumber the Pure Fashion divas ten to one. To alter this reality, alas, will require much more than fashion shows and etiquette classes. If we don't want seven-year-olds to wear hip-huggers before they have hips, then what we really need is a reversal of how we conceive female empowerment. Yet all too often, ideology collides with any commonsense discussion about appropriate dress, and anyone raising the question in public is invariably accused of "blaming the victim." But when there are actual victims, such as JonBenet Ramsey; and when killers at schools target little girls for sexual assault, one has to ask: Does barring discussion of age-appropriateness actually protect any girls, or does it simply create more victims?

When the term "muffin tops," referring to the flesh that can roll over the waistband of girls' low-rise jeans, began to gain currency, the reaction was revealing. Kate Freeborn, managing editor of *New Moon*, a feminist magazine for girls age eight to fourteen, was unsparing in her criticism:

> Anything that compartmentalizes girls and labels them according to body parts is negative. Again, we're not looking at the whole girl, but her legs, her butt, and now her muffin top. . . . These are girls whose hormones are working, whose bodies are changing in all kinds of ways.

They should have a little stomach out there. It means their bodies are doing what they're supposed to be doing.

Notice that Kate objects to the term "muffin top," but not the phenomenon. That's because it's politically incorrect to question young women's fashion choices. But what if the girls themselves don't want to be told to "have a little stomach out there"? What if, like Ella Gunderson, they are frustrated by their limited fashion options? In this light, adults' telling them to "have a little stomach out there" may not be as empowering as some people imagine.

It's unpopular to say this, but dress can turn a young woman, unwittingly, into walking entertainment for men, or it can do the opposite, and cause people to focus on her internal qualities. I have often seen a teenage girl at a bus stop or a supermarket, looking cheerfully ahead as a seventy-year-old man behind her leers at her exposed underwear or her white see-through pants. If you talk to her, she might say she's expressing her "individuality," but the man behind her happens to be noticing exactly the opposite—the body parts that all other women have. To be sure, it is one thing to be viewed as a piece of raw meat by a cute someone your own age, but it's something else to be seen that way by someone collecting Social Security. Some girls, were they to see the reaction beyond their peripheral vision, would scream "Gross!" and reconsider displaying a thong in public; others would surely maintain, "Well, that's his problem. *I'm* comfortable with my body."

Parents often share the latter view. In a book about raising confident daughters, "Clara" recounts how she bought her twelve-year-old daughter an extremely skimpy bikini, although reluctantly, since it "barely covered any piece of her anatomy." Her daughter was "furious" at the suggestion that this tiny bikini "could send the wrong message": "She didn't care what boys thought; why should she have to take them into account?" Her mother admits, "The trouble was, on the inside, I agreed with her." At the same time, "It was depressing for me to see her wanting to buy into this media image of girls as hot chicks, at twelve! She's this wonderful girl, with a great mind and funny sense of humor and a good heart, and I don't want people looking at her body and sizing her up that way. It's so demeaning!" Yet her mother posed a good question: "Why should a girl have to view her blossoming body as a liability?" Indeed, the body is an asset, not a liability (depending, I suppose, on what we do with it). But does it need to be viewed by everyone in order to prove that it is not a liability? To many, the answer is yes—but perhaps that is only because they misunderstand the concept of privacy.

Sandra Bem, a professor of gender studies at Cornell who prides herself on her progressive, egalitarian child rearing, writes about her ambivalence when her two-year-old daughter asked her to "kiss my vagina." Bem complied because she didn't want to communicate shame about the body:

> Kiss my ear, she would say, and I would. Kiss my nose, and I would . . . and so on through a whole array of body parts, including, on this particular day: kiss my vagina. Whoops, I thought to myself. This is a request I didn't anticipate, and it is definitely making me a little anxious. But, I continued in my private monologue, I don't really think there's anything wrong with the request, and I don't want Emily to think there's anything wrong with it either. So maybe I'll just go ahead and grant her request.

If she didn't, Bem was concerned that she would be "communicating" the wrong message—that genitals need to be treated differently, "as an untouchable part of her body in a way I've never done before and I don't really want to do yet." Therefore:

> I gave her a quick little peck on her vagina and we moved on. She never asked me to kiss her vagina again, so it's possible that my giving her just a quick little peck rather than a great big nuzzle communicated indirectly that I wasn't so keen on this.

Obviously, I am not an expert on the social construction of gender, but I think there is confusion here: that the only reason for privacy is being ashamed of something.

This is the same philosophy that recently brought a guest to tears on the popular makeover show *What Not to Wear*, when the hosts forced a woman to turn around and allow a camera close-up of her rear end in a new tight outfit. The woman—a mother and therapist—fought back physically so as not to submit to this shot, but to no avail; the male and female hosts literally turned her around and restrained her, so that the camera could focus on her derriere. Their explanation: Since she has such a fantastic rear end, why shouldn't the whole world see a close-up of it? By the time the camera had returned to her face, the woman was crying. The hosts—Stacy and Clinton—were baffled by her emotional reaction. Lest you think they are clueless, their subject, or victim, later tearfully returned to the camera to apologize for her problem—she deflects attention, she now realizes, and has trouble "accepting compliments."

This false philosophy of "body comfort" has also brought us a new industry: sex education for children in the early grades of school and those too young to go to school. *It's So Amazing!* by Robie H. Harris, a popular sex-ed book for seven-year-olds, is used in twenty-five countries. It teaches them all about abortion, ejaculation, and how to put on a condom—one of "the many kinds of birth control." It also teaches that "a homosexual person is sexually attracted—like a magnet—to the same sex or gender." Do seven-year-olds need to know all this? And do they need to know that "love and sex do not always go together"?

Perhaps. But what about four-year-olds? Robie Harris's new book—*It's Not the Stork!*—is for ages four and up. It features a discussion of artificial insemination along with the regular lesson about the birds and bees. Among other priceless illustrations, it includes a naked man and woman embracing under a cover (of course the woman is on top—we must be progressive). According to this book, four-year-olds should also learn details about why it's an "OK touch" to "touch or rub the private parts of your own body because it tickles and feels good."

Once upon a time, a preschool boy who pulled down his pants was thought to be a problem, but today he is considered precocious, ahead of his peers. The latest trend, as Jodi Kantor of *The New York Times* calls it, is "Sex Ed for the Stroller Set"—it is never too early to be talking about sex, because if you're *comfortable* with sex, then you ought to be talking about it. (A sex-ed volume aimed at two-and-a-half-year-olds is planned for 2008. No word about sex-ed for fetuses in utero as of yet.)

Dr. Justin Richardson, an assistant professor of psychiatry at Cornell and Columbia medical schools, told Kantor, "If you're talking about how babies are made, there's no age at which it is harmful to learn that the penis goes into the vagina."

I think "harmful" could be the wrong word here. The obvious problem with telling four-year-olds "The stork didn't bring you!" is that they have no frame of reference for what in the world you're talking about. They never thought that a stork brought them in the first place. In fact, I would bet that 90 percent of them have no concept of what a stork is. ("Tommy, it's time that you knew. The stork didn't bring you." "Fork? I'm using a fork, I'm a big boy!")

Try postponing that conversation a few years and you might have more luck. Parents understandably feel better imagining they are giving their kids a head start in life by bombarding them with sexual terminology; but I don't think this philosophy stands up to scrutiny. Experts are now rethinking the wisdom of letting children skip a grade, since a child's intelligence, it turns out, doesn't necessarily mean being socially and emotionally prepared for the next grade. Perhaps similarly, one day we will reconsider the advisability of skipping the entire latency period on the theory that society today is so sophisticated. Instead, it might make more sense to work harder to guard our children's innocence.

. . .

Perhaps we had the wrong idea about the body from the beginning. Most people think that Adam and Eve knew more after they ate from the forbidden tree, and only then realized that they were naked. But early rabbinic commentators on the Bible explain that after the sin, with evil internalized, Adam and Eve actually understood less about the world. Eating the tree's fruit introduced subjectivity.

Whereas before, Adam's and Eve's bodies and faces shone with a light that made it evident that they were spiritual beings, the moral uncertainty created by eating the fruit changed their physical appearance. Now only their faces retained a glimmering of the soul's light. (This is the origin of the idea that "the face is the seat of the soul.") Needless to say, this posed a problem: Bodies could be seen as mere animal bodies, instead of servants of the soul. To make sure they were perceived accurately—to retain their human dignity—Adam and Eve immediately covered up. They wanted to show that the most important part was still the soul, which came from God. The world may be superficial, but the right clothing keeps the focus where it should be.

Nowadays, we take pride in someone's saying, "Great body!" or "Nice legs!"—"Thanks!" we reply. But is this really liberating? We have become dependent on others' superficial assessment of us, and we begin to feel interchangeable. Perhaps it is no wonder that the most common problem facing postmodern women is low self-esteem. We are so accustomed to seeing ourselves in an external way that we are only dimly aware of having a self in the first place.

Dressing more formally indicates that what's inside is paramount. This is generally called the soul or—if you prefer—the evolutionary quirk that pricks us to posit something more than the body. In the Bible, women and religious scholars are encouraged to dress very carefully because their inner worlds are considered especially rich. Even today the general rule is still: The more respect you want, the more modestly you should dress. A wise woman won't show up at a job interview dressed like Britney Spears (unless she is interviewing for a spot in an MTV video).

Today people love to declare, "I dress for comfort." Yet it is still rare to see even the most laid-back individual walking down the street in a bathrobe. And the women who show the most skin also tend to wax the most, an activity hardly notable for its comfort. Vera Wang designs a number of beautiful sleeveless wedding gowns, but you never see her expensive creations at a royal wedding, where a modest traditional gown is always worn and conveys the great importance of the lady donning it. Can it be that princesses are generally not "comfortable with their bodies"? Probably not. The reality is that everyone dresses to project an image, not only for comfort, yet often we do not consciously stop and think of what we want that image to be.

It is certainly a given that every woman has the right to present herself as she wishes. But because we are so accustomed to political discussions, we rarely take the discussion beyond rights. When we do, we find that the inner self is a metaphor for the spiritual realm, and it needs to be protected: "The greatness of the daughter of the king is on the inside" (Psalms 45:14). Only the high priest could enter the Holy of Holies, and only on Yom Kippur. The holiest of all Jewish prayers is said in a whisper. Hanna, the mother of Samuel, prayed for a child by barely moving her lips. Initially, Eli the high priest thought she was drunk, but he later realized she was onto something. From then on, the Jews mouthed their most important prayers quietly. The most significant moments are always hidden.

Modesty is not about shame, then; it derives from knowing the true worth of something. For her doctoral dissertation at Harvard, Stephanie Wellen Levine spent a year among the Hasidic Jews in Brooklyn to see how the girls were faring, anticipating that their lives would be "the Platonic essence of feminine subjugation." Instead, to her shock, she found that these girls tended to be louder, more expressive, and more confident than their secular counterparts. "There they were—long skirts and remote synagogue seats notwithstanding—teasing, running, playing and downright enjoying; their personal styles shone through to any aware observer." Why, she asks, "would Lubavitch girls tend to hold on to the childhood voice and spirit that many in America at large seem to lose?" Levine concludes that their society, which "emphasizes internal scrutiny" and "spiritual grappling," makes the girls more confident; it even encourages the "independent personality" of the girls to "flourish beyond the levels many Americans reach."

People should feel confident that they have a right to make choices for themselves—long skirts or short—but the reality is that this is often difficult, especially for young women. Much academic ink has been spilled to uncover why previously confident girls mysteriously develop eating disorders and self-mutilating behaviors, but no one seems to know why these girls suddenly crumple the way they do. Part of the reason may be the pressure on girls to see their bodies as their truest selves. It's a path destined to lead to low self-esteem, as even the most perfect body starts to fall apart eventually. Girls correctly sense that there must be more to them than this.

I'll never forget a poll that appeared in *Marie Claire*, which found that a slight majority of American women would actually have a one-night stand with a stranger for money—57 percent. The amount for which these women would prostitute themselves was varied. Twenty-eight-year-old Jessica would need to be paid fifty dollars. "I've done it for nothing before," she explains, "so fifty dollars would be a bonus—it would cover a meal at a nice restaurant or a few CDs." Heather, also twenty-eight, an executive in public relations, was more particular: She would require a cool million. As she put it, philosophically, "I've never had a one-night stand before, but I don't think it would morally corrupt me to try it once—especially for a million dollars." Unlike the other women, she had standards, and stipulated that "any man I sleep with would have to be good at eye contact" and also "be a handsome J. Crew type."

Yet the same women were more reluctant when asked whether they would accept money to gain ten extra pounds permanently—only 41 percent would gain weight for money. To put on extra pounds would be shameful, for everyone could see that. Shari, a thirty-four-year-old nurse who wears a size two, explained her reasoning: "The ten extra pounds wouldn't pose a health risk, but it would be noticeable to others—and that would bother me. When you're thin, people offer flattering compliments like, 'Oh, you are so lucky to be that skinny.' If I gained weight, the positive feedback from others might disappear—and that could chip away at my self-esteem." Presumably, her self-esteem would vanish if she wore a size four.

That the same women do not find it "chips away at their self-esteem" to prostitute themselves suggests that they may not actually have real self-worth to lose. They are so totally dependent on others' opinions about their bodies precisely because they devalue what is happening inside their hearts. The scenario is hypothetical, to be sure, but still instructive. In many ways, fat has become the new adultery. *Sure, you can sleep with someone else's husband; but, baby, you'd better be thin.*

Part of this lopsided thinking is just human nature. We are, after all, social creatures, and although ideologically we may want to be nonjudgmental when it comes to matters of morality, we have to believe in something, and so we worship physical perfection.

Being in good shape is great, but today, superficial media messages have become toxic, filling the void where moral virtue used to be. Have you ever seen Tyra Banks berate one of her female contestants on *America's Next Top Model?* The usual infraction is looking insufficiently glamorous, but from the way she tears into these young women, you would think they had murdered her mother.

On some reality makeover shows, contestants are told in no uncertain terms that they are "ugly," and the women often have no contact with their families for months in order to totally remake their appearance. One winner of *The Swan*, DeLisa Stiles, was served with divorce papers as she was recovering from surgery (apparently she had been gone too long). Although the risk of medical complications increases with multiple plastic surgeries of the sort that are featured on these shows, the ideal of the perfect body outweighs all other considerations. No one even seems to mind that the newly plasticized women end up looking very much alike.

Manufacturers of breast implants may claim that plastic surgery boosts self-esteem, but if anything, the evidence seems to point the other way— women who have had breast implants are actually 21 percent more likely to commit suicide than women without implants. It could be that the operation attracts women who already have low self-esteem, but the implants don't seem to be helping much.

.   .   .

Today our worship of the body is so extreme that some women take it personally if men don't harass them on the street. Vicki Glembocki, writing for *Women's Health* in 2006, reported that her postpartum figure "had become invisible to construction workers." When no one complimented her backside, Vicki

> took matters into my own hands. . . . I experimented with the walk—
> a hustle one day, a sashay the next. Hair up. Hair down. One-inch heels.
> Three-inch heels. Suit. Skirt. Obscenely low-cut turquoise V-neck. I
> don't know what discouraged me more—that I'd become so desperate
> that I was prostituting my cleavage or that my prostituted cleavage
> wasn't even enough to make these men give me a second look.

The next morning, Vicki realized that she would need to confront the construction workers more directly: "I stormed up the street to the cheese shop, stopped in front of the guy with the bolt in his tongue, cocked my hip to the side and asked: 'What does a girl have to do?'" The man froze in mid-chew, uncomprehending, so Vicki realized she would need to elaborate: "What does a girl have to do to get checked out by you guys?" The construction worker claimed that she only had to walk by.

> "Walk by? Walk BY?!" I was mad now—so mad I wasn't concen-
> trating on what I was wearing or how I was walking. "Well, I WALK
> BY you every single day and you never check me out!" And then I
> unleashed—about the sashaying and the turquoise V-neck . . . and my
> waist going missing and . . . Someone walked behind me. He said some-
> thing to the boys I didn't hear that made them all nod like bobbleheads.
>
> "What did you say?" I asked, turning around.

He was an older man, perhaps a foreman, and what he said was, "Nice rack." Satisfied that her breasts had been officially praised, the author could finally return to work.

Every woman wants to be attractive, but hinging our entire self-worth on being attractive to everyone, and for our bodies alone, raises an obvious difficulty: Bodies change. We hear so much from feminists about not being "objectified by men," but we are learning that self-objectification is not a path to lasting confidence, either. As Beth Pope, from North Carolina explains to me:

> Once girls realize they don't have to be the way they are portrayed in those videos . . . All the songs sound the same, and the girls look so uncomfortable or mad half the time. They're just putting on masks. Once they see, "I don't have to be that girl in that video," they start to realize, "What else can I be?" That's one of the things I want to encourage. I've seen in my work in the inner city, when girls become more modest in dress, they become more forthright in speech.

To Beth, who is thirty-seven, "it's all about a deeper sense of self: I don't have to compare my butt to your butt to get his attention." She observes:

> You know, your Baby Phat is going to turn into baby fat, and it's not going to be pretty. But if there's something beyond the bod that captivates them, then you have a good chance. I've seen with my own eyes that once girls start putting more clothes on, they start talking more. It opens you up, because you're not worried anymore about comparing your butt to her butt. You're free to be confident in who you are; you can say what's on your mind. And you want someone who values that, because guess what. Your butt is going to be hitting the floor after awhile, so quit looking at it—it's just going to get wider.

In addition to making me crack up, Beth makes a valid point. Modesty is not about hiding your talents; quite the opposite, in fact. As I once heard Tali Gordon, a high school student from Los Angeles, put it, "Modesty is about having an internal approach to life, living life based on what's important to you."

Mary-Margaret Helma, a twenty-one-year-old college senior at Duquesne University in Pittsburgh, once worked with a job-prep organization program for underprivileged youth, Breachmenders International. The director had one particularly interesting rule: All the kids had to wear modest, appropriate business clothing to their jobs. "I held a dinner at Duquesne to help raise 500 dollars for gift cards for these kids so they could buy these clothes for their jobs," she said, and "the kids go on to colleges and successful careers. They see from an early age that what they wear matters and that in turn, they matter. They see for themselves that they are worth

too much to be dressing in any degrading way." Mary loves vintage clothing and even sews and sells her own modest clothing from Regency-
inspired patterns.

Those making modest clothing tend to be conservative, but many of the
liberal young women I spoke with were also eager to move on from showcasing their bodies as the primary thing. One such woman confessed to me
that she and her friends were getting sick of *The Vagina Monologues*, which
they had all seen many times in school. (Students today see Eve Ensler's
play the way those of a previous generation used to see *A Christmas Carol*.)
"I've seen it several times at school, and . . ." she trails off, because she is a
nice person and is clearly trying not to sound judgmental: "Maybe there are
older women out there who benefit from it and need to hear it, but it doesn't
really speak to [younger women]." I ask her if she thought it was embarrassing and she replies quickly, "No, I didn't think it was embarrassing, I
thought it was . . . cheesy. And most of my friends thought so, too. I think
young women need to hear the message that they are more than their bodies." (The performance includes a woman saying "It was ME, my vagina: it
was who I was," and women chanting various slang terms for female genitalia. Women's centers at several schools such as Boise State University pass
out vagina-shaped lollipops, while other schools, such as Arizona State University, float forty-foot inflatable vaginas on campus.)

The Vagina Monologues raises money for a good cause—to stop violence
against women—but some coeds are beginning to wonder if chanting slang
terms for female genitalia is really helping. At Saint Louis University, Katy
Willis and three friends—Maria Thorson, Jessica Navin, and Kathleen
Brennan—decided to organize a protest against *The Vagina Monologues*
and present a rival cultural event that would celebrate "the true mystery
and beauty of the whole female person instead of just focusing on her body
parts."

Their evening of music, art, dance, drama, and poetry "celebrated the
personhood of the woman and called for respect for her." They also raised
money for their local Birthright Crisis Pregnancy Center. The depth of the
performances was impressive; it included Marian hymns, comic songs, and
heartfelt verse. In 2006, the program also featured traditional Indian dancers
and the campus's all-female a cappella group. Katy's challenge to Eve Ensler is direct: "We think that anyone who opposes violence against women
should see that vulgarizing sexuality is itself a kind of violence to the value
of a person."

The majority of young women I spoke with actually agreed with Katy—though from the monopoly of *The Vagina Monologues* on campus, one would not expect this. It made me reflect on a comment Ella Gunderson had made about people's hidden attitudes. The chief thing she had learned from the reaction to her letter, Ella told me, was "don't wear things or do things just because of your friends." But, I asked her, what about girls who don't have the confidence to take on a public company as she had? Even so, girls could still do a lot: "If you don't want to go against a trend, just maybe only talk to one person and then you might find out someone else agrees with you. Just tell them that they're not the only ones, you know."

The only ones? Hardly. Thanks in no small measure to Ella and the other Pure Fashion divas, in just seven years I have seen modesty go from frumpy to the latest thing. "Now my daughters talk down about the girls who show too much," Wanda McDaniels told Ruth LaFerla of *The New York Times,* who wondered why "in a country addled by sex," knee-length skirts and twinsets are now the rage among teenagers. As seventeen-year-old Ashley Orfus explained to a quizzical reporter in 2004, around the time the tide began to turn, modesty "is very empowering for kids my age. You don't need to show your belly button to succeed in the world."

In Toronto, sadly oblivious to this trend, two teenage girls sashay past me wearing midriff-baring shirts and skintight pants. We all end up on the same bus, so I ask if I may interview them. "Sure," they chime in unison, casually popping their gum as if paparazzi follow them all the time. They are both fifteen, and they have just come from the beach, they tell me. They're on their way to the mall now to go shopping, so it seems the right time to quiz them about new trends. Well, midriff-exposing tops aren't "in" anymore, they volunteer, without batting an eyelash. "They're not?" I say, surprised. I feel it's rude to point out that their stomachs are visible this very moment, so I just nod politely. Perhaps they didn't realize they had put on cropped halter tops that morning. "Yes, you know, like, the long polka dot shirts? They're very 'in' now," they continue, seemingly without any self-awareness. "OK," I begin slowly, not sure of how to broach the topic of their clothing. "I'm taking notes here. *In the summer of 2006, polo shirts are 'in.'* . . . Thank you, OK—good. So do you guys see yourselves as . . . rebelling against this new trend?" They look at me as if I'm batty, and exchange glances. How could they resist a new trend? Why would they resist a new trend? The blonde rolls her eyes and explains to me, patiently, as if to a small child, "Nooo! The polo shirts, with like the V-necks and the collars? We're going to the mall to buy some now."

There was only one responsible thing to do, which was to let the girls get off the bus and buy those shirts as soon as possible.

HOW TO PUT ON YOUR OWN FASHION SHOW

Want to show off some modest fashions you've scoped out? The comedian and model Jen Dziura gives me the skinny on putting on your own fabulous production.

For a local production, six to eight models will be about right. Usually they do at least one outfit change, so two outfits per model will be twelve to sixteen. Some models might walk more than others—for instance, if you only have one plus-size model, she might go three times and someone else might only go once. This is OK. You just work out ahead of time who walks, in what order, wearing what, and post the list on a wall right in the place where the models will look before they walk down the "runway." For instance: "Melissa—red dress," or "Megan—blue tunic with suede skirt." Just make sure nobody's name is repeated without enough time for that person to change.

Arrange things so that the hardest outfits to get into come early in the show, so that a model's switch from first to second outfit can be done very quickly.

You don't need a real "runway" or anything on the floor. Just practice with the models where they should walk so everyone sees every angle of their outfits. For instance, one might walk from a back room, down an imaginary aisle—pausing halfway to do a little (modest!) pose with hand on hip, smiling—walk to the end, pause and smile, turn halfway around, pause and smile, turn and walk back.

The difficult thing is always getting the models to walk slowly enough, or the whole show is over in five minutes. Get them to practice, and tell them that they need to walk slowly, and also, when they stop to pose, that they need to stay there a minute. Tell them to imagine they have to get their pictures taken two or three different times on each walk down the runway. (You might have an actual photographer at the end of the "runway." Each model walks to the end of the runway and everyone watches as a photographer catches a few shots—this looks kind of official and glamorous, and of course everyone will want photos.)

The second before each model steps backstage, the next model starts. Think of this like a very slow relay race.

Music could be anything; just put someone in charge of it so that there's no uncomfortable "moment of silence" in between songs when someone's on the runway. For a modesty show, personally I think something like a little Doris Day or Edith Piaf—a retro, 1940s feel—would be both fashionable and appropriate.

As for the outfits, you could ask the models to bring any modest outfits they are especially fond of (someone with a modest wedding gown or formal dress might enjoy a chance to show it off again); but, yes, a store can let you borrow outfits. Ideally, the person from the store (if it's an independent local store) would also bring the outfits and decide what goes on which model, etc. (that is, serve as a stylist). You would offer all kinds of publicity, including printed credits on any announcements and advertisements, and spoken credits while the models walk.

Make the models bring their own shoes—generally we'd ask a model to bring black heels (no chunky heels) and something neutral (usually strappy heeled sandals that are inconspicuous and could go with anything).

There should be an announcer. That person says something like, "Melissa is wearing a cowl-neck wool winter dress from [name of store], with round-toed pumps from [store] and Melissa's own vintage earrings." The announcer should be someone who can ad-lib a bit, so maybe later while the model's walking, the announcer might say, "Wool is a great winter fabric . . ." or "This style of dress looks great with or without a belt," etc. The idea is to sloooow each model down. What seems like an eternity to her is generally about ten seconds in reality, so the more talking is happening, the more reminder she has that she has to stay out there.

Sometimes professional makeup artists and hairstylists will do fashion shows free to get credits and photos for their portfolios, but that's more likely in a big city where there is a fashion industry. You might try the people at salons who do hair and makeup for weddings; they might want publicity. But, honestly, I think that those people might go a bit overboard. For a modest fashion show, you could get by just fine with the models doing their own hair and makeup (and bringing a friend or a mother into the back area to help).

Have a staging and changing area set up, with mirrors and electrical outlets (and a clear marker somewhere stating "No men beyond this point!"), and make everybody get there a solid four hours ahead of time.

After all this, here's how the overall show might go.

An announcer at a microphone says some opening words, thanks everyone, etc. Someone else starts the music. Announcer announces each outfit as each model comes out and does a slow walk through the runway area and back. When all the models are done, you can bring them all back out to be seen together. Everyone always likes this (and it is great for photos).

Doing a fashion show brunch is fabulous. After the show everyone could mingle and have something to eat.

It's usually very easy to get volunteers for a fashion show (lots of women want a chance to be a model for a day), so put your volunteers to work. You can get everything but food free, so your costs should be minimal and incidental.

Whew!

CHAPTER SEVEN

People-Pleasing Bad Girls and Rebellious Good Girls

Dear Dr. Sylvia:
My nine-year-old daughter flirts with her uncle, her dad, and other adult men. They find it very annoying, as she won't leave them alone. I don't believe she's the victim of sexual abuse. I think she idolizes the blatant sexuality in the media and thinks that by flirting she'll gain approval. Do you have any suggestions as to how we can correct her behavior?

—from Sylvia Rimm's *Growing Up Too Fast*, 2005

When girls are flirting with their own fathers, child psychologists like Sylvia Rimm are understandably concerned.

In search of a solution, Dr. Rimm looked at headlines from *Seventeen* magazine in the 1970s ("How to Beat the Gossip Game," "Which Is Best—Oldest, Middle, Youngest Child?" "Prize Fiction," "What Your Voice Tells about You," "Poems and Reports from Worldwide Places"), and she discovered something odd. The headlines from the 1970s were much more interesting than those in *Teen* magazine in 2004 ("The Sexiest Hairstyles; The Sexiest Jeans," "On Girls, Geeks, and Going All the Way," "438 Ways to Meet Tons of Guys," "Turn-On Secrets He'll Never Tell You," "476 Ways to Look Sexy for Spring"). Rimm concluded that "the premature emphasis on using sex to attract boys" in girls' magazines today, meant to sweeten up the reading, can actually be stifling to a girl's self-image.

After reading Rimm's book, I flip through the Girl Scout catalog, hoping for an infusion of wholesomeness. That's when I see how much has changed since I was a Scout in the 1980s. I squint hard to see if I am reading correctly: There is a badge called "From Fitness to Fashion." It's an appliqué of a little black dress sewn next to tiny barbells, and it annoys me for some reason. I figure there's plenty of time to worry about the "little black dress" when girls grow up—do they really need to start quite so young?

But I don't want to rush to judgment. I know from experience that some patches grace the catalog but aren't important in the scheme of things. So I log on to the Girl Scouts' website to learn more, and I can hardly believe it. "From Fitness to Fashion" is prominently featured on the site under the American flag badge and the Girl Scout pin itself. It is apparently the patch of all patches, the über-patch, accompanied by this text: "The insignia on a girl's uniform are a record of her adventures and accomplishments as a Girl Scout." It's not clear how knowing how to wear a short black dress constitutes an accomplishment, and if it were indeed testimony to an "adventure," I would be very concerned.

The adventure continues with Girl Scouts' online magazine, *Girls' Life*, which offers a pull-down menu of "Style and Beauty," "Sneaky Crush Secrets," "Guy Shockers," "Ready Set Kiss," and "Boobs: An Owner's Guide"—you get the idea. The in-house expert, Carol, offers detailed advice on how to flirt:

> Once you do decide which specific guys you'd like to flirt with, get out there and smile and say hi and make eye contact and introduce yourself and give compliments. Picture dogs. Don't we all kind of prefer the tail-wagging sweet ones rather than the jumping, slobbering, scratching kind that sniff where they shouldn't? Bottom line: Be patient, not overeager, and things will work out.

Not really liking the comparison of girls to dogs, I turned to the only material on the page that seems substantive: "Seven Ways to Be a Daredevil," only to find, once more, a lesson in flirting (courageous flirting this time).

Finally, the top four quizzes in their "Fun and Games" section: "R U Irresistable?" [*sic*]; "R U a Flirt?"; "R U Body Confident?" and "R U Dateable?" These are all labeled "personality quizzes" for girls. Mind you, the old personality types had their limitations, too (but at least a choleric individual could have spelled "irresistible").

By contrast, the Boy Scouts' online *Boys' Life* website features games (archery, snowboard, and bowling challenge games), skills such as how to tie difficult knots, and the opportunity to peek at the "treasures of the Sierra." Not a word about girls appears anywhere.

You may protest that things were always this way—girls scouted boys while boys scouted the world—but that may be a bit too facile. Joy, sixty-three, a family therapist in Chicago, recalls, "When I was a Girl Scout, we rolled bandages for the Highland Park hospital or learned about nature, went on hikes, shellacked a gift box for pencils, helped older people across the street. It was a very big deal to be a Girl Scout. You were proud of it." Boys were not even in the picture.

Society is of course different now. The concept of "girl power" is at its height. But boys can be forgiven for thinking that the world revolves around their likes and dislikes, because, well, sometimes it seems to. In 2006, a report in the *Journal of Adolescent Health* found that when 425 ninth-grade students responded to an open-ended question about reasons for having oral sex, girls were most likely to list a desire to improve a relationship, whereas boys were most likely to mention pleasure. This confirmed a study published in 2000 by the Alan Guttmacher Institute that girls provide oral sex because they want to be popular or "make boys happy." Often a girl doesn't even feel she has the right to ask a boy she's with whether he has an STD. (This is unfortunate, given that girls bear the brunt of complications of STDs.)

At least as bad as all this are the girls who feel that they have to smooch other girls to entertain boys. A high schooler named Tiffany told a reporter for ABC's *Primetime* that boys at parties "they're like, 'Oh, my God, like I have to see two girls make out or I'm going to *die*,'" she said. "And girls will just be like, 'All right.'" Reporting on the same "craze" in *Salon* in 2006, Whitney Joiner found that none of the high school or college women actually enjoyed making out with other young women. Yet with boys increasingly under the influence of pornography, it had become a necessary way to get boys' attention. Julie, a twenty-year-old student at Northeastern University, told her, "It's definitely a good, well-worn, tried-and-true route to hooking up with a guy that you want. . . . It's showing him that you can be open, and if that's what he likes, that's what you'll do. Which makes him think you're better to sleep with than the 100 other girls in the room with you." Here, Joiner posed a key question: "But if these young women are not actually into kissing their girlfriends, why do they feel they need to do it to prove how sexual they are? Why can't a girl attract a boy by being her intelligent, hot self?" Julie responded that being able to attract a boy long-term is actually very difficult, and painted a picture of desperation:

"A lot of girls who do want long-term boyfriends will still settle for the hookup because it gives them that temporary feeling of being taken care of and being close to someone," Julie says. "It's sad to see that this is what it's come to—that guys will raise the bar and girls will scramble to meet it. Women just want to know what they have to do to get these guys to fall in love with them. And if guys will take them home after kissing a girl, then that's what they're going to do, because it's better than going home alone." She pauses. "Now that I'm saying it out loud, I'm like, Huh—that's a sad way of going about it."

Doing one thing you don't want, in order to get another thing you don't want. It's no wonder that these young women find it challenging to be themselves when they finally manage to take their liaisons home. Robin Sawyer, a fifty-five-year-old health teacher from the University of Maryland, told *The Washington Post* he was shocked to find out that 90 percent of his female students were only pretending to be sexually satisfied in their encounters. "Didn't want to hurt his feelings," explained one female student. (Or, to put it differently, "Didn't want to get dumped.")

In Montreal, a twelve-year-old girl told her fourteen-year-old friend Léa Clermont-Dion that she had given a guy oral sex. So Léa asked her, "Why did you do that?" and she said, "To please the guy." Wise beyond her years and politically conscious, Léa became livid:

It was to please? For hundreds of years feminists have fought to eliminate the phenomenon of "we serve men, we please men." Girls think that they're empowered in all this. They think it's their choice to degrade themselves for men. Is it really their choice? . . . I see a certain sexual submission. Before there was a submission period; now it's sexual submission and we don't even realize it.

If a hookup miraculously does lead to a relationship for a short time, many women have the idea that they must hang on for dear life, even if the guy doesn't treat them very well. A twenty-one-year-old caller nervously asks Dr. Joy Browne, on a radio show on WOR, what to do about her live-in boyfriend and fiancé, who is a "great guy" although he regularly asks her to "take care of herself" before he will condescend to be physically intimate

with her. Dr. Browne advises the young woman that with the right book and perhaps a video, this man can get over his "shyness" or whatever it is that's bothering him. Or better yet, if he has no interest in a mutually satisfying relationship, why not just leave?

A coed at Duke named Allison explained to Janet Reitman of *Rolling Stone* that the situation with her boyfriend "made me very uncomfortable and unhappy." Yet "if I didn't do [whatever he wants] and he broke up with me for some reason, two days from now he'd have somebody else. That's just how it works." Her friend Kasey observes, "You're just scared."

Reports are pouring in from all sides, and we can only wonder: Why, in a time of liberation, should girls and women live in abject terror of asserting themselves in relationships? Why, in the year 2007, should women's focus be completely on pleasing young men? In 1936, a group of coeds at the University of Michigan rated their prospects as either "A—smooth; B—OK; C—pass in a crowd; D—semigoon; or E—spook." Conversational banter and lots of flowers came well before sexual favors. The men had to prove themselves worthy of women. From a historical perspective, what's terribly ironic is that we thought that we had got rid of the "pleaser" when we got rid of the good girl.

. . .

The notion of "goodness" for girls was jettisoned partly for a valid reason: In the past, it had been taken to a stifling extreme. Professor Rosemary Agonito, who grew up in the 1950s and whose Italian immigrant parents had not wanted a girl, is well qualified to explain the problem:

> The "Nice Girl" Syndrome: Being a "Nice Girl" means putting ourselves last. It means pleasing others at all costs, accommodating their needs and wants—even when their agendas harm us. By striving always to be liked and accepted (which psychologists have long known to motivate women), we suppress our own desires and feelings, our own belief systems and values, to accommodate those of others. As Nice Girls we don't want to hurt anybody's feelings, so we don't talk back and we don't fight back, even when under siege. We go along; we take it. . . . Long-suffering and uncomplaining, the Nice Girl is ever dutiful. But being dutiful is defined as playing by somebody else's rules, rules that we had no say in creating.

Agonito's novel solution is for women to arrange their legs far apart at work, to "spread out in space like men," and even to put their feet up on the furniture whenever the opportunity presents itself. In short, to not be "nice."

Yet, significantly, this is not really the type of woman who replaced the stereotypical good girl. Agonito is concerned about girls' "passivity and deference," but today's girls are deferential to an entirely opposite script. In jettisoning the nice or good girl, we did not find in her place an army of schoolgirls putting their feet up on their desks. To be sure, girls certainly have become meaner—to other girls (see Chapter Nine)—and their eyes may be heavily lined with kohl, but they do not seem to be any more independent of boys. To the contrary, girls today are consumed by pleasing boys to a degree unknown in yesteryear. In April 2006, a thirteen-year-old girl in Zion, Illinois, reported being gang-raped by seven boys, but then later told the police that she had decided her experience was "consensual"— even though all the boys involved were strangers to her. (Only the eldest boy, seventeen, was charged with any crime.) Consent, while crucial, turns out not to be a sufficient guarantor of bodily dignity. If a girl believes that her reason for being is to please boys, and as many boys as possible, then the concept of consent actually becomes meaningless. To truly consent, one must first realize that one actually has a self. Today, unfortunately, this is no small matter. Many girls learn to preen and to please boys before they discover their own ideals and emotional needs.

Dave, a twenty-eight-year-old software developer on the East Coast, reflects on the imbalance between girls and boys at his high school:

> There was this guy—he was three years younger than me in school— and one day he asked this other ninth-grader if she'd perform oral sex on him. They were just friends and not in a relationship. Well, she said no, and then he said, *"Please?"* So she said, "Well . . . OK." It became a joke, that he just had to say "Please?" Another guy I knew would give pot to girls who performed oral sex on him, but it wasn't even real weed, that was the funny thing. It was fake, but they didn't know.

Or maybe they did know, but they just didn't care. Certainly others did not. "Her name was Miranda," Dave continues, referring to a different twelve-year-old girl.

We were all fourteen and playing video games at my friend's house, and somehow they decided to get oral sex from her under the covers, while I was there. His mother was in the other room. And then she finished and she was like, "Next!" And I didn't touch her. I was in front of the door on the chair; I just stayed there and said no. The whole thing made me very uncomfortable. Even for a guy who was interested, it was just too gross. Then, a few months later I found out she slept with my three friends: the same guy from the bed, and his friend, then this fat kid who lost his virginity. I started to feel sorry for her and so later I talked to her and [she] said she was doing it because that was what she did for her guy friends. Eventually the school therapist found out about it and had to report it because she was twelve, but nothing happened with the boys or anything. It still kind of amazes me that she thought she had to fool around with all these guys just because she was friends with them.

After a study published in 2006 in *Pediatric and Adolescent Medicine* revealed that 40 percent of teenage girls felt pressured into sex, the psychologist Neil Bernstein told the *Today* show that it was a "real wake-up call." "Girls are having a lot of trouble managing difficult situations—we've got to take these things seriously." In discussing girls' concern that boys would get angry if denied sex, Bernstein referred to the concept of "pleasing" directly: "When she's in a difficult situation, teach [your daughter] to say no. We're not in this world to please other people; they have to think independently, and be prepared for situations that arise."

As my defense of romantic hope in Chapter 4 should make clear, I am hardly arguing that girls should reject boys altogether. But wanting to build a life with someone is not the same as neurotic pleasing behavior, which usually derives from insecurity. Real love is a desire to give; to create a bond and a unit that is more than the sum of its parts. That comes from strength.

Setting high standards for your romantic life takes a lot of confidence, especially today. In *Girls Will Be Girls,* a book about how to "raise confident and courageous daughters," Dr. JoAnn Deak and Teresa Barker cast themselves in the tradition of Carol Gilligan. Gilligan "was the first to coin the phrase 'tyranny of niceness' to describe the way our culture stunts girls' emotional growth by training them to be pleasers, shaping their behavior, their expectations, and even their life dreams to accommodate or please others." Deak and Barker remind us, "Throughout history and well into the 1950s, girls were raised to be nice this way, to be compliant, and to devote their talents cheerfully as directed at home."

Yet unremarked by the authors is the fact that all their contemporary examples illustrate pleasing of a totally different and nondomestic variety:

The interview that was the epitome of the overpleasing girl was from Kim, a savvy and sophisticated seventeen-year-old senior. The interview question asked each girl to think of a time when she had faced a moral dilemma and describe what she did about it. Kim had a hard time coming up with an example, but then picked one she said "was kind of a moral dilemma because I was faced with deciding whether to do something that was wrong or not." She went on to talk about how she and her friends spent most weekends partying, going to friends' houses, drinking beer, having a good time. One Saturday night, the boy she was dating had had too much to drink at the party. As he staggered to the car, she knew he shouldn't drive. . . . She knew she should not go with him, but she just couldn't bring herself to say anything. She got in the car, and away they drove, careening off the road several times, but eventually making it home. When I asked Kim why she did this, she said that she hadn't wanted to upset him. "Even at the risk of losing your own life, you were willing to get in the car so he wouldn't be upset?" I asked. "Yes," she answered, without hesitation. "Would you do the same thing again?" I asked. Another yes.

Kim's story is actually quite cheery compared with Candace's. Deak recently attended a training camp for women who were to ride bicycles across the United States, and that is where she met Candace, the first woman to cross the United States with a hand-pedaled bicycle. Having read Candace's biographical sheet before coming to the camp, Deak knew that her physical handicap was due to an accident. After they had spent time together, Candace felt comfortable enough to tell Deak what that accident was:

She was a card dealer in Lake Tahoe at the time. As she said, "long fingernails, short skirts, and lots of makeup!" Her boyfriend and his buddy came to pick her up one early morning—3:00 or 4:00 A.M.—to go for a ride in the hills north of Lake Tahoe. As she started to get in the little sporty car, she noticed that he had been drinking heavily, and could barely talk or keep his eyes focused. She told him that she would drive and he could just rest. He said no, he wanted to drive and he was just fine. His buddy added in a taunting voice, "If you're so scared, just sit in the back—and put on your seat belt—we're going for a wild ride!" Candace stayed where she was, up front, and didn't put on a seat belt. She didn't want to seem the prude, didn't want to be a spoilsport, didn't want to ruin their fun. As they were rounding one of the big curves in the hills, her boyfriend lost control and the car rolled over. In the force of the impact, she hit her spine on the door and it snapped. The two guys suffered only scratches. In adjusting to her new life as a paraplegic, she jokes now, she eventually had to lose the long nails and high heels—they dragged on the ground from the seat of her new set of wheels, her wheelchair.

Note how the compliant girl, the pleaser, is the one who doesn't want to be a "prude" or a "spoilsport"—in other words, the good "bad" girl is so deeply ingrained in our cultural consciousness that in many cases living down to bad expectations is more important than one's very life. A good bad girl must be emotionally detached and hip—even if it kills her.

In sum, when compared with the stifling situation of having to constantly look good and make boys feel good, the old challenge of being good becomes more appealing with each passing year.

Consider *Gossip Girl,* the popular young adult novel series, whose characters are depicted entirely by looks, possessions, and how jaded they can act in their sexual encounters. We are told that Blair Waldorf, for one, was born and raised on New York's Upper East Side, is the sole owner of a tropical island, and "has worn a Rolex since sophomore year and is totally chummy with her stylist at the exclusive Red Door Salon." But the heart of the matter is that "she's got closets full of Chanel" and "diamond Bulgari earrings" to match, and "She's not afraid to play dirty to get what she wants."

This distinguishes Blair from "tall, blond, and drop-dead gorgeous" Serena van der Woodsen. "The fashion gods are always winking at Serena." Whether she's strutting down the runway or up Fifth Avenue, Serena looks effortlessly put together day in and day out." Like Blair, "she has a scandalous streak that can't be concealed behind a pair of Gucci aviators." This would include "a love triangle with her best friend's boyfriend" and "modeling for a racy photo that ended up plastered on every bus in Manhattan."

Once while waiting at a pediatrician's office, I made the mistake of asking a teenage girl reading a *Gossip Girl* book what she liked about the novels. I hadn't picked them up at that point, so though I gathered that the girl was not reading about bunnies, I didn't yet realize that the series was basically the Marquis de Sade for teens. I had, however, noticed throngs of teens toting the books around, so I innocently wanted to know what the big deal was. "I dunno," said the girl nervously. She was seated with her mother, and as her eyes darted back and forth, from me to her mother, then back, I became puzzled. "I'm just happy she's reading!" chirped the mother proudly, mussing her daughter's hair. I wouldn't be too sure about that, Ma. Then I read one of the tomes myself, and I got it—it was abject fear she had been telegraphing: *"You've read them, haven't you? Are you going to tell my mom what's between the covers?"*

Not to worry, my chickadee: Your secret is safe—until now, anyway. Ultimately it was not the casual sex, the crudeness, or the cynicism that shocked me in these young adult novels. It was the extreme difficulty of telling the characters apart. I had never had a reading experience like this in my entire life. Only by the middle of the novels could I divine who was who, and even then, only through the women's connection to the men— who tended to have at least a whiff of individuality. In explaining why "Serena" is different, for example, the *Gossip Girl* website offers this fair summation: "No one else we know . . . has been linked with everyone from rock stars to movie stars on Page Six." The path to uniqueness is by sleeping around while wearing the latest brands.

A quiz on the site is chock-full of probing questions, to better assess which character the fans most resemble. Do we favor linen pants or pencil capris? Strappy metallic stilettos or dainty kitten heels? Fishnets or vintage? Bobbi Brown makeup or Stila? Is our fave accessory a black leather cuff or sunglasses? My favorite date outfit is . . . zzzzzzz . . . Ooops, sorry about that. I must have fallen asleep there. Yes, all twelve of the questions, mind-numbingly, are related to fashion.

Finally, I understood why I was having so much trouble distinguishing between the characters in the books. It's not that the author is a poor writer; it's because the bad-girl ideal quashes personality with astonishing force. In real life, for example, when Koren Zailckas stops drinking, she discovers that she has nothing in common with her best friend. It dawns on her that she's been conforming to a "beer-ad version of herself":

> I agree to drink beer from a funnel, even though I know the boy channeling it through will pour too fast, and I will end up wearing the thick tar of beer and wet sand. When Natalie and the other girls strip down to their underwear, I do, too. . . . At the time, I write off these behaviors as a need to adapt. I don't want to stand out as a high-school girl, the type of baby who can't keep up with buxom sorority girls from Southern universities. . . . I concede to shifting my personality, just a hair, to observe the standards I think the situation calls for. . . . The process will be so incremental that I'll have no gauge of how much it will change me. I will wake up one day in my twenties like a skewed TV screen on which the hues are all wrong. My subtleties will be exaggerated and my overtones will be subdued. My entire personality will be off-color.

One fifteen-year-old girl I interviewed—whom I will call Zoe, since her remark is sure to anger some people—told me, "It's a generalization, but I've seen that most of the bad girls lack personality. I'm not trying to compliment myself; but in our group—I don't know—we were asking people and like a lot of people tell me, 'You have one of the best personalities I've ever met in someone.' And I truly think that girls that are quote-unquote 'Bad,' and feel they have to do things, they don't have personalities. They're like, 'Oh, hiiiiiiiiiiiiiii!' " She then does an imitation of a flirtatious girl acting phony. We then talk about how everyone has a unique personality, and Zoe quickly agrees. She then decides that what she really means is "not that they don't have personalities, of course," but that what they really want and believe is covered up by "this obsession with making the guys happy."

"Naomi," a young mother from the South, shows me just how right Zoe is. For her the "bad girl ideal" was extremely stifling:

> What I learned is that people treat you the way you portray yourself. Don't be surprised if he treats you like a toy if you look and act like one. After I graduated from university I stopped what I was doing and got dressed, and—literally—people took me more seriously overnight. I was so busy making sure that [the guys] liked me and they would call me back and enjoyed their time with me that I didn't worry about me.

It's so confusing and it does things to your mind. At a certain time you're never you. I couldn't say, "This isn't who I was raised to be," because my mom was saying it was OK [to sleep around]. Well, I finally figured out that I was wet, and I got out of the rain.

Actress Lindsay Lohan experienced a similar epiphany at the end of 2006, chalking up her late-night partying and "getting sick" to her desire to please. "I'm a people-pleaser," she disclosed to *InStyle* magazine. "But you can't always make everyone happy."

If today's bad-girl idols admit that they are pleasers, it makes sense that the fictional characters modeled after them in today's teen novels are so hard to keep straight. In the pathological aim to please, one's unique identity becomes compressed.

In contrast to the girls populating today's teen novels, whose characters I could barely keep straight while I was reading, the girls populating the novels I read fifteen years ago are still vivid in my mind. Anne of Green Gables, Jo March, Elizabeth Bennet: Each has her own distinct wit and outspokenness. And yet it is probably not entirely fair to compare today's bad-girl lit with the enchanted world of earlier classics. It's more useful, perhaps, to compare the *Gossip Girls* series with the novels of L. T. Meade (Elizabeth Thomasina Meade Smith), who was born in 1854 and churned out over 280 novels. She lived only to age sixty, so her novels were probably written quickly, much like today's young adult novels. But one difference is that whereas today's teen novels idealize the promiscuous, jaded girl, Meade's novels, though also didactic, inculcated a desire to be virtuous. (The bookseller who sold me these books had them filed under "Strange Grandmother Books.")

With titles such as *Wild Kitty* and *A Very Naughty Girl*, Meade introduced her readers to girls who were "naughty" in their own particular way, but who always, by the end of the novel, reformed. The plot required a very delicate operation; the character defect was expunged, but the girl's spirit remained in full force. Thus does the orphan Flower, excitable and disruptive to her adopted family, give up playing family politics after her adopted father goes blind. Once her pettiness is shed, she reveals her noble heart, which was there all along. Similarly, dreamy Angel falls off a horse, becomes paralyzed, and then discovers how superficial her previous life has been. Formulaic as her work sounds, Meade managed to paint portraits of girls that were vibrant and compelling. And unintentionally funny as some of the novels were—since many seem to culminate in a bump on the head—the characters are thoroughly engaging and distinct.

My favorite was Kathleen in *The Rebel of the School,* who started a society called the Wild Irish Girls to meet in secret and do terribly wicked things, such as attend an opera in London on their own. Kathleen bribes her little friends with special pins and trinkets from a wealthy relative, and before long brings the entire Shirley School to its knees. Her friend Ruth, who is poor, knows all about the secret society (of which she is no longer a member) but, out of loyalty to Kathleen, will not divulge the details to the schoolmistresses even though she is threatened with expulsion. Eventually, recognizing that Ruth's family depends on her scholarship to escape from poverty, Kathleen does the right thing and promises to dissolve her little bickering society of Wild Irish Girls. This is a victory not just for the school but for Kathleen herself, who had been so selfish that upon her arrival she locked the daughter of her boarding family out of the girl's own room. Kathleen always made a point of observing that her boarding mother was "tired," but she never connected her fatigue to her own impossible behavior. Here is one priceless scene:

"It is her room as much as yours. Let her in at once, my dear," [the boarding mother] demands.

"I am very sorry, darling Mrs. Tennant, but I am really privately engaged in my own half of the room. I am not interfering with Alice's."

"But you see, Kathleen, she can't get in her half."

"The door is in my half, you know," said Kathleen very meekly, "so I don't see that she has any cause to complain. I am awfully sorry; I will be as quick as I can."

"You annoy me very much. You make me very uncomfortable by going on in this extremely silly way, Kathleen."

"I will darn some more socks for you, darling, tired pet," whispered Kathleen coaxingly. "I really am awfully sorry, but there is no help for it. I must finish my own private affairs in my own half of the room."
She retreated from the door, and the scratching of the pen continued.

When Kathleen gets over her self-centeredness, as with all Meade's wayward girls who turn good, it's clear that she becomes more herself, not less so. Even the somewhat ridiculous, statistically improbable bump on the head has its rationale. Meade's heroines seem to suffer concussions as often as the *Gossip Girl* teens go shopping. It's a literary device perfectly suited for bringing out profound home truths—of the sort that are needed today perhaps more than ever, since they are not necessarily taught at home. A girl who had time to think was one who realized that we are more than just our physical bodies, and that idle gossip can truly destroy people's lives. Now, I'm not saying we should bump girls on the head so that they will appreciate what life is about. But even the worst of these novels was about the best of things. They were elevating to the same extent that today's young adult novels are depressing.

Consider *The Virginity Club,* one of the tamer contemporary young adult novels. Our heroine, Mandy, quickly discovers that remaining true to herself requires sleeping with her boyfriend. She will not bend to the pressure to join her school's virginity club, which offers a college scholarship (athough the idea of a high school today awarding a scholarship for "purity" is far-fetched). By the end of the novel, Mandy knows what's important: "Her second sexual encounter with Eric had gone much better than the first and since then, whenever they got around each other, well, let's just say they made up for lost time." Mandy also ends up at Princeton, but why dwell on that when there is serious stuff to be reckoned with? "Mandy had never thought she was capable of becoming a sex goddess, but she kind of was."

Formerly, being true to oneself meant doing the difficult thing over the easy thing, being true to one's soul or conscience. Now it always means, at a young age, releasing your inner "sex goddess."

There are, to be sure, young women for whom the role of public sex goddess does feel liberating, and no doubt being expected to be "good" would feel confining to them. But on balance, which is more wholesome for girls: to expect them to be bad, or to expect them to be good; to stress the sex goddess, or the altruistic goddess? Privately, one may be both; but publicly, when the external realm is stressed, the internal realm tends to get short shrift. I don't like the "us versus them" mentality, but it's clearly impossible for our society to be neutral on these questions. In our literature, movies, fashions, and popular songs, what we value in women comes through loud and clear, so let's be straight about what our priorities are, before all the girls jump through hoops, trying to become something that feels inauthentic to many of them. As Ella Gunderson, thirteen, puts it, "I don't think that people-pleasing is a bad thing because, like, it's natural for girls to want to make people happy. But some girls—I don't know—it's like they're trying to find what happiness is and our society is not letting them find it."

Ella points out something that few are willing to admit. When our contemporary girl tries to please her elders and her peers, she is typically led away from a path that could conceivably lead to happiness. (No, shopping + hooking up does not tend to = personal fulfillment.) A twenty-two-year-old woman whom I'll call Halley overheard her aunt talking to the aunt's ten-year-old daughter: "When you'll go out with boys, I'll give you condoms; don't worry about it." Halley confronted her aunt: "Why are you telling her that? She's only ten!" "Because my father didn't let me do anything," the aunt replied. (Even so, this mother is happily married to the man her father so closely supervised.)

How far must we go before we have conclusively demonstrated our emancipation? In avoiding the mousetraps of yesteryear, we may have unwittingly dug a pit fifty feet deep for our daughters. The popular contemporary dating guide *Read My Hips* recommends that a woman should flirt with married men, and not stop flirting even when she has the flu. It goes without saying that you must never "belly laugh at jokes"—a belly laugh is not appealing—and you should make a habit of tossing your hair "until you feel dizzy!" Also, "Suck in your tummy and stick out your chest," and that means always. "Do this even when you're waiting in line for the bathroom" because "you never know who might be on the way out of the men's room!" A truly resourceful girl should model herself after "Lisa," who has written out a "24-hour-flirt schedule" detailing how she will distract men at the office whom she has no intention of getting involved with. Later in the day, Lisa reveals her bra size to a stranger who instant-messages her: "She tells him anything she pleases since she knows she'll probably never meet him." As our heroine finally pulls her pink velvet sleep mask down over her face, she whispers to herself her special mantra, "I am the flirt queen."

I'm not a "greet your husband with a martini" type, but slogging through this manual sure made me nostalgic for that popular advice of yesteryear. In fairness to the martini lady, at least she invested her efforts to please in a mutually satisfying relationship, and didn't waste her energy presenting herself as a sex object to men she would never go out with. And say what you will about the martini lady, at least she was allowed a real "belly laugh," and at the end of the day she cuddled up to an actual man, not just a sleep mask and a mantra.

Thankfully, there are many young women who disregard our new set of confining expectations. But you may not have heard of them, because according to our contemporary standards they are the "problem" girls.

. . .

Stephanie Wellen Levine, now a professor at Tufts, compares secular girls' desire to please boys with the outlook of the Lubavitch girls she spent a year investigating, and turns up a surprising finding: The more observant the girl, the less likely she is to worry about "pleasing" boys. Levine gives as an example Brocha and Malkie, who join some modern Orthodox high school and college students for a coed ski trip—they had heard about the trip from a friend at Touro College and decided to tag along. Normally, coed trips are forbidden to Lubavitchers, but Brocha and Malkie are curious. As newcomers they might be expected to be shy, but in an interesting scene, Levine describes how they wrested control of the bus from the modern Orthodox boys, who insisted that the girls sit in the back:

> The modern Orthodox young women began trooping off to the back, but the Lubavitch girls complained: "Hey! What do you mean? What is this?" Malkie moved up a few rows, beckoning impishly to Brocha to join her. "Move back!" the boys yelled, but the Lubavitchers were intransigent. . . . A few last stragglers, all girls, ran toward the bus, and a chunky boy offered his expert assessment as each approached: "Ugly, ugly, ugly, so-so."

The modern Orthodox young women seemed uncomfortable and looked at one another apprehensively, but the Lubavitch girls were "shocked" and would not accept this with "quiet resignation."

> Such comments certainly plagued both of my high schools, where the girls were just as apt to shrink back and take their lumps. Brocha, normally a shy young woman who kept her rebellious leanings under careful wraps, yelled out, "Excuse me, but I know which bus never to take again!" For a long minute, the entire bus was silent. The boys' right to

hurt the young women had been questioned by someone new to girl-bashing.

Levine was shocked to discover that this boldness extends to the Lubavitch girls' behavior around their teachers. During an education class at the seminary, the instructor gave the girls a connect-the-dots exercise. One young woman asked if she had to follow the model, and wondered if she could learn more from forming her own designs. The teacher was horrified: "How do you think you're going to teach others? You can't wait, and direction means nothing to you." Levine took notes on the scene that unfolded:

> The girls, winking and laughing, pounced. . . . Why can't imagination be a tool? Were they being taught how to teach, or how to connect the dots? Why wasn't this teacher giving them the "positive reinforcement" she had been claiming was so important? The teacher finally gave the example of Torah. There, she said, you have to follow the rules. "This isn't Torah," was the immediate rejoinder. This incident exemplifies the mood at Bais Rivka. . . . God's demands range widely and demand impressive discipline, but where He leaves off, energy explodes. The goals of religious modesty and spiritual refinement join a clear encouragement of liveliness and force of personality.

The Lubavitch girls are quintessential rebellious good girls, but in one respect they have it easy: When they question authority, they have the backing of supportive peers. Brocha, for instance, had her friend Malkie on the bus. In the rest of the world, when a girl chooses to rebel and fight for her individuality, it often feels as if she must do battle with the entire universe. And sometimes she does.

*   *   *

If Brittany Hunsicker did not exist, no novelist could invent her, because her character—and society's reaction to her—would not be believable. And yet this sixteen-year-old girl, who caused a nationwide controversy by merely sharing her views on a book she had to read in class, does exist. Details of the story remain fuzzy, largely because no reporter has ever spoken to Brittany, although many articles have been written about her. The editors of *Seventeen* magazine wanted to speak to Brittany, but Brittany's mother, Tammy, didn't trust them.

I can certainly understand Tammy's wanting to be protective. At an age when most girls fret over whether they will get invited to the junior prom, Brittany has been publicly called a Nazi and a "national embarrassment" to the state of Pennsylvania, and the Hunsickers have had pork livers thrown at their home and backyard. Also, Tammy has been accused of manipulating Brittany to serve her own backward agenda. If you didn't know any better, you might gather, from the outrage surrounding the mention of Brittany's name, that these people must be racists.

In fact they are quite lovely, humble people, who have been vilified for a surprising reason: Brittany went to her school board and objected to a sexually explicit novel she had to read aloud in English class.

After driving two and a half hours from the Philadelphia airport, I find myself in Temple, Pennsylvania, a place I'd never heard of until I read about Brittany in *The New York Times*. I pass a row of children lined up outside an ice cream shop. Its sign actually reads, ICE CREAM. I have never seen such a sign before. The lack of franchises is refreshing and makes me feel as if I'm entering a different world.

But the Hunsickers live in a duplex that's much like every other home with kids. A younger sister who has just broken her nose during softball practice sits bandaged on the couch, with M&M's in a bowl nearby to soothe the pain. Still, it's clear that this is an unusual household. For one thing, Brittany just got back from a mission to Honduras, to deliver medicine to an orphanage. Brittany had raised the money for the trip by herself, plus 500 dollars to take care of some of the children's nutritional needs. She traveled with her grandmother. "We took the kids to the beach and—" Brittany's voice catches. "They never went to the beach before or anything." Brittany has long curly brown hair and a down-to-earth, open expression: "We had lots and lots of fun." She shows me the pictures of her with the children, who indeed look as though their whole lives have just been made.

They were anywhere from like age two to seventeen; there were seven boys and seven girls. They have many different stories—like the one, the youngest, her mom was a prostitute and an alcoholic and her mom burned her and she was eating dirt because that's all they had; they didn't give her anything else. And the boys, they were even sold as slaves, and they had these big muscles, [the director] said, when she first got them in the orphanage.

Brittany and other members of her church gave the kids food, boots, balloons, and stuffed animals. The biggest present of all, of course, is antibiotics. Brittany got special permission from the school to go on the trip, her third trip to Honduras. (It's gotten to the point where her friends, instead of giving her Christmas presents, now give her money to take to the orphans.) She took a picture of herself with every orphan, and she shows me each one: One of the little boys did not have pants; another had an abscess caused by a diaper rash; and there was a boy who was upset because the bottoms of his precious new boots got dirty. He looked a little sad and lonely in the picture, but eventually he arrived at a compromise, Brittany explains, with a gratified smile. He would wear his boots outside, but wipe them constantly so they wouldn't get "spoiled."

It's interesting that Brittany should talk about Honduras first, because the article in *The New York Times* noted that the controversy about the book began thus: "Miss Hunsicker had just returned from a two-week church mission in Honduras when, encouraged by her mother, she made her public complaint." Well, not precisely. As I would learn, the decision to come forward was entirely Brittany's. But what was the point of mentioning Honduras—or, for that matter, the fact that the Hunsickers' town is home to "a growing number of evangelical Christians"? It could just be thorough reporting, but if you consider all the references to Christians together with the (inaccurate) suggestion that Tammy was pulling the strings, there seems to be a subtle attempt to delegitimize Brittany's stance. The author may not have intended this subtext, but many would read it that way: This is not merely about a girl in a classroom; she is (wink, wink) one of *those* people—so don't give her views too much weight.

Full disclosure here: I am Jewish. But nowhere in the Establishment Clause have I ever seen the words, "God-believing people are to be relegated beyond considered judgment." And so if Brittany gets her kicks from visiting orphans in Honduras, I see that as an interesting fact about her—it certainly seems a worthwhile way to pass the time—and it's not going to prevent me from hearing her story.

Brittany's senior class alone has almost 500 students: "There are so many different types of people. Like you've got the jocks, you've got the emo kids, you've got the goth kids, you've got all different kinds." One thing they all had in common was that *The Buffalo Tree* by Adam Rapp has been on the eleventh-grade reading list at Muhlenberg High since 2000.

This novel is the story of young men at a juvenile detention center and includes some coarse passages, such as all the things that are "mad sexy," references to "titties," and various sights that cause the hero to develop "sex poles."

Not surprisingly, these passages and others were embarrassing to Brittany, especially since a fair portion of the book was read out loud in class. "Not all of it, but a lot of it" was read aloud—enough for the boys to be snickering and teasing the girls. "Everyone had to read the book and nobody wanted to, and I was just like, 'Do I have to read this book?'" Brittany asked her teacher if she could have an alternative assignment and the teacher said no. School policy, it turned out, was that if you say you object to a book on "moral or religious grounds" or "because of my values," then you can get an alternative assignment. But Brittany did not know of this; nor did anyone inform her of the option at the time. So she continued through the book like everyone else.

At this point in Brittany's narrative, her mother, Tammy, interrupts and adds that she doesn't blame the teacher for anything. "She was just doing her job. It wasn't her fault that the book was on the list." Tammy, a kindly, doe-eyed woman who looks way too young to have a daughter Brittany's age, is the opposite of the domineering character she was assumed to be in the media. She assures me at every turn that she "respects the school board's decision in trying to accommodate both sides." The problem was that "it was very shocking as a parent to discover the content in that book." Tammy works as a school bus driver; and as someone who struggles daily to keep kids in line, she feels they could be reading other novels that would be more beneficial to them:

> What used to be locker-room talk is now what they're teaching in English class. As a bus driver, when you hear obscene stuff, and you have younger kids on the bus, it's your job to say, "Hey, cut that out!" And then they say, "But I'm reading from my English book!" What do you say to that? You have eleventh-graders on the bus, reading this stuff to sixth-graders.

Soft-spoken Tammy doesn't seem the type to censor anyone. She knows what is going on, and she doesn't inhabit a strident, ideological universe. She is painfully aware that this debate involves real people, and she is very considerate of the feelings of others—even her opponents. For example, she asks that I not name individual teachers, because she doesn't want to embarrass anyone. (Even though those names are now part of the public record, I promise her that I will not name any particular teacher.)

This debate, of course, is much bigger than one book and its merits. In a follow-up discussion about the controversy, the author himself admitted that it was up to teachers to decide whether the book was appropriate for their classrooms. "When he was writing the book, Rapp said he never concerned himself with worrying if the content was appropriate for teenagers. That job is best left up to educators, he said." As far as Brittany was concerned, the educators at her school didn't make the right decision. So she decided to do something about it. "One of my best friends—well, she came over and we were talking about swearing and stuff, and then I said, 'Oh well, you should see the book we're reading in English class!'" Brittany's mom looked at the book and was quite taken aback, but Brittany insisted that it was her own issue. "I'm the one who suffered by having to read this stuff out loud in the class, so I want to tell them [the school board] about it." Tammy notified the superintendent beforehand to say that they would be coming and what they would be discussing, but she did have some qualms about Brittany's speaking. "I didn't want her in the limelight, you know. But she said, 'Mom,' she said 'if anybody's going to talk, I would like it to be me.' She said, 'I'm the one who sat in class.'"

So in April 2005, Brittany Hunsicker walked into the school board meeting and tried to read from *The Buffalo Tree*. "How would you like if your son and daughter had to read this?" she asked the board members. "I am in the eleventh grade," she said—in words that would be heard 'round the world—and "I had to read this junk." What wasn't reported, though, was that as Brittany began to read from the novel, she was prevented from continuing. "People talked about censorship," Brittany tells me later, laughing. "But I was the one who was censored! They wouldn't let me read my speech."

I told them my name, I told them what grade I was in, and then I said I would like to read you some of the book we are reading in English class. I had an excerpt at the beginning, and so I started reading to them, and they said, "Stop!" I said, "This is what I read out loud in my English class." And I said, "If you don't want me to be reading this, then *hello?*" I was reading this with my whole class out loud! But I wasn't allowed to read it to the school board. They said, "I don't want to hear any more; I don't want to hear that!"

Nonetheless, Brittany's point must have come through loud and clear. Less than an hour later, by a unanimous vote of the board, the book was removed from the curriculum. Brittany thought that "pretty much everyone in the room" was on her side; but a few months later—perhaps concerned about its national image as a hotbed of "censorship"—the board reversed its decision, and *The Buffalo Tree* was back in. (During its brief absence, the book was always available to students who wanted to read it, so it's not clear how the brief demotion from required reading constituted censorship.)

In another public forum, the teachers at the school determined that the redeeming value of the book was "the potential to save a child from juvenile delinquency." It is obviously hard to weigh an unknown potential benefit against an actual girl who claims to have been harmed by the book, so the teachers decided that to be on the safe side, they would go with the potential unknown benefit. I asked Brittany what she thought about this philosophy.

> WENDY: Did you feel like the boys in your class were very touched and resolved against juvenile delinquency after reading this book?
> BRITTANY: Are you kidding me? You should see what they're doing this year.
> WENDY: What are they doing this year?
> BRITTANY: Oh, man, the people that come in and—you know—they've just been smoking pot out on the corner of the school, you know. You can tell that they're high and you can tell what they do. And other stuff like—well, a lot of girls are pregnant, for example.
> WENDY: What do you think is going to make an impact on these boys, if they're to change?
> BRITTANY: Once they hit rock bottom.
> WENDY: The book won't change them?
> BRITTANY: Definitely not.

The period during which *The Buffalo Tree* was not required reading may have been brief, but the Muhlenberg community was still feeling the aftershocks and debating the issue a year later. In March 2006, a "panel on censorship" was held at a local college, Albright, and 125 teachers, parents, and school board members showed up. One teacher told the local paper, the *Reading Eagle,* that objection to *The Buffalo Tree* "was a coming out party for censorship" which was "influenced by a vocal minority of community members." He added, "*The Buffalo Tree* is a good book to introduce novels to teens who are not inclined to read on their own." At the same time, the teacher said that "he understood why parents wanted to shield their children from difficult topics and situations. But coarse language and questionable morals permeate American culture, he said. 'We really can't protect them, but we should prepare them,' [the English teacher] said."

I've never understood the argument that "we can't protect the children" as justification for exposing them to things they don't need to be exposed to in the classroom. "Questionable morals" do indeed "permeate" the culture, but we don't round kids up and lead them to strip joints, either. We obviously think there is some value to protecting them, and part of the idea of schooling, after all, is to expose kids to literature and experiences they wouldn't come across on their own, on cable television.

The Buffalo Tree is in many ways a fine novel. But does it need to be read aloud in a mixed classroom? Probably not. That was the issue for Brittany, and I agree with her that this is not a question of censorship. Do I feel censored because my book *A Return to Modesty* is not read aloud in high schools across America? No, I do not. Educators make choices about curriculums all the time, and waving the censorship flag is no substitute for explaining why certain books have been chosen above others.

Brittany has no regrets. "I knew that it was something I had to do because I didn't want to read anything like that again. The way it made me feel in class . . . it was humiliating, I guess, or—I don't know. It was just disgusting, like just the way the boys were reacting and stuff." The teacher had said "Stop it," but this was a difficult class to handle.

Eventually Brittany would learn how quickly people can change their minds, about books and in general: "It's funny, because everybody didn't want to read the book in the beginning but then when I said something, suddenly everybody wanted to read the book and it was sold out. So I guess I made the book sales go up." But the reaction of her peers surprised her: "Everybody was like, 'Oh, why did you do that?' You know, 'Everyone liked that book.' But in the beginning you didn't even want to read that book; you all agreed with me." As soon as Brittany came forward publicly, her support seemed to evaporate overnight.

There was just "my one best friend." Soon after, pork livers were thrown at the Hunsickers' house. "It was supposed to be buffalo meat because the book was *Buffalo Tree*, but it wasn't even buffalo meat." (Buffalo meat is expensive, it turns out.) "They actually bought them at the local markets, just hunks full of strange meat. They just threw them all over the grass, and all over our porch and backyard."

Then later, Brittany continues, matter-of-factly, "I was supposed to have porn books thrown at me when I walked out the door at school." Different people were telling her about the magazines that were being collected in her honor, but then at the last minute nothing happened. "My one friend told them not to," Brittany explains with gratitude.

> But people would still come up to me and start yelling, "Stop banning books!" And there was this one guy, he wore this HUNSICKER BANS BOOKS T-shirt, but instead of Hunsicker, it had "Hitler" crossed out and then my last name written in. So then he came up close to me and said something. I'm like, "What are you taking about?" So I texted my mom and said, "I can't stand this; come take me out or do *something*." So I went to the vice principal and they talked to him and then he said to the other teachers, "Don't let anybody beat her up"—because there were rumors that they were going to try and beat me up, and you know what, I really didn't care. . . . I knew that God was on my side, and that nobody was going to touch me.

In the end, after *The Buffalo Tree* returned to the curriculum, the school decided, as a compromise, to send home a big packet with a brief description of each book used in grades nine to twelve, and mark a big X if there was "sexual content, language, or violence." (Comically, in this very packet *The Buffalo Tree* is marked X for violence but not for sexual content.)

But at least students now know that they have the right to say, "I do not feel comfortable reading this book because of my values, or because of my religion"—if they can remember that gangly phrase—and that the teacher will have to give them another book. So thanks to Brittany, students are more informed about their choices, and parents are more informed about the books their children are reading (if school officials can manage to check the right boxes). So her speaking out really does seem to have made a difference. And she did get one e-mail of support, which Tammy shows me proudly: "I graduated from Muhlenberg two years ago and my teacher read this book to us, probably because she knew no one would read this trash on their own time. I commend the girl who went to the school board and had the courage to speak out on it." As evidenced by the fact that *The Buffalo Tree* was not popular initially, Brittany speculates that there are probably others who feel the same way, but people want to "go with the flow." Brittany then flashes her winning smile: "It seems like they're being rebellious to swear and be bad and stuff, but it's more rebellious being good because everyone's not now."

Deep down, her classmates seem to admire this stance. As Brittany puts on her puffy jacket to go to her night job, I ask her if the controversy has blown over eight months later. Are people at school nice to her again? "Are you kidding me? I'm more popular this year than I was last year." And with that triumphant declaration, she is out the door in a blaze of curls, off to her job at a wholesale club.

It would be nice if the story ended there, but unfortunately it does not. A supposed friend at Brittany's school later told her, "Whatever you do, don't Google your name on the Internet." I happen to be on the phone with her mother when the subject comes up, and I agree that self-Googling is never a good idea. I try to sound casual so as not to pique their curiosity, but I can already see that the end is inevitable. The friend has planted the seed and, "She's doing it! She's doing it!" explains her mother, laughing and giving me a play-by-play. My heart sinks, because I already know about a self-described "faithful husband, soccer dad" who has dubbed Brittany the "erection queen" of Muhlenberg High School, and published comments from anonymous readers questioning her sexual orientation. Of course there is no way of knowing whether this writer is really a faithful husband and soccer dad. I've never harbored much admiration for people who lob juvenile personal attacks at others from the safety of anonymous blogs. But the depressing thing is that he probably is a soccer dad.

"Brittany? Tammy?" Silence. I consider reminding them that people attack you only when they don't have a counterargument, but it seems pointless.

"She's reading some hurtful things right now," Tammy explains, her tone no longer playful. "I don't know. . . ." It's the first time I have heard Tammy lose her cool. "Maybe I made a mistake in letting her go to the board."

"But how can you say that?" I ask.

"I never thought it would go this far."

"But you really made a difference," I protest. "Parents know what their kids are reading; the kids know they have options," I remind her, "and now girls will probably feel more comfortable speaking out about things going on in their schools because of Brittany."

"You're right, you're right," she reassures me, and a flicker of the strong Tammy Hunsicker returns. But she doesn't sound convinced.

* * *

In researching the controversy at Muhlenberg High, I came across a rather astonishing news item from Todd Beamer High (between Seattle and Tacoma). In March 2004, fifteen-year-old Brandon Jerome didn't like the sexual references in *Balzac and the Little Chinese Seamstress,* a book that had been assigned and that includes a passage about a virgin having sex. According to the Associated Press, "Brandon told his mother, Lori Bridges, that a student drew an explicit picture of a boy and girl having sex as part of a class drawing exercise on the book."

> Bridges believes the novel isn't a bad book, but is inappropriate for high school students. "I think it's too mature. I think it embarrasses kids," she said. She and five others presented petitions signed by 32 parents asking the Federal Way School Board to ban the book. In an April 23 letter, [Superintendent] Murphy removed the book from district ninth-grade reading lists. He read the novel twice and said he found "many valuable literary elements. However, I have reservations that many students at the ninth-grade level possess the maturity and life experiences to correctly interpret the few sensitive scenes depicted in the novel without resorting to behaviors that demean the intent of the novel. . . ." he wrote.

So when the boy objected, the book was simply retired from the curriculum (although it is still in school libraries). There was no raging nationwide controversy, there was no cry of "censorship," there were no Hitler tees, and no middle-aged moms made fun of Brandon on the Internet. The boy wasn't happy, and the community responded.

There's a double standard, all right. It's just inverted. Female virgins are seen as freaks, but young men are admired if their virginity is a conscious choice (and not just due to a lack of opportunity). For instance, the basketball star A. C. Green was universally admired for saving his virginity until marriage, whereas Lakita Garth and Erika Harold (Miss America 2003) were publicly thrashed for doing the same. Erika Harold's account of being racially attacked as a child was loudly questioned as if she were making the whole thing up—just because a particular writer happened to disagree with her stance on abstinence. ("Incredibly, Harold had never publicly spoken of this torment before," sneered *Salon.*) And Lakita was told that, by waiting for the right man, she might have children with birth defects. One letter writer scoffed, "Come on! She'll have to be a medical miracle to bear a child by the time she gets married. She's already thirty-four years old, and the risk of having a child born with birth defects increases with age. To conceive when the child could be born with Down syndrome and/or other complications is just selfish." (Incidentally, Lakita gave birth to a healthy baby boy as this book was being completed.)

The scorn heaped on the "good" girl is part of a misguided attempt to correct the old double standard. Women now have to prove that they're liberated by being sexually active outside marriage, to a degree that men do not. Even teenage girls like Brittany Hunsicker bear the burden of proving that they aren't prudes—and proving it to middle-aged soccer dads. This is preposterous and damaging.

* * *

Yet Brittany Hunsicker can take heart: Even as we malign the good girl, it seems that, against our will, we are coming around to appreciating her. When I finally read *Why Men Marry Bitches*—and believe me, I had postponed reading it as long as I could—I was quite surprised to find out the nature of this modern "bitch."

> Relationship Principle 30: The way to weed out the contenders from the pretenders is to assess their attitude about waiting for sex. If he likes you, he'll be happy just being in your company. . . .

> Invite him in *before* you leave for your dinner date. . . . This helps break the ice, and prevents late-night access. Then when you send him on his way at the end of the date, it won't seem so impersonal.

> When you show a little, but not everything, his read is: "Now that's a woman who is in control."

When you move into someone's place, you don't just give up your personal space and belongings. More important, nearly always you also lose your *feeling of independence*. . . . This is often when the devaluing process begins. "Why do I need to prize and cherish her?" . . . And this is precisely the level of security a bitch will not allow a man to have.

Wait a minute—is the real bitch essentially the traditional, modest woman? How clever to sneak her in the back door like this, as the empowered modern viper we are all meant to love. But maybe there is more to it. Since, as we've already seen, the "good girl" is not really focused on pleasing other people, it makes sense that in the modern understanding, she would be considered the "bitchiest" of all. (In fact, this is the true origin of the word "bitch," as the female dog is difficult to mate with.)

Note that women who postpone sex these days are maligned as "manipulative" or "trying to trick men into marrying them." Unpacking this insult, we find that instead of being a reasonable goal or an ideal, marriage turns into the kind of shady, ulterior motive only a low woman would have at the back of her mind. The assumption is that the girl always wants the boy, and the trick is only to puff up that feeling into something more long-term.

But what if the boy is not right for her to begin with? The problem with relationships based on physicality is less that the man might not want to marry you than that you may be getting in deep with the wrong man.

The right man doesn't have to be manipulated. But if you're dating or perhaps even living with Mr. In the Meanwhile, then when Mr. Right comes along you may miss him altogether. Taking the opportunity to get to know someone on a deeper, nonphysical level first is the way you find out if you even want to marry him. I'm still mystified after hearing from one woman who "discovered" to her shock that her husband of six months did not want children—ever. She wrote to me as she was traveling to Europe with him, to try to "resolve the issue." Knowing that they'd lived together for three years before getting engaged, I asked her: How had they never discussed this before? There was so much "chemistry," she explained, and they were so obviously "perfect" for each other, that "it never came up."

It's easy to assume that our goal in dating is to be appealing, but it really isn't. While of course putting your best foot (and hairstyle) forward, you still have to be yourself in order to assess who is right for you, and vice versa. It's always hard to be objective about matters of the heart; but if you jump into bed, things get so much fuzzier. This is a known fact, and in male advice manuals such as *How to Succeed with Women*, it is used as a justification for rushing women into bed:

> When you are seducing a woman, you want to spend as little time with her as possible before having sex because the less time you spend with her, the less time you have to make a mistake fatal to the seduction. . . . Every unnecessary interaction is just another opportunity to bungle it up. Before the date, a woman is looking for reasons to get rid of you. Earlier we talked about how, when a woman dates someone, her orderly existence becomes shaken up. . . . In some corner of her mind, the woman you are interested in is looking for some justification to get you out of her life. The more time you give her to find one, the more likely she is to do just that.

On the other hand, happily, "Once a woman has had sex with you, the rules change. Now instead of trying to justify getting rid of you, she's trying to justify why you were worth having sex with in the first place. Instead of being on the hunt for your bad points, she's more likely to be on the lookout for the good." (If you must read advice manuals, it's better to read male than female guides: The male guides are so much more eye-opening.)

* * *

In *It's a Wonderful Life* (1946), Mary Hatch (played by Donna Reed) was a pillar of strength who eventually won George Bailey over. In *Mr. Smith Goes to Washington* (1939), Jean Arthur as Clarissa Saunders stands up for Smith, and only because she believes in him and lends him all her support are they able to accomplish their dreams in Washington. (She didn't even require any nip and tuck.) What defined Barbara Stanwyck in *Stella Dallas* (1937)—her social awkwardness or her giving heart and amazing self-sacrifice? Looking back, it was these characters' choices for the good that highlighted their unique strengths.

Today one hears a constant drumbeat of actresses complaining about the "inferior," superficial roles for women in the entertainment industry, but clearly it is not only the entertainment industry that has this problem. Inasmuch as we are only objects for men's sexual play, our roles in our daily lives will always be "inferior." It's no accident that one of the most popular advice books today is called *The Surrendered Wife*, or that according to this book your husband's pornography is "none of your business" and you shouldn't "make it more than it is." This is the liberated woman of today, and she has indeed "surrendered."

Consider, in contrast, the rebellious good girls of the Bible. Rebecca tricked Isaac into giving Jacob a blessing because her feminine insight told her that Jacob was worthier. Miriam argued with her own parents that they mustn't separate, an intervention that resulted in the Exodus from Egypt.

While pleasing others often reflects our own insecurity, being good is about something larger. Doing the right thing over the pleasing thing is harder than we assume, and perhaps it always was. But let's face it—it's the only way to get anything real done around here.

COMPARE, CONTRAST, AND OPINE:
WHAT DO *YOU* THINK?

One day in the late 1930s, Beverly Cleary (future children's book author) and her college roommate Norma heard a knock on their
kitchen door. It was a strange man who lived nearby, and he offered
them a basket of tomatoes. Cleary writes in her memoirs that she and
Norma were "delighted" for the fresh tomatoes; they "accepted
them, thanked him, and closed the door." The next afternoon, the
man knocked again—this time offering them his evening paper. Once
more, the coeds accepted his gift with thanks, and shut the door. That
the man desired to be invited in did not impress the ladies in the
slightest, and Cleary recalls that this routine "went on for several
days before he gave up and kept his paper." Young Beverly soon met
her match, a wonderful man named Clarence, and they wed despite
her mother's disapproval. (She had something against Catholics.)

Today it's fashionable to malign the modest woman as a "pleaser"
of the "patriarchy"—a typical negative comment on the Modestly-
Yours.net blog threatens that we gals will "never be anything but . . .
traitors of your own freedom: pliable, obsequious, sycophantic,
servile—complicit in your own oppression." But how pliable can
modesty be, when it usually means regularly *rejecting* the wrong sort
of man for oneself? Contrast Cleary's memoir with one from 1999, a
tragic catalog of self-mutilation in which the author, Caroline Kettlewell, careens through bouts of anorexia, self-cutting, and flings
with men who were downright annoying to her. Regarding one such
repugnant lover, she explains, "still I went along with a dull resignation . . . knowing it's pointless to resist. I just sighed to myself, *Oh
why not*. At that moment I didn't even care enough anymore to bother
extricating myself."

Does setting limits automatically mean you are "servile and pliable," or the opposite?

CHAPTER EIGHT

Feminism's (New) Fourth Wave

·

I think the thing that I was happiest about was going on the website a few weeks later and seeing that we had actually made a change, however small, in this huge company, and that somehow we made an impact. And that was just the coolest thing for me—and that other girls are thinking about it and girls are now aware of what they really are wearing and what it really does say about them, and about society as a whole.

—REBECCA ADELSHEIM, fifteen, one of the twenty-three Girlcotters who persuaded Abercrombie & Fitch to pull some of its "attitude tees"

If I identified as a feminist it would be as a nonradical feminist—someone who believes in equality and wants to better the lives of women, and, frankly, of men as well. In my school they say, "Oh, you know, she's so feminist; she's always for women," and that's not true. Like I think they have a wrong impression of us in a way. We just want to make things equal and then go from there—like, improve the quality of life for everyone.

—YAGMUR MUFTUOGLU, sixteen, another Girlcotter

I call Kim Gandy, president of the National Organization for Women (NOW), to find out her take on *Girls Gone Wild*. Does she agree with Helen Grieco, the executive director of California's NOW, that it's all about empowerment, and "Flashing your breasts on Daytona Beach says, 'I'm not a good girl. I think it's sexy to be a bad girl'"? Recently, what goes into attaining this socially optimal level of badness has been called into question, after allegations that particular girls were targeted, plied with alcohol by the crew, and sexually assaulted. Joe Francis has denied the charges, but traditionally these types of claims have concerned feminists.

So I ring up Ms. Gandy to see what her thinking is. We get off on the wrong foot, as she seems to be very offended by the question itself: "Remember that in our view, staff aren't allowed to speak for NOW. There's one thing that you should know. Also, I frankly get very frustrated when I get a lot of media calls about things like *Girls Gone Wild* and the Miss America Pageant and all of the things that we get called about all the time that are allegedly related to the feminist movement in some way."

I pose other questions, and then meander back. But she is a smart cookie: "We're still on question one, right?" I reassure her that we're making progress, since technically I've counted five questions by this point: "I think we're on question five." Ms. Gandy snaps, "Good!" Why good? She elaborates: "It's like you're trying to have a six-course women's studies lecture series on aspects of feminism in a conversation with one person who's the head of one organization. It just seems kind of—I'm not sure where you're going with it. We've been all over the place here and we haven't talked much at all about *issues,* issues facing women. . . ."

Here, I interrupt: "I guess I see this, for young women, as an issue facing them." Ms. Gandy is incredulous: "Whether they should take their clothes off at Daytona Beach?" The American Medical Association has just come out with a study about why such behavior on spring break is unhealthy for young women, so, feeling emboldened, I answer, "Yeah!" Ms. Gandy is now exasperated: "I think they should do it if they want to! What does that have to do with feminism?"

I admit that I am not entirely satisfied by this answer. I feel somewhat bad to be annoying a nice lady my mother's age—but something about her dismissal rankles me (especially given her colleague's enthusiastic support of *Girls Gone Wild*). I feel fairly certain that Ms. Gandy is not a fan, so why can't she come out and say so? She's the leader of one of the biggest feminist organizations in the world. Does she think that these drunk girls are being taken advantage of, or that they're empowered, or something in between? Nearly everyone has an opinion on *Girls Gone Wild*—except maybe the Amish and Orthodox Jews who don't have televisions (and even most of them have probably heard about it and have an opinion). So how can Kim Gandy not have an opinion?

Her strategy is to deny that it's a phenomenon at all, which I find rather confusing, until I realize this is her way of avoiding comment on it. So I persist, and after going back and forth no fewer than twenty-five times about whether drunk girls taking off their clothes at parties, on spring break, for videos is really happening and is something that some women (including Ms. Grieco) advocate as empowering, I finally settle, by sheer luck, on a formulation Ms. Gandy is comfortable with. I ask what she makes of the phenomenon itself, without attributing it to anyone in particular. Ms. Gandy now sounds supremely irritated with me, but at last answers the question: "If women want to take their clothes off, that's, you know, that's up to them to do that! Do I think that benefits women as a group in any way? No, I don't."

So there, forty-five minutes into our interview, was my answer. I try to sound upbeat, since Ms. Gandy sounds so ruffled—"OK, thanks, that's all I wanted to know."—but she adds bitterly, "You just want me to diss other people's view of feminism." I protest that I just wanted to know her opinion, but by then it is pretty clear that I am not going to be invited to her next dinner party.

To be fair, I certainly put Ms. Gandy in a difficult position, asking her to comment on remarks made by another executive of NOW. But if the majority of messages a young girl receives add up to "Take your clothes off; it's empowering," and "Have casual sex; it's empowering," and if those who disagree with such messages can't really articulate why, then we've got problems. If our top women leaders require forty-five minutes and the intellectual equivalent of root canal work to merely suggest that taking off your clothes and playing with dildos in public is not the be-all and end-all of women's happiness, and even they feel bad about having said anything against it—then, again, we've got serious problems. Either people believe in the bad girl as the only model, or they are simply too intimidated to challenge her rule.

You might wonder, as I did for some time, how the *Girls Gone Wild* mentality has been so successful in setting the terms of the debate. Essentially, I discovered, the exhibitionists rule by intimidation, by making others feel that there is something wrong with them if they think sexuality should be private, or special. Are we not "sex-positive"?

* * *

Still, though leaders of the feminist movement—and their opponents— might like to portray it as a settled question, in fact the meaning of feminism is up for grabs right now. The ground is rumbling, and the ideological fault lines are shifting, to such a degree that in April 2006, when a young conservative columnist attacked a professor of women's studies, he may have succeeded only in attacking someone more conservative than himself.

Nathanael Blake's attack on a women's studies course at his school, Oregon State University, was published on Townhall.com. The course, "WS 399: Sex and the City," did sound a bit unusual, setting out to examine the television series of the same name. Still, the columnist's over-the-top tone—"My demands that they get back in the kitchen and make me something to eat have been ill-received"—made me wonder if there was perhaps more to the story than I was getting. Blake explained that WS 399 had one of the largest enrollments on campus, capped off at 500 students, and that women who couldn't get into the class actually cried. But if the course was as frivolous as he claimed, why would women be weeping to get in? To me, it didn't add up.

I got my hands on the course syllabus and talked to the instructor, Amy Leer, in-depth; and I made a surprising discovery: The class wasn't celebrating the mind-set of *Sex and the City* but illustrating the poverty of it. Fluffy college classes analyzing various media are standard fare nowadays, but this one seemed actually fairly rigorous: The syllabus included a study by the University of Chicago and a work co-written by the conservative writer Maggie Gallagher, *The Case for Marriage*. When I went to college, professors of women's studies would have given up their tenure rather than allow students to read a conservative like Maggie Gallagher. This was indeed an odd class, but not for the reasons Mr. Blake had outlined.

In the end, there were actually 518 students taking Amy Leer's course (apparently the crying did help). For Amy, episodes of *Sex and the City* are springboards to discuss other issues, and primarily an opportunity to critique casual sex:

> One of my main critiques of the show is the casualness of the sex and
> the fact that they never talk about protection in sexual relationships.
> They don't talk about commitment or what it means to be in an adult
> committed relationship. Or consent even. Do they know what they're
> doing and the consequences that could happen? And there's alcohol in
> almost every episode, and then there's sex. It's pretty much the worst
> combination you can have. And we talk about that: how, you know,
> women tend to use alcohol to fit into that hypersex kind of box that so-

ciety has put them in; and how problematic that is for these women who are, you know, successful in their work and successful in other areas of their life—how they're putting themselves into that stereotypical hyper-sex box. . . . It shows how the sexual revolution's excesses have led to a devaluation of women and men. We're playing into the dumbness of men and the dumbness of women.

Hearing Amy speak, I found it hard to avoid the impression that many students were drawn to her course simply to hear advice they typically won't get anywhere else today. Amy is thirty-one—and as I would learn, she represented a new direction in feminism. "You know, there's been this kind of third-wave feminist thing to say that women should be 'where men are,'" she tells me. "But you know, I don't think for women to do that would be equality." Amy has girls in her class who start off wearing PORN STAR T-shirts, "It's just like, 'Oh, what are you *doing*? There's no power in that.'" When the class is over, "I've had countless students sending me cards after classes in the past, just talking about, you know: 'Your class changed my life.' Because they start opening their eyes. Because we're so normalized to sexuality and the devaluation of both men and women, and devaluation of commitment and responsibility, that we don't actually see the problem because it's normal."

Is this a feminist argument, or is it a conservative argument? "It's funny," Amy responds:

Conservatives assume that I'm a man-hating, abortion-loving lesbian or something. But that certainly is not who I am. I mean, I love men. And sometimes within the feminist community I get called a sellout. But I would self-identify as a liberal feminist, working within the system. It's just that we need to make some changes for both men and women.

In talking to women ages fourteen to forty-two about feminism, I came to see that feminism had become a sort of Rorschach test: The word itself has become almost meaningless—and can refer to diametrically opposed ideas—and yet hearing what feminism means to others is still interesting and can tell you a lot. Some people use the term to signal that they care about the dignity of women. Others use it to indicate that they want to fight the very notion of being dignified at all.

Usually to the youngest feminists, the idea of decency is tremendously appealing. Whereas to the older ones, it is the chief problem. Consider this bulletin, for example:

> Dear All,
> Please excuse my hijacking Temma's Afghan Women's Support list for another purpose. but I have a question some of you academics may be able to help me with. I am writing an essay partly about Wendy Shalit's book *A Return to Modesty.* . . . Wendy asks, "Why would so many young women be adopting modesty as the new sexual virtue?" But, being a twit, she never establishes that "so many" are doing anything of the kind. I'm kind of skeptical—I mean how many modestyniks are there—Three? Ten?
>
> So if any of you have a bead on the modesty biz at your campus I'd love to hear. Is this a trend? Are your female students distressed by coed bathrooms (a bugbear of Ms. Shalit's)? Are they calling for single-sex dorms? Eschewing sexy clothes? Calling for more ice cream socials and fewer rock concerts?
>
> Also, if you can think of people for me to call, I'd be grateful for names and if poss numbers (like: women's center, hillel house, campus ministries, etc.) if you have them at hand.
>
> I'd love to be able to say, well I made calls to counselors at twenty-five campuses and no one I spoke with saw modesty as a growing trend. "The miniskirt is really popular here," said Rabbi Greenbaum of Alaska State U. "As a matter of fact, I'm wearing one now."
>
> Deadline coming right up, of course.
>
> thanks in advance,
>
> in sisterhood,
>
> Katha [Pollitt], March 15, 1999

As a prominent second wave feminist—whose attack on me ended up, incidentally, in *The New York Times*—it's interesting to see how she settled on her conclusion in advance of undertaking her research. The word "modesty" clearly makes her see red.

To find out why modesty is more appealing to younger people, Pollitt might have talked to her own daughter, Sophie, who entered high school a few years later and, like many girls, was disgusted by contemporary sexual norms. As she put it in her diary, which was eventually published:

Guys in my classes are always looking at stupid magazines like *FHM* and *Maxim*, saying s——t like "oh her tits are so small" or "she's too fat." Who the F——K are these guys—they're like fifteen-years old with acne up the wazoo. Who gave them the right to comment on girls' bodies like that? OK, those girls are in a magazine, but they talk like that about girls in our school, too. But, of course, who cares what these guys look like, how flat their abs are or how much they weigh, because there will always be some girl to [provide oral sex] no matter what.

Like many intelligent young women, Sophie Pollitt-Cohen realizes that the boys' immaturity cannot be separated from the girls' willingness to provide sexual favors to those boys, "no matter what." Their relationship to the sexual revolution tends to be much more conflicted than their mothers'. When I contacted Sophie, a freshman at Wesleyan, she had been reading and enjoying Ariel Levy's *Female Chauvinist Pigs,* an indictment of some of the excesses of third-wave feminism. As she put it in an e-mail:

Women do so many un-empowering things (like girls thinking being on *Girls Gone Wild* is really cool). At my school, Wesleyan, which is obviously very liberal, there are many girls even here that dumb themselves down for guys or who consider "feminist" to be a dirty word that is only applied to ugly girls who hate men, which is definitely not true.

Sophie rejects sexual exhibitionism even though she identifies as a feminist. Some would say the original intention of the first wave of feminism was precisely this: for women to be taken seriously for their brains and not their bodies. But in recent years, feminism—particularly its third wave—has aligned itself with an entirely opposite attitude. Jennifer Baumgardner and Amy Richards, who are considered leaders of the third-wave movement, have equated "dancing at a strip club" with "volunteering at a women's shelter" in its potential to "radicalize" women in a positive way. This is the feminism you are most likely to find on the Internet today, in extensive discourses about the right to be sexual beings laced generously, always, with the f-word; and it is the feminism embodied by CAKE, which hosts parties where women disrobe and bump and grind in order to "explore, express, and define sexuality for themselves." ("Do-me" feminism and "lipstick" feminism are other derogatory terms referring to the third wave.) This is also the feminism that inspired a "countdown clock" to the time when the actor who plays Harry Potter—Daniel Radcliffe—becomes "legal": "Right now, he's at the tender age of sixteen . . . meaning there are less than two years left until I can legally seduce him!" Lynn Harris of *Salon*'s feminist blog, *Broadsheet,* reprinted these lines approvingly, adding that it's about time we had a countdown to a boy's becoming "legal," since people have been doing this for years to young female actresses: "607 days 'til we can legally play 'tonsil Quidditch.' Finally, a legal-age countdown clock for the ladies! Joining the handful of similar shrines to Emma Watson/ Hermione Granger and underage others."

The "girl power" movement of the early 1990s began idealistically, with the riot-grrrls producing fanzines or "'zines" complaining about sexual harassment, and hoping to create a more humane society. Sara McCool, age sixteen, from Pittsburgh, Pennsylvania, wrote in her 'zine *Sourpuss #3* about "when boys get together in packs" and "hassle" girls about wanting to have sex with them: "I have never seen a pack of girls do this. Maybe you have, but I haven't. I have never seen a pack of girls get together around some boy and yell at him how much they want to have sex with him."

Who could have guessed that only ten years later, feminist bloggers would do exactly this, descending on sixteen-year-old Daniel Radcliffe, counting down, and describing "how much they want to have sex with him"? If men lie in wait for teen actresses to come of age, then women must also crouch behind rocks, waiting for teen boys to come of age. We can be sexual predators, too.

As far as some women are concerned, this is what feminism has always been about. "Isabel," for example, who graduated from high school in the mid-1970s, shares this painful story:

> I was very into the women's liberation movement in high school, and attended a women's college. At the time, feminists were saying that women should be able to be as free as men are with regard to sexuality; we should experiment with our sexuality; virginity is for losers and goes against human nature; birth control should be available to teenagers; and abortion is OK. It was a very experimental time. It went completely against the moral strictures of our parents' generation. I was rebellious and free-spirited, so I went along with the feminist thinking. Now that I'm on the other side of life, I feel completely ripped off by the feminists. I ended up with herpes, pubic lice, and two

unwanted pregnancies which I terminated. I still have herpes outbreaks (rarely, thank goodness). No children—by the time I found my husband, I was too old to have kids. My supposed sexual liberation brought me lots of heartbreak and regrets, far outweighing the jollies. The feminists simply don't acknowledge the downside of this supposed liberation.

Although she had been a feminist since junior high school and was very idealistic about the movement, Isabel now thinks it would be "wrong of me not to warn others."

When I was a feminist in high school, I wanted more sports teams. I was really into it and fought strongly for it. With my best friend we contacted our local NOW [in the Northeast] and we said, "Why aren't we learning about Susan B. Anthony in school?" They put us in touch with a woman in her late twenties who had just had a baby. We visited her at her house, and she really turned the conversation around to, "Are you sexually active?" and "I know doctors who will put you on the Pill," and we were like, *"What?"* She said, "I know a physician who can write a prescription. Me and my husband have an open relationship and we sleep with whom we want." Well, we were totally flabbergasted. We didn't come for that. We were just sixteen years old.

Isabel laughs off the suggestion that the third-wave feminists originated any casualness about sex: "Sexual freedom was a huge part of it back then; it was always a part of it. Trying to deny that now—that's ludicrous. It was always about 'Look at your cervix in the mirror! Use your sexuality. We don't have these restrictions anymore.' As a girl in 1973–1974, I wasn't abstinent-minded myself, but it was so unexpected and weird, how this woman brought this stuff out of the blue. I wasn't going to sleep around with everyone!" Then in college, once again as a feminist, Isabel "stood for women to be doctors and lawyers, for more sports opportunities. But for the leadership it was always, 'We have the Pill; we can go experiment and be as wild as the men are, and that's our right.'" Then, she adds sadly, "You try that and it doesn't take very long before you feel very empty. You start thinking, 'They're telling me I should have a great time but I feel hollow.' You feel like you've been invaded."

Isabel's point is that since the 1960s, feminists were hostile to the idea of modesty or "hang-ups," which they perceived as a tool of patriarchal oppression. There were always, to be sure, a few antipornography feminists, but they invariably said their problem was that porn "discriminated" against women or that porn was "hate speech"—never that it violated our dignity as human beings. And in case you didn't notice, they lost that particular battle.

• • •

Melinda Gallagher is one of the leaders of third-wave feminism, and the cofounder of CAKE, with Emily Kramer. We meet in the winter of 2006 at a NewsBar in lower Manhattan. She has such a soft voice that I have to ask her at least three times to please speak up. Even though we're at a quiet coffee shop that's virtually empty—this is on Super Bowl Sunday—and there is no ambient noise, I'm genuinely concerned that the tape recorder will not pick up her voice. (It did, but barely.) That this gentle fair-haired creature in front of me could in any way be responsible for parties at which women strip and watch porn in public—well, this is like hearing that a white kitten with a cute pink bow, when not posing for calendars, kills alligators in its spare time.

Melinda admits that the kind of sexuality portrayed at a CAKE party "doesn't necessarily represent me."

> My role there is behind the scenes. If I came to a CAKE party (and wasn't working) my role would be to really watch—that's my personality. For a lot of women who aren't up on the stage, a CAKE party is about "Wow, that's really sexy; I'm going to try that with my boyfriend; I'm going to think about that." There's that level that's valuable and where I would personally put myself. But I also understand that there are many many women out there who it's really not for the men in the room, just for themselves; they love it—just being objects, just looking sexy and being sexy.

When people first meet Melinda, they'll say to her, "Why aren't you dressed a different way?" (She is dressed quite modestly in a long-sleeved V-neck sweater.) She has been in a relationship with the same man for eight years. People challenge her: "'If you're for sexuality outside a relationship, then you should be living that life.' Only I say, 'Yes, I'm choosing one way, and other women can choose another way.'"

Critics of CAKE protest that the company only reinforces the old misogyny, and that the women who attend its parties are duped into thinking they are feeling empowered, when really they're being oppressed. The theory is appealing, but ultimately I don't buy that line entirely. Melinda points out that the women really do enjoy their events, and there's no reason to believe that what she's saying isn't true. "Within the CAKE context, it's all about the women themselves," she assures me. "It's not about the men; it's all women-generated." Fifteen hundred women do pay $100 a year for membership in Club Cake, so clearly they are getting something out of the parties, other than merely wanting to feel oppressed for an evening. The question is what.

Melinda earned a master's degree in human sexuality and public health from New York University. She is very articulate as she explains the theory behind CAKE parties featuring extended strip-a-thons and themed events (mostly requiring women to show up in their lingerie). The first parties in New York City got a bit out of hand, especially one where porn stars had sex onstage. Melinda adds, "Of course it was totally illegal, and it was also when Giuliani was mayor." Rudolph Giuliani had a quality-of-life program in which broken windows were a definite no-no—to say nothing of public sex. On the other hand, CAKE's gaffe had an upside, since that party did make the front page of the *New York Post* the next day. But today "it's very rare that there's full nudity," Melinda clarifies.

I float the idea of sexuality as private and sacred, and Melinda responds staunchly: "That to me is inequality. We're public in the workforce, we're public in our social lives, we're public in every other realm. So if we're going to progress, [women] are going to have to carve out a public definition of our own sexuality." That was in fact the reasoning behind CAKE:

When we first started, the idea was really simple, Emily and I were both women's studies feminists, her [Emily] at Columbia and me at NYU. We were like—we had all these ideas in our heads: We will go and rent out a classroom at NYU for twenty people and like sit in a circle and put these ideas out there and maybe show some material or whatever [i.e., pornography]. And Matthew [Emily's brother and Melinda's boyfriend] actually said, "Why don't you have it be more New York-y and fun?" It was the summer, and, "Why don't you just do it in a more public forum?" And literally 500 people showed up. It was very much friends and family and friends of friends of friends. What is this new thing?—Women and sexuality, and also straight women and sexuality, as opposed to all this stuff that was going on through the 1990s of lesbian and bisexual clubs.

I ask Melinda about a friend of mine who went to a CAKE party and found that all the men were gay. "They are," she says, nodding. She admits, "The one challenge has been getting men who are not gay to come. Because the parties are for straight women. Gay men are more theatrical, more performance-y; they'll dance naked; it's much more of a cultural thing." CAKE began with the idea that men would have to pay double to get in, to see women being so outrageously sexual, but today the company sometimes pays for heterosexual men to show up at all. "We just want regular guys," the women would lament, and so Emily and Melissa sought them out—"We literally started casting [men] off the street."

If you step back and think about it, it is a bit odd. CAKE parties are about heterosexual women's "being sexual," yet the women are surrounded by individuals—gay men and other women—to whom, by their own admission, they are not in the least attracted. Since heterosexual men seem to be terrified of CAKE parties, it ends up as a kind of performance for all concerned. Even Melinda's longtime boyfriend and business partner seems ambivalent. "On my boyfriend's birthday," Gallagher told *New York* magazine, "I asked all the female Cake dancers to give him a collective lap dance. We are friends with the dancers, so it was cute and playful." But there was an irony: "I wouldn't hesitate to get him a lap dance at a strip club, but he usually prefers to get them for me instead."

The irony is rather doleful. Third-wave feminists embraced public sexuality in order to undermine gender stereotypes, while the men—untroubled by having anything to prove—seem to be hanging on to a basic modicum of modesty. "You know, when men see other men, gay or not, being sexual with women in public, it just provokes feelings of competitiveness and disgust," said one man who declined an invite to CAKE. Gary, a thirty-five-year-old southerner who now lives in Los Angeles, writes to me with a related issue—he describes himself as "good-looking and funny" and says he has no "problem meeting women and going out with them." But nonetheless Gary is lonely. By this point in his life he has parted with his "player ways":

Now I only look for a modest woman, but they are nowhere to be found and it only seems to be getting worse. I have gone out on three dates since moving here. Two were good and we really hit it off, but on the second date one girl asked me if we were going to have sex or not. I took her to her home, as I lost all attraction for her, and never called her again. The other date was the same thing. So for the past two years I have been bored with all the women whom I have met. It's all the same; they seem more sex-crazed than the men I know and it's rather boorish. . . . I hate that sex is somehow used as a form of validation these days. . . . Don't get me wrong, I like sex. (I am a man, after all!) But knowing that there is a challenge present does two things for me: It makes me feel like the person I am pursuing is worthwhile and has self-respect, and it makes me feel like a man should feel, like he has enough skill and compassion and gentleness to actually attract her.

After a rash of negative publicity implying that CAKE was promoting a sexist image of women as sexual objects, it is now diversifying and spending more time on producing books. Indeed, toward the end of our conversation Melinda told me, "CAKE is going to be deemphasizing the parties, and moving more into retail. Although the parties are successful, you know, I'm getting older and the parties go late, and you can't bring kids to events where you get home at 3:00 A.M." She looks hopeful as she says that at thirty-three she "wants to have children very soon," and so do her friends. "To become a mother," she admits, is something that nearly "every girlfriend that I know" wants. As I listen to Melinda, I feel our ideological differences melt away:

We're in our early thirties and there is that time that you have, and most of my friends do want that, and that is just the reality. That is one big difference between men and women. . . . Men can just run off, and that does add [an emotional element] to sex. . . . Just as I get older, I'm feeling differently than I did when I was in my twenties, when it's all open-ended. You hit thirty-three and you're, like, wow, forty is like right around the corner. We'd better start now or . . . oh, my goodness. And your priorities change.

Maybe we wish we could just bump and grind and be tough, but maybe at the end of the day, we're still just as vulnerable. Perhaps all this public display of their sexual power makes some women feel that we've equalized things. I don't think of this as false consciousness, which is condescending. But overcompensation might be at work here. Melinda would surely disagree, but when I ask her who the women are performing for—when there are no heterosexual men in the audience—she answers, "They're performing for themselves, as powerful, sexual beings. We've been going for five years and [there are] thousands of CAKE members, and the feedback is that it's a positive, reinforcing concept. Objectification can be a positive thing, if you own it, if you are in control of it."

She talks about control quite a bit, and that's when I finally get it. This is what CAKE offers women: the idea that you can be in control of something as messy as sexual vulnerability. "In my opinion it's only bad when you are not in *control*," Melinda continues. "The whole point of the CAKE atmosphere is to build a sort of utopia, a room where for that night, the women are totally in control and they set the agenda, and what happens is OK."

In building their utopia, whom are they trying to convince? Themselves. There are any number of reasons why a contemporary woman might not feel she is "setting the agenda" in her relationships, that what's happening, in fact, is often not "OK." Yet when she attends a CAKE party, for one night at least, she feels she has the upper hand.

If CAKE is indeed phasing out its parties, then what is next on the horizon? As Melinda talks about fantasy, I have my own little fantasy. I envision a business called KUGEL, named after the traditional Jewish noodle dish. People will pay to go to parties where it's guaranteed that others will keep their clothes on *the whole time*. Many different varieties of kugel will be served: sweet Yerushalmi kugel, plum noodle kugel, spinach kugel, pineapple upside-down kugel, potato zucchini kugel, tofu kugel, and of course the more traditional potato kugels as well. Only here's the catch: Instead of the women baking the kugel as they usually do, the men have to bake it. (All those husbands who, for example, reportedly made a mean carrot kugel when they were single will finally need to make their kugels materialize.) At last, women will have the opportunity to taste their husbands' or boyfriends' kugel. And of course KUGEL wouldn't pay for the kugel served— that would be too obvious. The men must bring two of their own kugels, or they won't be admitted.

KUGEL will spread like wildfire. People who formerly flocked to CAKE parties will now be flocking to KUGEL. Everyone would get a bit more *zaftig* and be less inclined to disrobe at the drop of a dime. Women would feel more empowered, alive, and well-fed.

I smile dreamily at Melinda, who seems to be waiting for me to say something. I quickly snap out of it: "Melinda, thanks so much for your time."

* * *

So the battle for the soul of feminism goes on. As I traveled around the country, I found that when girls did identify as feminists, they did not identify with the official leadership.

The younger feminists I encountered wanted a sharp departure from the "sex-positive" or pro-porn feminism of years past. They wanted a movement that stressed dignity more than rights. Growing up in a culture saturated with pornography, they consider it impossible that feminism should mean more of the same, even in a bid for equality. Many of them said things like, "I do agree with the initial meaning of feminism, which was that women have power by virtue of being women"; and, "I don't think the first feminists wanted us to be more like men." In *New Moon*, a feminist magazine for tween girls, Krystie, eleven, from Illinois, tells this story:

> I was listening to a Chicago radio station; they were having a contest to win a pair of tickets to something. In order to win the tickets, a woman had to show the DJs her breasts. The woman who had the biggest breasts would win tickets. That is one of the sickest things I've ever heard. I don't think I'll ever listen to that station again. Neither will my friends.

Will this girl grow up to believe, like Baumgardner, that "dancing at a strip club" can "radicalize" women? Probably not. As the third-wavers continue to advocate a public, crude sexuality and younger girls feel oppressed by how public sexuality is, the two sets of women are on course for an inevitable collision. In talking to them, I came to think of these younger feminists as part of a fourth wave, since their beliefs tend to distinguish them from the third-wave feminists who are usually quoted in the media. The fourth-wavers question pornography instead of wishing to star in it. They are more likely to be fans of Florence Nightingale than Nina Hartley. They are most taken with earlier feminists, the nineteenth-century women who were temperance advocates as much as suffragists. The suffragists argued that women should own property and have the right to vote precisely so that they might improve society with their moral perspective and their feminized heroism. The early feminists also believed in the sacredness of sexuality, it's interesting to note.

So do these young women.

. . .

Approximately 420 college students have arrived for a conference at l'Université du Québec à Montréal (UQAM) in March 2006. The conference promises: *"nous démystifierons le visage parfois tabou du féminisme en 2006 afin de lui redonner un élan"*—to "demystify the at times taboo face of feminism in 2006 in order to give it new momentum." That so many college students would attend such a conference is surprising, but perhaps less so when you find out that the keynote speaker is fourteen years old. Auburn-haired Léa Clermont-Dion, wearing a sophisticated pink scarf, takes the microphone. This is the fourth such conference she has helped organize on the "hypersexualization" of teen girls. Léa has delicate features but a determined look: *"Moi je réclame le droit de dire non merci . . . à tout ça!"* Her listeners seem excited, ready to hear more. The subject of this conference is *"L'égalité, acquise?"* ("Equality, Achieved?")—and the clear answer, according to Léa, is no. "Today I will speak of a problem that troubles me greatly. I can tell you that hypersexualization really exists; it's not just adults who are speaking about it."

The Beatles were a big influence on Léa's mother. But today's role models, Léa maintains—Eminem, Snoop Dog, 50 Cent for boys, Britney Spears and Paris Hilton for girls—are selling something that has a far more negative influence. It's not just that the boys wear pants below the buttocks, "XXL clothes, and for the girls it's XXXS, G-strings that show, see-through tops, exposed midriffs." It's more than that—"The word I would use to describe the look is 'slut.'"

I am surprised to hear a feminist use a word like that. (Léa uses the term *salope*, which has a connotation like our "ho.") "I know it's shocking when I say it, but this is the look that's seen as 'in,'" she continues. If one dresses like that, "one is well-perceived." Indeed, just last week, she reports, she heard some girls greeting each other with the expression "Hello, slut!" as if to say, "Hey, how's it going?" Léa points out, "This is a strange way to dialogue." Indeed, at about the same time as this conference, American media were reporting that "Hi, slut!" had become a popular greeting among girls in the United States; so apparently, whether it's "Hi, slut!" or *"Bonjour, sa-lope,"* the phenomenon is widespread. And for boys, of course, it's the "pimp" look.

Léa wants her audience to know that it's normal for young people to imitate their role models. But if we look at videos of Christina Aguilera, for example, "What do we see? We see Christina dressed in black leather underwear, with a whip, dancing around a pole while singing." In a magazine called *Filles d'Aujourd'hui* (*Girls of Today*) Léa saw an ad for running shoes—it showed Christina Aguilera dressed in black leather, holding a whip, and wearing the shoes. "Running shoes? What's the relationship between the black leather, the whip, and the shoes?" It doesn't even make sense, she points out. It's just that women must always be publicly sexual; that's the "stereotype" they must fit into.

The pressure on very young girls to perform oral sex, Léa reports, is as bad as the media portray, if not worse. "Young people find it very normal to practice it." She adds, "The problem is not having oral sex"—here she uses the *québecois* slang, "pipe":

> The problem is not the "pipe"—it's that there's no longer love, no inti-macy, no relationship. Young people don't know what a relationship is, really. There's also the phenomenon of "f——k friends." Have you heard of it? It's two partners who have sex with no strings. There are many of those. It's become very normal. Now, we don't say, "Would you like to be my girlfriend [*blonde,* in *québecois*]?" We say, "Would you like to be my f——k friend?" Are you fed up with beer ads [one of which includes a reference to ejaculation]? Are you fed up with that? I'm very fed up and disgusted. . . . If you're tired of this, then we have to react to it, we have to fight it!

Léa wants young women to rethink "what it is to be a liberated woman." She's heard girls say, "'Léa's a feminist, but what's the point? Feminism's useless; we can sleep with who we want, make ourselves up how we want, seduce who we want.' I don't think that's what it is to be a feminist. There's intimacy in all this." In case it isn't obvious, Léa identifies very strongly as a feminist. Indeed, she is such a staunch feminist that she actually refuses to meet with me after I make the mistake of telling her mother that I inter-viewed a former Miss America for this book. Léa, not surprisingly, is firmly against beauty pageants. Although I assure her that I'm no fan of beauty pageants myself, to my great amusement Léa wants nothing to do with me. Clearly, a young woman with standards.

As a young feminist, Léa wants older feminists to speak more about intimacy. "We have to speak to young people about intimacy and love, not just performance. Because now for young people, it's about performance, skin in exchange for skin." She says *cul*—literally, one derriere in exchange for another derriere.

But she didn't come just to bemoan the status quo. Léa believes that there are solutions. "It's not true that things have to stay as they are. It's your duty as citizens to say that you're against this. It's your duty. Everything is possible, my friends; everything is possible." Education campaigns must be run by young people and not by "moralizing adults," she tells her eager audience. More than that, women have a special responsibility to speak out about intimacy and love. "Schools don't do it, and neither do the pornified media. . . . You have to speak about it, and be able to speak about it with your children."

She ends her impassioned speech by asking her audience to consider what it means to be a woman today. "Is it to shave? To submit ourselves to sexual practices, not because we feel like it, but because of social pressure? Is that what it means to be liberated? Me, I say 'No, thank you to all this' and I hope that you will say 'No, thank you' to what the media offer us, and to what society offers us." In English this may sound banal, but in French it is a rousing anthem: *"Moi je réclame le droit de dire non merci . . . à tout ça!"* The college students in the audience have received their marching orders, and they are clearly moved and impressed.

Katherine Canty, reporting for the CBC on Léa's performance and how "enthralled" her audience was, observes: "The right to say no is a lot of responsibility for a fourteen-year-old, but Clermont-Dion is confident her generation of young women will find a healthier way to express their sexuality."

Later I speak to Cathy Wong, a friendly-looking twenty-year-old who wears red glasses and is involved with Léa in organizing these events. What feminism means is more varied than ever, in Cathy's opinion:

Today we're seeing younger women who want to be actually feminist and feminine at the same time. Before, in the 1960s, a lot of feminists would be like pro- the image of a guy. They would dress like guys, they would like act like guys, and even today a lot of feminists would act like guys sexually. And I believe that today feminism is not only about that and feminism has many facets and the women have to take responsibility for those many facets. And in the 1960s feminism was really divided too. For example, when we're talking about pornography, it was really, really divided. And I still believe that today, it is even more divided.

To Cathy, who is studying international and women's law, being a feminist means fighting pornography: "A lot of women feel that pornography, and the like, is actually affecting their life and their self-image, their self-esteem. It's affecting, for example, their way of living and the way of entertaining life with the opposite sex, for example. And I think that a lot of women actually feel powerless in front of those images."

At the same time, Cathy has many friends who have "totally different values," and they consider themselves feminists. She finds that the key to getting along is "respect." The notion of women who have mutually exclusive goals working together is a bit peculiar, but this spirit of tolerance is one positive inheritance of third-wave feminism.

Jennifer Baumgardner, for example, in the same speech in which she described her effort to write for *Playboy*, also allows for young women who choose more traditional lives: "Now that women are a little closer to having authentic choices, they're showing they are not just lemmings; they don't all want to work at the same job. Some of them found home life satisfying." As far as she's concerned, "Feminism has always been about valuing home life. Feminists were the ones that said that being a wife and a mother was a real job." Well, not exactly. Germaine Greer suggested that women should not even "enter into socially sanctioned relationships, like marriage" and should "refrain from establishing exclusive dependencies and other kinds of neurotic symbioses," which can lead to becoming "a vain, demanding, servile bore." She also said that mothers "sacrifice what they never had: a self," which was a nicer way of saying what Simone de Beauvoir said earlier: "She does nothing, she *has* nothing, she *is* nothing." Beauvoir also held that the stay-at-home mom was a slave, a "parasite," even a "praying mantis." Indeed, marriage by itself made even childless women into "praying mantises" and "leeches." Betty Friedan wrote that women at home constitute "a devaluation of human progress," and that the educated housewife is a "two-headed schizophrenic," akin to someone in "a coma." It's certainly nice of Baumgardner not to judge more traditional women as "stunted at a lower level of living," but Betty Friedan did exactly that.

More recently, in 2006, the feminist lawyer Linda Hirshman told stay-at-home mothers to *Get to Work* in her book of that title. Women who stay home "aren't using their capacities freely," she writes, and "their talent and education are lost from the public world to the private world of laundry and kissing boo-boos." Instead, all women should "aspire to something complex and demanding." They might, for instance, "own their own restaurant or start the next Starbucks, design the next wrap dress." That is, as long as the woman designs wrap dresses full-time; Hirshman has no patience for part-time work outside the home, which in her view cannot lead to a "flourishing life." As a mother who works part-time myself, I have to ask: the next wrap dress? I mean no disrespect to designers, but raising the next generation must be at least as creative and difficult as that wrap dress. It can seem less significant only if your sole criterion is external approval. Women may indeed get more social approval by designing a wrap dress than by comforting a child—primarily because of judgmental people who devalue the private sphere and relegate it to a silly collection of "boo-boos." But does this mean that our private actions are intrinsically any less significant?

Considered objectively, the second-wave feminists are not quite as tolerant as some might like to imagine them.

By contrast, feminists such as Baumgardner leave themselves open to the charge that in tolerating everything they believe in nothing. Critics have portrayed third-wavers as fluffy, "girlie" feminists, not believing in anything beyond knitting and stripping. I don't think this charge is quite fair. At least many third-wavers are tolerant in both directions, something that can hardly be said of their predecessors. To her credit, Baumgardner believes you can be pro-life and a feminist, although she is herself pro-choice: "I think you can be a feminist and be pro-life. A feminist pro-life person is someone who works actively to provide resources so that there are fewer abortions," she has said. And Rachel Kramer Bussel has written sensitively about the pressure on virgins to lose their virginity, certainly a brave undertaking for someone who wrote the "Lusty Lady" column for *The Village Voice*. Over e-mail, Rachel elaborates: "I believe in sexual freedom for everyone, not just people like me, and I think that has to include virgins, more modest people, etc. . . . I don't want to contribute to a culture that makes people feel ashamed of being virgins (or being whatever)."

So tolerance among some third-wavers was a refreshing development for feminism. And it just may be what opened the door to younger women like Léa Clermont-Dion and Cathy Wong and their more traditional concept of keeping sexuality significant.

Another difference: The third wave of feminism tries to smooth over contradictions within feminism in an attempt to be inclusive, whereas the fourth wave is stressing activism again.

. . .

I'm at the Frick Car and Carriage Museum in Pittsburgh, wandering around with the famous Girlcott girls. These are the girls who were offended by some of Abercrombie & Fitch's T-shirts for young women—such as WHO NEEDS BRAINS WHEN YOU HAVE THESE?—and led a boycott against them. Anyone who says that you can't go back to the nineteenth century has never been to the Car and Carriage Museum, where you can see a governess carriage (with high walls on the wagon, so the wee ones couldn't tumble out), and carriages from 1881 made for touring at a leisurely pace. I chose this location because it was convenient for the girls and also because it seemed to be a perfect place to schmooze about their postmodern battle for decency. We retire to the Frick café for a victory celebration, of sorts.

When the girls, as members of the Allegheny County Girls as Grantmakers program, decided to "Girlcott" the T-shirts in October 2005, the local newspaper was unimpressed. An op-ed in the *Pittsburgh Tribune-Review* laughed off their news conference denouncing Abercrombie's merchandise, and predicted that the protest would be ineffectual: Girls with "these items in their closet will continue buying similar clothing—if only to have something fresh to wear to the next wet T-shirt contest," smirked Eric Heyl. But the girls persevered, and they received thousands of letters from other girls who also found the shirts demeaning. Other shirts considered objectionable were BLONDES ARE ADORED, BRUNETTES ARE IGNORED, I HAD A NIGHTMARE I WAS A BRUNETTE, and DO I MAKE YOU LOOK FAT? Liz Clark, fourteen, told me, "Once we spoke out, we got tons of support from people who just thought, 'Oh, yeah, that's true; I don't like this either!'"

The *Pittsburgh Tribune-Review* may have dismissed the girls as "the next generation of feminist scolds," but the girls had the last laugh. Not only did Abercrombie & Fitch pull the most offensive shirts from its inventory; the company also invited sixteen of the Girlcott girls to visit its headquarters in Ohio, to help it create a new line of more empowering tees.

Sure, this was a bit of a public relations stunt on Abercrombie's part (as if they had thought the "bimbo" shirts were empowering until the teens from Pittsburgh came and enlightened them). But nonetheless, these girls ages thirteen to seventeen had accomplished what mothers nationwide could not—they made a peddler of "cutting-edge" shirts look clueless and out of touch with today's youth.

The Girlcott was thought up during a retreat in September 2005, at which the young women in the Girls as Grantmakers program were giving hypothetical money for proposed ideas, including staging a protest of Abercrombie's T-shirts. So many of the girls wanted to give their "money" to this protest, recalls Heather Arnet, the executive director of the Women and Girls Foundation of Southwest Pennsylvania, "that the girls started to say, 'Hey, why don't we really do this? The shirts really exist and it's a problem.'" They felt that these shirts encouraged bullying and cliques, and they wanted to start a project that would unify girls against the company instead of creating divisions among girls. As Emma Blackman-Mathis, age sixteen, put it in their public statement announcing the Girlcott, in October: "We, as young women and girls, do not need to create extra competition between our ranks. By Girlcotting these shirts, we not only create unity for a single project or battle; we create unity within the female community as a whole." Girls "won't be taken seriously if they wear those kind of shirts," added Jettie Fields, thirteen, who appeared on the *Today* show with Emma, asking girls to spread the word to other girls. Thousands of girls across the country agreed and refused to shop at Abercrombie until it pulled the offending shirts—as it promptly did after just five days of protests. (It took this action perhaps in the nick of time. In Connecticut, a group of girls circulated a petition against Abercrombie during their lunch hour and collected 600 signatures.)

To find out what happened in the aftermath, in the spring of 2006 I met with four young women who were involved from the beginning: Yagmur Muftuoglu, sixteen; Rebecca Adelsheim, fifteen; and Liz Clark and Katie Waronek, both fourteen. They attend different high schools in the Pittsburgh area, so it was interesting to hear about how students in their various schools reacted. Dark-haired Yagmur is the most formally dressed of the group, and resembles an elegant princess wearing a business suit. She is very confident, and just laughs about her peers' reaction: "No one ever came up to me directly, but it was always like, they'd come in wearing the shirt, and take their jacket off right in front of me, and I'd be like, 'What are you trying to play,' you know?" She knew that some girls supported the Girlcott, but "they couldn't say anything because everyone else was so much stronger against it."

Liz, who is fair-skinned and blond—yet nonetheless was not a fan of Abercrombie's shirt reading BLONDES ARE ADORED, BRUNETTES ARE IGNORED—tells me, "I don't know—a lot of the students I don't think really supported [the Girlcott] that much, especially guys. A lot of my guy friends were like, 'That's such a waste of time. Why would you do that?'"

Katie, who is wearing a T-shirt and jeans and has a cute wry expression, decides that she "had the weirdest experience. Half the people in my school hadn't heard about it, but those who did—I had one person who said, 'How's that, um, *thing* going for you?' Then a couple of guys turned around suddenly and they were kind of like, 'Why are you doing this? No one really cares!' There's another person who said, 'It doesn't matter, they're just shirts, so just give it up.'" Yet she discovered that "people at their own schools, they might be all smirky, but then, like, really in their hearts they might agree with you." Enough girls stopped buying the shirts, in any case, for Abercrombie to become concerned.

Rebecca, a passionate yet studious-looking young woman, received the most backing from her peers because she attends an all-girls school: "Everyone was very supportive—all the teachers, most of the students. But one of the coolest experiences for me was walking into a room and having people just sitting there talking about it and like I didn't have to say anything, and they didn't know I was involved. And they were like, 'Have you heard about the Girlcott?' And I was like, 'Yes, I've heard about the Girlcott!'" She dissolves into laughter.

Sometimes support came from surprising quarters. Heather Arnet tells me that one day during the Girlcott a large jock type veered toward Emma Blackman-Mathis and headed straight for her. Since Emma is just a little over five feet tall, she was concerned. He said, "Hey, you!" And Emma thought he might beat her up, but instead the jock said, "I heard about that . . . thing, and I think those T-shirts are really stupid, too." Then he walked away.

Other girl shirts made by Abercrombie include: SCHOOL IS A GREAT PLACE TO MEET BOYS, BOYOLOGY MAJOR, and I LOVE SENIOR BOYS/I LOVE SENIOR BOYS/I LOVE SENIOR BOYS. Girls in college can graduate to a tee with FRESHMAN 15 next to a list of fifteen guys' names on it (each in a different signature, like signatures on a tree trunk). Guys can wear shirts boasting, PLAYS WELL WITH D CUPS.

Liz reflects, "I feel like a lot of girls strive to be like these role models that aren't really good at all. I don't really know why; I think maybe just because they see them on TV, VH1 and MTV, all the time—just like they're rich, they have money, they're pretty. A lot of girls in high school think it's important to be like that. But like, I don't like Paris Hilton very much. I think a lot of girls just need to focus on other things."

Rebecca concurs: "a lot of it is media attention. The girls that people see all the time, those are the people who are role models, and when things are in the media, those are the things that people are thinking about at that time. That's why our Girlcott was so successful: because we got national attention, because people were hearing about it on the news, and then they started talking about it."

Yagmur, who reminded me of a budding philosophy professor, led the discussion:

> I heard somewhere that the people who should rule never rule, and the
> people who shouldn't rule are the only leaders—something like that.
> And I think that also goes for, like, role models. The people who seem
> to be role models are people with, like, I don't want to say, the wrong
> mind-set, because it's not wrong, but it's a different mind-set than what
> I think a real role model should be, in my eyes. I think a role model is
> someone who would want to change the world. But most of the role
> models on TV aren't like that, you know.

Most but not all of the Pittsburgh Girlcotters identified themselves as feminists, so I wanted to know what that concept meant to them. For Liz, "one of the big parts of equality is women being able to make their own decisions, and not having other people make them for them." She realizes that people might see this as a contradiction: "A lot of people accused the Girlcott of trying to censor stuff. But I mean, we weren't trying to make the company illegal or whatever." For her, girls are equal when they are aware that they don't have to go along with how women are portrayed in the media.

Since we had just seen so many charming old carriages, historical comparisons were inevitable. Rebecca says something genuinely profound:

A long time ago women had so many boundaries, and they had to follow those boundaries. There would be no fluctuation made. They couldn't decide those boundaries, but now it's like we have no boundaries. But if women are able to make their own decisions and set their own boundaries, that would be a huge step forward. Both genders should be making their own decisions and setting their own boundaries. If both can do that, that's so much more forward than in the 1900s.

Setting your own boundaries has its limitations, of course, when there's no guarantee anyone else will respect them. But the order of the day, at least, was to try. As Rebecca puts it: "I think one of the biggest problems for a lot of girls is fitting in and what they feel they have to do to fit in. Like, staying clean for girls, who feel that they have to get into drugs and drink and things like that, just because it's what girls around them are doing and people around them are doing. They think the only way to fit in is to do that stuff."

Yagmur agrees, and adds that even the most sympathetic parents don't get it sometimes:

I told my mom, you know, "I'm really proud of myself," and she was like, "What?" I said I'm proud of myself for getting through at least, like, most of high school, and like staying clean you know, like, without any moral scars and things like that, for not getting mixed in with the wrong people; and she was like, "Yeah, I know." She totally blew it off, but it's really the most important thing.

Liz thinks that Abercrombie's attitude tees are only popular because of peer pressure. A lot of girls feel pressure to look a certain way and act a certain way, to be like girls on TV, and I think the Girlcott worked because girls started to realize that they didn't have to act like that, and that they can be themselves and be smart, and not get laughed at by people."

Yagmur cuts in, "The majority is trying to be Paris Hilton," just so they don't get laughted at.

Then Katie has a brilliant insight, which I appreciate only later, when I listen to the tape (she is self-depreciating during the interview so her comment flies right by me). She says that it didn't matter what society valued, because being good was just plain harder:

Being good shows that you're willing to think about other people and not just yourself, because the whole world's like, "Oh, everything's about me." My Spanish teacher said, to help us learn the verb tenses, you have to think in the whole world, everything's about you. I don't know how it related to Spanish, but she was like, "Everything is about you," and I'm like, "Well, people always think that anyway." I want to think about other people, so I'm like, well, I'm probably never going to learn the tenses anyway. But seriously, acting like you care about other people—you need that in the world.

When the group finally took the three-hour bus ride to New Albany, Ohio, to meet with representatives of Abercrombie, the girls didn't get the sense that the company was taking them so seriously. "One woman was playing with her cell phone for a decent amount of time," someone pointed out. Another observed that the two women in the room (out of five representatives) kept pretty quiet throughout the meeting. One of the girls finally put a woman on the spot and asked her, "What do *you* think?" And her response was, "Well, I agree with Tom." This was simply unacceptable to the girls, who had suited up in their business best for the occasion, so they fired off a few follow-up questions. When the representatives' opinions were teased out of them, Abercrombie's position, as Rebecca summarizes it, was this: "They said a lot, 'You're not talking to deaf ears,' or something like that. And, 'We're with you, but this is what's popular now,' or something like that. But I mean, we got a lot of support, so I don't think their shirts were really *so* popular."

Yagmur, who also was one of the eleven girls in the boardroom, summarizes the company's party line: "The general consensus of the company was that these were T-shirts for the 'intelligent girl,' like they were supposed to be ironic and funny. And—I mean, I understand where they're coming from—but I told them, 'Well, none of it's being taken that way in school.'" Abercrombie had hoped to portray those who didn't get the joke as unsophisticated, but this didn't sit well with the girls, and especially not with Rebecca: "It's like if you're sophisticated, you'll be able to present yourself that way. But really, who is the joke on? Ultimately the joke is on the girl." Indeed.

It is really too bad that I was not in the room when Yagmur told the assembled representatives that they were "neglecting their social responsibility," but hearing her play by play was almost as good. I pictured the girls with their PowerPoint presentation and Yagmur speaking in her persuasive, idealistic way:

> I said Abercrombie is, like, so powerful; and in a way, I believe that you should take this power and use it productively. So what they're doing is using it destructively, I think. Like they're turning the tide back or forward—it depends on how you want to look at it—and I told them that recently morals have degenerated; everything's like slowly breaking down, whether or not they realize it. But, I said, "You know fifty years from now we're really going to say, yeah, that was happening." And I said, "You have the power to bring them [morals] back," and I don't know whether or not they understood.

Probaby not, but Rebecca tried to appeal to them from a different angle: "A lot of girls buy these T-shirts, just because they will buy Abercrombie, just for the brand name; and if Abercrombie would make empowering T-shirts, girls would buy them because it's from their store." That's what Rebecca also "tried to get across to them, their social responsibility—they have the power, but they're choosing not to [use it] at this point." Are they? Katie gives voice to my cynical side when she says that empowering tees would "kind of go against the whole image of Abercrombie." She reminds us that "OK, you have the half-naked guy, as soon as you walk in the store, and then to have a nice empowering T-shirt, right next to it? I think that kind of dampens what they're trying to send."

The controversy does remind me of environmentally friendly companies. Conventional wisdom once held that companies couldn't be both environmentally friendly and profitable, until it was discovered that being "green" could become a big selling point. Yagmur has, of course, thought of this already, and in fact she used an environmental metaphor when speaking to Abercrombie's representatives: "I talked about poisoning the water that they're going to drink. Well, these shirts are poisoning their own consumers." Did that go over big? Well, either way the reps heard her returning to the subject of "morals," which they must have loved:

> Morals. It's not like a T-shirt defines a person's ethics but it's definitely a reflection of it. And you show everyone. Everyone who sees the

T-shirts being worn thinks that girls, they're all like loose, or they're easy, or you know, they've done this and they're proud of it—and you show everyone that, well, it kind of reflects an idea that isn't true, and there's more to girls than just that.

Abercrombie may not become a company dedicated to girls' empowerment through T-shirts, but the slime factor has been reduced. The girls' influence is evident in some of the new tees Abercrombie is now offering, such as CUTE AND CLASSY.

* * *

The Women and Girls Foundation of Southwest Pennsylvania, which runs the Girls as Grantmakers program, is a feminist organization. And the Girlcott girls would not have gotten very far without the help of Heather Arnet, her expertise, and her media savvy. Yet it's not clear that, with their emphasis on "classiness" and "morals," the girls are a natural fit in any pre-existing feminist organization or movement.

This became obvious when a third-wave organization, the Real Hot 100!, attempted to co-opt the the Girlcotters to advance its agenda in July 2006. The attempt certainly made sense, since the Girlcotters were so popular—about 25,000 stories about them appeared online—that everyone seemed to want to take credit for them and claim them. (The only real surprise is that stuffed animals have not as yet been made of them.) Yet as you read Jessica Valenti's depiction of the Girlcotters, it doesn't take a genius to see why they and the third-wavers are not a natural fit:

> Meet this week's REAL hotties. . . . This week's 2006 REAL hotties fought Abercrombie & Fitch—and won! Because of their REALLY hot Girlcott, A&F pulled demeaning T-shirts from their shelves. How hot is that? Meet the Girlcott Girls . . . ages thirteen to eighteen, Pittsburgh, PA. What makes them REALLY hot? "Give me something to scream about!" is just what Abercrombie & Fitch did for twenty-four young girls after releasing a line of female T-shirts containing this sexually charged phrase along with some other sexist and racist messages, including, "Who needs brains when you have these?" . . . These T-shirts sparked a feminist uproar in this group of teens, and they decided to take action! The group of twenty-four REALLY hot girls originally came together to learn to be grantmakers, in a youth program.

The icing on the cake was the Real Hot icon, a red-hot drawing of a woman picking up her skirt, showing us her lingerie and her legs splayed up in the air. Wasn't this exactly the kind of thing the girls were fighting against? And did girls as young as thirteen really need to be called "hot" quite so many times? I sent the article to the Girlcotters, who were already well aware of the honor. One wrote back, "We actually read the report about us from the Real Hot 100 and thought it was interesting. . . . I think we all felt the form of the word 'hot' was used too often. While they probably meant well, I'm not sure why everything has to be redefined as hot." As for the symbol, another girl hadn't known about that: "Unless my Internet Explorer window is maximized I can't see everything on the screen. I never knew." Now that she saw the symbol, she found it "degrading—I guess that in a sense it was what our Abercrombie & Fitch campaign was also about." Another e-mailed me: "I dunno, it's kind of weird that feminists would call something 'hot.' . . . I must say that I disagree with a lot of the radical feminist things out there." Ironically, of course, the third-wavers got into all this "hottness" precisely to distance themselves from the "radical" antiporn feminists of yesteryear; but to many young feminists, it's making sex so casual that is radical—and unwanted.

One girl did like the Real Hot website, telling me that she felt all the hotness was innocuous, "simply a play on words" as an answer to *Maxim* magazine's annual lineup of 100 "hot women." She has a point—the group's slogan is "See how hot smart can be," and it aimed to show that women can do more than "look cute in a magazine." A terrific idea, but then why use the word "hotties" at all? Many are doing admirable work, such as teachers helping special-needs kids and lawyers advocating for the elderly. Is Bill Gates "hot" when he devotes himself to charity work? Do we need to see an illustration of him in his underwear with his legs splayed to the sky in order to appreciate what he is doing? Only for women, it seems, does every public act need to be redefined as "hot" for it to be socially acceptable— even or perhaps especially social service. After all, the more women are developed internally, the more this is threatening to a society that insists on seeing them merely externally. Hence the need to defuse the threat and reassure everyone: "Don't worry, you can still do what you want to us; we all just want to be porn stars, too!" It's no wonder that another girl told me, when she looked at the Real Hot 100! website, "I think we've been misunderstood."

If the third-wavers didn't really get the Girlcotters, neither did second-wave feminists. When I spoke to Kim Gandy, the president of NOW, she was shocked by my suggestion that the Girlcotters didn't want other girls to wear Abercrombie tees:

> MS. GANDY: Did you actually ask them whether they felt that if a girl wanted to wear one of those T-shirts that she ought to be able to?
> WENDY: Yeah, we talked about that.
> MS. GANDY: —because I think they would say yes!
> WENDY: Well, they wanted to "Girlcott" the shirts, remember, so obviously they wanted their actions to affect others' choices about what to wear. I mean, they're definitely not advocating that [the shirts] should be illegal, but the goal of a boycott is for the shirts to not be there anymore, so people couldn't wear them, right?
> MS. GANDY: Or so that people couldn't see them!

I don't appreciate the distinction, so she elaborates:

> MS. GANDY: I think it was more the seeing them than the wearing them. Because *they* wouldn't have worn them. They didn't want those messages to be out there for other people to absorb the negative messages about women. They're going to be honored at our conference . . . for taking action, but you know that is—I think it's more the issue of negative messages about women. Do we really want negative messages about women out there and not so much telling people what they're allowed to wear or what they're not allowed to wear. And I just want to make that distinction because I do think it's different.

It was fascinating to me that the Pittsburgh teens' strength—the fact that they stuck out their necks and made, essentially, a moral argument that these shirts were just plain demeaning, for all women—was precisely what Ms. Gandy wanted to downplay. She even seemed disturbed by it and at one point appeared unsure about why NOW was even honoring the girls: "They're going to be honored at our conference"—then a pause—"for taking *action*." Was that why? Activism is always a plus for a feminist, whereas judging other women's choices is a definite no-no.

But plainly, judging is what the girls were doing. Having grown up in an oversexualized culture, they were sick of it and were trying to rally other girls to not present themselves as mere sex objects. Still troubled, Ms.

Gandy later explains to me that what the girls were really doing was like objecting to posters: "If those messages had been on posters, for example, that people were putting in their rooms, I think they would have done the same thing." It was certainly a different way of looking at the episode, but didn't that presuppose the grounds in dispute? After all, these particular messages were not on posters but on T-shirts, which other girls were choosing to wear. I was left with the impression that she didn't really appreciate where the Girlcotters were coming from.

After the girls returned from the NOW conference in July 2006, I learned that the feeling was mutual. One girl, who is very tactful, had this to say: "I did go to the NOW conference. I thought it was interesting. To me, the workshops I attended seemed to be lacking something, though I'm not sure what. Maybe it was information; maybe it was the lack of seeing others' opinions; but something was lacking." Another girl was more forceful:

> We went to the NOW conference last week, and I support equality and would never like to be controlled by a man, but the NOW conference was more like a brainwashing feminist summit than anything else. They had this artistic performance that was so much about sex and how much all men suck; it really made me feel sick. You should've seen that artistic performance. It was frightening. I'd much rather see men and women being equal to one another and living well together than men asserting their masculinity and women trying to adopt that masculinity to make themselves superior. I don't know. . . . Those three days were awfully confusing for me. . . . I mean, we got that Women of Action award for what we've done, but, again, I think that we've been misunderstood. Everyone thinks that we are so feminist, but, frankly, most of us are not that radical. We just want to be on par with men.

I asked her what the other girls thought, but she was still recovering from the artistic performance:

> Ugh. The artistic performance was horrible. There was so much about "dykes" and sex. . . . It was pretty graphic about sex, too. . . . It was so weird, so vulgar. I can't say I felt victimized, but I did feel pressured into the radical feminist line of thought. I talked to many of the other girls. Now some of them (like two out of twenty-four) are very

feminist—not that this is a bad thing or anything, but still . . . Only like ten of us went [to the conference], but I'm pretty sure that eight out of that ten were also horrified by the trip. I mean, I LOOOVE the women advisers, but I felt kind of tricked. . . . I thought that they were very reasonable, middle-of-the-road like me, but I guess I was somewhat mistaken.

The women advisers, whom I have met, obviously really care about these girls and would never intentionally mislead them. But the Girlcott girls' going to a NOW conference was a train wreck waiting to happen, if for no other reason than that the feminist leadership tends to be vehemently opposed to the very moral message that the younger feminists espouse. For example, on the NOW website, one of the "misconceptions" supposedly leading to a bad body image is "the notion that women embody goodness and purity." This is a standard feminist line. Yet the site also puts forth another view, that it is against "the sexualization of girls' bodies at a very young age." Well, there is real tension between these two beliefs. If you want to fight the sexualization of girls' bodies and you want to do it effectively, then you have to allow for a concept of wholesomeness and a certain internal focus. But if you take the standard feminist line against "goodness and purity," then you're stuck. And you're also going to exclude girls like the Girlcotters who very much do believe in goodness.

If the feminist leaders were misguided in excluding "good girls" from their ideology, certain conservatives have been perhaps too hasty in declaring feminism dead. Feminism is clearly very much alive for young women, but it is a feminism that makes the leadership uneasy. For it is not as reflexively "bad-girl" as it once was, and its focus on personal dignity and on sex being sacred will mean the biggest shakeup of feminism since Seneca Falls in 1848.

Older feminists are now concerned that the sexual revolution and the concessions they made to pornography have not turned out as expected. They're discovering that promiscuity and public sexuality may not be the ticket to happiness, after all, even for men. So it makes sense that they would want to honor young women like the Girlcotters. The problem is that they are so committed to the idea of casual sex as liberation that they can't appreciate or even quite understand these younger feminists. They still don't understand that pursuing crudeness is the problem, not the solution. Or maybe they do understand this, but they don't want to admit they are wrong.

What will happen now is anyone's guess. Perhaps a new fourth wave of feminism really will take off, led by teen feminists such as Léa Clermont-Dion and the Girlcott girls. It will be a movement that is pro-woman but at the same time holds up high sexual standards. Alternatively, perhaps when these young women are older, they will simply cease to identify as feminists because the leadership cannot accommodate them.

I suppose we will just have to wait it out and see what happens.

Most interesting to me is the way that younger feminists are reclaiming older issues abandoned by some conservatives. As it stands, many younger feminists are now more conservative than some prominent conservatives—who are perhaps more properly described as libertarians on these cultural issues. At a time when Rush Limbaugh refers to the alleged rape victim at Duke as a "ho," and John Derbyshire of *National Review* objects to Jennifer Aniston's posing nude for *GQ*—not for reasons of privacy but because, according to him, only women ages fifteen to twenty are pleasant to regard in the nude—conservatives are plainly in danger of losing the moral high ground. Kathryn Lopez, *National Review Online*'s magnanimous editor, who always tries to keep discussions tasteful and aboveboard, reassures me, "Needless to say it's not a corporate opinion (thirtysomething gal editor says, thank you very much!)." That's good, because it would certainly be ironic if conservatives leaped to become "pornified" just as the young feminists finally recognize that things have gone too far.

Jane, a twenty-five-year-old former model who runs a nonprofit, confesses: "To be honest I am scared to grow old in a society that continues to devalue women. I am scared for my future baby girls to be raped, and I am scared for myself—perhaps I will be thrown to the wolves when I can no longer care for myself, as by that time a woman may be worth more as wolf food than as a person. Just kidding. Sort of." Then she reflects on "It's Hard Out Here for a Pimp," which won an Oscar for best song:

> It seems most "gangsta rap" has something to do with "pimping your ho," "slapping your bitch," or running away from law enforcement. I work in social services in an urban area in New Jersey, and can empathize with the urban experience, but I find it hard to believe that everyone born into socioeconomically disadvantaged situations becomes either a pimp or somebody's ho. The part of this whole situation that really worries me is not that a song about pimps won at the Academy Awards, but that such artistic outputs contribute to the overall de-

sensitization of America. Case in point: I spend most weekends at my boyfriend's apartment, which he shares with a roommate who is also a childhood friend. While always respectful toward me, Roommate (who is a big fan of gangsta rap and the hip-hop culture) has no problem speaking about his quest to find a woman for the evening, who will quietly leave later (I am putting this in the nicest of terms). Obviously, he sees nothing wrong with looking at women as subservient objects to provide services, and not as people with different reproductive organs.

Jane adds, "Roommate is your average twenty-eight-year-old male. He graduated from a good college with a profitable degree and has a job at which he earns a very good salary. He has friends, sometimes parties on the weekend, and has a good relationship with his family. He is what you would call Decent." And therein lies the problem:

It is now 2006, and the definition of Decent Man has been expanded to include misogyny and a general disrespect for women, the myth that women are something lower and to be treated as such. Perpetrated by large media outlets, peddled in the streets to our children so that little girls may know their roles as hos and little boys may grow up to be pimps. All of this contained in the psyche of Decent Man—without him ever even knowing it. It is just evidence of a New Decency. A Sad New Decency.

Who will challenge this "new decency"? Jane feels that both feminist groups and conservative groups are limited in terms of how much they can help young people. As far as she is concerned, "A revolution of this magnitude can't be brought to light by some sort of right-wing conservative group, because it will be immediately discredited." Neither does she have high hopes for organized feminist projects. "I just think that we need to lead the lives we choose with confidence, and let others see the fruit that such a choice produces." Since Jane herself feels that she escaped many bad situations in her teenage years simply by valuing herself, she wonders how "we can suddenly implement a program that teaches self-worth in a sex-saturated society. . . . It's beyond me. Instinctively, I want to say that it starts at home, with a mother who values herself, and a father who respects her. I am coming to the conclusion that it starts with us.

HOW TO START YOUR OWN GIRLCOTT

I collected some tips from the pros, the Girlcotters themselves.

1. Get lots of parents interested in and supportive of your cause. There's strength in numbers, after all. —Katie Waronek

2. The most important way to get the word out is to be organized. —Rebecca Adelsheim

3. Explain why the product is a problem. For example, if you're Girlcotting Bratz dolls, explain why it's so outrageous that these dolls are being sold to three-year-olds. —Katie Waronek

4. Just speak out, because chances are, no one's going to hate you forever if they don't agree with you or anything, and chances are a lot of people will agree with you. —Liz Clark

5. Say what you believe because the people who matter won't mind, and the people who mind don't matter. —Yagmur Muftuoglu

6. Set your goals. Do you want the items to be taken off the market? Or do you want to raise awareness? Who exactly is your audience? Parents? Kids? Who are you targeting? Use your answers to these questions to develop a plan of action. Do you want to hold a press conference? Protest with picket signs? Send out a chain mailing? Tell your friends and family to stop buying? Then, fight! Take a strong stand. Be prepared to answer questions from people you don't agree with. If you want to go through with this, you will need to push and push for it. Be passionate! People will agree with you! Convince people who don't! Keep repeating these steps until the world is perfect. :) —Liz Clark

7. If other people freak out when you want to make a change, do it anyway. Don't be afraid that you're the only one, because you're probably not the only one. There are almost always people who share your ideas. And if you are the only one, cool, that's fine too. It doesn't matter. Then you're an original. —Rebecca Adelsheim

CHAPTER NINE

From Diapers to Bitches—and Back

•

Stitch 'N Bitch Nation (knitting book)
Skinny Bitch (diet book)
The Bitch in the House (marriage book for women)
Why Men Love Bitches (dating book)
The Bitch Posse (chick lit)
Any Bitch Can Cook (cookbook)
Bloodthirsty Bitches and Pious Pimps of Power (political book)
Bitchfest (compendium of articles from feminist magazine)

The bitch industry is big. In 2006, the Dixie Chicks' new album *Taking the Long Way* showcased their anthem, "Not Ready to Make Nice," and the singers' thickly kohl-lined eyes on the CD cover photo drove home the brassy message. This featured song, concerning why they're "still mad as hell," would go on to earn two Grammy Awards for Song Of The Year and Record Of The Year in February of 2007. After the singers swept up five Grammy Awards total, it was hard to avoid the impression that *not* making nice was the new making nice.

Blue Q offers a "Total Bitch Spa Kit" for $19.95, "for those who demand the very best." Each kit contains samples of bath salts, body wash, Total Bitch lip balm, four moist towelettes, and "a 'Let It Go' journal!"

Alas, we may have "let it go" just a bit too much. Shanelle Matthews, a student at Louisiana State, notices that her male professor uses the term "bitch" to refer to a woman—"as a synonym for woman"—and she realizes that "most of the students seemed to find it funny." In some books, like *Skinny Bitch*—the term "bitch" is used so positively that I assumed *Book of the Bitch: A Complete Guide to Understanding and Caring for Bitches* must be a husbands' guide for a happy marriage. Even the dogs on the cover did not dissuade me; perhaps they were ironic dogs. One day in a bookstore I opened the book and then I figured it out: "Lack of exercise may have resulted in the overgrowth of toenails, so have them clipped or take her for a walk on a shingle beach." Thank goodness that the book really was about dogs, or else this would have been one domineering husband.

The term "bitch" referring to a woman—and intended as a compliment—has become commonplace; it practically constitutes a new ideal. In an attempt to trace how this happened, I ordered some back issues of the feminist magazine *Bitch*, to be sent to my parents' address. I've found that mail to Canada can get lost, or an envelope might be delivered, for example, with its contents removed (which kind of ruins it for me, I'm rather picky). So my plan was simple: I was to see my parents soon, and I would collect my magazines at the same time. I warned my mom by e-mail that they would be arriving: "Do not be alarmed, Mommy, when you receive a pile of magazines called *Bitch*. It is for my book." At the time, one of my sisters was pregnant and about to go into labor, so Mom did not receive this critical message in time. Thus when I asked if my magazines had arrived, I was informed of their untimely demise: "Those were for *you*? Why didn't you tell me? Of course I threw them right out!"

"You threw out my *Bitch*es?" I was aghast, but already starting to laugh. "I can't believe you threw them out, Mommy—that was, like, sixty dollars' worth of *Bitch*es!" Since I'm not the type of person who goes around calling other women "bitches," hearing the spiky b-word tumble out was new for me, and oddly liberating. (Had I been repressing my inner bitch all along?) I imagined my mother's stunned face as she opened her package of *Bitch*es, and suddenly I couldn't stop laughing.

My mom laughed too, although somewhat more nervously: "Well, I don't know, hon. I was just so offended that they would send me that kind of thing, right to my doorstep. I thought, 'Why are they targeting me?'"

Although my mom was quite hip in her day, her generation did not yet see "bitch" as a term of empowerment. I assured her that I understood, since I myself was not certain whether the attempt to "reclaim" the word had been successful.

But then suddenly, Mom put down the phone—"Wait a minute!" I heard a few muffled yet impassioned tones from my father, followed by a note of surprise from my mother. She returned to the phone sounding very relieved: "Everything is OK, hon. Your father saved them. I told him not to save them, but he took 'em out of the garbage when I wasn't looking."

Saved, as it were, by the patriarchy.

"He thought maybe you would find them interesting."

I most certainly did—and not only because of all the ads for sex toys, "alternative porn" sites, and reusable menstrual pads. ("Think positively about your period!" exhorted one such Orwellian ad.)

Launched in January 1996 by the founding editors Lisa Jervis and Andi Zeisler, *Bitch* is a fascinating read. Billed as a "feminist response to pop culture" and with a rather impressive circulation of 50,000 in the United States and Canada, it aimed to "reclaim the word 'bitch' for strong, outspoken women, much the same way that 'queer' has been reclaimed by the gay community," as Andi Zeisler explained. This reclamation project, I soon saw, encompasses diverse subject matter. One is confused by a defense of female facial hair—why is removing facial hair "unnatural," but piercing perfectly acceptable? But then comes a surprising, equally impassioned defense of scrapbooking in which the author, Andy Steiner, observes wisely that people look down on scrapbooking because they don't value the detailed personal histories of women and children. There are compelling critiques of pornography just a few pages away from ads for pornography.

Bitch is predictable in only one respect: its unwavering support for the aggressive girl. An article about Pamela Anderson hopes for a time when she "gets another dread disease or her implants explode." Those concerned about mean girls are merely using "a safe cover for hostilities and fears about teenage girls and their power." In another article, the film *Alive* (based on a true story of passengers stranded after a plane crash) earns the author's disapproval because a female character, Lilliana, refuses to succumb to cannibalism in order to survive. Her "inherent gentility" is criticized. Annie Garrett, in the fictional *Vertical Limit* (2000), is criticized for refusing to steal vital supplies from a stranded companion who is suffering from altitude sickness. While this author acknowledges that Annie is the group's "moral center," her resistance to "the temptation to give in to savage instincts, even at the peril of her own survival" is looked at askance: "By straitjacketing female characters into the position of civilized society's spokespeople, these movies deny women both moral complexity and credit for having a dark side—a side that deserves to be examined for its real-life and metaphorical implications for gender roles."

Now, I actually had the misfortune of viewing *Vertical Limit*, and the self-aggrandizing, immoral behavior of the lead explorer, Eliot Vaughn, was painful to watch. Little did I know that he ought to be a role model for women exploring their "dark side." But as I learned from *Bitch*, the character Sal in *The Beach* (2000), who rules over a dystopian paradise, is far preferable to poor Annie, who is *sans* dark side. That's because Sal "readily flouts the restrictive mores usually placed on women, demanding sexual favors from underlings, then using a kiss-and-tell approach to keep dissenters in line."

When did the bitch become so praiseworthy, and why? As with many social problems, the idealization of the bitch began with good intentions. Some men, it was observed, thought of strong, powerful women as being bitches; therefore, women needed to "take back" the word and "reclaim" it. With this vision the feminist magazine *Bitch* began, aiming to celebrate "women who simply speak their minds and don't back down from a viewpoint, even if it's controversial." But somewhere down the line, women being strong and outspoken somehow morphed into women being aggressive and mean—and often to each other. Some writers may still hope for more films with aggressive heroines, but the women who actually sew up adolescents when they're bleeding (due to violence) tend to be much less wistful. Dr. Deborah Prothrow-Stith from the Harvard School of Public Health, for example, and Dr. Howard Spivak, a Professor of Pediatrics and Community Health at Tufts University School of Medicine, found the number one reason for "the statistical increase in bullying and violence among young girls across the country" is "the shift toward violence in the images of women and girls in the media"—a trend that they call the "feminization of the superhero."

Sarah Pevey, twenty-three, from Knoxville, Tennessee, cyber-sighs to me: "Ahh . . . chick-fighting. I'm a veteran. I've heard some people say that the world would be more peaceful if women ruled the world. I don't think so. I think that if women ruled the world, we wouldn't just bomb the enemy. We would turn their friends against them and crush their spirits so badly that they would bomb themselves."

One would hope not, but certainly the idea of female strength has been corrupted. In the late 1990s, in her book *Bitch*, Elizabeth Wurtzel tweaked the "strong woman" formula and added a dash of selfishness: "For a woman to do just as she pleases and dispense with other people's needs, wants, demands, and desires continues to be revolutionary." In this revolution of discarding others' needs, the finer points of social interactions got lost. Wurtzel begins her book by praising Amy Fisher, a teenager on Long Island who shot her lover's wife, because Fisher had the enlightened attitude "gimme gimme gimme" and didn't believe "that a lady must wait and all that stuff." Wurtzel also admires Amy for receiving "more than twenty disciplinary citations" at Albion State Correctional Center and for being "found guilty of sexually harassing a guard. Which, I'm sure the Riot Grrrls would agree, means she must be doing something right." By contrast, Wurtzel compares the woman Amy shot, Mary Jo Buttafuoco, to "an alligator who has been flushed down the toilet bowl." Mary Jo was not "revolutionary."

Amy Fisher may have reformed and turned her life around, but today a sampling of the books popular among adolescent girls and their mothers— *See Jane Hit, Queen Bees and Wannabes, Mean Girls Grow Up, Girl Wars*— reveals that the biggest problem facing girls is not sexism but female nastiness. Whereas before, a strong woman could be perceived as a bitch (wrongly), now many are genuinely acting like bitches, and relishing it. Women no longer merely refer to other women as alligators; they now proceed to hunt them down like alligators, too. Doctors Prothrow-Stith and Spivak summarized the trend in *Sugar and Spice and No Longer Nice* (2005):

> Girls are committing significantly more acts of violence than they did even one generation ago. The episodes are not only more frequent but they are also more serious, thus resulting in arrests and incarceration. We fear the more deadly consequences ahead as girls predictably increase their use of weapons, particularly guns, in altercations. Even though girls' physical violence has not received the same professional attention that girls' bullying, backstabbing, and cliques have, there are no legitimate ways to discount what is happening with girls. Parents must deal with the fact that physical violence among girls is a significant problem for some communities and on the horizon for others. Now is the time to focus on prevention.

I certainly don't lay the blame for this on *Bitch* magazine, which is a lively forum for discussions about feminism and pop culture. But plainly, the effort to reclaim the term "bitch" has not turned out quite as hoped.

Even Andi Zeisler, one of the cofounders of *Bitch*, admits that it's "tough" to answer whether "the word 'bitch' has or hasn't been reclaimed."

Certainly the "definition of 'bitch' hasn't been reclaimed to the extent that we'd like to see," Andi explains to me by e-mail. "The main thing that's happened to the word over the last decade or so is that it's become a lot more likely to be applied to men as well as women, and thus a lot more general. . . . It's still used to disparage women in the usual ways, but now you're at least as likely to hear it directed at men as well."

To me it is no victory if men are as mean as they perceive women to be, or if women are as mean as they perceive men to be. Badness, whether sexual or social, has its limitations. And so, though the effort to reclaim the word "bitch" did not work, you might say that the word may well have claimed *us*. Today young women aren't more comfortable being strong, but they do seem vastly more comfortable being mean.

GIRLS RULE, BOYS DROOL is a popular T-shirt, along with DO I MAKE YOU LOOK FAT? A strong female must be thinner than the rest; she "rules" over boys and, especially, over other girls. The makers of these T-shirts inform us that the messages are "ironic," but needless to say, young girls rarely take them that way. Six-year-old Lily, wearing a furry white bikini top, explains to the photographer Lauren Greenfield, quite seriously: "Girls rule better. . . . They rule, and boys drool. . . . I'm proud to be a girl 'cause girls do whatever so good." What exactly do girls "rule" at? Lily explains: "To dress up cool so boys like them. I saw it in a movie. They get dressed so fashionable, like a doll and stuff." She then adds, in case this wasn't already obvious, "I really want to be a teenager. Now. Really fast." Lily's role models include "Madonna, Britney [Spears], and Christina Aguilera."

"Ruling" always packs a one-two punch: It entails styling yourself as a sex object for boys, even as you avow that you're "better" than they are. Does seeking the approval of boys so desperately create an emotional vacuum that "ruling" and bitchiness attempt to fill? If so, the attempt is unsuccessful. As I studied the intricacies of "girl power," I came to see that the progression was typically as follows: (1) Girls rule—they're better than boys. (2) Girls rule—because we can please boys. (3) *I* rule, so get out of my way, you bitch!

The singer Pink, who sang "Stupid Girls," lampooned girls who become overly sexual boy-toys, yet she is often photographed in extremely aggressive postures, sneering or screaming, as if to say, "Instead, be strong and mean like me!" But the prematurely sexualized girl and the mean girl are often two sides of the same ideal. Despite the "Hottie Handbook" announcing the owner's intent to steal her friend's boyfriend, and despite the T-shirts bragging DON'T HATE ME BECAUSE I'M BEAUTIFUL. . . . HATE ME BECAUSE YOUR BOYFRIEND THINKS I AM, so-called girl power is anything but powerful. "I Rule" is supposed to express female strength, but it always seems to end in backstabbing and sexual competitiveness.

Though the number of girl bullies is on the rise—both in schools and in virtual areas such as MySpace—and though the U.S. military is still reeling from the revelations of torture at Abu Ghraib and the participation of a woman, Lynndie England, many parents remain in denial. Defending her daughter's taunting of naked male prisoners, Lynndie England's mother, Terrie, told reporters, "They were just doing stupid kid things, pranks." Many parents go further and see girls' being mean as the highest level of empowerment—for them, although not, presumably, for their victims. In 2003, after girls at Glenbrook North High were beaten, smeared with feces and animal guts, and forced to eat raw meat in a football hazing ritual, two mothers were charged with providing alcohol for the event. Five girls were hospitalized, one with a broken ankle and another with a cut in her head requiring ten stitches. The columnist Debra Pickett of the *Chicago Sun-Times* wrote of the incident, "The girls—both the ones doing the pounding and the ones sitting there and taking it like Marines—looked just as strong, fierce and stupid as any guys ever have."

In *Ophelia's Mom,* Nina Shandler writes that Patricia Raglin was "determined to nurture a feminist." Patricia then explains how proud she was of her outspoken daughter, who began hitting at a young age: "The nursery school complained that even at age two, Melissa bullied the five-year-olds, jumped up to hit them. So it started early. I encouraged her to 'go for it' or 'do it.' All my life, I had been told 'Girls don't act that way' and asked 'Are we ladies?' You know, the regular junk that kept women in their place." If they are given a choice between being docile and being a bully, many mothers and experts today choose bullying. But are those really the only two choices for young women? What about being confident, and also kind? That to me would be true girl power.

But kindness in women is now suspect. In her guide to young married women, Mandi Norwood seems to endorse women being mean to their own husbands. Norwood explains: "Giving, devoting, sacrificing . . . these are the actions of a good wife, no? No. These are the actions of a drudge, a sucker, a sap." A woman like this will find that society is uninterested in her, we are told; she will be "fearful" for her own "future," and her husband will soon have an affair.

What a nightmarish scenario! To avoid losing our "self-worth," we are instructed not to be "caretakers." But if there are uncaring spouses—and, unfortunately, it seems that there are—why not urge them to be caring? If neither partner is willing to be a "caretaker," a marriage is not likely to survive for long.

Norwood tells the reader that she comes "from a family in which divorce always followed marriage" (her mother, aunt, and grandmother all divorced). If "modern marriage" means marriage heading for divorce, then Norwood's guide is not an altogether poor one. But when women seeking to "protect" themselves within marriage take up an adversarial stance prematurely, they precipitate trouble. From the first pages of Norwood's book, divorce is a black cloud hovering above us day after day. Naturally, this makes daily interactions extremely unpleasant. One prickly, aggressive woman admired by Norwood throws her husband's clothes into the garden if he leaves socks on the floor—"he understood I meant it," this woman grimly remarks. (I should think so.) A woman named Melanie does even better: She drops the laundry in front of her husband when he dares to watch television, and calls him "a f——king retard":

> I said, " 'Scuse me! Do you not see?" And then he said, "What? What did I do?" So I said, "What? Are you a f——king retard that you don't see me running up and down stairs?" Are you effective? I ask. "Most of the time," says Melanie. "He might start giving me attitude and then I'll say, 'Listen, I'm asking you for help, so listen to me and stop your bulls——t.' "

Most of Norwood's profiles are of women who have been married only a few years, yet she presents their advice—"I'm not passive-aggressive, I'm very aggressive. It's the better way to be"—as if it were holy writ. But it's not even clear whether any of these women were still married at the time of the book's publication.

I do wonder about Joely, twenty-six and married for just one year, who offers this kernel of wisdom to friends who "don't want to be their mothers": "Just stand there and start screaming. If you stand there and scream long enough, someone is going to realize that you're standing in the middle of the room screaming." Then people will have to ask, "Why are you screaming?"

This is no doubt true the first few times you scream; but in the long term, treating your spouse with such a lack of respect tends to make a marriage spiral downward with astonishing rapidity. For these women, though, there is no alternative other than "the quiet submissive wife" and the screaming banshee. Many are children of divorce themselves, and they've never learned how to communicate their needs in an assertive yet respectful manner.

Is being mean an effective way of engaging the world, or is it the problem? Theorists of meanness cannot make up their minds. Rachel Simmons's book *Odd Girl Out: The Hidden Culture of Aggression in Girls* is a case in point. She begins: "Our culture refuses girls access to open conflict." Thus "it forces their aggression into nonphysical, indirect, and covert forms. Girls use backbiting, exclusion, rumors, name-calling, and manipulation to inflict psychological pain on targeted victims. Unlike boys,who tend to bully acquaintances or strangers, girls frequently attack within tightly knit networks of friends." There is much that is valuable in Simmons's study, but I just can't agree that girls are relationally aggressive because they can't "fight it out like the boys." In fact, the theory is so common that Simmons says "you will not find statistics or scientific conclusions about girls and aggression" in her book, because "few would argue that boys have access to a wide range of ways to express their anger. Many girls, on the other hand, are forced to cut themselves off from direct aggression altogether. . . . Our culture has long been accustomed to celebrating the 'niceness' of girls."

Simmons is standing on solid ground here. Academically, at least, this theory has supposedly been proved many times over. *Social Aggression among Girls*, a scholarly analysis that appeared in 2003—a year after Simmons's book—summarizes the literature: Girls' "social aggression is covert," writes the author, Professor Marion Underwood, "thereby maximizing the effect/danger ratio (Bjorkquist, 1994) and complying with strong gender stereotypes dictating that girls do not fight and that women's anger is something that must be managed and controlled (Lutz, 1990)."

However, there is a glaring problem with the standard "repressed good girl" theory: If social aggression were truly evidence of repressed physical aggression, then we should find girls becoming less socially aggressive as they become more physically aggressive. But instead the opposite is true. In recent years, as girls have become increasingly—and alarmingly—

physically violent, we've had an opportunity to test the theory that they just need to "get it out of their system," as boys supposedly do. And contrary to our expectations, the experts agree that girls are becoming more socially aggressive *and* more physically aggressive at the same time. Girls are becoming worse on both counts. In short, repressed-good-girl theory is a sham.

The first sign of this is that repressed-good-girl theory is utterly illogical, once you stop to think about it. Girls are said to be mean because we're teaching them to be nice, but that doesn't make sense. You have to twist your brain into a pretzel to simply process the idea, although once you've got it, it sounds so sophisticated that no one dares challenge it. Simmons's own examples prove that the theory of repressed good girls is wrong. There is no "niceness" being redirected here; it is all just meanness from the start. Nor is there anything "covert" about girls' social aggression, since everyone, it turns out, is quite clear about who the bullies are.

Consider Brianna and Mackenzie, who started a club called "Hate Harriet the Hore Incorporated." Members of the club would walk by their victim, sigh "Hhiiiiiii," and then laugh to one another—they were sounding out the initials of the club (HHHI). When that grew tiresome, they would body-slam the girl and send her and her books smashing to the ground. She tried to smash them first, figuring that they would stop if preempted, but they didn't. Simmons reports, "She ended up with a lot of bruises, missing papers, and an uncanny ability to predict when the bells would ring. There was no teacher in the hallway to see." Only in junior year, when the victim had an opportunity to steal her tormentor's boyfriend, Eric, did things quiet down.

Here is another telling example from *Odd Girl Out:*

> When thirteen-year-old Sherry's friends suddenly stopped speaking to her, her father, worried for his devastated daughter, approached a friend's mother to find out what happened. She was underwhelmed. "Girls will be girls," she said. It's typical girl behavior, nothing to be worried about, a phase girls go through. It will pass. "You are making a mountain out of a molehill," she told him. . . . Her remarks echo the prevailing wisdom about alternative aggression between girls; girl bullying is a rite of passage, a stage they will outgrow.

Well, which is it? If girls' bullying is indeed considered "a rite of passage"—as today, it seems to be—then expecting girls to be "good" cannot be the problem. What we learn from Simmons's examples is that in fact the adults expect girls to be *mean*. Simmons interviews a number of mothers who are reluctant to report bullying by girls; it is simply taken for granted. No one wants to be the classroom's "hysterical mother." With good reason:

> Parents seeking justice for their daughters face cultural and personal obstacles. . . . School officials downplay the problem or blame the victim. Many parents described daughters being sent to psychological counseling for treatment when there was nothing wrong with them, encouraged to get costly social skills training when it was the perpetrator who in fact needed the help, or ignored because the perpetrator was stealthy and it came down to a case of she-said, she-said. Not surprisingly, plenty of parents opt for silence.

"Suzanne" told Simmons that had she made a big deal over her daughter's being bullied, "you know, it would be like, 'Well what's wrong with your kid if she can't deal with her issues? Why doesn't she just walk away and get over this?'" The message, clearly, is that it's a tough world, so you've got to be tough. Teaching girls to be "nice" is not a priority; it is more often perceived as a liability. According to Simmons, one forty-one-year-old mother from Ridgewood, New Jersey, "closed down at even the thought of coming forward," even though the aggression against her daughter had gotten "really, really bad." As evidence that her daughter needed to handle her bully by herself, the mother pointed out how mean her daughter's own friends were. She wanted her daughter to become "an independent woman."

Clearly, this mother is not passing on any "strong gender stereotype" to her daughter; it is simply a matter of pain and anger. And the parents are evenly divided, sometimes internally ambivalent, about whether anger should be controlled. Maybe it is "empowering." Although one bully was a close friend's daughter, "Faye"—the victim's mother—never confronted the woman, instead blaming her own daughter's "low self-esteem" for her troubles: "She'll have this for the rest of her life. We all do," she said. Being able to "handle" girls' "bitchiness," then, is taken to be part of life.

Rachel Simmons offers sensible suggestions, such as describing aggressive behavior in less inflammatory terms. She has found that parents and teachers are more comfortable discussing things like "relational aggression" or "rumor spreading" than saying, for example, "My, your daughter's certainly a mean one!" No doubt. But if we really want bullying to stop, I think we have to face the problem and see it without ideologically tinted glasses. Plainly, girls (and women) are not expected to be good; the problem is precisely that there are no standards for correct behavior.

We are accustomed to reacting against the good girl of yesteryear, so no one seems to have noticed that girls are no longer taught to be nice and quiet. The "good girl" is like a phantom limb that seems to be causing pain; we still blame her, even when she's no longer the culprit. Who is teaching girls to be nice? Not their teachers, and certainly not their parents. Most adults stopped doing that about twenty years ago. Any idea of "niceness" that does trickle down is usually a very superficial notion. A bully who tells adults that she is trying to be "nice" by spreading rumors instead of hitting—let's just say the girl has a lot of chutzpah. And any adult who believes her is being conned. The problem here is not niceness. The problem is that there is no real understanding of what true kindness means, nor a recognition that all people have dignity and deserve to be consistently treated as such. These girls already know how to "vent." Now it's time to change their thinking.

Erika Harold, Miss America 2003, had to leave her school as a child in Illinois because she was subjected to racial harassment by the other kids (both girls and boys). From ninth grade to sophomore year, it was simply decided that she was to be a victim, that she stood out. Her family's home was vandalized; the police had to be called eight times; and she received actual death threats. Since Erika often lectures on teenage violence, I ask her about the theory that girls are trying to be nice, and that's why they become bullies. We meet for dinner in Cambridge, where Erika is studying law at Harvard, and I find her to be quite brilliant:

Well, you have to never have been around kids for a long time if you think that. We live in a culture where reality TV is pervasive, and we're entertained by other people's humiliation and by pulling on people's weaknesses and watching a weak person be embarrassed; and I would maintain that's the cause—glorifying humiliation of others—not being good. With bullying it's about thinking you have the right to devalue other people, and there are some people who think people should just toughen up, grow up. But bullying, I think, is a much more pernicious problem than that. If people don't value other people, they just see it as acceptable to bully other people. Again, very few people say, "No, you should not do this." That sounds very simplistic but even a school would need to have a policy. A lot of schools don't have any sort of policy against just persecution of other kids.

I cite academic theories suggesting that programming girls to be good is to blame, and Erika dismisses them totally: "It's not at all that; it's telling people that there are no boundaries for your behavior and you can choose whatever you would like to do and there are no consequences. I've never— in all of the work that I've done with bullying, I've never heard that advanced by anyone who works in the field."

So we may have made the debate over "mean girls" too complicated. Or, to put it another way, we may be tilting at windmills: We may be seeing good-girl programming when it doesn't in fact exist. And that is preventing us from making things better. In this case, the obvious explanation is also the right one: Girls today are mean because we're telling them to be mean. Or sometimes, we punish them for being nice.

In April of 2006, five-year-old Savannah from Maynard, Massachusetts received a big hug from her pig-tailed friend, Sophie, and then got in trouble with her teacher. Savannah was actually forced to write a note home saying that "I didn't like when she hugin me," and six other students had to write their parents about the "incident." When she got home, Savannah told her parents, "I'm really sad that I got in trouble for hugging."

What we value and advocate in girls has social consequences. If we want girls to be nicer, then we've got to stop telling them that being nice is the problem.

Yet if you've ever broached the subject of inner virtue to those people age thirty-five and up, you may have noticed an instinctive recoiling from the idea that young women might be encouraged to cultivate anything "good" (except a good body). Giving me a withering look, a forty-two-year-old lawyer barks, "I am *very suspicious* of telling girls they need to be morally good. That's sexism right there!" Her reaction is typical. Yet this suspicion of altruism and basic goodness, as usual, does not extend to young men. The Girl Scouts website may emphasize "From Fitness to Fashion," but when I visit the Boy Scouts merit badge page, I learn that boys can earn "badges of honor" for signaling, the ability to read and send

Morse code; for first aid; and above all for "twenty good marks for various good deeds."

. . .

In a groundbreaking study, a group of parents in Montreal allowed their ten-year-olds to wear microphones so that these children's interactions on the playground could be recorded. The result was *It's a Girl's World: How Girls Use Their Social Power to Hurt Each Other* (2004), a film written and directed by Lynn Glazier and produced by Gerry Flahive of the National Film Board of Canada. The girls eventually forgot about the presence of the microphones and, along with frequent "behind the scenes" contact with the parents and the school, the viewer gets a rare look at what girls' everyday exchanges are really like.

Ten-year-old Marina, an adorable long-haired brunette with warm brown eyes, is shown shooing other girls away at the jump rope, and later saying, amid a cluster of girls, "I mean, there's a lot of people I don't like!" At first, Marina's mom praises this behavior as displaying confidence and "leadership": "She has a vision of where she wants the group to go." Her teacher agrees: If she doesn't like that outfit, she's going to tell you she doesn't like that outfit." A mixed blessing, this type of leadership.

Cut back to Marina, on the playground, now shouting at eight girls gathered around her, and pointing to a girl on the pavement next to them. That girl is shivering and crying. Marina is unmoved, calling the girl "sensitive," and reminding her gang that she cries "every time."

Later, speaking in low tones into audio recorders from the privacy of their bedrooms at night, the girls recount the challenges of their school day. The contents of these audio diaries were unknown to their parents and friends, but each girl independently complains about how Marina crumples up their school papers, erases their computer screens, or talks about them disparagingly. Marina herself is then seen literally conducting the girls in a song on the playground, and directing: "OK, let's stop!" Everyone stops. She is the smallest of the bunch, but her rule is unquestioned.

Marina's mother admits that this year she noticed her daughter wasn't just "cutting people off," but influencing other girls to act mean as well. To her credit, she drew the line there, and told Marina that she had to stop. Her privileges are soon taken away. Shifting uncomfortably under her parents' scrutiny, Marina seems to improve, and, finally, to consider the consequences of her behavior.

By contrast, consider what happens when pint-size Diana picks on Amy, a gentle girl with glasses. Diana, Marina's henchman, questions Amy's right to be in their group because Amy had dared to make other friends. When the parents, sitting around a coffee table, meet to discuss the bullying behavior, the difference in attitude between Marina's parents and Diana's mom, Natasha, is striking. Natasha seems to brush her daughter's behavior aside: "Kids can do really stupid things. They just do really stupid things, and they're mean, and they're nasty." Natasha is not malicious, but she does take a permissive attitude, which is common for parents of bystanders of aggressors. She is just not overly concerned: "Sometimes they're bullies, sometimes they're bullied, sometimes they're on the in, sometimes they're on the out. They're going to be OK in the end." Except, of course, when they're not.

Hilary, Amy's mom, understandably disagrees with Natasha's attitude, and points out that every night her daughter dreads the prospect of going to school the next day. Amy in fact does not seem to be OK (her greatest aspiration is to be invisible).

Natasha replies by asking Hilary if they have sought family counseling. The answer is yes. Then Natasha wants to know if the counseling has been helpful, if they found "someone good." Natasha looks strained, and subjects Hilary to a battery of rapid-fire questions. Consciously or not, she seems to be deflecting the attention from her daughter's bullying behavior to the victim, who has "problems." Hilary finally absorbs this irony and, exasperated, points out, "We can counsel her till she's blue in the face,"— then she becomes emotional and stops. Natasha's next query says it all: "Are you beginning to question your skills as a parent?" Why should the victim's mother question her own skills as a parent? But none of the other mothers sipping coffee will challenge Natasha. "Perhaps," Hilary says, weakly. Then she breaks down, sobbing: "Tell me something I could do differently, to make my daughter not want to be invisible!" No one really has anything to say, because Hilary is not the problem here. But no one wants to face the real problem.

The bullying of ten-year-old Amy is indeed a serious problem, but if truth be told, it is not a very complicated one. In my opinion, the problem is actually this belief that girls are "mean and nasty," and that bullying is part of life. Hence the mothers in the group break their heads over how to get counseling for the victim and her family.

Public health researchers at Tufts and Harvard tell us that bullying is learned behavior—learning to feel good at someone else's expense—and that this pattern can be unlearned. And Jennifer Connolly, the director of York University's LaMarsh Centre for Research into Violence and Conflict Resolution, has found that 90 percent of the time bullying will stop if adults in authority respond speedily and let the aggressor know that their behavior is completely unacceptable. Can it be "live and let live" attitudes are actually more likely to cause bullying than any belief in girls' niceness?

Shelley Hymel, a psychologist at the University of British Columbia, makes a very astute observation in *It's a Girl's World*. After studying some of the more aggressive girls and the harm they cause, Dr. Hymel noticed that girls are beginning to see meanness as "normative," and that this prevents them from morally developing. After the camera cuts to one girl who is shown screaming at her friend, Dr. Hymel observes: "We're moving away from the girl as the sweet, petite, quiet stereotype to a real advocacy I'm seeing in girls of, 'Being a bitch is cool!'" And the more we do this, she points out, the more girls will become violent toward one another. Probably because of her work in the trenches, Dr. Hymel is able to acknowledge something that many intelligent adults today cannot: The script has changed.

Fourteen-year-old Dawn-Marie Wesley, a kind, shy brunette from British Columbia, was tormented by a group of girls day after day. They played a game in which one girl would invent rumors of things Dawn said about the most aggressive girl, D.W.—or D.W. herself would invent things, just to pick on Dawn. It always ended with D.W. threatening to beat Dawn up (another girl already had). Although she was scared, Dawn swore her best friend to secrecy, fearing that things would only get worse if she did something about the aggression. To keep their minds off all the abuse, the girls clowned around together in front of their bedroom mirrors. One day in 2000, walking through the forest with her group, D.W. upped the ante: "I'm going to f——king kill you," she screamed at Dawn over the phone.

Two hours later, Dawn killed herself. While the gang padded on, crunching the leaves underfoot in the forest, Dawn-Marie was hanging herself with her dog's leash from a rafter in her basement bedroom. Her mother found a note from Dawn-Marie, apologizing for killing herself and saying how much she loved her parents. Her action was preemptive, she tried to explain, since she would soon be killed anyway. According to the *Globe and Mail*, her suicide note read, in part:

> If I try to get help, it would get worse. . . . They are always looking for a new person to beat up and they are the toughest girls. If I ratted, they would get suspended and there would be no stopping them. I love you all so much.

Thirteen-year-old Corinne Sides from Rockdale, Texas, excelled at academics, singing, and charming her family with her big blue eyes. For years, a group of girls took it upon themselves to wish Corinne dead, to her face, because she was supposedly "really fat, ugly," and "had ratty hair." More likely, they wanted Corinne dead because she was actually none of these things and they were quite jealous of her. On October 6th, 2004, in PE class, one of these girls slapped Corinne, which marked the start of an incredibly brutal day. A series of girls began telling her directly to "go home and kill yourself"—it was to be their "Theme of the Day," apparently. Corinne cried all day and scrawled over her school desk, "This school hates me." When she got home, Corinne finally took her "friends'" advice and killed herself with a gunshot to her forehead.

Corinne's suicide was not an isolated tragedy, and neither was Dawn-Marie Wesley's. In recent years, a frightening number of teens have taken their lives after being abused by their peers, and often both the victim and the perpetrator are girls. For example, April Kimes, Cassie Gielecki, Kristina Calco, and Jessica Haffer were all victims of bullying, and aged thirteen to fifteen when they committed suicide. A new term has emerged, "bullycide," to refer to this new phenomenon. Yet to this day, I still hear of experts telling parents, "don't tell your daughters to be nice," because niceness is supposedly the problem. How many teens have to buried before we can bury this theory along with them?

* * *

Repressed-good-girl theory is based largely on the findings of a group of Norwegian researchers, who observed in 1992 that girls were expressing anger in "unconventional" ways. Here "unconventional" simply means nonmasculine. The researchers deduced that this was because the girls were denied physically aggressive outlets: "When aggression cannot, for one reason or another, be directed (physically or verbally) at its target, the perpetrator has to find other channels." They called the girls' social lives "ruthless" and "cruel," and they attributed all this to cultural rules against overt aggression in girls. They never really tested their theory, but it nevertheless became the basis for modern repressed-good-girl theory.

As noted previously, one way of testing the theory is to observe if social aggression in girls goes down as their physical violence goes up. (It does not; it becomes compounded.) Another interesting avenue would be to speak to girls who have rigid rules against being mean, and see if those girls are more relationally aggressive, or less so.

I spoke to three girls, all fourteen years old, who attend a Jewish Orthodox school in the Northeast. Theirs was not a *Bais Yaakov* ("House of Jacob"), the strictest type of Orthodox girls' school, but neither was it modern Orthodox. It was, rather, an "alternative" school for girls where they could learn about Judaism and strive to incorporate Judaism into their lives. Some of their parents were not religious or were newly religious. I told the girls that I was reading books about bullying and wanted to know if it happened at Orthodox schools too. Were girls not nice? Were there cliques? My heart sank as they nodded and said, "Absolutely! We were just talking about this!" The problem, apparently, was a universal one. Come and sit down, they motioned to me. So I asked them what they meant by "not nice."

Miriam, a blond, twinkly-eyed girl wearing a crisp oxford cloth shirt and black skirt, answered first. "Well, if you don't like someone . . ." She lowered her voice until it was almost a whisper, and smiled impishly: "It's like, then you don't go out with them *Moṭei Shabbos*"—after the Sabbath—"or you don't ask them to hang out with you on Sunday." I understood that the girls considered this "mean," but clearly a girl couldn't invite the entire class to hang out with her on Sunday. This was quite different, needless to say, from picking on one girl until she killed herself.

"There are a few girls in school who really like everyone and get along with everyone," added shy Ahuva, who had an auburn ponytail and cute dimples, "but that's unusual." Most of the girls have cliques, their own groups of friends. "But we're still *nice*," they all stressed. For example, when Miriam and her friends were at a coffee shop studying for an exam, they saw a girl in their class who was studying for the same exam. "She wasn't our friend but we invited her to study with us because it's not nice to sit by yourself and study alone."

When I praised them for doing that, they protested: "But we're hypocritical." How so? "We'll be nice to girls even if we don't like them; that's hypocritical." Well, is it? Being nice to girls when the teachers are not there is still quite different from being nice only as long as the teachers are looking. They haven't gotten to the point that they consider ideal—truly liking and seeing the good in everyone—but for the most part, these young women do control their behavior. For them, being good is a value they have internalized.

Are there hate lists? "Oh, yeah, there was a whole incident this year because there was this girl who had a list of everyone she hated." But at most schools, girls create outcasts by singling out a few girls that a group hates, whereas in this case the girl who had drawn up the hate list was herself the outcast. She was called "the hate girl." "It's sad, the hate girl," said Sabrina, who wore a long-sleeved shirt under a short-sleeved blue T-shirt, a remnant of the public school she had recently left. Bespectacled Miriam nodded, adding maternally: "She's obviously struggling, and you just hope . . . you just hope she'll get back on the *derech*" (literally, "path," meaning "the right way").

According to repressed-good-girl theory, girls gossip and backstab because society teaches them to be "nice" and to suppress negative emotions. Yet in subcultures where kindness is explicitly valued, girls are actually much more direct. As Stephanie Levine observes in *Mystics, Mavericks, and Merrymakers,* "mainstream girls' most serious problems often come from their 'good friends.'" Hasidic girls, in contrast "tend to be boisterous and direct, and passive-aggressive subterfuge carries less allure when people share their emotions directly." One incident from Levine's year "undercover" stuck in her mind. On a trip made by Bais Rivka—that's the school's name, meaning "House of Rebecca"—

Shira stormed into the dining area, crying. Someone asked what was wrong, and she bellowed: "Feigie said I'm fat and ugly!" Then Feigie herself ran in, yelling, "I didn't mean it like that!" Soon about ten girls were involved in moderating the dispute. The discussion was very open, and eventually Shira realized that she had misunderstood Feigie's comment. Sobbing, Shira apologized to Feigie for accusing her of meanness. If a similar dispute had developed in a suburban middle-class high school, Shira might have been mortified to confront Feigie directly, let alone shout about her gripe in a room filled with her classmates. Shira's anger would have rankled beneath the surface, and friends would turn against Feigie. The short blowup I witnessed might have averted unbearable long-term tension. Shira's honesty and openness startled me, but the girls found this scene unremarkable, a typical spat that played itself out like hundreds before it.

Stephanie Levine found this incident remarkable because her "gut expectation" was that Hasidic life "would stunt girls' personal voices with much more force than in America at large." Her professors shared this expectation. But these girls were able to resolve conflict so openly because they shared clear standards of what is acceptable behavior. So the expectation to be good does not cause aggression in relationships. It is more likely to resolve such aggression.

* * *

Not only educators are becoming alarmed by the increase in both physical and emotional aggression in girls. After a fistfight between women forced a plane to land in 2006, and at a time when our public discourse has become so debased that pundits and commentators regularly wish death on their ideological enemies, many of us are rethinking whether a superaggressive society is one we really want to inhabit. Just as, sexually, young women were pushed to imitate the most detached, adolescent males, only to discover that promiscuity wasn't making men very happy either, so women have been urged to imitate the most ruthless males in order to be "successful," only to find that the most ruthless are not necessarily the happiest, and not ultimately the most successful either. Women (myself included) tend to look down on assertive male social networking as insincere "schmoozing," but maybe we could learn something from such men. We think we are being empowered and authentic by being bitchy, but we may discover that we are now held back in a different way—by one another. In a sense, our ideal is Jane Austen's Miss Caroline Bingley: catty to other women, totally obsequious to men. It didn't get Miss Bingley very far in *Pride and Prejudice*, and it's not getting us very far either.

One business manager observed to Cheryl Dellasega, the author of *Mean Girls Grow Up*, "Women destroy each other. They haven't learned the win-win concept. For them, it's 'I win, you lose' or vice versa." At this writing, a very popular management book for women is *The Girl's Guide to Being a Boss (Without Being a Bitch): Valuable Lessons, Smart Suggestions, and True Stories for Succeeding as the Chick-in-Charge.* We seem to be approaching a paradigm shift. Women often feel they need to put on a bitch persona in order to battle sexism and move forward. Now, these authors explain, the patience, strength, wisdom, resourcefulness—and even nurturing—that women are so good at may actually be assets in the office. So forget about *Why Good Girls Don't Get Ahead;* apparently, they just might.

Robin Koval, an ad executive in New York and coauthor (with Linda Kaplan Thaler) of *The Power of Nice: How to Conquer the Business World with Kindness,* explains that truly being nice does not mean letting people walk all over you. Rather, it means "having the courage and creativity to stand up for what you want, but doing it in a way that is not ugly or threatening." She points to studies showing that niceness can also increase a company's productivity and help with networking: "The old command-and-control way of doing business is clearly over. . . . Meanness is so last millennium. Niceness is the future."

Some young women, it seems, would agree. Audrey, seventeen, from Fort Wayne, tells me that she is "respected" at school because she doesn't swear: "Things like language and like gossip and stuff—there's a lot of things that I won't say, and people will respect me for that, because like I won't tolerate foul language or anything like that."

The young women who were involved in the Pure Fashion program in Fort Wayne had broken with their peers not only because of their modest dress but also by speaking out about bullying. They were rebelling by being good in every sense.

Curly-haired Elizabeth, seventeen, shares a story that sends the girls into hysterics: "During my junior year this girl called another girl the 'b' word and I was like, 'Do not call people that; that's mean, you know; it's, like, not right. They don't deserve to be called that.' And this girl goes, 'Oh! I just cannot get away from your family.'"

And consider what's happening at the Harvard Westlake School, a top school in Los Angeles. Among its students are the Barta sisters, who started a nonprofit, Kid Flicks, to collect and distribute videos and DVDs to children in hospitals. To date they've collected more than 16,000 films. Reina Factor, also from Westlake, read about a project undertaken by Do One Nice Thing to make get-well cards for sick children, so she assembled her friends and they made hundreds of cards. At her sweet-sixteen party she asked her guests to make more cards, and she then matched the number they made.

Reina said she wanted to add a dimension to her party, to share her joy with some children. She is now in the process of starting a nonprofit organization to encourage more teenagers to make cards for hospitalized kids.

Not to be outdone, twin sisters Julia and Sarah Steinberg co-founded Farm to Family (http://www.farmtofamily.org) to collect produce from farmers' markets for hungry people. At age seventeen, these young women launched a related nonprofit in Los Angeles. A cynic might say that these girls are just getting a head start on padding their college applications, but that doesn't explain why these young women should compete at being altruistic instead of padding their résumés in other ways.

I visited Kellenberg High on Long Island in 2006, after it canceled its senior prom. Administrators were concerned about houses in the Hamptons being rented to the tune of $20,000 for thirty-six hours, without supervision. When I thumbed through a binder of letters objecting to the cancellation, nearly all of them were from parents. The students I spoke with seemed relieved that the prom had been canceled, and were looking forward to an alternative event (a boat ride, with dancing, around Manhattan). Some students were going to make sandwiches for the poor in lieu of the prom. I asked one senior, Christine Keane, who was excited about the alternative event, whether she would let her own kids go to a prom someday. "Maybe," she considered, adding, "if there even is one" by the time her kids are in high school. She suspected that the prom as we know it may be on its way out. I focused on her navy blue skirt and black penny loafers, to make sure I was not dreaming. The prom on its way out? Making sandwiches for the poor instead? Other girls, huddled in packs between classes, seemed bored with the drama over the prom. One reached into her fashionable red fabric bag and took out a pair of knitting needles. She is knitting a sweater for someone in a local women's shelter, she tells me.

Despite violence among girls being on the rise, I don't despair of the millennial generation, because in many places goodness is also on the rise.

*   *   *

One of the first things people will say to someone who is feeling down is, "Volunteer! Stop thinking about yourself." It's revealing that this often works, but not because—as some would have it—"in giving, we're reminded of people worse off than us." In this calculation, altruism is reduced to *schadenfreude* (thank God I'm not like them!). In fact kindness acts like a tonic because it helps us to realize our lives have a larger purpose.

Toby Kleinman, from Jerusalem, once said something I considered very profound. "You know, what's missing in our lives is the background music," she announced. Of course we have iPods, but they rarely play the right music at the right time, because we do not understand the true significance of our actions. We had been studying the part of the Midrash that claims, had Aaron known his lack of jealousy of his brother Moses would be recorded for posterity, "he would have come to him with drums and dances." Being truly happy for his brother took spiritual greatness, a greatness which even Aaron did not fully appreciate at the time. Similarly, the prophetess Miriam—who rebelled against the pharaoh and defied his decree to kill every Jewish male child, thus saving a generation of children; the same Miriam who led the women in song after they crossed the Red Sea—is introduced in the Torah as the midwife "Puah," who would coo gently to newborn babies to pacify them. Why is she introduced in this way? The greatness of Miriam was that she showed the same enthusiasm in comforting a crying baby and in leading all the Jewish women in song. She understood the "bigness" of private actions; she understood that to calm a child who is not hers, when the child will never find out, is nonetheless significant. This is what real goodness is about.

* * *

I never appreciated my friend Chaya. Busy with four young children in Israel, she nonetheless managed to track me down all the way to Brooklyn, where at the time I was camping out at a friend's house and deciding whether to marry a certain man (I didn't). Being self-involved, I was not in the least surprised to receive her call. What, after all, could be more interesting than my dating life? Of course she should call me all the way from Israel to see how it's going! Now that I have a child of my own, and see how hard it is to keep up with friends, I appreciate her so much more.

Unfortunately, I never got to tell her this, because at the age of thirty-eight, Chaya died of cancer shortly after I got married three years ago. When I visited her in a hospital in Jerusalem on the day before she died, I fed her ice chips, which were all she could keep down. She could barely speak or lift her head for the five hours I kept vigil, and yet when I first walked through the door, she weakly motioned to me to present my hand for inspection. She fingered my wedding ring happily, then patted me and rested her head back on her pillow, smiling contentedly.

When I have a mere cold, I find it challenging to be pleasant and to smile, yet here was Chaya, in terrible pain, still concerned for me and able somehow—but how?—to share in my happiness. On your deathbed, it occurred to me, you really can't fake the kind of person you are. And this was who she was, and who I wasn't. A year later, as a new mother, I would wonder, "How in the world was Chaya, with four kids, able to track me down and talk to me about *dating?*" I was barely capable of tracking down two coats and organizing an escape to the park. Then I thought back to her reaching for my ring and smiling and I realized that there was my answer. She was such a good friend for the same reason that she was a good person: She was internally developed. It wasn't merely that she cared about other people; her sense of self was expansive and included other people, and so their triumphs were hers. Her goodness and her spiritual focus didn't stifle her; they made her great.

Before her illness, Chaya had been writing a book about women. So sometimes, when there is a rare quiet moment in our house, I find myself returning to some detail that a girl shared, and wondering what Chaya would have thought about it. Sometimes I cannot sleep because certain details I learn don't add up for me. Like the young woman who told me she had "no regrets" in starting an "alternative" porn site in 2002, but she took down her site by January of 2005. If she had no regrets, why take down the site? When I visited her blog in the wee hours one morning, I learned that her boyfriend at the time would not be intimate with her "unless there was a webcam on us, unless we were performing for an audience." This, naturally, had unsettled her. On the other hand, she wrote, one "great" part of running a porn site was "documenting my life and having people care."

It's been about a year since I spoke to this young woman, but I remain haunted by this idea: *creating pornography so that people will care?* Clearly, we need to find other ways of showing girls that we care about them, even if they don't take off their clothes. And as I've learned from my friends, who are truly good, it is never too late to show that you believe in someone.

Growth is always possible.

Until it happens, though, one can always write about it.

A RECIPE FOR PLEASING WITH INTEGRITY

Is there a way for a young woman to impress others, without having to be mean or compromise her value system? Yes, there is, and it's called apple pie. Here is my favorite apple pie recipe, from my friend Talya, who picked it up when she was working at St. Clare's Hospital in New Jersey.

It is really so easy to make, and delicious. It makes a nice gift for those you care about, or—more strategically—it can be a way to open doors socially without spreading rumors or taking off any clothing whatsoever. I made it for my grandmother one morning, then got on a flight to Chicago, and the pie was still warm when I arrived. All the people on the plane—even the first-class passengers you can't pay to turn their heads—stopped what they were doing to sniff the air, and put down their newspapers: "Wow, is that apple pie?" Yes, it was, but it wasn't for them. Customs also entirely forgot that you're not supposed to take food from Canada to the United States and only asked, "Wow, is that a homemade apple pie?" Yes, it was, but it wasn't for them either.

So, my friends, don't believe what you've been told about motherhood and apple pie. Every rebellious good girl should have this recipe in her arsenal.

You will need:

- 2 frozen premade pie crusts (I never said I was Martha Stewart.)
- 5 to 7 apples: Any combo of Granny Smith, Delicious, Rome, and McIntosh will work fine.
- 1½ to 2 cups fresh cranberries
- ¼ cup flour
- 1 cup sugar (You can halve this if you're trying to be virtuous in the modern sense.)
- 2 teaspoons cinnamon
- Milk or soy milk
- 1 egg

Directions:

1. Make a few slits in bottom pie crust.
2. Core apples and cut into big slices—maybe eighths. Pile them into pie, then mix in the cranberries.
3. Combine flour, sugar, and cinnamon and add to pie. Stir.
4. Add top crust, pinch it in place, and make it look nice. Then make slits in top.
5. Brush top with milk or soy milk, then with egg lightly beaten.
6. Sprinkle additional cinnamon and sugar on top.
7. Preheat oven to 400 degrees Fahrenheit. Bake at 400 degrees for 10 minutes, then at 300 degrees for 35 minutes.

CONCLUSION

Who's Afraid of the Big Bad Good Girl?

●

> "Try hard," said her father, "try very hard to be good. Don't let
> goodness go. Grasp it tight with both hands and never let it go. So
> may God indeed help you." Ogilvie said these words in a strained
> voice. Then he covered her up in bed, drew down the blinds, and
> left her.
>
> —Father tucking in his eight-year-old daughter while undergoing a moral
>   crisis of his own. (From *Daddy's Girl*, by L. T. Meade, 1891)

In April of 2006, I learned that my alma mater had sponsored T-shirts
reading GAY? FINE BY ME! for freshmen. The shirts were free—that is,
paid for by the Office of Campus Life to encourage tolerance. The general
idea was a fine one, but given the tenor of campus life, a bit unnecessary in
my view. When I was at Williams in the late 1990s, our sidewalk was always
graced with obscene chalkings during Gay Pride Week, and there were
daily "coming out" opportunities in the announcements section of our
"Daily Advisor." Coming out to your classmates was always received well
over breakfast. The Jewish Center was defaced with "F——k Moses and
His Homophobic Laws," to celebrate another gender-bending event—I
think it may have been transgendered awareness this time. And during a
"community building" exercise during first-year orientation, we all had to
say, "Hi, my name is [name] and I'm gay!" Later on, Bisexual Visibility
Week saw a flowering of VISIBILITY stickers made available to us all, to
make sure that our high level of tolerance would be evident to all onlook-
ers. So perhaps you can begin to see why, the GAY? FINE BY ME! T-shirts
seemed rather redundant.

I contacted the current president and asked him if he would consider, the
next time the college did a run of shirts, printing tees saying VIRGIN? FINE

BY ME! or *WAITING UNTIL MARRIAGE?* FINE BY ME! I explained that during my own stay at Williams, there was little tolerance on display for those who wanted to lead a more conservative lifestyle. I recounted how students would give me "the finger" after I opposed the coed bathrooms, and how I later learned that many people agreed with my views but didn't want to be stigmatized by being seen with me. Wouldn't it be great for students to learn tolerance not just for views they already agree with, but for those they don't?

The president, an affable fellow, wrote to me right away. "Students do all sorts of T-shirts," he explained, "but we don't print them in Hopkins Hall [the administration building]. In other words, I don't think it is correct to call them 'your' T-shirts. Interesting ideas for alternatives." But wasn't it true that the administration had sponsored the *GAY?* FINE BY ME! tees, through the Office of Campus life? Free of charge? Therefore, I thought if The Office of Campus Life could also sponsor T-shirts of a different variety, then that would send a strong message that the college was not advocating simply one brand of tolerance, but rather tolerance in general.

The president said that he would "copy the Dean's Office about the T-shirt idea." I appreciated this. But months passed and no word came, so I contacted him again. I didn't mean to annoy him, but I really did love the idea of *WAITING UNTIL MARRIAGE?* FINE BY ME! tees floating around my alma mater. I felt they would shake things up in a good way. Finally the president said that he had talked with a dean about it but could "no longer remember what she said."

Why do adults staunchly resist presenting a "traditional" approach to young people? I can understand not wanting it presented as the only way, but adults often are deeply suspicious of merely allowing traditional choices to be options. For example, for a year I have been campaigning for the American Library Association (ALA) to include ModestyZone in its list of sites for young people. The ALA has a "healthy relationships for teens" resource section, which includes websites like the Coalition for Positive Sexuality, Go Ask Alice!, Scarleteen (Sex Education for the Real World), and Sex Etc. Many of these organizations promote a cavalier attitude toward sex. Sex Etc. provides a detailed description of how to have anal sex, with the caution, "Some people find it very pleasurable. Some people don't." Fifteen-year-olds wondering if they are "too young to have sex" are told yes, "if you're afraid to do any of this stuff"—such as visiting a family planning clinic. So here we go again: The bold and mature have sex, while the scared, immature chickies huddle and wait. Since some of the sites recommended by the ALA discuss even bestiality and sadomasochism in a nonjudgmental manner, at the very least I felt that they could include a link to our site to get an opposing view. But no. My queries were never answered, and when I finally tracked down (no small feat) the person in charge of making decisions for that specific page, the professor said she would decide on the matter within a few weeks, only to later delegate the decision to a committee that wouldn't meet for months. (After the committee finally did meet, I never heard from the professor again.)

Experts love to blame advertising and music videos for the pressure on nine-year-old girls to look "sexy." But perhaps even more blameworthy is our reluctance to consider, even for a moment, a more wholesome alternative.

The problem, I hope, is obvious by now. If the only public voices girls can hear are those who advocate wildness, and if those who believe in wholesomeness seem afraid to make their case, girls don't have much of a choice. Being an exhibitionist then becomes the only way of being "good."

Why are people so terrified of the good girl? In truth, it's often with good reason. Take Elsie Dinsmore, the eponymous heroine of a popular didactic series written by Martha Finely in the late nineteenth century. Elsie is ridiculously, preposterously good. She refuses to tell her teacher that a boy spilled ink on her paper and made a large blot—she much prefers to be scolded unjustly for being a "careless, disobedient child!"

Arthur, a boy who teases Elsie, later asks her to lend him money from her meager allowance so that he may buy a toy ship he has his heart set on. Elsie buys him the ship and insists that he not repay her. This was not without its advantages: "Arthur kept his word [not to tease her] and for many weeks entirely refrained from teasing Elsie, and while freed from that annoyance she was always able to have her tasks thoroughly prepared." When some other children break adults' watches, she intervenes and offers to pay to replace the watches rather then see anyone get whipped. When the family's carriage is about to topple and death seems imminent, "Elsie alone preserved a cheerful serenity." It must have been frustrating for human girls to be compared with the angelic Elsie, as they would always come up short.

So those of us who wish for slightly more respect between men and women face a real problem: Does this entail resurrecting the impossible, long-suffering Elsie Dinsmore? Certainly no one wants to become *her*— hence we are stuck with the long-suffering cast of *Desperate Housewives* as our alternative role models.

Thankfully, there is a whole range of possibilities between these extremes, and the good girl of today bears no resemblance to the repressed terror of yesterday. Yet the extravagant use of propaganda continually gets in the way of striking a more reasonable balance. Namely, these eight myths:

1. THE MYTH OF TIME TRAVEL   In the 1920s, women seemed to have more sexual power; they certainly got taken out more, and marrying a good man was a far simpler proposition. On the other hand, in some circles it was thought that women's smaller brains indicated inferior intelligence. (This theory was later discredited when people noted that elephants have the biggest brains of all—it turns out that brain size has to be related to body size for the comparison to be meaningful.) Given all this, if women and men began to value modesty more, would women be regarded as dumb? No. This is for the simple reason that *we cannot go back in time*. Hence, Ella Gunderson's wanting Nordstrom to carry more modest clothing doesn't interfere in the slightest with her aspiring to become a veterinarian. If men would refrain from taking advantage of drunk, barely legal-age girls and filming their escapades, we would still have commercial air travel and all the modern amenities we've come to love. If men ceased to see themselves as predators and women as prey, there would be no movement at Harvard to revisit the question of women's brains and elephants' brains—since that particular debate has been settled. Society would just be a bit more pleasant, that's all. So the debate over the possibility of innocence and kindness is not ultimately a question of whether time travel is possible, even though some political hacks like to make it seem that way. The question is simply what we're going to value now.

Every age has its challenges. Let's not allow the problems of the past to get in the way of incorporating ideas that are eternal and remain helpful to us now.

2. FEAR OF THE TALIBAN   The most common argument I hear from those who promote exhibitionism is that some shady individuals believe in modesty. Hence, if one does not want to be like those scary extremists, the case for modesty must not be made. For example:

> Can someone pay for Wendy to go to Saudi Arabia and see what enforced modesty is like? :-)
>
> —comment by Anne on Pandagon website (February 28, 2006).

> When you force your views of proper family life, proper public modesty, how is that different from the Taliban?
>
> —comment by "graphic truth" on the ModestlyYours.net blog (June 22, 2006).

If you examine this view in terms of formal logic, you should be able to spot the flaw:

> The Taliban say they believe in modesty.
> Wendy says she believes in modesty.
> So Wendy must be the Taliban, or is as bad as the Taliban.

This is known as the *association fallacy*. Cats and dogs both like to eat, but a cat is not a dog. The fact that individuals say they value modesty doesn't mean they are taking the same perspective, or that they value the same things. Here is another common, related fallacy:

> Either Britney Spears or the Taliban.
> The Taliban is fearsome.
> Therefore, we must all dress like Britney Spears.

This is known as an *appeal to fear*. "Either Tide or dirty clothes. You don't want dirty clothes, so you'd better buy Tide." The first premise is fallacious, because it sets up a false dichotomy that ignores the vast range of ways to get clothes clean without using Tide. Similarly, we ignore the vast range of human experience between Britney Spears and the Taliban.

I'm pointing this out for two reasons. First, and more important, I want my parents to feel that my majoring in philosophy was not a complete waste, and that I am using my degree in some small practical way. Second, I couldn't help noticing that instead of addressing my arguments, certain individuals like to compare me to a warlord. It's hard to know who is more insulted by this comparison, but it would certainly make a great *New Yorker* cartoon. (A warlord in Afghanistan opens his e-mail and looks horrified: "Can you imagine? They compare me to the infidel Wendy!")

But let's be honest—this is not really about the difference between imploring and imposing. Nor is wishing for better advice for teenagers quite the same as advocating illiteracy and oppression. Ironically, people who liken everything that seems "old fashioned" to being a warlord or a Nazi are the ones who really restrict choice. Their strong rhetoric puts more conservative choices out of reach for most young people. "I think girls will take on the 'bad girl' persona just because they don't want to be stigmatized by the labels," as sixteen-year-old Lauren from Indiana put it.

So people who cry "Taliban!" or "prude!" when they hear something with which they disagree are actually closer to the Taliban than they realize. Whether their weapon of choice is physical acid or verbal acid, the goal is the same: to make it impossible for others to choose a different lifestyle.

In the literature about self-cutting, a recurring theme is girls' pain in being born female, a considerably odd sentiment in a society claiming to have female empowerment at heart. Erin started cutting when she was fifteen. First she started to starve herself to look like a model; then, when everyone told her how great she looked, she graduated to other harmful behaviors. She explains to Lauren Greenfield, "Most of my cuts are on my lower belly."

> It took me a long time to figure out why. First of all, I could hide them. Secondly, I just hated being a woman. It brought me nothing but pain. Everything that represents being a woman is in your pelvic area. It's where your uterus is. So I didn't feel sorry for making scars on it, because it was just like bringing the scars to the outside. Now they're visible. . . . Women aren't taught to use their voices. So they use their bodies instead. Many girls are not taught that it's special to be a woman, and a lot of girls find out that it hurts to be a woman.

It's particularly hard for Erin, now in her mid-twenties, to gain weight because thinness is what she is known for. Her nickname is "Itty Bitty," and her lowest weight was sixty pounds. If girls were taught that being good, not just looking good, was valued, I think this would expand their notion of self. They might be happier to be female if they understood that their bodies were OK as they are, and that it's their personalities which make them unique. Thus, extremist, ridiculous rhetoric such as "Morality is like the Taliban" is not innocuous drivel. It does real harm, because it deprives girls of the more wholesome alternatives they so desperately need.

3. THE "GOOD GIRL" IS LINKED TO A DOUBLE STANDARD The double standard is real, but its history is more complex than we have been led to believe. In the beginning of her book *Slut,* Leora Tanenbaum points out that there are twenty-eight negative words referring to a sexually active woman (such as "slut") but only three referring to a sexually active man. In contrast, she comes up with twelve positive words for sexually active men (such as "stud" and "player") and only two for women. Yet, significantly, this is a modern list.

Boys couldn't always do whatever they wanted. The reality is that for most of world history both sexes were severely and sometimes oppressively constrained, but often with an eye to bringing out the best in them. Girls, for example, were enjoined at the turn of the twentieth century in the *Little Book of Courtesies* to "Look round on the world. Every flower in the garden is lovelier than you can hope to be in person, and it is by gentleness and virtue that you will shine all your life, even in that far-off day . . . when you will be old and grey."

And a typical issue of the *Boy's Own Paper,* on December 29, 1888, shows the paper's constant concern with helping to develop respectful, courageous gentlemen. In one illustration, "Death Rather Than Dishonour," a pure-looking young man walks the plank on a ship where knife-wielding ruffians have been trying to conscript him as a pirate. Advice books aimed at boys contain continual reminders to treat one's sister—and all ladies—respectfully and "with reverence."

As recently as 1948, you'll find that the sexually promiscuous boy was looked down on. Let's consult *The Stork Didn't Bring You!* one last time:

> You'll recognize the boy. . . . He'll be tall, dark, and dreamy, with the wavy hair, wonderful physique, smooth fast line, and sleek clothes. But this long-lashed Lothario, who expects the gals to gush and swoon in his wake (and they do), is due for the low-value mark too. He'll run with older crowds, date only "women," and anything his own age will be kid

stuff and a waste of time. [He is] more to be pitied than feared as we shall see. Exactly how he got that way is hard to say. We can only deduce that he is a very mixed-up mixture of both sex and self-consciousness, making it difficult for both himself and society to put up with.

Here are a few words that didn't make it onto Tanenbaum's list: "mixed-up," "due for the low-value mark," "more to be pitied." It turns out that male promiscuity wasn't always idealized the way it is today. And, our authors continue, there is also the "masher" or the "wolf"—insecure, hollow, and "full of emptiness":

> Underneath that aggressive veneer, he is hiding a very deep feeling of mental and physical inadequacy toward those about him . . . as expressed in his constant conquests. . . . If you care to bother about wolves at all, you'll discover they aren't really interested in sex, or any other kind of human relationship, except perhaps to defile it. They're out only to destroy—because deep inside they're displeased with themselves. They don't really want to share anything, because they have nothing to share. They can't return a favor or kindness, because they never learned the art or the pleasure of giving. Thus no wolf is the strong man he appears. He's rather a straw man—hollow and full of emptiness. He chooses sex as his strongest weapon, because of its very personal nature and the fact that most normal human beings hold it in awe and respect.

So the supposed "double standard" of times past really depends on which time—and society—you're talking about. In Jewish life, for thousands of years the men have been equally obligated to avoid premarital sex and adultery, and to satisfy their wives. (The woman's sexual rights are included in the marriage contract; one such right is the understanding that if the woman doesn't want to have sex, or if the husband is even thinking of another woman, relations are prohibited.) In general society, could men "get away with more," sexually, than women? Probably. But let's not always assume that these men were any happier.

Today, with women disproportionately bearing the emotional and physical consequences of sex, with promiscuity idealized, and boys taught to be players rather than to be responsible, in a very real sense the double standard is worse than it ever was. As M. J. Davis, a student at the University of North Carolina at Chapel Hill, puts it, "for too many women, at the end of the night, sex still becomes a power struggle, often one they lose." Romantic life increasingly resembles a battlefield, but we can hardly blame all this on the good girl. Quite the opposite, restoring a single high standard will be impossible without her.

4. BUT HOW CAN WE IMPOSE?   As early as high school, children are taught that everyone has opinions, that all opinions are equally legitimate, and the only thing to remember is not to "impose" your opinion on someone else. Where are they getting this from? One source, certainly, is their parents. In the PBS documentary *The Lost Children of Rockdale County,* parents and students were interviewed to explain an outbreak of syphilis in their middle-class suburb. It emerged that girls as young as twelve were engaging in group sex and that they were often angry with their parents for not setting any boundaries. "I wish you'd be stricter," was an often-expressed lament from child to parent. Many also wished that they had kept their virginity. One of the mothers who received such a rebuke (from both a son and a daughter, as it happens) fretted openly that she could only "tell them how I feel."

With such advice issuing from the home these days, it is left to the schools to provide anything resembling a moral code. But instead, teachers tend to reinforce the message that there are only arbitrary opinions, and that the only truth is that there is no universal truth to be had.

In a popular guide by the National Council of Teachers of English (NCTE), *Teaching for a Tolerant World, Grades K–6: Essays and Resources,* Professor April Nauman of Northeastern Illinois University concedes that young students should learn about the Holocaust "to recognize the dangers of growing intolerances in their own country and lives." Yet, in Professor Nauman's telling, "the Judeo-Christian cultural construction of Nazis" is flawed, holding as it does "that the Nazis were simply monsters." Authors who have a "negative manner of characterizing the Nazis" thus promote a "danger[ous] . . . cycle" of "stereotyping." So instead, teachers should ask questions about "the origins of group hatred," and then quickly proceed to the real issues. They are to ask, "What are examples of intolerance toward groups of others in the United States today (especially attacks against gays and lesbians, the burning of African American churches, violence against women)?" And, she carefully prods, "what can the students do to protest such incidents?"

One really despairs of knowing which is more astonishing here: raiding the Holocaust like a cookie jar, in order to steal a fashionable lesson one wants to force-feed; or that the very lesson the author seeks to inculcate— that there is no universal good or bad—happens to have been lifted from the Nazis. Typically, Professor Nauman doesn't even believe her own lesson, for when it comes to attacks against gays or violence against women, she has her bad guys and good guys just like the rest of us.

Rarely, in fact, are any of us neutral about important matters. This relativism we wear like a second skin—really a radical skepticism—is quite selective, and certainly with regard to sexuality we are skeptical only of traditional choices. When we are "imposing" exhibitionism, suddenly our skepticism is folded away. As this book was going to press, my alma mater publicized something called "Sex Week," including but not limited to: a "Bang-quet," a visit from "feminist pornography expert and star Annie Sprinkle and a Sex Toy Raffle (for every orientation and inclination)," a "Passion Party (like Tupperware parties but with sex toys)" and also something called "Vulvapalooza," a massive student performance night to be held in the college's main hall. I don't begrudge anyone their "Bang-quet," but let's be honest: Are we really against "imposing" our views? In fact, the expectation that the young will be publicly—and promiscuously—sexual is imposed all around us, all the time. Offering an alternative to this morass is not an imposition. It's giving young people more opportunities.

5. THE GOOD GIRL IS LINKED TO THE PATRIARCHY When sixteen-year-old Amy Fisher's father took her to Complete Auto Body, where she first met Joey Buttafuoco, he reportedly overheard Joey make an extremely crude reference about wanting to sleep with his daughter. "Somehow that remark hadn't bothered my father," Amy says. "He dismissed it as a compliment."

This is the view of the modern, enlightened father. In 2004, Jessica Simpson's dad told *GQ* that "Jessica never tries to be sexy. . . . She just is sexy. If you put her in a T-shirt or you put her in a bustier, she's sexy in both. She's got double Ds! You can't cover those suckers up!"

Then there is Donald Trump, age fifty-nine, who appeared on *The View* in 2006 and joked about dating his twenty-four-year-old daughter, Ivanka. Trump was asked how he would feel if Ivanka appeared in *Playboy,* and he considered it: "I don't think Ivanka would do that—although she does have a very nice figure. I've said if Ivanka weren't my daughter, perhaps I'd be dating her." Again, Trump was joking, but he got me thinking.

By now we have all learned to smirk at the patriarch of yesteryear, who would "protect" his daughter from suspicious characters she supposedly needed no help with, but perhaps it is time to ask: Who has replaced him? In truth, the anti-patriarch may turn out to be far scarier. Think of Sarah's father, who was so concerned because his twenty-nine-year-old daughter was still a virgin that he publicly voted on candidates for her deflowering ("Sarah's Dad's Pick"). His intentions may be perfectly good, but in practice the anti-patriarch is difficult to distinguish from a kind of pimp.

Which, in the end, is more misogynistic?—the message "I love you, you're special, and the guy who will marry you had better be pretty special, too," or "Work it, baby, work it! The men out there in the world deserve a piece of you, so don't be stingy. Shake those double Ds!"

People link goodness in girls to the expectations of "patriarchal fathers," whom they do not want to resuscitate.

But I still say, beware the anti-patriarchal father.

6. THE SEX-NEGATIVE MYTH In an important opinion piece in *The New York Times,* Lawrence Downes lamented that a talent show at his ten-year-old daughter's middle school had featured a parade of girls dancing to sexually explicit songs. He was not prepared to see girls flaunting their bare bellies, splaying their legs, thrusting out their chests, and even straddling chairs "like lap dancers without laps"—all to the clapping of proud teachers and parents at their public school on Long Island. He feared "sounding like a prig" for wondering if the lyrics "Jerk it like you're making it choke. . . . Ohh. I'm so stimulated. Feel so X-rated" were appropriate for middle-school girls at an official school function. Downes had reason to tread delicately. In response, a director of programming for girls, Patti Binder, wrote that she was "ambivalent" about setting restrictions for such "talent" shows: "In no way do I want to teach girls that sexuality is bad, that moving their bodies in any kind of way is inherently bad. There are so few messages for girls that their pleasure is important, and that their sexuality is okay and positive."

The 1960s set in motion a dualism about sexuality, and we remain deeply influenced by it. Either one is "sex-positive," in which case there are no limits on the expression of sexuality; or, if one believes in age-appropriateness or sex being for private delectation, one is then "sex-negative."

But as we have seen, sex is much more of a "negative" experience when there are no barriers to desire. Children are sexualized for the enjoyment of adults—although any normal person can see that this is plain wrong—and once they start to develop feelings as teens, they are told not to be "prudes." Yet barking at young people to do what is expected and simply "think of England" doesn't exactly capture the erotic imagination either.

Viva Las Vegas, a stripper, writes in a separate feature in *The New York Times* that despite her "delectable" boyfriend, and despite being childless and having more time than many married people, she rarely wants to have sex. So Viva packs her boyfriend off to couples therapy—which happens to take place at a tryout for a new reality show—to find out how to get her libido back. She worries that the show "could ruin my career. A stripper and sex writer who doesn't like sex?" But instead of biting the therapy bullet, Viva decides that there's nothing wrong with her low libido. She ends up agreeing with a sixty-year-old bartender who tells her, in the oracular way bartenders have, "Honey, no woman really loves sex. That's why you strippers make so much money."

Is that right? Or is there a relationship between stripping for strangers and ignoring the boyfriend? When sexuality is public, some of the zip does seem to get lost. Listen to Paris Hilton, who spills this revealing tidbit to *Seventeen* in the issue of December 2006: "I get in so many fights with guys who are like, 'In public you're the sexiest sex symbol, but you're not sexual at all at home.' I'm like, 'Whatever, shut up. I don't wanna be.'" (Ariel Levy reports that on one of her tapes Hilton actually takes a cell phone call during intercourse.) When a symbol of the sexual revolution experiences total boredom, you have to ask what is going on.

The perils of casual sex are encountered by men as well. A popular Internet writer was asked why his sexual tastes have become so bizarre of late (please don't ask), and he explained his motivations with startling candor: "At this point in my life, I have been with hundreds of girls. I was into triple digits before I put up my site four years ago (September 2002), and after four years at the peak of my game—with a dash of internet celebrity thrown in—I am past the point of even being able to round to the nearest hundred. Because of this, normal sex has lost its novelty, and become almost rote to me." When you are with "that many girls, the excitement of random sex disappears. I have to find novelty in weird places."

This is a man who is admitting that he has essentially destroyed his own sexuality, and his adventures have gone from strange to just plain sad. Evidently, it's hard to treat another person as an object without coarsening your own heart, and the coarsening process tends to preclude one's own sexual satisfaction.

We need to tell young people this, instead of encouraging ten-year-old girls to perform sexualized dances for their teachers. Both boys' and girls' sexual experience—and their lives—will be much more positive when they do not treat sex as a recreational sport.

7. WHAT ABOUT THE GUYS? People sometimes ask me why I do not address men more directly. Men do, after all, make up half of the population. Unfortunately, if a man does not behave like a gentleman and treat women with respect, there is very little a woman can say to change his behavior. Boys need better male role models. Rick Reilly once wrote about taking his fourteen-year-old son Kellen to Hawaii for the "knee-buckling treat" of viewing, upclose, the naked "swimsuit" models of *Sports Illustrated*. There is plainly nothing I could say to Mr. Reilly to convince him that this might not be the best father-son activity for a fourteen-year-old boy. I suppose I could go around trying to persuade teenage boys to boycott Axe deodorant, but if their own fathers are playing with the "shower hottie" and spanking games on the Axe promotional website, it would probably be an uphill road.

Girls, on the other hand, even when they do not have the best role models, can learn to let a boy go if he wants more than they are willing to give. And in learning how to do this—to say no to the wrong ones and yes to the right one—a girl can come to appreciate her own worth even when her own mother does not seem to.

8. MISUNDERSTANDING HYPOCRISY Of all the myths getting in the way of giving better advice to young people, most dangerous is the view that we must be perfect angels in order to have an opinion on anything. Obviously there is such a thing as a genuine hypocrite, someone who preaches one thing and makes no attempt to live by the code he or she professes to believe in. But simply failing to live up to one's ideal is just being human. In an age of little privacy, round-the-clock media coverage, and whole blogs devoted to examining people's failings and shouting "Hypocrite!" many people are understandably reluctant to come forward with anything resembling normative advice.

I don't think this makes sense. Since ordinary parents and not angels are usually entrusted with children, it must be that we are meant to tell children *something*, despite our failings. It can't be right that we can never learn from experience, that we must merely clothe, bathe, feed, and shelter our babies, and then tell them, "Sorry, can't say!" when they ask for our opinions. "You'll have to figure it all out for yourselves!"

Ridiculous—yet that is, in essence, what many intelligent people seem to believe. I had to laugh when a prominent cultural commentator deemed it a "hypocrisy tip-off" that her opponent had said it's great to have more children, while he "himself married at thirty-eight and has two children." If our lives are not identical to our ideals, even down to the number of children, then we are hypocrites. Isn't that a bit much? Isn't it possible to appreciate the value of children later in life, when you can't have any more? Or not to have met the right person right away?

It would be nice if we could worry less about hypocrisy and more about living lives that are authentic and meaningful.

*   *   *

I once traveled by car with some elderly friends going to a family event, and it was a very humbling experience. The wife was suffering from Alzheimer's, and every twenty seconds she would ask somewhat fearfully, "Where are we going?" After ten minutes of this, I am not proud to admit that I felt my own sanity slipping, and that I needed to get out of the car. (I didn't.) Yet her husband would always respond gently and cheerfully, as if for the first time: "We're going to a bris!"

Years later, I heard from my grandparents about this couple, and how the husband gallantly continued to care for his wife during her mental degeneration. By the time she died, she no longer recognized her husband of fifty years. But she did tell him, offhand, something very beautiful: "You know, I don't know who you are, but you're the best," she had said.

Most of us, I think, are looking for that kind of love. It's the love that brings out the best in us and in others; it's the ennobling love that persists even when the brain cells are long gone. But how can we find it, in a society that often values taking over giving, and the superficial over the profound?

To me, this is what our new female role models are trying to change. They are not just reclaiming "sexual power" as the media pundits would have you think. What these young women have, plainly, is a gift—a gift to inspire others, and to uplift society.

Maybe the good girl isn't so bad, after all.

ACKNOWLEDGMENTS

This book would not exist if not for the support and dedication of Will Murphy, my editor. From the beginning he understood and cared about the perspective of the girls I had talked to. I am extremely grateful to him and to the entire Random House team for giving voice to the girls we don't usually hear from. Robbin Schiff went beyond the call of duty in working with me on the cover. Jennifer Rodriguez was a paragon of patience.

My agent Kathy Robbins has been more than an advocate; she is a wonderful adviser whose sense of humor has kept me afloat. Special thanks to David Halpern for his innumerable thoughtful suggestions.

All those who participated in my website and group blog, even those who have disagreed, are much appreciated for the way they have helped me to think about these issues. It's thanks to them that a vibrant online community exists, and to Mr. and Mrs. Fox for enabling it all to happen. Alexandra Foley warned me about Bratz dolls years before anyone was talking about them, and her many insights have been of incalculable value. So were Abby Fradkin's.

I am deeply grateful to my sources for enlightening me and sharing their lives. It is one thing to ask parents to quote minor daughters off-the-record, but many parents trusted me enough to let me quote real names, which is of a totally different magnitude. Their willingness to stick out their necks has made a real difference, not just for this book but for society at large. Kudos to all of these families for their brave and unpopular stands.

I am indebted to the good folks at Cherniak Software for their ongoing technical assistance and especially to Robert Cherniak for his friendship and generosity. My friends Rivky, Aliza, Brindy, Ruth, and Judy have sustained me and they are the best friends anyone could have.

Without my parents' love, inspiration, and seemingly endless supply of newspaper clippings, this book would never have seen the light of day (I wouldn't have, either). My sisters and grandparents believed in me, and my in-laws fed and cheered me on numerous occasions.

I'm leaving my husband for last because it is really impossible to thank him properly for all his support, and for being who he is. But I can thank him for disconnecting our Internet router so that I could finish this book.

NOTES

PREFACE

xii as others have regretted • See, for example, Claire Hoffman, "Baby Give Me a Kiss," *Los Angeles Times* (August 6, 2006).

xii "not doing it right" • Ariel Levy, *Female Chauvinist Pigs: Women and the Rise of Raunch Culture* (Free Press, New York, 2005) p. 10.

INTRODUCTION

xvi The dolls are officially • Rachel in MGA Entertainment's public relations department confirmed that all Bratz Babyz are for ages four and up on August 4, 2006.

xvi "Ages three . . ." • *The Princess Rules!* Copyright MGA Entertainment (Grosset and Dunlap, New York, 2003), pp. 19, 29.

xvi The book *BRATZ Xpress* • *BRATZ Xpress Yourself!* Copyright MGA Entertainment (Grosset and Dunlap, New York, 2003), pp. 54, 59.

xvi The *BRATZ Holiday* • *BRATZ Holiday Shoppin' Spree: A Guide to Totally Hot Shoppin'* Copyright MGA Entertainment (Grosset and Dunlap, New York, 2003), p. 42.

xvii When I called • When I called MGA (August 4, 2006), Rachel in PR told me that the company had over 420 licensees pushing various products, so someone "would have to go through piles and piles of papers" to find out what age group this particular book was aimed at. She herself was not eager to do this, and when I asked if someone else could get back to me at a later date, I was told that she had "no idea who to bounce [me] to."

xvii Bratz already puts • The *Bratz Magazine* is now published every three months. According to their promotional website, this "young girls' glossy" is aimed at a core audience of girls ages seven through twelve. This is how they depict their target audience: "So whether you like to get out there and be active or are more suited to hanging out at hot parties looking your best, we have something for you!" From www.titanmagazines.com. For background on how Bratz came to claim the doll market, see Margaret Talbot, "Little Hotties," *The New Yorker* (December 7, 2006).

xviii under pressure • James Montgomery, "Hasbro Decides Not to Stickwit Pussycat Dolls Toy Line," MTV.com (May 26, 2006).

xix "Inside every woman . . ." • From the website pussycatdolls.com.

xix It's revolting • E-mail to author (May 7, 2005).

xix People wonder • Claudia Wallis, "The Thing about Thongs: Why the Bottom Line Has Become a Battleground for Parents of Tweens," *Time* (September 28, 2003).

xx Target's website • "Xhilaration Juniors Ruffle Edge TBack Thong Red Pop and Baja Coral," www.target.com.

xx "eye candy" and "kiss me" • See "Abercrombie's Sexy Undies 'Slip,'" CNN.com (May 28, 2002); also Diana Walsh, "Abercrombie and Fitch is at it Again," San Francisco Chronicle (December 3, 2003).

"in the minority" • email to author, March 10, 2007.

xx Limited Too • Limited Too bills itself as "fun fashion for tweens." Their "Lace And Rhinestone Lowrise Panty" is available on their website, limitedtoo .com, in the Pjs/underwear section.

xx Hot Topic • Hot Topic became popular among tweens and teens by making itself as "all about the music." See www.hottopic.com.

xx I'M TOO SEXY FOR MY DIAPER • J.C. Penny pulled this onesie from its stores in October, 2006, after child-rights groups objected.

xx Kohl's Department store • See Kohls.com, Girls 7–16, Bras section.

xx Shops catering • I first learned about this from a program on Canadian Broadcast Corporation (CBC), "Buying into Sexy: The Sexing Up of 'Tweens'" (January 9, 2005); the store that sells the size 30AA padded push-up bra is called "Miss Teen" and caters specifically to preteens.

xx A newspaper in Philadelphia • Jane Von Bergen, "Tweens Buying Secret Lingerie," *South Bend Tribune* (January 3, 2006); see also Vivian McInerny, "Pink Casual Loungewear Brand Nicely Colors Teen Girls' Word," *Oregonian* (May 7, 2006).

xx-xxi Studies show • "Study: More Kids Exposed to Online Porn," CNN.com (February 5, 2007). This article was based on a study by New Hampshire researchers, and published in the February 2007 *Pediatrics*.

xxi Liz from Maryland • E-mail to author (July 23, 2006).

xxi Even owners of nail • Ruth La Ferla, "Fashion Aims Young," *New York Times* (August 24, 2006).

xxi Consider *Packaging* • Sharon Lamb, Ed.D., and Lyn Mikel Brown, Ed.D., *Packaging Girlhood: Rescuing Our Daughters from Marketers' Schemes* (St. Martin's, New York, 2006), see especially p. 125.

xxii You can't just dismiss • Ibid., p. 131.

xxiii Let's be realistic • Ibid., pp. 65–66.

xxiii The druglike effect • See, for example, Marie Winn, *TV: The Plug-In Drug* (Penguin, New York, 2002).

xxiv Across the political spectrum • See, for example, Pamela Paul, *Pornified* (Times Books, New York, 2005), pp. 7–8.

CHAPTER ONE

3 There is a metal • Janet Reitman, "Sex and Scandal at Duke," *Rolling Stone* (June 1, 2006).

3 Numerous studies from left • See, for example, Independent Women's Forum, "Hooking Up, Hanging Out, and Hoping for Mr. Right" (2001), a study of college women on eleven campuses. See also Duke's Women's Initiative report (2003), and Barrett Seaman, *Binge: What Your College Student Won't Tell You* (Wiley, Hoboken, N.J., 2005), especially pp. 42 and 50.

3 Even an article • Lori Gottlieb, "Down with the Husband Hunt!" *Glamour* (September 2006).

4 The number of unmarried women • Barbara Dafoe Whitehead, *Why There Are No Good Men Left: The Romantic Plight of the New Single Woman* (Broadway, New York, 2003), p. 10.

4 the percentage of childless • In 2004, about one in five women in their early forties was childless, compared with one in ten in 1976. Jane Lawler Dye, "Fertility of American Women: June 2004," *Current Population Reports* P20-555 (U.S. Census Bureau, Washington, D.C., 2005), table 6.

4 I first read • Regina Lynn, "The Naked Truth about Sex," Wired.com (June 16, 2006).

5 Katha Pollitt called me • Katha Pollitt, "Favorite Things: 207," Slate.com (March 15, 1999). See also query on "m-fem" Listserve, March 15, 1999; *Subject to Debate* (Modern Library Paperbacks, New York, 2001), p. 260.

5 Camille Paglia simply declared • see Sharon Krum, "Save Our Sex," *The Guardian* (April 1, 1999).

5 *The Nation* solemnly foretold • Kim Phillips-Fein, "Feminine Mystiquers," *The Nation* (March 11, 1999).

5 the *New York Observer* • After being criticized for portraying me as an SS officer, the illustrator claimed that the SS insignia on my lapels really stood for Save-a-Soul. How many readers realized this? There's no way to know, of course, but it was certainly nice that the *Observer* had such good intentions.

6 You basically laid • Letter to ModestZone.net (September 16, 2005). The full letter is posted under "Women's Studies?"

6 Your book honestly • E-mail to author (July 12, 2006).

6 "Have I ruined . . ." • E-mail to ModestyZone.net (August 9, 2006).

6 Somehow with it being perfectly normal • E-mail to author (October 31, 2004).

7 "Teenagers Want More . . ." • Kate Zernike, *New York Times* (December 16, 2003).

7 And the experts tell us • According to *Journal of Adolescent Health* (Vol. 38, 2006), pp. 193–200, a study in 2004 of 530 African-American and Hispanic high school students in New York City found that "among adolescents who perceived a high percentage of their peers to be sexually active, those who reported that their mothers had above-average responsiveness were 1.6 times

more likely to plan to delay intercourse than were adolescents who reported that their mothers had average responsiveness."

8 Recently Todd • William Nobel, MD, "I Don't Want to Lose This One, Too," *Journal of Adolescent and Family Health* (Vol. 2, No. 3, March 2004), p. 98. Nobel is with the Pediatric Association of the University of Texas Medical Branch at Galveston.

8 In a survey of 1,000 girls • Survey conducted by The Lab, a British mobile telephone company; see *Manchester Evening News* (June 6, 2005). Twenty-five percent of fifteen- to nineteen-year-olds "thought being a lap dancer would be a good profession," as compared with 3 percent who picked teaching.

8 Jessica, a twenty-one-year-old • In-person interview, Toronto (July 29, 2006).

9 One Internet-based sex educator • Cory Silverberg, "Your Guide to Sexuality," sexuality.about.com (March 29, 2006).

9 In a study of 279 female adolescents • This study of June 2006 was conducted by Margaret Blythe, MD, and colleagues at Indiana University Medical Center. *Archives of Pediatrics and Adolescent Medicine* is one of the JAMA/Archives journals.

9 According to a study • This study, which polled sexually active twelve- to seventeen-year-olds, found that 63 percent of boys and 69 percent of girls wished they had waited longer; in 2000, the numbers were boys, 55 percent; girls, 72 percent.

9 as Diane Sawyer was • ABC *Primetime Live* special on Norplant (May 1994).

9 The marriage educator • Marline Pearson, "Ignoring Teens' Romantic Lives," keynote address at Smart Marriages Conference, Reno, Nevada (June 2003).

10 In a survey done in 2005 • Bella English, "Countering Hypersexualized Marketing Aimed at Young Girls," *Boston Globe* (March 12, 2005).

10 "Are you sure she's a virgin?" • Gaby to Xiao Mei, *Desperate Housewives* (May 7, 2006). The episode was "Desperate Moment."

10 In May 2006 • This study was published in *Archives of Women's Mental Health* (May 2006) and was funded by the National Institute on Drug Abuse. The study also found that boys who binge-drank were about 2½ times as likely to be depressed, and that boys who experimented with sex were also more likely to exhibit depressed symptoms than boys who did not experiment. However, these symptoms were "mild to moderate," whereas the girls' symptoms "from engaging in low to moderate risk behaviors" were "significantly greater." At the highest-risk behaviors, there were no significant gender differences.

10 For some time now • See, for example, National Longitudinal Survey of Adolescent Health, Wave II (1996), in which 25.3 percent of sexually active girls ages fourteen to seventeen reported that they felt depressed "a lot of the time" or "most or all of the time," as compared with 7.7 percent who were not sexually active. (Of sexually active boys, 8.3 percent reported they were depressed, as compared with 3.4 percent who were not sexually active.) And 14.3 percent of sexually active teenage girls attempted suicide compared with 5.1

percent of non–sexually active teens. (Boys' rates were 6 percent versus 7 percent.) More recently, in *Journal of Adolescent Health* (March 2006), links were found between adolescents' low self-esteem, emotional distress, and sexual activity. Critics say that there is no way of isolating the variables; it could be that those with low self-esteem and depression try to self-medicate with sex, not that the sex itself is the cause of the depression. But even if it is the latter, or a little of both, sex is still far from being the empowered activity that is presented in the media. If indeed the causality is opposite from what social scientists assume, and those with low self-esteem are drawn to sexual activity the way they're drawn to drugs and other self-destructive behaviors, then that's hardly an endorsement of this behavior.

10 In an important study • Hallfors, D. D., et al., "Which Comes First in Adolescence—Sex and Drugs or Depression?" *American Journal of Preventive Medicine* (Vol. 29, 2005).

11 "Researchers tell us . . ." • Sharon Lamb, Ed. D. and Lyn Mikel Brown, Ed. D., *Packaging Girlhood: Rescuing Our Daughters from Marketers' Schemes* (St. Martin's, New York, 2006), pp. 185–186.

11 Since the great • Tracy A. Lambert et al., "Pluralistic Ignorance and Hooking Up," *Journal of Sex Research* (Vol. 40, No. 2, May 2003), pp. 129–133.

12 For many women • A. S. Kahn et al., "Hooking Up: Dangerous New Dating Methods?" in A. S. Kahn (chair), "Sex, Unwanted Sex, and Sexual Assault on College Campuses" (August 2000), symposium, Annual Meeting of the American Psychological Association, Washington, D.C.

12 Irene, fifteen • Both Irene's and Jeanette May's quotes are taken from Benoit Denizet-Lewis, "What Ever Happened to Teen Romance?" *New York Times Magazine* (May 30, 2004).

13 Studies have • Data from National Longitudinal Study of Youth from 1979 to 2000. This study of more than 7,000 men and women (at age eighteen and again at age thirty-eight) found that individuals who were abstinent until marriage had only half the risk of divorce of non-abstinent individuals, that they had on average a 20 percent higher income, and that they had gone further in higher education than those who were non-abstinent. Reginald Finger, MD, et al., "Association of Virginity at Age 18 with Educational, Economic, Social, and Health Outcomes in Middle Adulthood," *Journal of Adolescent and Family Health*, Vol. 3, No. 4 (April 2005). "These findings were not due to avoiding teen pregnancy or teen fatherhood, and they persisted after controlling for ethnicity and measures of previous educational or economic disadvantage. . . . Possible explanations for the impact on divorce include the influence of preexisting poor relationship skills as well as that of extramarital affairs." The Add Health data of 1994 and follow-ups in 2001 indicate that teenagers who were sexually abstinent were also more likely to graduate from college.

13 and the happier • "Marital Status and Health: United States 1999–2002," Report from Centers for Disease Control (2004). This study, based on interviews with 127,545 adults age eighteen and over, found that married adults were in

better psychological and physical health than cohabiting, single, or divorced adults. Married adults were also less likely to smoke, drink heavily, and be physically inactive.

13 Also, marital sex • See, for example, Linda J. Wait and Kara Joyner, "Emotional and Physical Satisfaction with Sex in Married, Cohabiting, and Dating Sexual Unions: Do Men and Women Differ?" in E. O. Laumann and R. T. Michael, eds., *Sex, Love, and Health in America* (University of Chicago Press, Chicago, 2001), pp. 239–269; Edward O. Laumann, John H. Gagnon, Robert T. Michael, and Stuart Michaels, *The Social Organization of Sexuality* (University of Chicago Press, Chicago, 1994).

13 Margaret Atwood • Address to American Booksellers Association Convention, Miami, Florida (June 1, 1993).

13 As various media • Stephanie Rosenbloom, "The Taming of the Slur," *New York Times* (July 13, 2006); see also Leora Tanenbaum *Slut! Growing Up Female with a Bad Reputation* (HarperCollins Perennial, New York, 2000).

14 Witness Jessica Cutler • April Witt, "Blog Interrupted," *Washington Post* (August 14, 2004), p. w12; Amy Sohn, "The Vagina Dialogues: Sex Columnists Compare Notes," *New York* (November 21, 2005).

14 In 2005 • Andrea Lavinthal and Jessica Rozler, *The Hookup Handbook: The Single Girl's Guide to Living It Up* (Simon Spotlight, New York, 2005), p. 180.

15 Men report • Barbara Dafoe Whitehead and David Popenoe, "The State of Our Unions: The Social Health of Marriage in America National Marriage Project, 2002." See especially the section "Why Men Won't Commit." Reason 1: "They can get sex without marriage more easily than in times past."

15 *The Hookup* • Lavinthal and Rozler, op. cit., p. 2.

15 "Dating is a thing" • Ibid., back cover.

15 Increasing numbers of men • Pamela Paul, *Pornified* (Times Books, New York, 2005), pp. 157–159; and Ian Kerner, *DSI: Date Scene Investigation* (Regan Books, New York, 2006), pp. 14, 20, 177. Kerner, a sex therapist, calls this phenomenon "sexual attention deficit disorder (SADD)."

15 There is now talk • Julian Dibbell, "Is the World Ready for Libido in a Nasal Spray?" *New York* (November 21, 2005).

15 Professor Chyng Sun • Chyng Sun, "Revisiting the Obscenity Debate," *Counterpunch* (January 31, 2005). In her rebuttal, Nina Hartley accused Professor Sun of being an "anti-sex feminist" and displaying "neo-Victorian erotophobia." See Nina Hartley, "Thus I Refute Chyng Sun," *Counterpunch* (February 2, 2005).

16 members of Single • Lori Gottlieb, "The XY Files," *Atlantic Monthly* (September 2005).

16 Indeed, researchers • For instance, at UCLA, Professor Daniel Russel, and at the University of Chicago, John Cacioppo. Leaving aside emotional pain, increasing loneliness is also of concern because socially isolated people have significantly poorer immune systems and are prone to a number of illnesses.

17 Amy Sohn • Foreword to Ian Kerner, Ph.D., *Let's Face It: You're Not That into Him, Either: Raise Your Standards and Reach for the Love You Deserve,* (Regan Books, New York, 2005), p. xvii.

17 It is now sex therapists • Ibid., pp. 25, 27, 32.

17 just as George Gilder • Gilder argued that married men were happier and healthier in *Sexual Suicide.* (Quadrangle Books, Chicago, 1973). This book would eventually be called *Men and Marriage.*

17 Listen to the executive • Elizabeth Strickland, "Just Desserts," *San Francisco Weekly* (March 29, 2006).

CHAPTER TWO

21 "Sibyl, just" • Mrs. L. T. Meade, *Daddy's Girl,* (Donohue, Chicago, 1891), p. 105.

21 Mollie, a sophomore • Nina Shandler, Ed. D., *Ophelia's Mom: Women Speak Out about Loving and Letting Go of Their Adolescent Daughters* (Crown, New York, 2001), p. 257.

21 A girl named Regina • E-mail to ModestyZone.net (October 22, 2006).

22 When I log • Jake Tapper, "Brains 1, Barbie 0," Salon.com (September 25, 2002).

22 A visit • Jennifer Axen and Barbara McGregor, *Striptease Kit: A Guide to the Art of Striptease* (Chronicle, San Francisco, 2005).

22 according to the *Philadelphia* • Jenice M. Armstrong, "Exotic Class Reveals Your 'Body Rhythm,'" *Philadelphia Inquirer* (March 31, 2004).

23 Aradia Fitness • From www.aradiafitness.com.

23 In London • Vanessa Feltz, "Inside Out: Pole Position," bbc.co.uk (November 1, 2004).

23 a gym teacher • "Children Are Taught Pole Dancing," news.bbc.co.uk (December 12, 2006).

24 *Marie Claire* • *Marie Claire* (October 2005).

24 Now girls as young • Sandy Kobrin, "More Women Seek Vaginal Plastic Surgery," WomenENews.com (November 14, 2004). See also Debra Ollivier, "Designer Vaginas," Salon.com (November 14, 2000); and Amy Chozick, "U.S. Women Seek a Second First Time," *The Wall Street Journal* (December 15, 2005).

24 The hip, acclaimed • Joshua Glenn, "Literary Cheesecake," *Boston Globe* (September 18, 2005). Interview with Rebecca Wolff.

24 Some models • Randy Dotinga, "SuicideGirls Gone AWOL," *Wired News* (September 28, 2005).

24 *in 2004 a survey* • This survey found that 79 percent of adults, 63 percent of boys and 67 percent of girls, half of younger girls (ages twelve to fourteen), and 74 percent of girls ages fifteen to nineteen agreed that looking sexy is one of the most important things teenage girls do. Bill Albert, "With One Voice: America's Adults and Teens Sound Off about Teen Pregnancy," National Campaign to Prevent Teen Pregnancy Survey (December 2004).

24 "There are no good girls" • Naomi Wolf, *Promiscuities* (Random House, New York, 1998), flap copy.

25 which twelve-year-olds • A call to *Teen Vogue*'s editorial department (July 27, 2006) yielded "fourteen to seventeen" as the target audience. Carrie, in the publicity department, later said that the magazine was "written for the sixteen-year-old," but especially after the acquisition of *YM* magazine, it was "always likely," she conceded, that younger children were reading it. In my own informal poll of teenage girls, readers of *Teen Vogue, Seventeen*, and *CosmoGIRL!* were more likely to be twelve or thirteen than seventeen. Generally, seventeen-year-olds have graduated to *Cosmo* or *Glamour*. The authors of *Packaging Girlhood* also found that "the average reader of teen magazines is twelve, which means many ten-year-olds are reading them," (pp. 192–193).

25 "It's a little too . . . " • E-mail to author (February 8, 2006).

25 Nate Beckenson • Phone interview (February 10, 2006).

25 The same issue • Lauren Waterman "The Good Girl," Lauren Waterman, "Northern Star," *Teen Vogue* (May 2006).

26 HPV can be • Lisa A. Manhart and Laura Koutsky, "Do Condoms Prevent Genital HPV Infection, External Genital Warts, or Cervical Neoplasia?" *Sexually Transmitted Diseases* (vol. 29, No. 11, 2002), pp. 725–735.

26 Now Claire wants • Leigh Belz, "Close Contact," *Teen Vogue* (May 2006).

26 She reassured • Lola Ogunnaike, "That Dirrty Girl Cleans Up Real Nice," *New York Times* (July 30, 2006).

26 Taking off your shirt • Professor Mary Valentich, in a study of women flashing in Calgary, noted that "some participants felt they were part of history." Jill Mahoney, "When Women Bare Breasts, the Context Is Everything," *Globe and Mail* (April 17, 2006).

27 Now that some *Playboy* • Izabella St. James, *Bunny Tales: Behind Closed Doors at the Playboy Mansion* (Perseus, New York, 2006). St. James reports that the sex was "impersonal," took place in front of an audience, never involved kissing, and was essentially a "charade."

27 Jennifer Saginor • Lisa Carter, "Daddy Dearest," Nerve.com (June 2005).

27 After being cheated • Interview with Jen Singh, *Toronto Life* (May 2006).

27 *The Hookup Handbook* • Andrea Lavinthal and Jessica Rozler, *The Hookup Handbook: The Single Girl's Guide to Living It Up* (Simon Spotlight, New York, 2005), pp. 55–57.

28 This passage • John H. Young, *Our Deportment: Manners, Conduct, and Dress of the Most Refined Society* (F.B. Dickerson, Detroit, Mich., 1887), p. 179.

29 Scientists have • Larry J. Young and Zuoxin Wang, "The Neurobiology of Pair Bonding," *Nature Neuroscience* (Vol. 7, No. 10, October 2004), pp. 1048–1054; K. M. Kendrick, "Oxytocin, Motherhood, and Bonding," *Experimental Physiology* (Vol. 85, March 2000), pp. 111S–124S.

29 Consider a fifteen-year-old • E-mail to author (April 23, 2006).

29 Richard Blaquiere • *Sounds Like Canada,* CBC (November 4, 2004). The guest host was Bernard St. Laurent.

30 As Marc Fisher • Marc Fisher, "Are You a Toxic Parent?" *Washington Post* (July 30, 2006).

31 Amy would later • Interview with Amy O'Neill, onmilwaukee.com (October 18, 2004). When I fact-checked to confirm my memory, intending to contact Amy, I learned that she had become a talented artist and had discussed this event in an interview: "I learned to walk in the lobby of the Oriental. I had my 12th birthday party at the Oriental. . . . My dad put my name in huge letters on the marquee. He told me that my present from him was that he would get any movie I wanted to play at my party. I chose 'Harold and Maude.' All the girls there thought it was the dumbest movie ever. I thought it was heavenly."

31 Some people were taken aback • Ryan Kim, "Bump, Grind Your Way to Riches, Students Told," *San Francisco Chronicle* (January 14, 2005).

31 In 1993 • Debra Koenig, speaking to girls from the University School of Milwaukee (May 28, 1993). I checked my memory with the help of Google, which has her saying, "Frankly, sleep around all you want, but whatever you do don't get married." I could be wrong, because I wasn't present; but at the time, those who attended her talk reported the emphatic "whatever you do."

31 twenty-one-year-old woman • Cary Tennis, "My Queer Radical Feminist Peers Are Aghast That I Want to Marry," in "Dear Cary," Salon.com (June 8, 2006).

32 Twenty-nine-year-old blond • "The 29-Year-Old Virgin," janemag.com (August 23, 2006).

32 Cece • In-person interview, Manhattan (February 5, 2006).

33 "downplay" their virginity • "Ask Him Anything," *Cosmo* (August 2005).

33 Amy Alkon" • "I Take It Up the Bum" jewelry, from advicegoddess.com (December 25, 2005).

33 Scarleteen's philosophy • Heather Corinna, "SexYOUality: Is That All There Is?" Scarleteen.com.

35 "Go Ask Alice" • www.goaskalice.columbia.edu

35 how to clean their cat-o-nine tails • Go Ask Alice. This answer was published on December 8, 1995, and is still up as of February 1, 2007.

35 "Alice answers" • This answer was titled, "Freaked Out About First Kiss," but had been taken down when I searched for the date. However, responses to this particular Q & A, from July 21, 2000, to November 25, 2005, are still up on the site.

36 "Sexual contacts . . ." • This is the revised answer currently posted on the "Alice" site (and dated April 14, 2000). The original answer was even more of an endorsement of bestiality.

36 Margaret • Interview (February 29, 2006).

36 in London • "Contraception: Doctors Put Girls Aged 10 on the Pill," *Sunday Times* (May 11, 2005).

36 in the United States • This case occurred in Crystal Lake, Illinois, in 1997; the

child molester took his student repeatedly to a Title X–funded clinic for Depo-Provera. To protect the child's "privacy," the parents were not contacted; nor were the police. There are 4,800 of these clinics nationwide serving 1.2 million adolescent girls (out of 5 million served by all clinics).

37 In September • "Mom Guilty of Rape for Arranging Daughter's Sex Date," Associated Press (September 22, 2005).

37 A woman afraid • Lisa Medendorp, "Daughter Given Away for Sex, Police Say," *Muskegon Chronicle* (August 10, 2006).

37 I know a couple • Comment on the Modestlyyours.net blog (August 15, 2006).

38 In her disturbing • Koren Zailckas, *Smashed: Story of a Drunken Girlhood* (Viking, New York, 2005), p. 190.

38 I barely knew • Ibid., pp. 212–213.

38 During another night • Ibid., p. 205.

38 Her friend Elle • Ibid., p. 220.

39 her mother • Ibid., p. 276.

39 Debbie in Montgomery • Emily Wax, "Coed All-Nighters Put Trust on Line," *Washington Post* (November 16, 2000).

39 When a group • Bella English, "Countering Hypersexualized Marketing Aimed at Young Girls," *Boston Globe;* (March 12, 2005). Dr. Steiner-Adair works with adolescent girls.

40 One mother • "Buying into Sexy: The Sexing Up of Tweens," CBC (January 9, 2005).

40 Elizabeth Wurtzel • Elizabeth Wurtzel, *Bitch: In Praise of Difficult Women* (New York, Anchor Books, 1998), p. 3.

40 The psychologist • Shandler, op. cit., p. 112.

40 Sixteen-year-old • Quotations from Lauren: telephone interview (June 26, 2006).

44 "Say what you will" • Posted by "The Big E" on the thread "Modest and Immodest Ephs," Ephblog.com (December 5, 2005).

44 Bucknell • Allison Kasic, "Strippers on Campus: Outrageous or Empowering?" iwf.org (June 2, 2006).

44 Wesleyan • For example, COL 289, an interdisciplinary course in the College of Letters, was called "Pornography: Writing of Prostitutes."

44 Occidental College • Occidental College Course Catalog (2006–2007). See Women's Studies Department.

44 an employee of Miko Exoticwear • Abe Lubetkin, "On-Campus Female Orgasm Workshop Draws Curious Males," *Brown Daily Herald* (November 29, 2006).

45 As Dean Joe • Telephone interview (April 5, 2000).

45 At the women's college • Phone interview at the Office of Residence Life (April 4, 2000).

45 As Lynn Peril notes • *College Girls: Bluestockings, Sex Kittens, and Coeds, Then and Now* (Norton, New York, 2006), p. 284.

45 Yale's website • Timothy Dwight Residential College, rules (website).

46 At Spelman • Phone interviews (June 21, 2006).

47 In January 2006 • Discussion on ModestlyYours.net, thread started by Meghan Grizzle (January 13, 2006).

47 Studies have indicated • Leslie M. Janes and James M. Olson, "Jeer Pressure: The Behavioral Effects of Observing Ridicule of Others," *Personality and Social Psychology Bulletin* (Vol. 26, No. 4, April 2000), pp. 474–485; Elizabeth N. Duncan-Ricks, CSW, "Adolescent Sexuality and Peer Pressure," *Child and Adolescent Social Work Journal* (Vol. 9, No. 4, August 1991), pp. 319–327.

47 Amanda • E-mail to the author (March 7, 2005).

48 One senior • Letter to author (March 25, 2004).

48 Professor Susan Shaw • Telephone interview (May 9, 2006).

CHAPTER THREE

51 The adolescent must learn • Lois Pemberton, *The Stork Didn't Bring You!* (Hermitage Press, New York, 1948), pp. xii, 183.

51 Fifteen-year-old Taylor • From Taylor Moore's speech at Abstinence Clearinghouse, Los Angeles (August 3, 2005).

54 When Taylor • Interview with Taylor and Trudy Moore, Los Angeles (August 3, 2005).

55 in March 2006 • for Generation Life Chastity Days, Philadelphia (March 2006).

58 The following summer • Post on the ModestlyYours.net blog (July 19, 2006).

59 dollars allocated • For fiscal year 2002 $1.6 billion was allocated to funding sex education and contraception (including Title X Family Planning, TANF, Health Education in Schools, Community Coalition Partnership for the Prevention of Teen Pregnancy, and so on) and about $400 million to funding sex education and contraception for teenagers. The figures for abstinence education were $119 million and $102 million respectively. For fiscal year 2006, $283 million was appropriated for Title X alone, compared with $172 million for abstinence programs. According to a study done in 2000 by the Kaiser Family Foundation, nine out of ten of the nation's 22,000 to 23,000 public secondary schools teach sex education. Only 34 percent of those programs were abstinence-only. Kaiser Family Foundation, "Sex Education in America: A Series of National Surveys of Students, Parents, Teachers, and Principals" (September 2000), p. 3. Sex education, whether federally funded or not, seems to be entrenched.

59 A Hamilton College/Zogby • Professor Dennis Gilbert of Hamilton, in conjunction with Zogby International, "Youth Hot Button Issues Poll" (released January 5, 2006). Findings include: "Two-thirds of high school seniors would require parental consent before a woman under the age of 18 could legally obtain an abortion; the majority of high school seniors do not believe that a woman who is poor and unable to afford another child should have a legal right to an abortion; 70 percent of females in the class of 2006 say they would not consider abortion if they became pregnant while in high school; yet,

more than 60 percent of high school seniors want the Supreme Court to preserve the Roe v. Wade abortion decision."

59 William Strauss • Telephone interview (May 9, 2006).

60 Best Friends • See Robert Lerner, Ph.D., "Can Abstinence Work? An Analysis of the Best Friends Program," *Adolescent and Family Health* (Vol. 3, No. 4, 2004), pp. 185–192. Excerpt: "Despite the fact that BF [Best Friends] schools have reading scores similar to and math scores lower than the District of Columbia as a whole and despite the fact they are located in wards that have higher rates of out-of-wedlock birth, girls who have attended the Best Friends program are substantially less likely to smoke, drink, take illegal drugs, and have sex than a comparable sample of YRBS [Youth Risk Behavior Survey] respondents."

60 Educators are correct • A study of 2004 by National Campaign to Prevent Teen Pregnancy found that 94 percent of teens want a strong message from society to not have sex, at least until they are out of high school.

60 teens who pledge abstinence • Hannah Bruckner and Peter Bearman, "After the Promise: The STD Consequences of Adolescent Virginity Pledges," *Journal of Adolescent Health* (April 2005), pp. 271–278. These authors claimed that adolescents who made virginity pledges were as likely as non-pledgers to have sexually transmitted diseases (STDs) later, in young adulthood. Bruckner and Bearman also implied that adolescents who make virginity pledges were more likely to engage in risky oral and anal sex. This article was widely reported and interpreted as "discrediting" abstinence education. However, see Robert Rector and Kirk A. Johnson, "Adolescent Virginity Pledges, Condom Use, and Sexually Transmitted Diseases among Young Adults," Heritage Foundation Conference Paper (June 14, 2005). Rector and Johnson (and some other scholars) argue that Bearman and Bruckner's own data do not support the original conclusions. For example, Bearman and Bruckner conceded in their report that as young adults virginity pledgers did have lower STD rates than non-pledgers, but they concluded that the differences were not "statistically significant." Rector and Johnson claim that Bearman and Bruckner used only one measure of STD: the presence of three STDs in urine samples. When Rector and Johnson used five STD measures (based on urine samples, STD diagnoses, and STD symptoms), the differences were found to be statistically significant. Rector and Johnson also claim that Bearman and Bruckner did not hold constant relevant variables such as race, gender, and family background. When these variables were held constant, virginity pledgers were found not only to have lower STD rates but also to be less likely to have children out of wedlock, less likely to become pregnant as teenagers, less likely to give birth as teens or young adults, less likely to have sex before age eighteen, and less likely to engage in sex outside wedlock as adults. According to Rector and Johnson, the Add Health database shows that pledgers are less likely than non-pledgers to engage in oral or anal sex, and pledgers who do become sexually active are

less likely to engage in oral or anal sex or to have sex with prostitutes (compared with sexually active non-pledgers). Here is Rector and Johnson's explanation: "The assertion that virginity pledgers are more likely to engage in anal sex does not apply to all virginity pledgers or even to sexually active pledgers. Instead, the claim is limited to pledgers who have engaged in anal sex but not vaginal intercourse. This 'at risk' subgroup comprises only 21 persons out of the entire Add Health sample of 14,116 individuals. This 'at risk' subgroup amounts to less than one percent of all virginity pledgers. By stating that a minute subsegment of virginity pledgers were more likely to engage in risky anal sex, while failing to inform the reader that virginity pledgers as a whole were substantially less likely to engage in this behavior, Bearman and Bruckner severely misled their readers. Their sensationalistic implication garnered widespread media attention, but distorted the truth, and unfairly maligned abstinence education."

67 My last stop • From interview with Rashida Jolley, Washington, D.C. (January 16, 2006).

72 a respected sociologist • Telephone interview (June 22, 2006).

72 Mashadi decides • E-mail to author (September 11, 2006).

73 A young teacher • E-mail to author (December 7, 2006).

73 In 2004 • Jennifer Alsever, "The Sleepover Sales Pitch," *Business 2.0*, (October 2005).

74 *Mizz* magazine • Rachel Bell, "It's Porn, Innit?" *Guardian* (August 15, 2005).

74 More broadly • Since 2001, the National Campaign to Prevent Teen Pregnancy has commissioned nationally representative surveys of adults and teens. In both 2002 and 2003, the survey asked, "Do you think it is embarrassing for teens to admit they are virgins?" In 2002, 48 percent of adults said yes, compared with 26 percent of teens. In 2003, 39 percent of adults said yes compared with 19 percent of teens. So the overall numbers have gone down, but the disparity between adults and teens remains approximately the same.

74 71 percent of girls • Bill Albert, "With One Voice: America's Adults and Teens Sound Off about Teen Pregnancy," National Campaign to Prevent Teen Pregnancy Survey (December 2004).

74 Harris poll • The pollsters state, "The most striking, and surely the most important differences among various demographic groups are the differences between younger and older adults." Fifty-six percent of people ages eighteen to twenty-four, and 60 percent of those twenty-five to twenty-nine think abstinence programs effectively reduce or prevent the occurrence of HIV/AIDS; but only 43 percent of thirty- to thirty-nine-year-olds felt abstinence programs were effective against HIV/AIDS; this number went down to 41 percent among those forty to forty-nine, 37 percent among those fifty to sixty-four, and 31 percent for those older than sixty-five.

74 Edith Stein Project • From www.edithsteinproject.org; also Welcome Talk from the organizers of the 2007 event.

74 Anscombe Society • See www.princeton.edu/~anscombe.

74 the New Sexual Revolution • Annalyn Censky, "Students Start 'Revolution' to Promote Abstinence," *Arizona State Press* (November 1, 2006).

75 One young woman, Helen Vera • "Traditional Dating Could Mean Perfect Match," *Yale Daily News* (February 17, 2004).

76 *Harvard Business Review* • Phillip Longman, "What Sells When Father Knows Best," *Harvard Business Review* (February 2007). This article was part of its "Breakthrough Ideas for 2007" series.

76 As Lakita Garth • E-mail from Garth to author (August 28, 2006). Comment on her opposition is from a website post, "Parenting through the Generation Gap," ModestlyYours.net (December 6, 2005).

CHAPTER FOUR

78 So right away • Telephone interview (October 13, 2005).

78 a swinging couple • Em and Lo, "The New Monogamy: Until Death Do Us Part—Except Every Other Friday," *New York* (November 21, 2005).

79 Then I happened • "To Breed or Not to Breed," *Daily Siege*, Nerve.com (June 27, 2006).

79 In one online forum • Commentator Dirtwood, *Daily Siege*, Nerve.com (June 30, 2006).

80 "Nutbag!" • WGN News (February 28, 2006).

80 *Elle*'s expert • "Ask E. Jean," *Elle* (April 2001).

80 *Cosmo* tells • Editors, "You're Dying to Get Married If . . ." *Cosmopolitan* (April 2005).

81 A typical issue of *Cosmo* • "Your Burning Sex Questions Answered" and "Stealth Ways to Keep Him Interested," *Cosmopolitan* (April 2005).

81 A woman who • Jonathan Small, "Ask Him Anything," *Cosmopolitan* (August 2005).

81 Over and over again • Small, op. cit.; Morgan Swett, "Low-Down and Dirty Breakups," *Cosmopolitan* (May 2006).

82 "The Booty Call . . ." • *Cosmopolitan* (April 2005).

82 "Always Keep Your Expectations Low" • *Cosmopolitan* (June 2002).

83 Mashadi Matabane: E-mail to author (September 11, 2006).

83 Consider the manual • Cynthia Rowley and Ilene Rosenzweig, *Swell: A Girl's Guide to the Good Life* (Time Warner Books, New York, 1999); "naked Saturday," p. 42; pretend someone is chasing you, p. 43; go out with married men "platonically," p. 49.

84 You're pillow-talking • Ibid., p. 38.

85 The no-pajama • Ibid., p. 39.

85 Scarleteen's widely circulated • www.scarleteen.com/sexuality/ readiness_2.html.

86 It seems that • Heather Corinna, "Safe Sex . . . for Your Heart," Scarleteen.com.

86 Jeanette May • Benoit Denizet-Lewis, "What Ever Happened to Teen Romance?" *New York Times Magazine* (May 30, 2004).

87 parents who didn't know • "There are a lot of kids whose parents are not comfortable talking about this and there are parents who've contacted us and said this information is so great and I'm glad you're out there," Jeanette May, interview in Washington, D.C. (January 15, 2006).

87 After we settle • Ibid.

88 Amy Sohn • Foreword to Ian Kerner, Ph.D., *Let's Face It: You're Not That into Him, Either—Raise Your Standards and Reach for the Love You Deserve* (ReganBooks, New York, 2005), p. xvii.

89 Of a dozen • Survey of 1,000 girls conducted by Emory University, 1993.

89 Catharine MacKinnon • MacKinnon, *Feminism Unmodified* (Harvard University Press, Cambridge, Mass., 1987), p. 82.

89 Katie Roiphe • Roiphe, *The Morning After: Sex, Fear, and Feminism on Campus* (Little, Brown, New York, 1993), pp. 70–71.

90 Consider a nineteen-year-old • E-mail to ModestyZone.net (August 27, 2006).

91 Dear Experts • "Ask the Experts," Teenwire.com (question posted February 25, 2003). This question was still featured in August 2006.

91 well over two-thirds • According to a study by the National Campaign to Prevent Teen Pregnancy, which polled sexually active teens ages twelve to seventeen in 2004, 63 percent of boys and 69 percent of girls wish they had waited longer to have sex. In 2000, the numbers were boys, 55 percent; girls, 72 percent.

91 SIECUS • Sexuality Information and Education Council of the United States (SIECUS), "Facing Facts: Sexual Health for America's Adolescents," PDF from siecus.org, pp. 12–13. Originally published in 1995, and still featured prominently on its website in 2006.

94 Indeed, about half • Richard Crosby et al., "Condom Use Errors and Problems among College Men," *Sexually Transmitted Diseases* (Vol. 29, No. 9, 2002), pp. 552–557. In September 2002 Crosby and his colleagues surveyed 158 male students at Indiana University-Bloomington, each of whom had used condoms in the past three months. They found that 30 percent of the students reported placing the condom upside down and having to flip it over; 40 percent reported not leaving enough space at the tip of the condom; 43 percent reported putting on a condom after beginning to have sex; and 15 percent reported taking off a condom before they were finished having sex. Even when the condom was kept on, one-third of the time it slipped off (owing to these errors, the researchers concluded).

93 In the July • Entry, LiveJournal (August 2005).

94 First let me • Letter to ModestyZone.net (received September 20, 2005).

96 Robin Gunderson • In-person interview, Seattle, Wash. (February 26, 2006).

96 Rashida Jolley • Interview Washington, D.C. (January 16, 2006).

97 Ten years after • Interview with Orna, April 31, 2006, in Toronto, Ontario.

97 In a remarkable • Elizabeth Marquardt, *Between Two Worlds: The Inner Lives of Children of Divorce* (Crown, New York, 2005) p. 176.

99 "fear and loathing of sex" • Andy Katz, in reference to my review of "Ushpizin" in the *Wall Street Journal,* "soc.culture.jewish" newsgroup (December 5, 2005). See also letter from Adam Brooks, Salon.com (July 21, 1999), to the effect that modest women, even in marriage, "should never make an effort to enjoy the physical act."

99 "unsatisfying sex was the norm" • Mandi Norwood, *The Hitched Chick's Guide to Modern Marriage: Essential Advice for Staying Single-Minded and Happily Married* (St. Martin's Griffin, New York, 2003), p. 82.

99 "it's all out in the open at last . . ." • Lois Pemberton, *The Stork Didn't Bring You!* (Hermitage, New York, 1948), p. 4.

100 "Letter about Whoring" • Carol Queen, *Real Live Nude Girl: Chronicles of Sex-Positive Culture* (Cleis, San Francisco, 1997), p. 3.

100 "every time I see a client . . ." • Ibid., p. 5.

100 "sex work" • Ibid., p. 187.

100 Carol complains • Ibid., p. 53.

100 "clumsy, selfish male" • Ibid., p. xv.

100 A mother • Phone interview (March 6, 2006).

100 In 1911 • Theodore Schroeder, "Obscenity, Prudery, and Morals" and "Psychologic Study of Modesty and Obscenity," in *"Obscene" Literature and Constitutional Law* (privately printed, New York, 1911), pp. 1–2, 276. Cited in Rochelle Gurstein's *The Repeal of Reticence: A History of America's Cultural and Legal Struggles over Free Speech, Obscenity, Sexual Liberation, and Modern Art* (Hill and Wang, New York, 1996), pp. 114–115.

101 defense of bestiality • Steven Rinella, "Depraved Indifference," Nerve.com, (January 2006).

101 "The answer . . ." • Attributed to Annie Sprinkle, in Eric Rich, "Wesleyan Brings Porn into the Classroom," *Hartford Courant* (May 8, 1999).

101 The chapter • Boston Women's Health Book Collective, *Our Bodies, Ourselves: A New Edition for a New Era* (Touchstone, New York, 2005), p. 206.

102 "*If you make love . . .*" • Ibid., p. 207.

102 "the institution of marriage . . ." • Ibid., p. 163.

102 Even Freud • Sigmund Freud, *Civilization and Its Discontents,* trans. and ed. James Strachey (Norton, New York, 1961), p. 71.

102 Dr. Paul • Telephone interview (May 22, 2006).

103 "Catherine doesn't pretend" • Lauren Henderson, *Jane Austen's Guide to Dating* (Hyperion, New York, 2005), pp. 11–12.

104 "a few weeks of anticipation" • Ibid., p. 22.

104 Tzipporah Heller • "In a Different Voice," speech at a Jewish Women's Conference, Toronto (April 30, 2006). Mrs. Heller, who resides in Jerusalem, is the author of *Our Bodies, Our Souls* (New York, Feldheim 2003).

105 In this incident • Molly Jong-Fast, *The Sex Doctors in the Basement* (Villard, New York, 2005), p. 41.

105 "Evidence that Dart . . . " • Ibid., p. 69.

105 At the time • Ibid., pp. 98, 108.

105 "When you're twelve . . . " • Ibid., pp. 115–116.

106 They tend to smirk • See, for example, Lucinda Rosenfeld, "Sex, Drugs, Etc.," *New York Times* (July 16, 2000): "if Miranda's real-life inspiration, Molly Jong-Fast, weren't the daughter of a famous novelist (or two), it seems doubtful that this book would have found a publisher."

106 when interviewing her • Molly Jong-Fast, "My Mother, the Sex Writer." *Glamour* (April 2006).

107 "So my parents . . ." • Quotations hereafter from my interview with Molly Jong-Fast, Manhattan (February 6, 2006).

108 In a touching essay • Erica Jong, *What Do Women Want?* (HarperCollins, New York, 1998), p. 5.

CHAPTER FIVE

110 I have come • Posted on the ModestlyYours.net blog (October 30, 2006).

110 One day at work • Erin Palazzolo on ModestlyYours.Net (November 25, 2005).

111 In their literature • Information from the website www.CuddleParty.com.

111 The official rule • Ibid.

111 WHAT TO BRING • E-mail to the author from Cuddle Party facilitator (January 16, 2006).

113 This kind of advanced training • See CuddleParty.com, "Cuddle Party Facilitator Training."

113 only twenty-two people so far • E-mail to author from Reid Mihalko (June 22, 2006).

118 "make the world a better place" • E-mail to author from Reid Mihalko (June 26, 2006).

118 According to a study • Lynn Smith-Lovin, "Social Isolation in America: Changes in Core Discussion Networks over Two Decades," *American Sociological Review* (June 2006). The study compared data from 1985 and 2004.

121 Debbie Stoller • Stoller, *Stitch 'N Bitch: The Knitter's Handbook* (Workman, New York, 2003).

123 Lindsay, a bright • Telephone interview with Lindsay and Audrey from Fort Wayne (May 6, 2006).

123 Such involvement • Karen V. Hansen, "Rediscovering the Social," in Jeff Weintraub and Krishan Kumar, eds., *Public and Private in Thought and Practice: Perspectives on a Grand Dichotomy* (University of Chicago Press, Chicago, 1997), pp. 269, 281.

124 Lately I've taken • "Healthy Place" forums (October 1, 2006).

126 In 2003 • Thelma Gutierrez and Kim McCabe, "Parents: Online Newsgroup Helped Daughter," Cnn.com (November 11, 2005).

126 Another visitor • Google groups, alt.suicide.holiday (September 11, 2006). Topic: "My Psych, My Therapist, and My Death."

126 "Two are better than one" • Pirkei Avot, 6:6.

127 "Dembe" • E-mail exchange (January 11, 2006).

128 Many mothers echo Comment by Debbie, ModestlyYours.net blog (March 10, 2006).

128 The writer Ariel Levy • Phone interview (March 8, 2006).

129 Consider Cathy Gallagher • Alex Johnson, "When You Care Enough to Risk Everything," MSNBC.com (August 17, 2005).

129 Secret Lover • See www.secretlovercollection.com.

130 In 2005 • Em and Lo, "The New Monogamy: Until Death Do Us Part—Except Every Other Friday," *New York* (November 21, 2005).

130 *Undressing Infidelity* • Diane Shader Smith, *Undressing Infidelity: Why More Wives Are Unfaithful* (Adam Media, Cincinnati, Ohio, 2005), p. xiii.

130 "amazing women" • Ibid., p. xv.

130 More typical • Ibid., pp. 20, 124, 137, 177, 191, 199.

130 "Anna" scoffs • Ibid., p. 204.

131 *Homewrecker* • Daphne Gottlieb, ed., *Homewrecker: An Adultery Reader* (Soft Skull, Brooklyn, New York, 2005). As reviewed in *Bitch* (No. 32, Summer 2006).

131 In *Against Love* • Laura Kipnis, *Against Love: A Polemic* (Pantheon, New York, 2003), p. 28.

131 Norwood is somewhat • Mandi Norwood, *Hitched Chick's Guide to Modern Marriage: Essential Advice for Staying Single-Minded and Happily Married* (St. Martin's Griffin, New York, 2003) p. 175.

131 "a range of negative effects on children" • Ibid., p. 180.

131 Consider thirty-two-year-old • Ibid., pp. 199–200.

132 "All work" • Ibid., pp. 206–207.

132 "Sometimes an affair" • Ibid., p. 214.

134 After three girls • Christine Armario, "Young Love Spurred Attack," *Newsday* (January 17, 2007).

CHAPTER SIX

138 Walking around a crowded city • Comment from Paul, on the Modestly Yours.net blog (September 14, 2006).

138 In the autumn • Phone interview (November 29, 2006).

138 Not long after • E-mail to author (May 10, 2006).

139 Chloé Hurley • "Pennetiquette," *The Daily Pennsylvanian,* (September 15, 2006).

140 Chloé has already • E-mail to author (October 10, 2006).

140 Now when I • In-person interview (February 28, 2006).

141 P. Diddy • See (or don't see) "Pee Diddy," YouTube.com (August 28, 2006).

141 *A Modest Revolution* • Quotations from Denise Richards, *A Modest Revolution: Today's Girls Say What They Really Think!* (Covenant Communications, American Fork, Utah, 2006). Copyright: Brigham Young University Department of Communications. Documentary film

142 Her mom, Pam • Quotations from interview with Ella, Robin, and Pam Gunderson, Seattle, Wash. (February 26, 2006).

143 The story of Ella • Nick Perry, "More Modest Clothing Please, Girl Asks Nordstrom," *Seattle Times* (May 21, 2004).

144 On CNN • Transcript of *American Morning*, Cnn.com, (aired May 28, 2004).

145 Ella did receive • "More Girls Push for Modest Fashion," Associated Press (June 2, 2004).

145 In Tucson • Scott Simonson, "Local Teens Score One for Modesty," *Arizona Daily Star* (September 18, 2004); about thirty percent of those who signed the petition were between twelve and twenty-one; the rest were older.
Postshow press release, "2006 Pure Fashion Show Demonstrates That Teens Can Dress Trendy but Still Tasteful."

146 "My mom is agnostic" • E-mail to author (September 20, 2006).

147 "As I have outlined earlier . . ." • Katha Pollitt, *Subject to Debate: Sense and Dissents on Women, Politics, and Culture* (Modern Library Paperbacks, New York, 2001), p. xxvii.

147 Fort Wayne, Indiana • The Pure Fashion show took place on May 5, 2006. I conducted a teleconference with the girls on May 6, 2006.

148 "cleavage crackdown" • "Texas School District Bans Cleavage," CBS local news, (August 4, 2006).

149 The first time • In-person interview (February 28, 2006).

149 Nene Kalu • Post on ModestlyYours.net blog (August 18, 2006).

150 Consider a ninth-grader • E-mails to author (February 26, 2006).

151 I saw a lot of crazy stuff • In-person interview (January 15, 2006).

152 Brands On Sale • Joe Kovacs, "Pimp and Ho Kids," WorldNetDaily.com (August 25, 2004).

152 fishnet stockings • Fishnets for girls are carried by Le Chateau.

152 "Shaggles" • Comment on HuffingtonPost.com (September 14, 2006).

154 "Maggie" • "The Art of Modesty," *Seventeen* (June 2004).

156 Tom Ford • "When she was on the set I think she felt uncomfortable, and I didn't want to make anybody feel uncomfortable," Ford told ABC's *Good Morning America;* see also "Vanity Fair's Tom Ford Moment," Editor's Letter, *Vanity Fair* (March 2006).

156 Halle Berry • Jeff Simon of the *Buffalo News* and Edward Guthmann of the *San Francisco Chronicle* called Berry's performance in *Swordfish* "brave."

156 Even top-ranking • For example, Maria Manokova; see Dylan Loeb McClain, "Sex and Chess: Is She a Queen or a Pawn?" *New York Times* (November 27, 2005).

157 I saw a little · ModestlyYours.Net (August 29, 2006). When I e-mailed Bethany, she said that she saw the tee at an international H&M store in Turkey.

158 Kate Freeborn · Freeborn, "Muffin Tops Distasteful, Some Say," New Moon.com (August 15, 2005).

158 "Clara" · Jo Ann Deak Ph.D. and Teresa Barker, *Girls Will Be Girls: Raising Confident and Courageous Daughters* (Hyperion, New York, 2002) pp. 9–11.

159 Sandra Bem · Sandra Lipsitz Bem, *An Unconventional Family* (Yale University Press, New Haven, Conn., 2001), p. 113.

160 *It's So Amazing* · Robie H. Harris, illust. Michael Emberley, *It's So Amazing! A Book about Eggs, Sperm, Birth, Babies, and Families* (Candlewick, Cambridge, Mass., 2002), pp. 24, 30, 32, 39, 42.

160 According to this book · Ibid., pp. 28, 50.

160 The latest trend · Jodi Kantor, "Sex Ed for the Stroller Set," *New York Times* (November 17, 2005).

161 But early rabbinic commentators · Rashi on Genesis 2:25.

163 Stephanie Wellen Levine · Levine *Mystics, Mavericks, and Merrymakers* (New York University Press, New York, 2003), pp. 13, 15, 225, 23.

163 I'll never forget · *Marie Claire* (June 2001).

164 On some reality · In 2004, according to a lawsuit filed by Deleese Williams's family, the crew of "Extreme Makeover" went so far as to interview her family and push Williams's sister Kellie and her own husband into making cruel comments about Deleese's looks. Just hours before she was to begin her makeover and jaw surgery, the show's producers reportedly told Deleese that it would take too long for her jaw to heal, so she was sent home. Kellie, distraught over what she had said about her sister, eventually killed herself. See Michelle Caruso, "Extreme Tragedy," *New York Daily News* (September 18, 2005).

165 women who have had breast implants · L. A. Brinton et al., "Mortality among Augmentation Mammoplasty Patients," *Epidemiology* (Vol. 12, 2001), pp. 321–326. This study was based on the medical records and death cerificates of almost 8,000 women with breast implants. It also found that implant patients were four times as likely as compared with women without implants to die of lung cancer, emphysema, and pneumonia.

165 Vicki Glembocki · Glembocki, "What's a Girl Gotta Do?" *Women's Health* (March 2006).

166 As Beth Pope · Telephone interview (March 6, 2006).

166 Tali Gordon · From *A Modest Revolution*, op. cit.

167 Mary-Margaret Helma · See www.luthientiuviel.com for Mary's own designs.

168 Katy's challenge · St. Louis Genius Girls, ModestyZone.net (February 2006).

168 "Now my daughters . . ." · Ruth LaFerla, "Sex Doesn't Sell: Miss Prim Is In," *New York Times* (February 15, 2004), p. 1.

168 Ashley Orfus explained · "Teens are Covering Up Again for School," *National Post* (September 7, 2004).

CHAPTER SEVEN

173 Dear Dr. Sylvia • Sylvia Rimm, *Growing Up Too Fast: The Rimm Report on the Secret World of America's Middle Schoolers* (Rodale, New York, 2005).

173 In search • Rimm, op. cit., pp. 112–113.

173 "premature emphasis" • Ibid., p. 110.

174 There is a badge • "From Fitness to Fashion" badge (patch 09563); "Looking Your Best" Badge (09306); "Healthy Relationships" (09210).

174 *Girls' Life* • see www.girlslife.com "Fun Stuff" for the personality quizzes.

175 *Boys' Life* • See www.scouting.org.

175 Joy, sixty-three • Phone interview (October 20, 2006).

175 In 2006 • Jodi L. Cornell, MSW, MA, and Bonnie L. Halpern-Felsher, Ph.D., "Adolescents Tell Us Why Teens Have Oral Sex," *Journal of Adolescent Health*, Vol. 38 (2006), pp. 299–301. Girls also listed "fear," "popularity," and "pleasure," but the number one reason was to make their partners happy or "to improve an intimate, romantic relationship" (25 percent of girls came up with that on their own, as compared with only 5 percent of boys who thought oral sex would improve a relationship). The percentage of young people participating in oral and anal sex doubled from 1994 to 2004, according to a study at Johns Hopkins, which was also released in 2006. (Dr. Emily Erbelding from Johns Hopkins Bayview in Baltimore presented this study, which examined the medical records of 2,598 twelve- to twenty-five-year-olds in 1994 and 6,438 subjects of the same age in 2004, who attended STD clinics in Baltimore. The rates of oral sex doubled among males and females, and the prevalence of self-reported anal sex rose from 3 to 5.5 percent.) Previously, when the Centers for Disease Control released data in 2005 suggesting that rates of oral sex were on the rise among boys and girls, the results were hailed by champions of the sexual revolution as evidence of equality. Not quite. Much more important than the numbers are the underlying attitudes. That is why the largely ignored study in *Adolescent Health* seems to me to be the far more significant one.

175 a study published in 2000 • Lisa Remez, "Oral Sex among Adolescents," Alan Guttmacher Institute, *Family Planning Perspectives* (Vol. 32, No. 6, December 2000).

175 Often a girl • College students' reasons for nonuse of condoms in dating relationships included that they would rather assume their partners were disease-free than actually ask. See *Journal of Sex and Marital Therapy* (Vol. 26, No. 1, 2000), pp. 95–105.

175 A high schooler • "What Parents Don't Know About Their Teen Daughters' Sex Lives," ABC's *Primetime* (May 18, 2006). Based on a taped slumber party for fourteen girls ages thirteen to seventeen.

176 Whitney Joiner • Joiner, "Live! Girl on Girl Action!" Salon.com (June 30, 2006).

176 Robin Sawyer • Laura Sessions Stepp, "Beyond the Birds and the Bees," *Washington Post* (October 10, 2006).

176 In Montreal • *"L'égalité, acquise?"* Conference at l'Université du Québec à Montréal (March 6, 2006).

177 Dr. Joy Browne • Elizabeth Neville on ModestlyYours.net (December 21, 2005).

177 A coed at Duke • Janet Reitman, "Sex and Scandal at Duke," *Rolling Stone* (June 1, 2006).

177 In 1936 • Beth L. Bailey, *From Front Porch to Back Seat: Courtship in Twentieth-Century America* (Johns Hopkins University Press, Baltimore, Md., 1988), p. 28.

178 The "Nice Girl" • Rosemary Agonito, *No More Nice Girl* (Adams, Holbrook, Mass., 1993), pp. 17–18.

178 Agonito's novel solution • Ibid., p. 81.

178 thirteen-year-old girl in Zion • "Zion Girl Who Claimed Rape Recants Story," *Chicago Sun-Times* (May 8, 2006).

179 Dave, a twenty-eight-year-old • In-person interview (March 28, 2005). To protect her privacy, the girl's name has been changed.

179 Neil Berstein • The *Today* show, NBC (June 9, 2006). Bernstein was speaking to Ann Curry.

180 The Indiana School • J. Spencer and G. Zimet, "Self Esteem as a Predictor of Initiation of Coitus in Early Adolescents," *Pediatrics* (Vol. 109, April 2002), pp. 581–584. For boys, early intercourse is slightly related to increased aggression and substance abuse, but not, interestingly, to low self-esteem. It seems that boys who feel good about themselves will try to get more girls.

180 Then in 2003 • W. Pedersen et al., "Intercourse Debut Age: Poor Resources, Problem Behavior, or Romantic Appeal?" *Journal of Sex Research* (November 2003).

180 In *Girls Will* • JoAnn Deak, Ph.D., with Teresa Barker, *Girls Will Be Girls: Raising Confident and Courageous Daughters* (Hyperion, New York, 2002), p. 22.

180 The interview • Ibid., p. 225.

181 She was a card • Ibid., pp. 225–226.

183 "beer-ad version of herself" • Koren Zailckas, *Smashed: Story of a Drunken Girlhood* (Viking, New York, 2005), p. 190.

184 "Naomi" • Telephone Interview (March 6, 2006).

184 today's bad-girl lit • Naomi Wolf, "Young Adult Fiction: Wild Things," *New York Times* (March 12, 2006).

185 My favorite was • *The Rebel of the School* (M. A. Donohue, Chicago, 1913) p. 50.

186 *The Virginity Club* • Kate Brian, *The Virginity Club* (Simon Pulse, New York, 2004) p. 305.

187 As Ella Gunderson • In-person interview, Seattle (February 26, 2006).

187 shopping + hooking up • We have already covered hooking up elsewhere. With regard to shopping, some studies suggest that overindulgence in consumer products increases self-absorption and mental health problems. Williams Damon, director of the Stanford University Center on Adolescence, said, "You sit around feeling anxious all the time instead of figuring out what you can do to make a difference in the world." Peg Tyre, Julie Scelfo,

and Barbara Kantrowitz, "The Power of No," *Newsweek* (September 13, 2004).

187 The popular • Eve Marx, *Read My Hips: The Sexy Art of Flirtation* (Polka Dot, Cincinnati, Ohio, 2005), p. 11.

187 you must never • Ibid., p. 120.

188 "24-hour flirt schedule" • Ibid., pp. 53–60.

188 As our heroine • Ibid., p. 60.

188 Brocha and Malkie • Stephanie Wellen Levine, *Mystics, Mavericks, and Merrymakers* (New York University Press, New York, 2003), pp. 20–21.

189 The girls, winking • Ibid., 49–50.

191 They were anywhere • Quotations from interview with Brittany Hunsicker in Temple, Penn. (March 20, 2006).

191 "Miss Hunsicker . . ." • Bruce Weber, "A Town's Struggle in the Culture War," *New York Times* (June 2, 2005).

192 This novel • Excerpts from Adam Rapp, *The Buffalo Tree* (HarperTeen, New York, 2002).

193 What used to be locker-room talk • Initial telephone interview with Tammy Hunsicker (January 30, 2006).

193 In a follow-up • Darrin Youker, "Novel at Heart of Forum on School Censorship," *Reading Eagle* (March 28, 2006).

195 One teacher • Ibid.

198 In March 2004 • "Book Off Ninth-Grade Reading List," Associated Press (March 11, 2004).

199 Erika Harold's account • Lara Riscol, "Miss America's Stealth Virginity Campaign," Salon.com (October 28, 2002).

199 One letter writer • Quia S. Querisma, Letter to the Editor, *Essence* (February 2004).

200 Relationship Principle 30 • Sherry Argov, *Why Men Marry Bitches* (Simon and Schuster, New York, 2006), pp. 74, 76, 165, 209.

201 When you are • Ron Louis and David Copeland, *How to Succeed with Women* (Reward, New York, 1998), p. 206.

202 according to this book • Laura Doyle, *The Surrendered Wife* (Fireside, New York, 2001), p. 216.

203 One day • Beverly Cleary, *My Own Two Feet: A Memoir* (Avon Books, New York, 1995), p. 85

203 a typical negative • comment by "Maja Parla" on the ModestlyYours.Net blog (February 1, 2007).

203 Regarding one such • Caroline Kettlewell, *Skin Game: A Cutter's Memoir* (St. Martin's Press, New York, 1999), p. 134.

CHAPTER EIGHT

204 I think the thing • Quotes from Katie and Rebecca from in-person interview with Girlcotters, Pittsburgh, Penn. (March 17, 2006).

204 girls were targeted · Claire Hoffman reports "Baby Give Me a Kiss," *Los Angeles Times* (August 6, 2006). Hoffman reports that one eighteen-year-old woman, Jannel, was invited to the *Girls Gone Wild* VIP area with Joe Francis, given shots of tequila, and then pressured to masturbate with a dildo and have intercourse with Joe Francis, although she claims to have said no and to have been in pain (being, at the time, a virgin). Mr. Francis's lawyer denies that the sex was anything but consensual, despite Ms. Szyszka's "discomfort during the encounter."

205 So I ring · Telephone interview (May 26, 2006).

205 The American · American Medical Association (AMA, March 8, 2006). This study of women ages seventeen to thirty-five found, "More than half of women (57 percent) agree being promiscuous is a way to fit in. . . . Nearly three out of five women know friends who had unprotected sex during spring break. Twelve percent felt forced or pressured into sex. An overwhelming majority (84 percent) of respondents thought images of college girls partying during spring break may contribute to an increase in females' reckless behavior. An even higher percentage (86 percent) agreed these images may contribute to dangerous behaviors by males toward women." However, some of the methodology of the poll has been criticized, including the age bracket (which was said to be too large to be meaningful), and the fact that the poll could be shared with friends.

207 Nathanael Blake's attack · Blake, "Sex and the City in the Classroom," Townhall.com (April 29, 2006).

207 One of my main critiques of the show · Telephone interview with Amy Leer (May 22, 2006).

209 Dear All · Katha Pollitt, "Query re: Student 'modesty'?" from m-fem mailing list archive, www.archives.econ.utah.edu

210 Guys in my classes · Julia Baskin, Lindsey Newman, Sophie Pollitt-Cohen, and Courtney Toombs, *The Notebook Girls* (Warner, New York, 2006).

210 Women do so many · E-mail to author (April 17, 2006).

210 Jennifer Baumgardner · Jennifer Baumgardner and Amy Richards, *Manifesta: Young Women, Feminism, and the Future* (Farrar, Straus and Giroux, New York, 2000) p. 14.

211 607 days · Lynn Harris, "Broadsheet," Salon.com (November 23, 2005).

211 "that guy says he likes you" · Hillary Carlip, *Girl Power: Young Women Speak Out! Personal Writings from Teenage Girls* (Warner, New York, 1995), p. 41.

212 I was very · E-mail to author (August 20, 2005).

213 "We have the Pill" · Phone interview (April 25, 2006).

213 My role there · Quotations from interview with Melinda Gallagher, New York City (February 5, 2006).

215 "On my boyfriend's birthday" · Em and Lo, "The New Monogamy," *New York*, (November 21, 2005).

215 Gary, a thirty-five-year-old · E-mail to author (September 4, 2006).

218 I was listening • "How Aggravating!" *New Moon* (February 2004).

219 The conference promises • From www.journeeinternationaledelafemme 2006.blogspot.com/.

219 *"L'égalité, acquise?"* • Conference at l'Université du Québec à Montréal (March 6, 2006).

221 Katherine Canty • CBC *World Report*, (March 8, 2006), with the reporter Judy Madden.

221 Cathy Wong • Quotations from phone interview (May 11, 2006).

222 Jennifer Baumgardner • Q&A at Commonwealth Club, 21st Century Speaker Series (March 4, 2004).

222 Germaine Greer • Greer, *The Female Eunuch* (McGraw-Hill, New York, 1971), p. 21; "servile bore," p. 109; mothers who sacrifice never had a self, p. 171.

222 "She does nothing" • Simone de Beauvoir, *The Second Sex* (Knopf, New York, 1989), p. 357; "vegetate as a parasite," p. 430, "parasitic," p. 456; "praying mantis," p. 467; "marriage makes women into 'praying mantises,' 'leeches,' 'poisonous' creatures," p. 482; woman is "a parasite" p. 594; "woman parasite" p. 596; "once she ceases to be a parasite," p. 676. (Originally published 1949.)

222 "devaluation of human progress" • Betty Friedan, *The Feminine Mystique* (Norton, New York, 1997), p. 254; "two-headed schizophrenic," p. 23; "virtual schizophrenics," p. 67; "parasites," p. 271 "coma," p. 79; "stunted at a lower level of living," p. 316. (Originally published 1963.)

223 Women who stay • Linda Hirshman, *Get to Work: A Manifesto for Women of the World* (Penguin, New York, 2006), p. 2.

223 second-wave feminists • Shulamith Firestone, *The Dialectic of Sex* (Farrar, Straus and Giroux, New York, 1970), pp. 92, 114, 180. Firestone also said that children who dream of "no marriage at all" are the "smarter children, who realize the fault lies in the institution, not in their parents"; that "women are a parasitical class living off, and at the margins of, the male economy"; and that pregnancy was "barbaric" and a "deformation."

223 "I think you can . . ." • Baumgardner, Q&A at the Commonwealth Club, op. cit.

223 Rachel Kramer Bussel • Bussel, "Like a Virgin," *Village Voice* (October 22, 2006); also e-mail to author (October 16, 2006).

224 An op-ed • Eric Heyl, "Who's the Brains Behind This T-Shirt Girlcott?" *Pittsburgh Tribune-Review* (October 28, 2005).

224 "Once we spoke . . ." • Quotations from my interview, Pittsburgh (March 19, 2006).

224 "the next generation" • Dimitri Vassilaros, "Feminists, to a T," *Pittsburgh Tribune-Review* (January 27, 2006).

225 The Girlcott was thought • Interview (March 19, 2006).

225 "We, as young . . ." • Susan Aschoff, "It's Grrrl Power vs. Abercrombie & Fitch," *St. Petersburg Times* (November 5, 2005).

231 Meet this week's • Feature on TheRealHot100.org (July 24, 2006).

232 One wrote back • E-mails from three Girlcotters (July 26, 2006).

233 Kim Gandy • Telephone interview (May 26, 2006).

234 After the girls • E-mails about NOW conference • from Girlcotters (July 26 and July 29, 2006).

235 "notion that women" • NOW website (May 2006), to celebrate "Love Your Body Day."

236 Rush Limbaugh • Limbaugh referred to her during the March 31, 2006, broadcast of his nationally syndicated radio program.

236 John Derbyshire • www.nro.com (November 30, 2006). "Did I buy, or browse, a copy of the November 17 *GQ*, in order to get a look at Jennifer Aniston's bristols? No, I didn't. While I have no doubt that Ms. Aniston is a paragon of charm, wit, and intelligence, she is also 36 years old. . . . a woman's salad days are shorter than a man's—really, in this precise context, only from about 15 to 20. The Nautilus and the treadmill can add a half decade or so, but by 36 the bloom is definitely off the rose."

236 Kathryn Lopez • E-mail (June 23, 2006).

236 Jane • Comment on ModestlyYours.net (March 13, 2006).

237 we can suddenly • E-mail to author from Jane (March 13, 2006).

CHAPTER NINE

239 "Not Ready to Make Nice" • *Taking the Long Way*, Dixie Chicks, Sony (May, 2006).

239 Shanelle Matthews • Matthews, "The B Word," *Said It* (Vol. 4, No. 2, 2006).

239 *Book of the Bitch* • J. M. Evans and Kay White, *Book of the Bitch: A Complete Guide to Understanding and Caring for Bitches* (Interpet, Dorking, Surrey, 2002), p. 228.

241 circulation of 50,000 • From Andi Zeisler by e-mail (June 15, 2006).

241 it aimed to • Deborah Solomon, "Pop Goes the Feminist," *New York Times* (August 6, 2006).

241 defense of female facial hair • Aimee Dowl, "Beyond the Bearded Lady," *Bitch* (No. 28, Spring 2005); defense of scrapbooking: Andy Steiner, "Scrap Happy," *Bitch* (No.18, Fall 2002).

241 critiques of pornography • Shauna Swartz, "XXX Offender: Reality Porn and the Reign of Humilitainment," *Bitch* (No. 26, Fall 2004); see also ad for the Suicide Girls.

241 An article about • Jennifer Mathieu, "Jane Petty Criticism Corner," *Bitch* (No. 29, Summer 2005).

241 "a safe cover . . ." • Gabrielle Moss, "Teen Mean Fighting Machine," *Bitch* (No. 27, Winter 2005).

242 the character Sal • Julie Craig, "Lord of the Butterflies," *Bitch* (No. 18, Fall 2002).

242 "women who simply" • E-mail to author from Andi Zeisler (June 15, 2006).

242 "feminization of the superhero" • From Howard R. Spivak and Deborah Prothrow-Stith, *Sugar and Spice and No Longer Nice: How We Can Stop Girls' Violence* (San Francisco, Jossey-Bass, 2005), p. 80.

242 "Ahh . . ." • E-mail to the Author from Sarah Pevey, August 18, 2006

243 "For a woman   " • Elizabeth Wurtzel, *Bitch* (Random House, New York, 1998), p. 26.

243 "gimme gimme" • Ibid., p. 156.

243 "more than twenty . . ." • Ibid., p. 153.

243 Wurtzel compares • Ibid., p. 149.

243 "Girls are committing" • From Howard R. Spivak and Deborah Prothrow-Stith, *Sugar and Spice and No Longer Nice: How We Can Stop Girls' Violence* (San Francisco, Jossey-Bass, 2005), p. 26.

243 Andi Zeisler • E-mail to author (June 15, 2006).

244 "Girls Rule" • Lauren Greenfield, *Girl Culture* (Chronicle, San Francisco, 2002), p. 77.

245 "the girls . . ." • Debra Pickett, "Hazing Could Affect College Plans," *Chicago Sun-Times* (May 13, 2003).

245 "The nursery school" • Nina Shandler, Ed. D., *Ophelia's Mom: Women Speak Out about Loving and Letting Go of Their Adolescent Daughters* (Crown, New York, 2001), p. 255.

246 "Giving, devoting" • Mandi Norwood, *The Hitched Chick's Guide to Modern Marriage: Essential Advice for Staying Single-Minded and Happily Married* (St. Martin's Griffin, New York, 2003), pp. 13–14.

246 "from a family" • Ibid., pp. 1, 2.

246 One prickly • Ibid., p. 38.

246 A woman named • Ibid., p. 39.

247 But it's not even • I tried to contact Mandi Norwood several times by e-mail and regular mail to find out whether the women she profiled were still married, but I did not receive a response. Of course, it is possible that she did not receive my messages.

247 treating your spouse • Studies have found that talking about emotions in a nonconfrontational way beats expressing your anger to your spouse. See, for example, Hara Estroff Marano, "The Downside of Anger," *Psychology Today* (August 12, 2003).

247 "Our culture" • Rachel Simmons, *Odd Girl Out: The Hidden Culture of Aggression in Girls* (Harcourt, New York, 2002), p. 3.

247 "you will not" • Ibid., pp. 8, 16.

248 Girls' "social aggression" • Marion Underwood, *Social Aggression among Girls* (Guilford, New York, 2003), p. 141.

248 "Hate Harriet the Hore, Inc.," • Simmons, op. cit., p. 26.

249 "Girls will be girls" • Ibid., p. 33.

249 "School officials downplay" • Ibid., p. 204.

250 "an independent woman" • Ibid., p. 206

251 Well, you have • Interview with Erika Harold, Cambridge, Mass. (March 19, 2006).

251 Savannah and Sophie's hug • Amalia Barreda, "Girl's Controversial Hug," WCVB news (April 6, 2006).

252 Boy Scouts • See www.meritbadge.com.

bullying is learned behavior • See Howard R. Spivak and Deborah Prothrow-Stith, *Sugar and Spice and No Longer Nice: How We Can Stop Girls' Violence* (San Francisco, Jossey-Bass, 2005), p. 110.

252 In a groundbreaking • Kaj Bjoerkqvist and Pirkko Niemela, "New Trends in the Study of Female Aggression," in K. Bjoerkqvist and P. Niemela, eds., *Of Mice and Women: Aspects of Female Aggression* (Academic, San Diego, Calif., 1992).

254 Jennifer Connolly • Kim Honey, "Everyday War Zone" *The Globe and Mail* (March 30, 2002).

another girl had already done so • "B.C. Girl Convicted in School Bullying Tragedy," CBC News (March 26, 2002).

255 her suicide note read • Caroline Alphonso, "Bullies Push Their Victims to Suicide," *The Globe and Mail* (November 27, 2000).

255 "bullycide" • See www.jaredstory.com for more information about bullycide.

256 I spoke to three girls • Group interview (December 2, 2005).

257 "On a trip" • Stephanie Wellen Levine, *Mystics, Mavericks, and Merrymakers* (New York University Press, New York, 2003), p. 12.

258 Not only educators • Jeffrey Kluger, "Taming Wild Girls," *Time* (May 1, 2006).

258 After a fistfight • "Female Fistfight Forces Plane Landing," Associated Press (June 25, 2006).

258 pundits and commentators • When Laura Ingraham was diagnosed with breast cancer in 2005, the website "Democratic Underground" was deluged with wishes from liberals that she would "choke on her own vomit," or "go into remission and f——king choke to death." Huffington Post printed comments on Dick Cheney's heart problems "hoping" he would be in his "last throes"; one reader said, "I was thinking more along the lines of a stake through his heart" (June 24, 2005). The conservative pundit Ann Coulter wrote that the "9/11 widows" she disagreed with seemed to be "enjoying their husbands' deaths." See Ann Coulter, *Godless* (Crown, New York, 2006), p. 130.

258 One business manager • Cheryl Dellasega, *Mean Girls Grown Up: Adult Women Who Are Still Queen Bees, Middle Bees, and Afraid-to-Bees* (Wiley, Hoboken, N.J., 2005), p. 82.

259 management book • Caitlin Friedman and Kimberly Yorio, *The Girl's Guide to Being a Boss (Without Being a Bitch): Valuable Lessons, Smart Suggestions, and True Stories for Succeeding as the Chick-in-Charge* (Morgan Road Books, New York, 2006). See also Jean Hollands, *Same Game, Different Rules: How to Get*

Ahead without Being a Bully Boss, Ice Queen, or Ms. Understood. Hollands, a counselor, coaches female executives on how to cry and how to be free of the "internal mush" that women often feel they must cover up with aggressive behavior.

260 I asked one • interview with Christine Keane at Kellenberg High, February 6,
2006.

260 part of the Midrash • Vayikra Raba 34:8.

261 "Puah" • The biblical commentator Rashi says, "Puah is Miriam. She was
named 'Puah' because she would coo [the *poah* in Hebrew means cooing] and
gently speak to a baby, in the manner of women who know how to pacify a
crying infant." Shemos 1:15.

262 "no regrets" • telephone interview with Lux Nightmare, June 18, 2006.

262 "having people care" • Posted on August 23th and 27th, 2006, www
.thatstrangegirl.com.

CONCLUSION

267 "Try hard" • L. T. Meade, *Daddy's Girl* (M. A. Donohue, Chicago, 1891).

267 I contacted • E-mail exchanges with President Morton Schapiro (April 28,
2006; June 22, 2006).

269 the professor said • E-mail to author from Melanie Kimball (October 20,
2006).

269 "Kids have always . . ." • "Too Sexy, Too Soon?" CBSnews.com (September
27, 2006).

270 In the series • Martha Finley, *Elsie Dinsmore* (Routledge, London, 1906).
Other titles in the series are *Elsie's Girlhood* and *Elsie's Womanhood.*
Elsie Dinsmore, p. 13.
Ibid., pp. 40–44.
Ibid., p. 148.
Ibid., p. 157.

273 "Most of my cuts" • Lauren Greenfield, *Girl Culture* (Chronicle, San Francisco, 2003), p. 105.

274 In the beginning • Leora Tanenbaum, *Slut! Growing Up Female with a Bad
Reputation* (HarperCollins, New York, 2000), front matter.

274 "Look around . . ." • Katherine Tynan and Charles Robinson, *Little Book of
Courtesies* (Dutton, New York, 1906), pp. 24–25.

274 You'll recognize • Lois Pemberton, *The Stork Didn't Bring You!* (Hermitage,
New York, 1948), pp. 86–87.

276 As M. J. Davis • student M. J. Davis, "Weekend America" radio segment,
"Sexual Assault on Campus" (September 23, 2006).

276 In the PBS • *The Lost Children of Rockdale County,* PBS, (October 19, 1999).

276 A popular guide • Judith P. Robertson, ed., and April D. Nauman, "Re-
Reading the Bad Guys: Sixth Graders' Understanding of Nazi Soldiers in
Number the Stars," in *Teaching for a Tolerant World, Grades K–6* (National
Council of Teachers of English, Urbana, Ill., 1999), pp. 107-120.

277 "Sex Week" • Sex Week was to take place from February 23–March 4, 2007, according to ephblog.com (February 15, 2007). It is sponsored by the Women's Center of Williams College.

277 Amy Fisher • Elizabeth Wurtzel, *Bitch: In Praise of Difficult Women* (Doubleday, New York, 1998), p. 136.

278 In a wonderful • Lawrence Downes, "Middle School Girls Gone Wild," *New York Times* (December 29, 2006).

278 Patty Binder • See www.whatsgoodforgirls.blogspot.com.

279 Viva Las Vegas • "A Reality Show for Couples Therapy? Sign Us Up," *New York Times,* "Modern Love" column (April 23, 2006).

279 Paris Hilton • "'People Shouldn't Judge Me,'" *Seventeen* (December 2006).

279 A popular Internet • TuckerMax.com.

280 "knee-buckling treat" • Rick Reilly, Back-page column, *Sports Illustrated* (Vol. 94, No. 8, Winter 2001).

281 "hypocrisy tip-off" • Katha Pollitt, "Bah, Humbug," *Nation* (June 3, 2003).

Agonito, Rosemary, Ph.D. *No More "Nice Girl": Power, Sexuality and Success in the Workplace*. Holbrook, Massachusetts: Adams Media Corporation, 1993.

Argov, Sherry. *Why Men Love Bitches: From Doormat to Dreamgirl—A Woman's Guide to Holding Her Own in a Relationship*. Avon, Massachusetts: Adams Media Corporation, 2000.

————. *Why Men Marry Bitches: A Woman's Guide to Winning Her Man's Heart*. New York: Simon & Schuster, 2006.

Artz, Sibylle, Ph.D. *Sex, Power, & the Violent School Girl*. Toronto, Ontario: Trifolium Books, 1998.

Austen, Jane. *Pride and Prejudice*. New York: W. W. Norton & Company, 1993 (first published in 1813).

Baskin, Julia, Lindsey Newman, Sophie Pollitt-Cohen, and Courtney Toombs. *The Notebook Girls*. New York: Warner Books, 2006.

Bem, Sandra Lipsitz. *An Unconventional Family*. New Haven, Connecticut: Yale University Press, 1998.

Boston Women's Health Book Collective, The. *Our Bodies, Ourselves: A New Edition for a New Era*. New York: Touchstone, 2005 (first published in 1984).

Brian, Kate. *The Virginity Club*. New York: Simon Pulse, 2004.

Cleary, Beverly. *My Own Two Feet: A Memoir*. New York: Avon Books, 1995.

Coloroso, Barbara. *The Bully, The Bullied, and the Bystander: From Pre-School to High School—How Parents and Teachers Can Help Break the Cycle of Violence*. Toronto, Ontario: HarperCollins Canada, 2002.

Deak, JoAnn, Ph.D., with Teresa Barker. *Girls Will Be Girls: Raising Confident and Courageous Daughters*. New York: Hyperion, 2002.

Dellasega, Cheryl, Ph.D. *Mean Girls Grown Up: Adult Women Who Are Still Queen Bees, Middle Bees, and Afraid-to-Bees*. Hoboken, New Jersey: John Wiley & Sons, Inc., 2005.

Deyo, Sue, and Yaacov Deyo. *Speed Dating: The Smarter, Faster Way to Lasting Love*. New York: Collins, 2002.

Doyle, Laura. *The Surrendered Wife: A Practical Guide for Finding Intimacy, Passion, and Peace with a Man*. New York: Simon & Schuster, 1999.

Finley, Martha. *Elsie Dinsmore*. London: George Routledge and Sons, 1906.

Flora Selwyn; Or How to Behave. A Book for Little Girls. New York: Cassell & Company, 1869.

Freud, Sigmund. *Civilization and Its Discontents.* Translated and edited by James Strachey. New York: W. W. Norton & Company, 1961 (originally published in 1929).

Gilder, George. *Men and Marriage.* Gretna, Louisiana: Pelican Publishing Company, 1993.

Greenfield, Laura. *Girl Culture.* San Francisco: Chronicle Books, 2002.

Gurstein, Rochelle. *The Repeal of Reticence: America's Cultural and Legal Struggles over Free Speech, Obscenity, Sexual Liberation, and Modern Art.* New York: Hill and Wang, 1996.

Hartley, Florence. *The Ladies' Book of Etiquette and Manual of Politeness: A Complete Handbook for the Use of the Lady in Polite Society.* Davenport, Iowa: J. S. Locke & Company, 1993 (originally published in 1872).

Heller, Tziporah. *Our Bodies Our Souls: A Jewish Perspective on Feminine Spirituality.* New York: Feldheim, 2003.

Henderson, Lauren. *Jane Austen's Guide to Dating.* New York: Hyperion, 2005.

Hirshman, Linda R. *Get to Work: A Manifesto for Women of the World.* New York: Penguin, 2006.

Howe, Neil, and William Strauss. *Millennials Rising: The Next Great Generation.* New York: Vintage Books, 2000.

Humphry, Mrs. *Manners for Women.* London: Ward, Lock & Co., 1897.

———. *Manners for Men.* London: Ward, Lock & Co., 1897.

Jong-Fast, Molly. *The Sex Doctors in the Basement.* New York: Random House, 2005.

Kerner, Ian, Ph.D. *Be Honest—You're Not That Into Him Either: Raise Your Standards and Reach for the Love You Deserve.* New York: ReganBooks, 2005.

Kettlewell, Caroline. *Skin Game: A Cutter's Memoir.* New York: St. Martin's Press, 1999.

Krulik, Nancy E. *BRATZ! Yasmin: The Princess Rules!* New York: Grosset & Dunlap, 2003.

Lamb, Sharon, Ed.D., and Lyn Mikel Brown, Ed.D. *Packaging Childhood: Rescuing Our Daughters from Marketers' Schemes.* New York.: St. Martin's Press, 2006.

Lavinthal, Andrea, and Jessica Rozler. *The Hookup Handbook: A Single Girl's Guide to Living It Up.* New York: Simon Spotlight, 2005.

Levine, Judith. *Harmful to Minors: The Perils of Protecting Children from Sex.* New York: Thunder's Mouth Press, 2002.

Levine, Stephanie Wellen. *Mystics, Mavericks, and Merrymakers: An Intimate Journey Among Hasidic Girls.* New York: New York University Press, 2003.

Levy, Ariel. *Female Chauvinist Pigs: Women and the Rise of Raunch Culture.* New York: Free Press, 2005.

Louis, Ron, and David Copeland. *How to Succeed with Women.* New York: Reward Books, 1998.

Marquardt, Elizabeth. *Between Two Worlds: The Inner Lives of Children of Divorce.* New York: Crown, 2005.

Marx, Eve. *Read My Hips: The Sexy Art of Flirtation.* Avon, Massachusetts: Polka Dot Press, 2005.

Mayer, Melody. *Friends with Benefits: A Nannies Novel.* New York: Delacorte Press, 2006.

Meade, L. T. *Daddy's Girl.* Chicago: M. A. Donohue & Co., 1900

———. *Girls: New and Old.* New York: The Cassell Publishing Company, 1894

———. *Polly: A New-Fashioned Girl.* New York: New York Book Co., 1911.

———. *The Rebel of the School.* Philadelphia: J. B. Lippincott, 1902.

———. *A Sweet Girl Graduate.* Chicago: M. A. Donohue, 1891.

———. *A Very Naughty Girl.* New York: Grosset & Dunlap, 1901.

———. *Wild Kitty: A School Story.* Chicago: M. A. Donohue & Co., 1897.

Morse, Jennifer Roback. *Smart Sex: Finding Life-Long Love in a Hook-Up World.* Dallas, Texas: Spence Publishing, 2005.

Norwood, Mandi. *The Hitched Chick's Guide to Modern Marriage: Essential Advice for Staying Single-minded and Happily Married.* New York: St. Martin's Griffin, 2003.

O'Connor, Charles, Executive Brand Editor. *Bratz Holiday Shoppin' Spree: A Guide to Totally Hot Shoppin'.* New York: Grosset & Dunlap, 2003.

———. *Bratz Xpress Yourself! Friends, Family, School, and You!* New York: Grosset & Dunlap, 2003.

Pemberton, Lois. *The Stork Didn't Bring You! The Facts of Life for Teenagers.* New York: Hermitage Press Inc., 1948.

Peril, Lynn. *College Girls: Bluestockings, Sex Kittens, and Co-Eds, Then and Now.* New York: W. W. Norton, 2006.

Pollitt, Katha. *Virginity or Death! And Other Social and Political Issues of Our Time.* New York: Random House, 2006.

Queen, Carol. *Real Live Nude Girl: Chronicles of Sex-Positive Culture.* Pittsburgh, Pennsylvania: Cleis Press, 1997.

Reynolds, Kimberley. *Girls Only?: Gender and Popular Children's Fiction in Britain, 1880–1910.* Philadelphia: Temple University Press, 1990.

Rimm, Sylvia, Ph.D. *Growing Up Too Fast: The Rimm Report on the Secret World of America's Middle Schoolers.* Emmaus, Pennsylvania: Rodale, 2005.

Robertson, Judith P., ed. *Teaching for a Tolerant World, Grades K–6: Essays and Resources.* Urbana, Illinois: The National Council of Teachers of English, 1999.

Roiphe, Katie. *The Morning After: Sex, Fear, and Feminism on Campus.* Boston: Little, Brown, 1993.

Rowley, Cynthia, and Ilene Rosenzweig. *Swell: A Girl's Guide to the Good Life.* New York: Warner Books, 1999.

Sangster, Margaret E. *Winsome Womanhood.* Chicago: H. Fleming Revell Company, 1900.

Schaefer Riley, Naomi. *God on the Quad: How Religious Colleges and the Missionary Generation Are Changing America.* New York: St. Martin's Press, 2005.

Seaman, Barrett. *Binge: What Your College Student Won't Tell You.* Hoboken, New Jersey: Wiley, 2005.

Shandler, Nina, Ed.D. *Ophelia's Mom: Women Speak Out About Loving and Letting Go of Their Adolescent Daughters.* New York: Crown, 2001.

Simmons, Rachel. *Odd Girl Out: The Hidden Culture of Aggression in Girls.* New York: Harcourt, Inc. 2002.

Spirak, Howard R., and Deborah Prothrow-Stith. *Sugar and Spice and No Longer Nice: How We Can Stop Girls' Violence.* San Francisco: Jossey-Bass, 2005.

Stark, Christine, and Rebecca Whisnant, eds. *Not for Sale: Feminists Resisting Prostitution and Pornography.* North Melbourne, Australia: Spinifex Press, 2004.

Straus, Jillian. *Unhooked Generation: The Truth About Why We're Still Single.* New York: Hyperion, 2006.

Tanenbaum, Leora. *Slut: Growing Up Female with a Bad Reputation.* New York: HarperCollins, 2000.

Tynan, Katherine, and Charles Robinson. *A Little Book of Courtesies.* New York: E. P. Dutton & Co., 1906.

Underwood, Marion K. *Social Aggression Among Girls.* New York: The Guilford Press, 2003.

von Ziegesar, Cecily. *Only in Your Dreams: A Gossip Girl Novel.* New York: Little, Brown, 2006.

Weill, Sabrina. *The Real Truth About Teens & Sex.* New York: Penguin, 2005.

Weintraub, Jeff, and Krishan Kumar, eds. *Public and Private in Thought and Practice: Perspectives on a Grand Dichotomy.* Chicago: The University of Chicago Press, 1997.

White, Emily. *Fast Girls: Teenage Tribes and the Myth of the Slut.* New York: Berkley Trade, 2002.

Winn, Marie. *The Plug-In Drug: Television, Children, & the Family (Revised Edition).* New York: Penguin Books, 1985.

Wiseman, Rosalind. *Queen Bees & Wannabes: Helping Your Daughter Survive Cliques, Gossip, Boyfriends & Other Realities of Adolescence.* New York: Three Rivers Press, 2002.

Wolf, Naomi. *Promiscuities: The Secret Struggle for Womanhood.* New York: Random House, 1997.

Woodall, Trinny, and Susannah Constantine. *Trinny and Susannah: What You Wear Can Change Your Life.* London: Weidenfield & Nicolson, 2004.

Wurtzel, Elizabeth. *Bitch: In Praise of Difficult Women.* New York: Doubleday, 1998.

Zailckas, Koren. *Smashed: Story of a Drunken Girlhood.* New York: Viking, 2005.

Zarzour, Kim. *The Schoolyard Bully: How to Cope with Conflict and Raise an Assertive Child.* Toronto, Ontario: HarperCollins Canada, 1994.

The Good Girl
REVOLUTION

WENDY SHALIT

A Reader's Guide

Questions and Topics for Discussion

In *The Good Girl Revolution: Young Rebels with Self-Esteem and High Standards*, Wendy Shalit examines a youth-led rebellion that is challenging the status quo. Shalit questions our assumptions about "repressed good girls" and, drawing on numerous studies and interviews, uncovers a new approach towards relationships that values intimacy and trust over sexual exhibitionism.

1. How do you feel about a coloring book for ages "three and up" that asks young readers what they'd wear to look "hot", or cartoon characters that sing about the importance of girls looking "hot"? Who benefits from this sexualization of very young girls, and who loses out? Explain.

2. Wendy Shalit says in her Introduction: "For girls to have meaningful choices and genuine hope, the 'wild girl' or 'bad girl' cannot seem like the only empowered option" (p. xxv). What do you think she means by this statement? The author quotes a teenager who was upset when her five-year-old neighbor put on makeup, platform shoes, and a miniskirt to show off in front of some boys playing basketball. But how is the neighbor different from a girl who plays "princess" at home? Why does the author find it problematic that girls at such a young age preen to please boys? Do you agree or disagree?

3. Why might the fifteen-year-old boy involved with a much older woman feel that his mother doesn't love him because she doesn't ask where he is going at night (p. 8)? What do you feel is a parent's role in setting boundaries regarding sexual activity?

4. Are you surprised by the findings, published in *The Journal of Sex Research*, that many college students are hooking up because of peer pressure and not because these casual encounters are particularly satisfying? How does the author use the concept of "pluralistic ignorance" (p. 11) and apply it to college life? What are college students ignorant of when it comes

to hooking up? And why do you think alcohol plays such a large role in these encounters?

5. What evidence does the author present to support her claim that being "publicly sexual" has become the new female ideal (p. 25)? Do you think the popularity of "stripper fitness" and teen magazines glorifying "hot chicks" constitutes a trend, or reflects isolated examples? Do you share the belief that women who wear less clothing are more confident? Why or why not?

6. If a child does not want to take a particular sex education course offered in school, do you think her parent should force her to? Why or why not?

7. How do some teen-advice websites send the message that sexual abstinence is not a valid option? Do you agree with Scarleteen that postponing sex until marriage is not a "manageable" choice (p. 34)? What does the author mean by writing that we have made "a swear word of 'innocence'" (p. 38)?

8. Why might boys be "scared" of Lauren because she's not a "booty call" (p. 42)? Does one have to be sexually active in order to be liberated?

9. Who do you consider to be your role models, and why are they important to you? Do you agree with the fifteen-year-old boy who told Rashida, "'Far too often, it's the adults who are saying we can't accomplish our dreams, and they expect us to fail instead of encouraging us to aim high'" (p. 69)? Are there people in your life who demonstrate that they believe in you?

10. Wendy Shalit claims that nowadays, the desire to connect emotionally to a sexual partner is seen by many to be problematic. "Emotional repression," as Shalit dubs it, serves to dull feelings of disappointment which often follow "no-strings attached" sex. Do you think that this is a good thing? What do you see as the role of emotion in a healthy sexual relationship? And how do Molly Jong-Fast's views about sexuality differ from those of her famous mother (p. 105)? Whose views best reflect your own on this subject?

11. The author looks to the past—to the custom of "friendly visiting" (p. 123) in the 1850s, for example—to contrast with those of today's teenagers, who report that it can be difficult to form lasting friendships. Do you agree or disagree with seventeen-year-old Audrey, who says, "You can't

just go up and talk to somebody because they're texting on their cell or talking on their cell"? What social changes come to mind when you think of the evolution of technology?

12. Wendy Shalit proposes that our "sexual free-for-all" has made it more difficult to form female friendships and she argues against those who consider adultery to be just another lifestyle choice. Do you agree with the author that if you can't trust other women, it is more difficult to befriend them? What other factors beyond sexual competitiveness can contribute to the breakdown of friendships?

13. Have you ever considered writing a letter to a business or advertising company, only to think that it wouldn't make a difference? Why do you think eleven-year-old Ella Gunderson's letter to Nordstrom was so effective? Given the rash of teen protests against companies that sell racy clothing, do you think sex will always sell with the younger generation, or will there be increasing demand for a bit of mystery and glamour?

14. The danger of overpleasing (p. 180) is an important issue in this book, and the author is troubled by girls who risk their lives with drunk drivers because they don't want the boys to be "upset." How does the author distinguish between giving out of love, and pleasing out of insecurity? Brittany Hunsicker (p. 190) is an example of a very traditional yet outspoken teen, having complained to her school board about a "dirty book" read aloud in English class. Do you think the author is right to call her a rebel, or would you consider her more of a pleaser since her parents are traditional? Think of ways in which your own values conflict with what society considers normal, and how you might change things for the better.

15. Shalit cites Helen Grieco, executive director of the California National Organization for Women, who defended the *Girls Gone Wild* videos because " 'flashing your breasts on Daytona Beach says, "I'm not a good girl. I think it's sexy to be a bad girl" ' " (p. 18). Do you think such feminists—who value being "bad"—are typical, or the exception? The author draws a parallel between the new fourth wave of feminists, such as the Girlcotters who boycotted Abercrombie and Fitch's attitude tees, and the original feminists who believed in women's power to uplift society. Do you identify with this new fourth-wave feminist, or more with the third wave, which places more emphasis on sexual experimentation? Explain.

16. How do you think adult expectations can worsen the problem of relational aggression (or bullying) or alternatively, help to prevent it?

17. Why would a young woman launch a pornography site as a way of "documenting my life and having people care" (p. 262)? What does this example say about what our society values? And how can parents or friends demonstrate caring so that young people do not have to go to such extremes to feel cared about?

18. Why are people "afraid of the good girl," according to the author? Do you think that, as a society, we are overcorrecting for the past oppression of women and we have now become too exhibitionistic, or have we struck the right balance? Why does the author find the "sex-negative" versus the "sex-positive" dichotomy to be unhelpful (p. 275)?

19. How do your personal experiences relate to Wendy Shalit's argument? How do you feel about students who are "sexiled" from their dorm rooms? Coed sleepovers for tweens? The role of pornography in our society and the decline of romance? Parents who pressure their college-age sons to "score," or their daughters to lose their virginity?

PHOTO: © HELEN TANSEY

WENDY SHALIT is the author of *A Return to Modesty: Discovering The Lost Virtue*. The enthusiastic response to her book from young women around the world prompted her to launch the online community, Modestly Yours. Today she lives with her family in Toronto, Ontario, where she enjoys various modern amenities such as the dishwasher, and has no desire to return to the nineteenth century. Read more at www .goodgirlrevolution.com.